Collected Works of Velimir Khlebnikov

volume 1

Letters and Theoretical Writings

Collected Works of

Velimir Khlebnikov

volume I

Letters and Theoretical Writings

translated by Paul Schmidt

edited by Charlotte Douglas

Harvard University Press

Cambridge, Massachusetts, and London, England

1987

Library of Congress Cataloging-in-Publication Data

Khlebnikov, Velimir, 1885–1922.
    Collected works of Velimir Khlebnikov.

    Translated from the Russian.
    Contents: v. 1. Letters and theoretical writings.
    Vol.   includes indexes.
    1. Khlebnikov, Velimir, 1885–1922—Translations, English.
    2. Khlebnikov, Velimir, 1885–1922—Correspondence.
    3. Poets, Russian—20th century—Correspondence.
    I. Douglas, Charlotte, 1936–   .
    II. Title.
PG3476.K485A23   1987   891.71′3 [B]   87-8399
ISBN 0-674-14045-1 (alk. paper)

Designed by Gwen Frankfeldt

Preface

Our work on this volume was supported by the Dia Art Foundation, New York, and by a grant for work in the USSR from the International Research and Exchanges Board. Many other people and organizations also assisted in its preparation. In the Soviet Union we received sympathetic help and especially enlightening information concerning Khlebnikov and his colleagues from Alexander E. Parnis, Mai Miturich, and Vasily Katanian. In this country, Ronald Vroon of the University of Pennsylvania read our manuscript with great care and made many valuable suggestions.

We would also like to express our gratitude to the following people for their gracious help in many and varied ways: Henryk Baran, John Bowlt, Nina Bruni, Ann Helgeson, Nikolai Khardzhiev, Evgeny Kovtun, Vladimir Markov, Igor Palmin, Robert Palter, Serafim Pavlovsky, Alla Povelikhina, Vasily Rakitin, Elena Rakitina, Serafima Blokh Roitman, Stephen Rudy, Dmitry Sarabianov, Marina Schwartz, and Victor Tupitsyn. We are indebted for their generous assistance to the administration and staff of the Central State Archive of Literature and Art, Moscow, and the State Russian Museum, Leningrad.

Special and heartfelt thanks go to our co-worker Katherine Theodore, whose daily labor on this book finally made it a reality.

About sources: This volume includes all of Khlebnikov's theoretical writings and autobiographical material that appeared in the five-volume *Sobranie proizvedenii Velimira Khlebnikova* (Collected Works of Velimir Khlebnikov), ed. N. Stepanov and Iu. Tynianov (Leningrad: Izdatelstvo pisatelei v Leningrade, 1928–1933), and in *Neizdannye proizvedeniia* (Unpublished Works), ed. N. Khardzhiev and T. Grits (Moscow: Khudozhestvennaia literatura, 1940). We also made liberal use of the commentary and notes given in these two publications. A few texts have been translated from the added material published as part of volume III of Vladimir Markov's republication of these two editions,

Sobranie sochinenii (Collected Writings; Munich: Wilhelm Fink, 1968–1972), and from original published sources and unpublished archival material. As this volume reached the first stage of proof, a newly edited collection of Khlebnikov's writings appeared in the Soviet Union: *Tvoreniia* (Works), ed. M. Ia. Poliakov, V. P. Grigoriev, and A. E. Parnis (Moscow: Sovetsky pisatel, 1986). We were able to make last-minute changes in page proof to reflect the alterations and additional material offered by the new Soviet edition.

The date and source for each Russian text is indicated at the end of its translation. Abbreviations are as follows:

Roman and arabic numbers—volume and page of *Sobranie proizvedenii* (Collected Works)

NP—*Neizdannye proizvedeniia* (Unpublished Works)

M.III—volume III of *Sobranie sochinenii* (Collected Writings)

TsGALI—Central State Archive of Literature and Art, Moscow

T—*Tvoreniia* (Works, 1986)

Transliteration throughout follows the U.S. Library of Congress system, slightly simplified. In the text we have used the normal spelling for proper names when an English common usage has been established; for example, the Russian *-skii* ending has been rendered *-sky*.

Places in the text marked "[illegible]" are so marked in the Soviet editions. Ellipses in the Russian text—it is sometimes difficult to ascertain whether they are Khlebnikov's or the editor's omissions—are marked here by five dots; our ellipses are represented by three.

In Russia a change in the civil calendar was made shortly after the Bolshevik revolution. Officially, January 31, 1918, was followed by February 14, 1918. Dates in this volume follow the system in use in Russia at the time in question. That is, the Julian calendar—the old system (O.S.)—is used up to January 31, 1918; thereafter, the dates coincide with the Gregorian or Western calendar (N.S.). To convert dates in the twentieth century prior to January 1918 to Western dates, add thirteen days; for nineteenth-century dates, add twelve days.

Contents

Contents

Contents

Illustrations

Letters and Biographical Writings

VELIMIR KHLEBNIKOV

Viktor (Velimir) Khlebnikov was born on November 9, 1885, into the family of the Russian administrator of the Kalmyk nomads, Mongolian Buddhists who inhabited the grassy steppes on the west bank of the Caspian Sea.[1] He was the fourth of five children: Boris, Ekaterina, and Alexander were older; Vera, who became a recognized artist and was always very close to him, was six years younger. Vladimir Alexeevich Khlebnikov, the poet's father, graduated with the equivalent of an American Ph.D. from the University of St. Petersburg and was a prominent naturalist and ornithologist. His mother, Ekaterina Nikolaevna Verbitskaia, was an intelligent woman who studied history in school and had close connections with the Populist movement.[2]

The Khlebnikov household was informal, cheerful, and active. Ekaterina, although devoted to her children, was indifferent to domestic chores and preferred to spend her time gardening and reading. Vladimir collected specimens of birds and plants, wrote scientific articles about land management, and took a warm interest in the life of the Kalmyks, their religion, games, and stories. His work on birds reflected his capacity for patient observation: he was skilled at gathering and recording details and at systemizing the multiplicities of the cultural, as well as the natural, environment. By all accounts he was a gentle, perceptive man and, although in later years father and son quarreled, in childhood and adolescence Viktor wholeheartedly adopted his father's freethinking and scholarly way of life, showing a similar talent for close observation and the scientific propensity to classify. Vladimir's profession and his interest in ethnography gave his family an unusual under-

1. Khlebnikov was born in what is now the village of Malye Derbety in the Kalmyk Autonomous Republic, about 50 miles south and east of the present city of Volgograd.

2. Verbitskaia knew Vera Figner and was especially close to her first cousin, Alexander Mikhailov, both well-known members of the Populist terrorist organization, the People's Will. See Mikhailov's 1882 letter to her in A. P. Pribyleva-Korba and V. N. Figner, *Narodovoletz Aleksandr Dmitrievich Mikhailov* (Leningrad, 1925), pp. 186–188.

standing of diverse ways of life. Friends noted their tolerance and respect for one another, and the keen interest in reading and learning that was supported by a large home library. They shared their house with a variety of small wild animals—hedgehogs, turtles, and gerbils lived inside unrestrained; outside there were well-populated animal sheds and cages. To develop the habit of recording observations of natural phenomena, Vladimir encouraged his children to keep notebooks. By the time he was eleven, Viktor had begun to chronicle his daily activities and to note sightings of birds.

Until he was six years old, the young Khlebnikov lived in the only house in a settlement of nomadic tents, surrounded on the steppe by camels and other animals belonging to the Kalmyks. Later he observed, "a camel knows the essence of Buddhism, and suppresses a Chinese smile,"[3] and saw himself as permanently residing in a dual country situated in both the West and the East, Russia and the Orient, a man of two worlds, possessing two identities, born on the banks of the "Caspian-China" Sea. Ultimately this prompted him to consider that only "Planet Earth" could describe his true home.

Led primarily by his desire that the children experience the abundant variety of nature, Vladimir left the eastern steppe and took a position as district supervisor in the extreme western province of Volynia, bordering Poland. In the course of the move, Viktor with his siblings made his first visit to St. Petersburg, spending the summer of 1891 with his maternal grandmother, Maria Petrovna Verbitskaia. At his grandmother's dacha outside the city, Viktor, almost six years old, was first introduced to the natural world of northwestern Russia, so different from the grassy plains of the east.

In Volynia the Khlebnikovs spent the next four years in a rural idyll, a dramatic change from their life on the steppe. Their house, an abandoned estate, was surrounded by ancient forests and luxurious parkland filled with fruit trees and rare plants. The children played among castle ruins, learned about mushrooms, and scoured the woods for berries and birdnests.

Vitya [Viktor] learned avidly to recognize and distinguish the herbs and flowers from his mother, and he was always interested in their properties. He was very proud when he succeeded in mak-

3. From "O Garden of Animals!" as sent to Viacheslav Ivanov in letter 15, June 10, 1909.

ing ink from wild cornflowers . . . He had his own herbarium and flowerbed that he tended, and people remember that he paid particular attention to the periwinkle, that simple humble flower.[4]

The family's next move, when Viktor was ten, was to the province of Simbirsk (now Ulianovsk) on the northern Volga. There they lived in the Mordovian village of Pomaevo while Vladimir served as district steward. It was here that Viktor learned the myths and folklore of the Mordovians, tales of sword-carrying knights and treasure-laden burial mounds that lay hidden beneath apparently ordinary hills and woods. Although the Khlebnikov family did not ordinarily indulge in parties and socializing, on holidays the Mordovians were invited for festivities organized by Ekaterina; they came in their exotic embroidered costumes, tall and stately, with glittering necklaces and high hats, thrilling the children with their exuberant dancing and singing.

Viktor was a handsome child, self-possessed, willful, smart, and given to thinking. He was fair and tall, and everyone who saw him remarked on the intensity of his eyes, "a constant play of color, pale bluish and green, as if a water-lily leaf were floating on a lake."[5] The boy thrived in the protection of an indulgent home and when, at age twelve, he was sent off the 60 miles to Simbirsk to school, he was so unhappy at being surrounded by strangers that the family found it necessary to move into the city so that their son might live at home.

In 1898 the family moved north to the city of Kazan, home of one of the most prestigious universities in Russia. Khlebnikov continued in school to develop particular interests in mathematics, literature, and art. From an early age he had begun to draw—a natural extension of his observational skills—and now the family engaged a student from the Kazan Art School to instruct him seriously; after three years a reputable graphic artist took over the children's lessons. When not making the obligatory drawings from plaster casts, the young Khlebnikov sketched his beloved birds and animals, and when he progressed to oils and canvas, trees and fields were his subjects.[6]

After graduation from secondary school, Khlebnikov enrolled at the University of Kazan in mathematics. In doing so, he was entering

4. Unpublished memoirs of his mother, E. N. Khlebnikova (1923).
5. Velimir Khlebnikov, "Kolya was a handsome boy" (1912–13).
6. Many of Khlebnikov's early drawings and paintings are kept in the Central State Archives of Literature and Art in Moscow.

the domain of the geometer Nikolai Ivanovich Lobachevsky, who would acquire mythological stature for Khlebnikov's life and work. Misunderstood and unacknowledged in his own time, Lobachevsky with his revolutionary non-Euclidean geometry challenged the common understanding of the nature of space and the world itself. In many ways Kazan was Lobachevsky's town: he dominated it not only as an internationally known mathematician but as a native son who had been personally responsible for the growth of its university and the organization of its journals and scholarly scientific societies. At the end of the nineteenth century, owing to the efforts of the scholar Alexander Vasilev, Lobachevsky was receiving belated recognition. Vasilev, who headed the department of mathematics in which Khlebnikov was enrolled, published dozens of books and articles about the mathematician and his work.[7] By the time Khlebnikov entered the university, Lobachevsky's spirit, his courageous commitment to academic freedom and intellectual inquiry, had again become a vital force in Kazan. Khlebnikov's identification with the geometer must have been strengthened by the coincidence of their other interests: the Russian language, history, art, and Eastern cultures. In some sense Khlebnikov would have no choice but to become the "King of Time," for Lobachevsky had long been for him the "King of Space."

In Kazan Khlebnikov's pursuit of science continued as a way of life. After his first year at the university, he changed his major from mathematics to natural science and joined the famous Kazan Society of Natural Scientists, of which his father was also a member. Under the auspices of the society in the spring of 1905, Khlebnikov and his brother Alexander made an ornithological expedition to the Pavdinsk Preserve in the northern Urals, where they remained for almost five months, gathering specimens for their father's collection and recording songs and sightings. Later they reported the results of their trip at a society meeting and eventually, as coauthors, published their work.[8] Although presented in a scholarly format, the ornithological descriptions pub-

7. See, for example, A. V. Vasilev, *Nikolai Ivanovich Lobachevskii* (Kazan, 1894), and *Nikolai Ivanovich Lobachevskii* (St. Petersburg, 1914). The address on Lobachevsky given by Vasilev in 1893 at the hundred-year jubilee celebration in Kazan was published in English as *Nicolai Ivanovich Lobachevsky,* trans. George Bruce Halsted (Austin, Texas, 1894).

8. Khlebnikov read the report about the trip to the Natural Science Society at Kazan University on December 3, 1906; Nikolai Khardzhiev, "Novoe o Velimire Khlebni-

lished by the poet and his brother are exceptionally lively, filled with local lore gained from provincial hunters and with remarkable descriptions of birdcalls:

> The nutcracker often sits for a while with closed eyes after feeding, ruffling its feathers and evidently reveling in the sound of its voice, as if recounting something of its impressions of the day in its own strange language: "pee-oo, pee-oo, pee-oo," it moans painfullly and piteously; "pee-ee, pee-ee, pee-ee," it pipes in a delicate voice, like the cry of the hazel grouse; then insistently and intelligently, "knya, knya, knya"; then switches to muttering, "kya, kya, kya"; then trembling with intensity, almost as if it were angry, and ruffling its feathers, it makes a rude hoarse hiss.[9]

Khlebnikov's interest in birds continued throughout his years in Kazan. In 1907 he published a short account of ornithological observations made the previous spring.[10]

It seems clear that by this time Khlebnikov had a knowing, intimate relationship to the natural world, one that was appreciative and at the same time probing, as if by keeping accounts he could make nature yield up the system governing its wisdom and variety. While he was still in the village of Pomaevo, the eleven-year-old Khlebnikov had already begun to write poems. His earliest extant poem is a sympathetic observation of a bird in a cage.[11] This early image of nature trapped and tamed remained a very powerful one throughout Khlebnikov's work; later it proved central to a variety of his projects.

But in addition to his scientific interests, in Kazan Khlebnikov became an eager reader of the Symbolist literary journal *Libra*[12] and began to write his first serious poetry, often taking for his images the birds he studied so attentively. Many of these poems were among those Khlebnikov sent to the well-known Symbolist poet Viacheslav Ivanov for

kove," *Russian Literature* 9 (1975), 9. The article was published in *Priroda i okhota* 12 (1911). Vladimir's bird collection was eventually given to the Astrakhan Regional Museum; Khardzhiev, "Novoe o Velimire Khlebnikove," *Den' poezii* (Moscow, 1975), p. 203.

9. "Ornithological Observations," included in this volume.

10. "On finding a cuckoo."

11. "Ptichka v kletke" (Bird in a cage), quoted by Khardzhiev in "Novoe," *Den' poezii*, p. 203.

12. Memoirs of B. P. Denike, quoted in Khardzhiev, "Novoe," *Russian Literature*, p. 7.

comment in March 1908. We do not have Ivanov's reply, but we can assume that either then or later in the summer, when the young poet met Ivanov in the Crimea, the older man was not completely discouraging: within six months, the twenty-two-year-old Khlebnikov had moved to St. Petersburg, enrolled at his father's alma mater, and began to publish his literary efforts.

Probably it was Khlebnikov's intention to please his father by pursuing scientific interests in Petersburg. At the university he enrolled in natural science, but from the time of his move to the capital city his active study of science yielded place to literary work. The following year, after an extended stay at home, he changed his major to Russian and Slavic languages and began to study Pushkin.[13]

Technically Khlebnikov's first publication in St. Petersburg was an anonymous manifesto posted in a university corridor, a call to defend the Slavic countries of Bosnia and Herzegovina against annexation by Austria; it was not long before the bellicose document found its way into a Petersburg newspaper.[14] "Montenegro and Belgrade have sworn eternal brotherhood, and with the madness of those whose divine lot is to be victorious they are now prepared to oppose their wills to the will of an incomparably stronger enemy . . . Holy War! Unavoidable, approaching, immediate—war for the trampled rights of the Slavs, I salute you! Down with the Hapsburgs! Hold back the Hohenzollerns!"

Sentiments favoring a Pan-Slavic cultural and political renaissance were widely shared in the Russia of 1908. In the summer of that year the All-Slavic Congress held in Prague issued a program for Neo-Slavism. Slavic circles at the universities sponsored speakers and planned study tours, and as part of the heightened cultural awareness there was a broad interest in creating a Pan-Slavic language.[15] When

13. Among his other courses, Khlebnikov was a participant in the famous Pushkin seminar of S. A. Vengerov, an experience that had long-lasting reverberations in his work. See A. E. Parnis, "Iuzhnoslavianskaia tema Velimira Khlebnikova," *Zarubezhnye slaviane i russkaia kul'tura* (Leningrad, 1978), p. 232.

14. *Vecher* 133, October 16 (29), 1908. It was reprinted under Khlebnikov's name in the Cubo-Futurist collection *Riav! Perchatki!* (Roar! Gauntlets!; St. Petersburg, 1913), p. 3.

15. There is reason to suppose that Khlebnikov himself belonged to such a Slavic circle. On this and the Pan-Slavic issue generally, see Parnis, "Iuzhnoslavianskaia tema."

Austria annexed Bosnia and Herzegovina in the fall (with the tsar's secret complicity), vociferous objections were raised by the Russian intelligentsia, including leading figures of the literary establishment.[16] Khlebnikov's Pan-Slavic views were no doubt reinforced by the Populist convictions of his mother and grandparents, and by the fact that his Aunt Masha had lived in Montenegro for several years.[17] His letters home from Petersburg at this time attest to his friendly visits with Masha and other members of his mother's family. And by the end of 1909 he had changed his name to the south Slavic form, "Velimir," and was contemplating a trip to Montenegro.[18]

A romantic inclination to democratic utopianism had been evident in the young poet for some time. Along with other Kazan students in 1903, he was jailed for taking part in an anti-tsarist protest over the death of a young Social Democrat.[19] He was delighted when, on his first trip to Moscow the following year, his cabdriver spoke enthusiastically of a house built in the Neo-Slavic style: "Since ordinary people don't really appreciate architecture," he wrote his parents, "that evidently means this style feels closer and more accessible to Russians, otherwise the cabdriver wouldn't have singled it out."[20] It is easy to understand that, with the general burst of Slavic feeling in 1908, Khlebnikov saw himself in the vanguard of the new revivalist spirit. "Long live the Slavic Renaissance!" he urged his fellow students. "Slavic youth unite! Slavic youth of St. Petersburg unite! The Slavic spring lives!"[21]

Khlebnikov was also being drawn toward literary circles, obviously pleased to meet writers he had known before only in print. Within a few weeks of his move to Petersburg, he wrote home about having seen "Sologub, Gorodetsky, and the rest of the zoo" at a public reading, and in the following year he reports, "I have met almost all the young writ-

16. See Leo Tolstoy's "On the Annexation of Bosnia and Herzegovina to Austria" in several issues of the Moscow newspaper *Golos Moskvy* (December 4–7, 1908), as cited in Parnis, p. 223.

17. His maternal uncle's wife, Maria Konstantinovna Timofeeva, had spent several years in Montenegro as tutor to the daughter of Prince Nikolai Negosh. See Parnis, "Iuzhnoslavianskaia tema," p. 228, and "Neizvestnyi rasskaz V. Khlebnikova," *Russian Literature Triquarterly* 13 (Fall 1975), 472n7.

18. Letters 22, December 28, 1909; 23, December 30, 1909; and 25, February 1, 1910. On the change of Khlebnikov's first name, see notes to letter 23.

19. Letter 1, December 3, 1903.

20. Letter 3, 1904 (?).

21. Parnis, "Iuzhnoslavianskaia tema," p. 225.

ers in Petersburg—Gumilyov, Auslander, Kuzmin, Hofman, Count Tolstoy, and others including Guenther."[22] Right away he had taken his work to Vasily Kamensky, a writer only a year older than himself and the editor of a literary almanac, *Spring*.[23] Kamensky has described his first meeting with Khlebnikov:

> Once I was all by myself, bogged down with manuscripts in Shebuev's apartment, where we had the editorial offices. It was getting late, and I had opened the front door wide; I was waiting for Shebuev's return, so I could get off to the theater.
>
> At first I heard someone's hesitant footsteps on the stone stairs. I went out onto the landing—the steps stopped.
>
> I went back again. And again the steps. I went out—and again they stopped. Then I started quietly down the staircase: a student in a University overcoat was pressed against the wall and looked at me with frightened blue eyes.
>
> Knowing from experience the timidity with which beginning writers approach editorial offices, I asked him gently: "Are you looking for the editorial offices? Come on in."
>
> I repeated the invitation. "Please don't be bashful. Even though I'm an editor, I'm just a student like you. The editor-in-chief isn't here and I'm alone." My directness won out and the student quietly, thoughtfully, came up after me and into the anteroom.
>
> "Would you like to take off your coat?" I put out my hand to help him with his coat, but he suddenly backed off and hit the back of his head on the coatrack. "Well, never mind, come into the office in your coat. Sit down, and let's talk."
>
> The student sat on the very edge of the chair, took off his cap, rubbed his high forehead, messed up his blond hair, opened his mouth a bit like a child and fixed a pair of heavenly eyes on me.
>
> We looked at·each other silently that way, smiling.
>
> I liked the mysterious creature so much I was ready to hug him. "Did you bring us something?"

22. Letter 6, October 13, 1908; letter 18, October 16, 1909. For biographical information on the writers mentioned, see notes to letters 6 and 18.

23. Vasily Kamensky, the editor of *Vesna* (Spring), was a writer, artist, and aviator. He began his literary career at seventeen in Perm, writing about the town's social problems for the local newspaper. He moved to St. Petersburg in 1906. For more information on Kamensky, see notes to letter 11.

The student got a blue notebook out of his pocket, nervously rolled it up and handed it to me like a candle.

"Well here is . . . . . something . . . . . I don't know." And not a word more.

I smoothed out the notebook. On the first page, as if written with a hair, were some kind of almost invisible calculations; on the second page were random beginning lines of verse; on the third was written in large letters "Sufferance in Glances," but this was crossed out and in a different handwriting was "A Sinner's Seduction" . . .

"We'll print your 'Sinner's Seduction,' I'm sure Shebuev will like it." The student quickly jumped up, happy, and wiped his forehead: "That's wonderful. I didn't expect . . . . . I don't know."

"But your story isn't signed; would you sign it please?"

And he signed: "V. Khlebnikov."[24]

Just one month after his arrival in Petersburg, Khlebnikov had placed his first piece of literary prose.[25]

The aspiring writer began to frequent Viacheslav Ivanov's Wednesday evenings, where poets and writers of every stylistic persuasion assembled for talk and readings. At Ivanov's he met Mikhail Kuzmin, a fine poet who at the time was enjoying a considerable reputation for a recent book of verse, *Nets*.[26] Kuzmin used to hold court in his own rooms at Ivanov's, and he apparently took a particular interest in the young writer from Kazan. In the fall of 1909 Khlebnikov happily wrote home to his mother, "I am an apprentice and my teacher is Kuzmin."

The circle of Symbolists led by Ivanov began calling itself the Academy of Verse in the spring of 1909, when Ivanov began a series of lectures to his friends on Russian versification. The group maintained a sympathetic association with the Petersburg painters of the former World of Art group, including Sergei Makovsky, Lev Bakst, and Alexandre Benois. In October this connection was embodied in an elegant new journal *Apollo*, edited by Makovsky and devoted to the latest currents in Russian and Western art and literature. Khlebnikov, writing furiously, was open in his admiration and delighted to be included, if only on the fringes, of such elevated company. To his brother he wrote,

24. V. V. Kamensky, *Put' entuziasta* (Moscow, 1931), pp. 92–93, 95.

25. "Iskushenie greshnika," *Vesna*, October 1908, p. 2.

26. For Kuzmin, see notes to letter 18.

"I am going to be a member of an 'Academy' of poets . . . I value them for their depth and sincerity and originality, which I don't have much of. My prose poem will be published in *Apollo*," and to his doubting father he reported having read his poems at academy meetings.[27]

But "O Garden of Animals," written in the style of Walt Whitman[28] and the work Khlebnikov had in mind for *Apollo*, never saw publication there. Probably the editors found it paradoxical, if not downright incomprehensible, and lacking in literary finish. The lean language and abundant images of Khlebnikov's early work trace the materials out of which his life had so far been formed: closely observed nature, ethnic cultural traditions, Slavic mythologies and the religion of rural Russia, a homely blend of Christian beliefs and the pantheistic anthropomorphizing of natural forces. The bird images of the early lyrics, the identification with animals and the rough wisdom of hunters found in stories such as "Usa-Gali" and "Nikolai," are a unique rendering of deep-felt personal experience.

Khlebnikov had arrived in Petersburg with a rich and keenly developed way of seeing the world that was vastly different from the views of the cultivated literary establishment in the capital. His acquaintances at the "Academy of poets" were Symbolists; they viewed the world as a system of correspondences and attempted to decipher mysterious hints of higher realities. The refined exoticism of their art, and the philosophy associated with it, served them as a kind of arcane religion; in this their aesthetics were far from Khlebnikov's. In just over a year the disparity became obvious, and the poet began to feel betrayed by his former friends. Adding to his misery at the time was the position he had taken as tutor in a merchant's house to two daughters, a situation that he found insufferable. Early in 1910, the predictable disagreements with *Apollo* and the academy intensified, and he left Ivanov's circle.

It was Vasily Kamensky, Khlebnikov's editor at *Spring*, who introduced him to a new, more congenial group of writers and painters; they immediately recognized the poet's talents and for the next few years

27. Letter 19, October 23, 1909; letter 20, November 13, 1909.

28. At this time Khlebnikov composed at least one more prose poem relying on Whitman's poetic forms. It went unpublished until recently: "Ia pereplyl zaliv Sudaka" (I swam across the Sudak gulf), quoted by Khardzhiev in "Novoe," *Russian Literature*, pp. 12–13.

gave him crucial moral and financial support. Hurt and indignant at his rejection by the academy, Khlebnikov found Kamensky's introduction to Mikhail Matiushin and Elena Guro providential. Matiushin was a violinist and Guro a writer, but both painted as well, and in their comfortable apartment on Litseiskaia Street, Khlebnikov met David Burliuk, poet, painter, and the "father of Russian Futurism," who rescued him from his difficult living situation and brought him to live on the Fontanka Canal with Kamensky and his new wife.[29]

> Khlebnikov couldn't make up his mind about quitting, so I went to the girls' mama and told her I was taking her student away with me. She didn't seem a bit surprised—in fact she even seemed somewhat relieved. He packed up his "things" in a hurry—he didn't have much. A small suitcase, and a sack that Vitya dragged out from under the bed . . . It was a pillow case, stuffed with crumpled pieces of paper, pages torn out of notebooks, whole sheets or even just torn-off corners of pages . . . "My manuscripts," Vitya muttered.[30]

Probably at Matiushin's he also became acquainted with Nikolai Kulbin, a physician, painter, and publicizer of the new art, for in just a few weeks, in March, they all—Kamensky, Matiushin, Guro, David Burliuk and his brother Vladimir—took part in the large Triangle exhibition organized by Kulbin. Khlebnikov was included in a section showing drawings and autographs by writers, along with Tolstoy, Gorky, Pushkin, Chekhov, and many of the academy poets.

Almost simultaneously, in his collection *The Impressionists' Studio,* Kulbin published Khlebnikov's poem "Incantation by Laughter," a feat of verbal acrobatics that came to be known as the epitome of Russian Futurism and his most famous work.

Hlahla! Uthlofan, lauflings!
Hlahla! Ufhlafan, lauflings!
Who lawghen with lafe, who hlaehen lewchly,
Hlahla! Ufhlofan hlouly!
Hlahla! Hloufish lauflings lafe uf beloght lauchalorum!
Hlahla! Loufenish lauflings lafe, hlohan utlaufly!

29. Kamensky had only recently returned from his native Perm. The previous August he had married Avgusta Viktorovna Yugova, a widow with two young children.
30. *Tvorchestvo* I (1920), 13.

Lawfen, lawfen,
Hloh, hlouh, hlou! luifekin, luifekin,
Hlofeningum, hlofeningum.
Hlahla! Uthlofan, lauflings!
Hlahla! Ufhlofan, lauflings![31]

For over a year Khlebnikov had been writing verse based on neologisms, and his new friends recognized the revolutionary character of this work and readily adapted their aesthetic principles to it. The group—later they were to call themselves Futurians and Cubo-Futurists[32]—intended to publish a selection of prose and poetry that would scandalize the literary establishment and draw immediate attention to themselves. Khlebnikov eagerly joined in the plans for this united assault on Russian Symbolism. Kamensky, who served as editor of their first miscellany, remembered its planning:

> Khlebnikov was living with me at the time, and I had never seen him happier or more excited than during those busy days . . . Mussing up his hair, doubling over and straightening up, turning the blue haze of his eyes upon us [he] paced nervously, thrusting his body forward and glistening with a shower of ideas. "Well . . . . . the Futurians should establish islands and dictate things from there. . . . We'll communicate with the mainland by plane—like birds. We'll fly in in the spring, have various ideas, and fly home in the fall." David Burliuk, the super-realist, trained his lorgnette on the abstracted poet and asked, "But Vitya, what are we going to eat on this island?" Khlebnikov literally jumped back. "What? Fruit. And we can be like hunters, more or less, and we can live in tents and write. We'll be a fighting tribe."[33]

A Jam for Judges—the title, literally "a small trap for judges," was invented by Khlebnikov and reflects the image of his imprisoned birds—appeared in April 1910.[34] In deliberate contrast to the luxurious *Apollo,* it was printed on the reverse side of ordinary wallpaper, without

31. *King of Time,* p. 20.
32. The group did not designate themselves Cubo-Futurists until 1913; earlier they called themselves Hyleans, Futurians, or Futurists. In the interest of simplifying terminology, I have used the "Cubo-Futurist" appellation throughout.
33. Kamensky, *Put' entuziasta,* pp. 114–115.
34. *Sadok sudei* was published by Matiushin in an edition of three hundred copies.

punctuation and other typographical niceties. Here at last "O Garden of Animals," newly expanded, appeared; among Khlebnikov's other contributions was his play *The Marquise Des S.*, a wry spoof aimed at *Apollo*. That journal responded by quoting *A Jam for Judges* mockingly in a column reserved for the lunatic fringe. Only after thirteen months did it mention Khlebnikov's contributions to *Jam* in earnest. Then the poet Gumilyov wrote:

> Khlebnikov is a visionary. His forms are convincing by their ab-
> surdity, his ideas by their paradoxicalness. It seems as if he dreams
> his poetry and then writes it down, preserving all of the incoher-
> ence of the course of events . . . [He] preserves all the nuances, so
> his verse loses in literariness but gains in depth. From this comes
> his sometimes incomprehensible neologisms, rhythms, and far-
> fetched turns of speech, which offend even the most unassuming
> taste. But really, what isn't dreamed? And in a dream everything is
> significant and valuable in itself.[35]

But almost no one else took the publication seriously, certainly not enough to be scandalized.

With money borrowed from Matiushin and Guro, Khlebnikov re-turned to his family for eight months the following winter; they were then living in Alferovo, another Mordovian village about 100 miles northwest of the present city of Ulianovsk. Compelled by his father to remain in "this most sordid of all towns" longer than he would have wished, Khlebnikov devoted himself to studying the Laws of Time that were to concern him for the remainder of his life. "I spend all my time working on numbers and on the fates of nations as dependent variables of numbers," he wrote to Matiushin in April 1911, and to his sister Vera: "I'm working on numbers. They keep fascinating me all over again."[36]

In June, still in Alferovo, Khlebnikov was officially expelled from the university for nonpayment of fees. When he returned to St. Peters burg in the fall, he briefly considered entering the Archeology Institute in Moscow, but was quickly caught up in the increasing pace of Cubo-Futurist activities.[37] Through Burliuk he met Vladimir Mayakovsky

---

35. *Apollon* 5 (1911), 76–78.
36. Letters 30 and 31.
37. For a general description of Cubo-Futurism in 1913, see Vladimir Markov, *Russian Futurism* (Berkeley, 1968).

and Alexei Kruchonykh,[38] both of whom had come to Moscow as young artists but had changed their primary creative efforts to poetry. When, early in their acquaintance, Kruchonykh brought his first poems to Khlebnikov in his room, there began a collaboration between the two poets that was to be of the greatest importance for Russian Futurism. Kruchonykh describes the process of their first collaboration:

> I pulled two pages of drafts out of my calico notebook, about 40 to 50 lines of my first poem "A Game in Hell." I showed it to him humbly. Suddenly, to my surprise, Velimir sat down and began to add his own lines above, below, and around mine. That was a characteristic feature of Khlebnikov, he caught fire creatively from the smallest spark. He showed me some pages covered with his minute handwriting. We read it together, argued, and corrected it again. And so we became coauthors unexpectedly and involuntarily.[39]

During the next two years the two men collaborated in the publication of five more books[40] and developed notions of poetic language that were central to literary modernism in Russia.

Khlebnikov left at the beginning of spring to visit the Burliuk family at Chernianka, an estate in Tavrida province managed by the Burliuks' father.[41] He was still working on the Laws of Time. On April 9, 1912, Burliuk wrote to Vasily Kandinsky in Munich: "Viktor Khlebnikov is here with me; I will bring you his article or mail it—about his discoveries in history and geography. He should be published, but in Russia for some reason they always publish the less deserving, and he doesn't have any energy at all."[42] Before he left on a six-week trip to western Europe in the middle of April, Burliuk loaned Khlebnikov some money to publish his booklet *Teacher and Student,* which included the first of several published studies of equations governing the fate of

38. Alexei Kruchonykh, a graphic artist from Kherson province, was a friend of the Burliuks. He had visited Moscow in 1907 and settled there in the winter of 1910–11. He gave up painting and began to write poetry early in 1912. See also letter 43.

39. Kruchonykh's unpublished memoirs quoted by Khardzhiev in NP 438.

40. *Mirskontsa* (The World in Reverse, 1912), *Slovo kak takovoe* (The Word as Such, 1913), *Bukh lesinnyi* (Forestly Rapid, 1913), *Starinnaia liubov. Bukh lesinnyi* (Oldfashioned Love. Forestly Rapid, 1914), *Te-li-le* (1914).

41. Letter of Alexander Khlebnikov in Miturich collection, postmarked March 21, 1912: "Vitya is leaving for the Burliuks at Chernianka."

42. Letter in Gabriele Münter-Johannes Eichner Stiftung, Städtische Galerie im Lenbachhaus, Munich. I am grateful to Rose-Carol Washton Long and Armin Zweite for a copy of the letter.

nations and principles determining the location of major cities. Here Khlebnikov also introduced his concept of the "internal declension" of words.[43] To the doubts expressed by his father about the intellectual respectability of certain parts of this work, Khlebnikov responded, "I am convinced the day will come when you will be proud of me, for I will have spread out a magic tablecloth upon which will appear a spiritual feast for the whole of humanity."[44] Khlebnikov continued to work on numbers, preparing to publish another booklet on the cycles of time and the nature of language.[45] Early in the fall with money supplied by Mayakovsky's summer neighbors, Georgy Kuzmin and Sergei Dolinsky, *A Game in Hell,* written jointly by Khlebnikov and Kruchonykh, was published in Moscow; it was illustrated with sixteen striking primitivist drawings by Kruchonykh's friend Natalia Goncharova.[46]

After a visit to the Black Sea and his aunt's family in Odessa— "Every day I go swimming in the ocean and I am becoming amphibian since I travel as far by sea as I do by land," he wrote to his father[47]— Khlebnikov went to Moscow, where he was near the Burliuks, Kruchonykh, and Mayakovsky. He lived then in a small room in apartment 3 at 11 Novo-Vasilevsky Street, with "one window, no sun, a bed near the floor like a turtle on its iron legs. Under the bed, a pillowcase in which he kept his work . . . a table and chair, an open wardrobe."[48] Evenings they would all gather in Marusia and David Burliuk's room on the fourth floor of the Hotel Romanovka on Malaia Bronnaia Street, a

43. D. Burliuk, "Tri glavy," p. 15. See also letter 36, April 23, 1912. Khlebnikov mentions the sum of 15 rubles for printing the booklet; Burliuk puts it at 20. *Uchitel' i uchenik* (Teacher and Student) was published in Kherson with a picture of Vladimir Burliuk on the cover.

44. Letter 37, June 5, 1912.

45. "Razgovor dvukh osob" (Two Individuals: Conversation) was published only the following March in *Union of Youth.*

46. Kruchonykh's first book of poems, *Starinnaia liubov'* (Oldfashioned Love), with illustrations by Mikhail Larionov, was published about the same time as *Igra v adu* (A Game in Hell). Georgy Kuzmin was a pilot and lived near Mayakovsky during the summer of 1912. From the fall of that year until early 1914, he and the composer Sergei D. Dolinsky financed five more publications by Kruchonykh and two collective publications, *Poshchechina obshchestvennomu vkusu* (A Slap in the Face of Public Taste) in January 1913 and *Trebnik troikh* (Trio Tract) in April. A second edition of *A Game in Hell,* with illustrations by Olga Rozanova and Kazimir Malevich, was published by them at the end of 1913.

47. Letter 37, June 5, 1912.

48. D. Burliuk, "Tri glavy," p. 17. For the address see letter 39; the street is now Iulius Fuchik Street.

residence favored by music students. There amid the red overstuffed furniture—Khlebnikov occupied the armchair by the piano, Mayakovsky the couch—taking tea from an enormous steaming samovar, the young poets and artists began their most important and productive winter. During the next two years the Cubo-Futurists published, in both Moscow and St. Petersburg, more than a dozen small collections of radically new prose and poetry, illustrated by avant-garde artists such as Mikhail Larionov, David and Vladimir Burliuk, Goncharova, Kazimir Malevich, and Pavel Filonov, and published mainly by Matiushin, Kruchonykh, and Kuzmin and Dolinsky. In all of this, and in spite of periods of depression occasioned by difficult relations with his father, Khlebnikov was an prolific participant.

That fall, the Cubo-Futurists began to put together a new edition of *A Jam for Judges* for publication by Guro and Matiushin's Crane Press in Petersburg. Khlebnikov, perhaps rashly, had promised a young friend, a thirteen-year-old girl identified in a letter only as "Militsa" and "El. Al.," that her poems would be printed in *A Jam for Judges II*. Both David Burliuk and Kamensky were opposed to it. Khlebnikov appealed to Matiushin, not on the basis of the new aesthetics—children's art had already been hung at modern exhibitions—but on the basis of the historical interest the poems would acquire in the future.[49] At the Romanovka the group also assembled the material for *A Slap in the Face of Public Taste,* a collection of prose and poetry by Khlebnikov, Kruchonykh, Nikolai Burliuk, Mayakovsky, Kandinsky, and others. It was prefaced by a manifesto of the same name, which declared the poets' right to harbor "an insuperable hatred for language as it existed before them" and extolling the "self-sufficient word." *A Slap* came from the printers on December 18; determined to be outrageous, it was printed on gray and brown wrapping paper and published in coarse burlap covers. Over half the collection is Khlebnikov's work, "written to astonish the world," and includes "BO BEH O BEE" and several other poems that put to creative use his ideas about a universal alphabet.[50]

By the time Khlebnikov moved back to Petersburg early in 1913, he was again thinking about Neo-Slavism. In Moscow he had met Janko Lavrin, a well known Slavist and publisher and an associate of the newspaper *Slav.* He lived with Lavrin for some two months after

49. Letter 39, October 5, 1912.
50. Letter 41, December 13, 1912. On the date of *Slap* see Nikolai Khardzhiev, "Poeziia i zhivopis'," *K istorii russkogo avangarda* (Stockholm, 1976), p. 16.

his move to Petersburg and, perhaps in response to hostilities in the Balkans and the buildup of the German army, the poet wrote several articles for *Slav,* attacking Austro-Hungarian and German militarism and exploring the cultural roots of various Slavic groups.[51] Khlebnikov in these essays remarks on the traditional narrowness of Russian literature, suggesting that its viewpoint be expanded to include neglected historical periods and peoples such as Jews, Pomeranians, and Bulgars. Here, as elsewhere, he mentions the importance to Russia of Persian and Mongol influences and even proposes a political alliance with the East: "To the ring of European allies we might reply with a ring of Asiatic allies—a friendly alliance of Moslems, Chinese, and Russians."[52]

Khlebnikov's move to Petersburg in 1913 coincided with a general Cubo-Futurist shift to that city. Kruchonykh also moved and set up his new publishing enterprise, EUY, that spring. In March, Burliuk, Kruchonykh, and the other Cubo-Futurist poets became officially allied with the Petersburg Union of Youth, a connection that gave them access to Union financial support for their public debates and for the production of a Cubo-Futurist opera, *Victory over the Sun.* The common alliance also made official Khlebnikov's relationship with Mikhail Matiushin, a leading member of the Union and one of the poet's most reliable publishers and supporters, and with Malevich and Filonov, two of his favorite artists. It was his friendship with the Cubo-Futurists that led to the publication of Khlebnikov's first books of poetry—Burliuk printed *Works* (1914), and Kruchonykh, under the EUY imprint, published *Roar! Gauntlets!* (1913) and *Selected Verse* (1914).

Although their ideas differed, Khlebnikov and Kruchonykh together were responsible for a large part of Cubo-Futurist theory. Kruchonykh's major article, "New Paths for the Word," quotes Khlebnikov's poetry and spells out some of the aesthetic principles of Cubo-

51. It may have been to this that Khlebnikov refers in letter 41, December 13, 1912, to his cousin: "I'm getting a job with a magazine for 40–50 rubles." *Slavianin* (Slav) began its twice-a-week publication in February 1913 as "the organ of the spiritual, political, and economic rapprochement of the Slavs"; it lasted for half a year. Parnis, "Iuzhno-slavianskaia tema," pp. 229–230.

52. "A Friend in the West." On Leibniz's similar suggestion, see the introduction to Theoretical Writings in this volume. "Who Are the Ugrorussians?" and "Expanding the Boundaries of Russian Literature" were also published in *Slav,* all between March and July 1913.

Futurism. The two poets' collaborative statements from 1913, "The Word as Such," and "The Letter as Such," call attention to the word and letter as physical objects, sensual signs that may be manipulated in various ways to carry expressive meaning. To both men *zaum*, beyonsense, was an extension of poetic language that rejected the mediation of common sense and deemphasized denotative meaning. Kruchonykh's beyonsense was created through devices such as intuitively invented neologisms, grammatical confusions, sound puns, and non-sequiturs, while Khlebnikov concentrated on a more analytical construction of neologisms, building new words carefully from meaningful linguistic elements.[53]

Matiushin's wife, the poet Elena Guro, died of tuberculosis on April 24, 1913, at their summer house in Uusikirkko, Finland. She was thirty-five. A gentle and sensitive person, Guro had greatly admired Khlebnikov—for his love of animals and birds as well as for his poetry. She saw in him the figure of the ideal poet, whose work "rings with the voice of love." Such a poet is a "giver, not a taker, of life."[54] Khlebnikov received the news of Guro's death in Astrakhan, where he was home for the summer. Her death and daily life with his father made him melancholy once again about his work and himself. "How stupid that people die," he wrote to Matiushin, "which means that we'll die too, and still we go on writing and publishing. And I am dying spiritually. Some sort of change; a disenchantment; a failure of belief, coldness, callousness."[55]

In July, Kruchonykh and Kazimir Malevich went to visit Matiushin, still in Uusikirkko recovering from his wife's death. They intended to develop a program of Cubo-Futurist work for the coming season and invited Khlebnikov to join them. He responded joyfully to the prospect of leaving Astrakhan: "I have tried in vain to get something done here, and something has been doggedly hindering my work,"[56] he wrote to Matiushin, and asked him for money to make the trip. But when he received Matiushin's check, he accidentally dropped it in the

53. On Eastern mystical concepts associated with Cubo-Futurist theory and the sectarian basis of Kruchonykh's beyonsense, see Charlotte Douglas, "Beyond Reason: Malevich, Matiushin, and Their Circles," *The Spiritual in Art: Abstract Painting, 1890–1985* (New York, 1986), pp. 184–199.
54. Elena Guro, as quoted in E. F. Kovtun, "Elena Guro, poet i khudozhnik," in *Pamiatniki kul'tury: novye otkrytiia. Ezhegodnik, 1976* (Moscow, 1977), p. 321.
55. Letter 46, June 18, 1913.
56. Letter 47, July 1913.

water while swimming and so was unable to join them. For the rest of the summer he continued his literary collaboration with Kruchonykh by mail and otherwise occupied himself with theories of time and resonance. Only in the fall did he return north.

In Petersburg, Khlebnikov was instantly swept up in the most active season yet for the Cubo-Futurists. David Burliuk read lectures entitled "Pushkin and Khlebnikov" in both Petersburg and Moscow, and Khlebnikov appeared on stage with the Burliuks, Igor Severianin, and others to read his poems.[57] To the astonishment of the public, the Cubo-Futurists frequently paraded the streets with bright pictures and lettering painted on their faces; the newspapers faithfully reported each shocking sight. This kind of publicity ensured that their two major events would be well attended: the opera *Victory over the Sun* and Mayakovsky's lyrical play *Tragedy* were presented under the auspices of the Union of Youth at the end of the year. Kruchonykh's absurdist libretto for *Victory* was preceded by Khlebnikov's long prologue; Matiushin composed songs for the opera and Malevich devised geometrical costumes and sets. Filonov worked on the backdrops for *Tragedy*. The two productions alternated nights at Petersburg's Luna Park Theater from the second to the fifth of December. *Victory*'s defiant coarseness and apparent meaninglessness caused an uproar and general pandemonium at each performance.[58]

The notorious founder of Italian Futurism, Filippo Tommaso Marinetti, made his sole visit to Russia at the beginning of 1914.[59] The only representatives of the avant-garde who were in Moscow when Marinetti arrived were Natalia Goncharova, Mikhail Larionov, and their followers. Larionov immediately established the tone of the three-week visit by writing inhospitably that sour milk and rotten eggs might be the most appropriate reception for their Italian guest. When, after three lectures and considerable publicity, Marinetti arrived in Peters-

57. Burliuk spoke at the Tenishev School in Petersburg on November 3 and at the Polytechnic Museum in Moscow on November 11, 1913. Khlebnikov participated at the lectures and in a reading at the Women's Medical Institute with Severianin on November 2, 1913. *Kolokol* 2260 (November 5, 1913), 3.

58. For details see Charlotte Douglas, "Birth of a 'Royal Infant': Malevich and 'Victory over the Sun,'" *Art in America*, March-April 1974, pp. 30–41.

59. Marinetti arrived in Russia on January 26 (February 8) and left on February 17 (March 2), 1914.

burg, Khlebnikov set upon him with uncharacteristic bitterness. At the first lecture Khlebnikov angrily handed out a printed statement accusing his compatriots of "falling at the feet of Marinetti" and calling them "traitors to Russian art."[60] The physician Nikolai Kulbin, who was Marinetti's host in the city and responsible for the lecture arrangements, attempted to restrain Khlebnikov. As Marinetti looked on, the loud public argument ended when an enraged Khlebnikov challenged Kulbin to a duel and furiously left the hall.[61]

On the following day as part of an account of the lecture, Khlebnikov's leaflet was printed in the *Stock Exchange News* with a snide comment about his being considered a "genius." This elicited still further angry reactions; in vituperative letters to Nikolai Burliuk and Marinetti, he attacked them and Kulbin, and disassociated himself from the Cubo-Futurists.[62] Marinetti had arrived in Russia just when the avant-garde felt they were at last achieving a reputation independent of their Italian namesakes. This, combined with a quite justified fear of the native tendency to admire excessively anything foreign, prompted the Russians' reactions to him. Marinetti must have been disappointed to have had so little substantive contact with the Cubo-Futurists, but he nevertheless criticized them for their religious and cosmic interests, which he saw as inappropriate to Futurism. Not everyone was as hostile to him as Khlebnikov; the Burliuks, Mayakovsky, and others were grudgingly cordial. Although they appreciated Italian Futurist art, the Russians were offended by Marinetti's manner, his bellicose statements, and even his moustache. Most of all they were disturbed by his lack of understanding of their work. The poet Ilya Zdanevich summarized, as soon as Marinetti left, "He's very nice, but he talks a lot of nonsense. Furthermore, he is a bourgeois and doesn't know much about art."[63]

Khlebnikov developed a wide acquaintance among Petersburg's creative elite at this time. In 1913–1915 he often spent holidays in the Finnish countryside north of Petersburg, included as a guest at the

60. The text of Khlebnikov's leaflet is given in the notes to letter 56.
61. Khardzhiev, "Veselyi god," p. 131.
62. Letters 56 and 57.
63. For details of Marinetti's reception in Russia, see N. I. Khardzhiev, "'Veselyi god' Maiakovskogo," *Vladimir Majakovskij: Memoirs and Essays,* Bengt Jangfeldt and Nils Åke Nilsson, eds. (Stockholm, 1975), pp. 108–151; Bengt Jangfeldt, "Šeršenevič, Kul'bin and Marinetti," *We and They: National Identity as a Theme in Slavic Cultures* (Copenhagen, 1984), pp. 158–165; and Charlotte Douglas, "The New Russian Art and Italian Futurism," *Art Journal,* Spring 1975, pp. 229–239.

comfortable summer homes of new friends. There he drew and wrote poems and was the object alternately of affection and bewilderment.[64]

The First World War brought devastation to Russia. In the struggle to defend itself, the country consumed all its energy and resources and normal living ceased. Revolution, when it came first in February of 1917 and again in October, was the reaction of an exhausted populace to the demands of a war that seemed never to be over. Along with many of the Russian Cubo-Futurists, Khlebnikov was opposed to the war. Much of his poetry after 1915 was strongly pacifist, and his calculations of time took on an added sense of urgency. In the story "Ka" he speaks as the artist who, asked whether he is going to war, responds "I'm already at war . . . only it's a war to conquer time, not space. I crouch in my trench and grab scraps of time from the past. It's a rough assignment, just as bad as you'd have in a battle for space."[65] On April 8, 1916, the thirty-year-old poet, who had been working on his "alphabet of the mind" at home in Astrakhan during the Easter holidays, was drafted and sent to the 93rd Infantry Regiment in Tsaritsyn. No one could have been more unsuited to military life. He wrote sadly to a friend just after he was drafted:

> The King is out of luck,
> The King is under lock
> and key.
> Infantry Regiment Ninety-Three
> Will be the death of the child in me.

Khlebnikov appealed for help to Nikolai Kulbin, the object of his wrath during Marinetti's visit and the publisher six years earlier of his "Incantation by Laughter" (despite his activities in the cause of the avant-garde, Kulbin was still a respected professor at the Military Medical Academy in Petersburg): "Marching, orders, it's murdering my sense of rhythm, and makes me crazy by the end of the evening detail, and I

64. Among Khlebnikov's new friends were the family of Baron and Baroness Alexander Budberg, especially their daughters Irina and Vera, the popular writer Boris Lazarevsky and his daughter Vera, the playwright Nikolai Evreinov, A. E. Belenson, editor of the journal *Strelets* (Sagittarius), and the artists Ivan Puni and Xenia Boguslavskaia. See the excerpts from Khlebnikov's diaries of this period, in this volume.

65. *King of Time*, p. 88.

can never remember which is my right foot and which is my left . . . Thanks to the continual, monotonous cursing and swearing, my feeling for language is dying within me."[66]

Khlebnikov's career in the army was spent mainly in training camps and awaiting responses from his various medical appeals and reviews. On leave the summer after he was drafted, he met Grigory Petnikov and the poet Nikolai Aseev in Kharkov, where they published as a poster-sized sheet "The Trumpet of the Martians," a manifesto declaring a new worldwide organization and attacking the older generation. In Kharkov, Khlebnikov, Petnikov, and Aseev were often at the lively and friendly home of the Siniakovs. Maria, one of their daughters and an artist, was a signatory of the manifesto.[67] In November, Petnikov published Khlebnikov's "Alphabet of the Mind," "A Second Language," and "Letter to Two Japanese" in his journal *Chronicle*.

The revolution in February 1917 saved Khlebnikov from active service. At the time he was at an army training camp in Saratov. By the middle of April he had been given leave and, again in Kharkov with Petnikov, wrote "An Appeal by The Presidents of Planet Earth," a Futurist-style manifesto with anarchist overtones, proclaiming a world government and openly advocating peace.

It was during the war that Khlebnikov's work on numbers gradually cohered into the idea of a "government of time." Dubbed "the King of Time" by the Cubo-Futurists at the end of 1915, Khlebnikov with his friend and disciple Grigory Petnikov founded the Society of 317. It was planned to be an association of 317—a key number in Khlebnikov's calculations then—creative scientists, writers, and thinkers from various countries who would constitute themselves into a government of time and oppose the evils worked by political states, those "governments of space." In the course of the next months, Khlebnikov's name for himself and a changing group of friends evolved from 317 and Martians to the Presidents of Planet Earth, "inventor/explorers" who took a stand against the "investor/exploiters" of the world. From the time of the first 1917 revolution, appeals, directives, and manifestos were written in bureaucratic language in the name of the Presidents of Planet Earth.

The turmoil of revolutionary Russia, the exhilarating mixture of childish pranks and general irreverence, combined with sobering un-

---

66. Letter 77, April–May 1916.
67. Krasnaia Poliana, the Siniakov estate, was just outside Kharkov. Another daughter, Oksana, married Aseev.

certainties about the "unknown conqueror," are strikingly conveyed in "October on the Neva," Khlebnikov's very personal account of the Bolshevik revolution in Petersburg and Moscow:

> We rushed outside. The cannons were silent. We ran through the streets of the city like kids after the first snowfall, looking at the frosty stars of bullet holes in windows, at the snowy flowers of tiny cracks; we walked through the shards of glass, clear as ice, that covered Tverskoy Boulevard. Pleasant, those first hours, when we picked up bullets that had smashed against walls, all bent and twisted, like the bodies of burnt-up butterflies.[68]

In Petersburg, Khlebnikov's and Petnikov's closest friends were artists. They stayed for a time with Lev Bruni, whose apartment in the Academy of Art building was a well-known gathering place for the avant-garde, especially those who were now admirers of Khlebnikov. "Khlebnikov was the trunk of the age, and from it we were germinating branches," the critic Nikolai Punin wrote about the frequenters of "apartment no. 5."[69] Khlebnikov was exhilarated by the events around him, in spite of the extreme practical difficulties they caused. In Moscow he spent much of his time with the artist Vladimir Tatlin. The revolutionary clashes taking place in the streets seemed only to herald vast new possibilities for art, and the two occupied themselves with plans to stage Khlebnikov's plays.[70]

In the revolution the Russian modernists saw an opportunity to advance their art, to create autonomously but with government approval and support, and to serve a society demonstrably in need of their help. Under the new Soviet of Workers and Peasants, Khlebnikov looked forward eagerly to the social changes that seemed possible in Russia, and for the first time he himself found outlets for his work. In Astrakhan during the Civil War, he worked as a journalist for a Bolshe-

---

68. *King of Time*, p. 108.

69. In his unpublished memoirs Punin discusses the special relationship he, Bruni, and Pyotr Miturich, residents of the apartment in 1916, had to the work of Khlebnikov. See also the letter from Petnikov to A. E. Parnis, quoted in "V. Khlebnikov—Sotrudnik 'Krasnogo Voina,'" *Literaturnoe obozrenie* 2 (1980), 108. In December, Punin approached Anatole Lunacharsky, the head of Lenin's new Commissariat of Enlightenment, for permission to stage *Oshibka smerti* (Miss Death Makes a Mistake), but the idea was not pursued. N. Punin, "V dni Krasnogo Oktiabria," *Zhizn' iskusstva* 816 (1921), 1.

70. Khlebnikov and Tatlin planned to stage *Miss Death Makes a Mistake, Gospozha Lenin* (Mrs. Laneen), and *13 v vozdukhe* (13 in the Air). Khardzhiev, *NP* 413.

vik newspaper, *Red Soldier*, the organ of the local military-political section.[71] He was involved, together with his father, in organizing a nature preserve on the Volga delta and took part in the Technical Union, a club for people interested in scientific ideas.[72]

In the winter of 1919 in Kharkov, while the city fell alternately into the hands of the Red and White armies, Khlebnikov avoided the military altogether by spending four months in a psychiatric hospital. He went to the institution on his own, presenting an official request to be evaluated on his fitness for military service. Khlebnikov's psychiatrist, who made a detailed and generally sympathetic assessment of his mental condition, concluded:

> And so this presence of outstanding qualities in the talented Khlebnikov clearly indicates that it is unnecessary to protect society from him and, quite the reverse, the distinctive qualities of this gifted personality have postulated a special approach to him on the part of the collective, in order to derive the maximum benefit from him. This is why in my conclusion as a specialist I pronounce him not fit for military service.[73]

But, once at the hospital, Khlebnikov seemed to find little opportunity to leave, especially because of the chaos in the city, and he remained there until February 1920. During this time he suffered two sieges of typhus, a disease rampant at the time, but, apart from his legs, which continued to pain him, he appeared to make a good recovery. Khlebnikov finally left his refuge when A. N. Andrievsky, a young instructor with the political section of the Red Army and an admirer of his work, offered the poet room in his communal lodgings.[74]

Upon release, Khlebnikov wrote anxiously to Moscow about publication of his work, long promised but repeatedly postponed, and reports that he is "beginning to work once again, which for a long time

71. The newspaper *Krasnyi voin* (Red Soldier) was initially the organ of the Astrakhan Military Council and the Provincial Military Commissariat, subsequently the organ of the political section of the Eleventh Army. Parnis, "V. Khlebnikov," p. 105.

72. For a discussion of the Technical Union, see Parnis, "V. Khlebnikov," p. 108.

73. V. Ia. Anfimov, "K voprosu o psikhopatologii tvorchestva. V. Khlebnikov v 1919 godu," *Trudy 3–i krasnodarskoi klinicheskoi gorodskoi bol'nitsy* 1 (Krasnodar, 1935), 71.

74. On Khlebnikov in Kharkov, see Ronald Vroon, "Velimir Khlebnikov's 'I esli v "Khar'kovskie ptitsy"': Manuscript Sources and Subtexts," *Russian Review* 42 (1983), 249–270.

I simply could not do."[75] Sergei Esenin published a few of Khlebnikov's poems in his collection *Dawnlight Diner*, and in the hungry and war-torn city the artist Vasily Ermilov managed to print fifty copies of *Ladomir*, a long evocation of the land of the future.[76] Ermilov had just been appointed artistic head of the local propaganda organization but, even so, his resources were limited. He recalls:

> He said to me: I have to have this printed, then, like Antaeus touching the ground, I will renew my strength. I resolved to help him do it, and proposed that he recopy the text in his own hand using lithographic ink (he couldn't stand recopying), and this is what he did. The book was printed with the help of my brother, who at that time worked in the lithography shop of the Southern Railroad.[77]

Throughout 1920 and 1921 Khlebnikov worked as a civilian publicist with the army and navy on the southern front. He was desperately poor, badly fed and clothed, but seemingly content. In wry good humor he even poeticized his body lice as "All the citizens, all the men and women / Of the Government of ME."[78] At first in Kharkov and then in Baku, he lectured soldiers on his various projects for the future and the cycles of time, for which work he received food allotments and small sums of money. In Baku he joined two old friends, Kruchonykh and the poet Gorodetsky, whom he had known at Ivanov's Academy of Verse, in writing propaganda posters for the cultural section of the Volga-Caspian fleet. There he lived with the graphic artist Mechislav Dobrokovsky, who also was working on the posters, at the Maritime dormitory, and it was here that he formulated the Laws of Time, the fundamental algorithms that he believed govern natural and historical events. "I possess equations for the stars, equations for voices, equations for thoughts, equations of birth and death," he wrote to Vera, and reported reading an account of his calculations at evening classes for workers: "I announced to the Marxists that I represented Marx squared, and to those who preferred Mohammed I announced that I

---

75. Letter 101, April 30, 1920.

76. Later in Moscow Esenin published Khlebnikov's "Noch' v okope" (Night in the Trenches) separately. A. E. Parnis, "Vstrecha poetov," *Literaturnaia Rossiia*, December 12, 1975, p. 16.

77. Parnis, entry for October 28, 1885, in *Pamiatnye knizhnye daty* (Moscow, 1985), p. 168. See also Zinovy Fogel, *Vasilii Ermilov* (Moscow, 1975).

78. "Russia and Me," *King of Time*, p. 35.

was the continuation of the teachings of Mohammed, who was henceforth silenced since the Number had now replaced the Word."[79]

It was in connection with his propaganda activities that the poet suddenly received the chance to go to Persia as a lecturer and journalist with the Red Army. In mid-April 1921, an extremely happy Khlebnikov sailed for Enzeli (now Bandar-e Anzali, Iran). He was elated by the sun and sea and with the opportunity finally to be in the East. To his mother he sent leaves from a quinine tree, and to his sister he wrote triumphantly: "The banner of the Presidents of Planet Earth follows me wherever I go, and waves now over Persia."[80] Tanned, dressed in Persian robes, and living on handouts, he explored coastal and inland villages, staying for a time as tutor in the house of a Talysh khan, where he became enamored of the khan's young daughter.[81] At the garrison club in Resht he read poems to the soldiers and published many of those he was writing in *Red Iran,* the army weekly.[82] Dobrokovsky had preceded Khlebnikov to Persia and was working as before, producing revolutionary posters and linoleum cuts for *Red Iran.* Long-haired and barefoot, the two friends walked the narrow streets of Resht together. The local people took them to be religious men and labeled them "Russian dervishes":

> Only with Dobrokovsky did he talk about anything and often walked with him around the town, eliciting from the Persians a certain, almost religious, respect. Dobrokovsky had the same style, walking in some kind of florid caftan and the same long hair. Dobrokovsky, it seems, got his caftan from an ecclesiastical wardrobe, which had been taken by the Baltic sailors along with several thousand White Guard trunks.[83]

They spent many of their days reclining in cafes drinking tea and smoking the opium-based teriak. While Khlebnikov composed poetry, Dobrokovsky, who had picked up the local dialect quickly, sketched portraits, talked politics, and propagandized for the revolution: "Down with the English! Land to the peasants! Welcome the democratic re-

79. Letter 102, January 2, 1921.
80. Letter 109, April 14, 1921.
81. Ronald Vroon, "Velimir Khlebnikov's 'Razin: Two Trinities': A Reconstruction," *Slavic Review* 39/1 (March 1980), 81–82.
82. A. E. Parnis, "Khlebnikov v revoliutsionnom giliane," *Narody Azii i Afriki* 5 (1967), 157, 159.
83. A. Kosterin, "Russkie dervishi," *Moskva* 9 (1966), 218.

public! Friendship with Soviet Russia!" Spontaneous contributions from their listeners kept them well supplied with food, drink, and smoke.

In the fall Khlebnikov returned with the army to Russia and spent the next few months in the town of Piatigorsk in the Caucasus. From the Persian seashore, autumn in the mountains came as a disorienting shock:

> A tree burned like a torch in the golden air,
> Turning, bending.
> Autumn's steel is angry,
> Striking sparks of golden days . . .
> The golden wind of autumn
> Has scattered me everywhere.[84]

Here he came face to face with the brutal starvation brought on by the Civil War. He sympathized especially with the children, many of whom he tried to help. The cycle of poems "Hunger" bears painful and ironic witness, as the desperate children and their families turn for food to the small woodland creatures with whom the poet also felt a kinship.

> Last night
> by the fire they chattered
> cooked their frogs
> and ate them.
> I wonder if maybe today
> they get butterfly borscht? [85]

Khlebnikov had his most prophetic visions of the technological future in the midst of this extreme privation. He wrote the essay "The Radio of the Future" in Piatigorsk at this time, predicting coast-to-coast concerts by means of radio and art exhibitions transmitted on illuminated screens. Understandably, perhaps, he was especially optimistic when it came to food: "we will have learned to transmit the sense of taste . . . A simple, ample meal will wear the guise of a luxurious feast." [86]

84. "Vozdukh raskolot na chernye vetki" (The air splits on black branches), III.186.
85. "A boy down by the creek," *King of Time,* p. 47.
86. "The Radio of the Future," *King of Time,* p. 158.

Khlebnikov arrived in Moscow for the last time late in December 1921. He had been away for over two and a half years, and it took him a month in a hospital car on the overcrowded and marginally functioning railroad to travel the 2500 miles from Piatigorsk. In a cold and ravaged city staggering beneath enormous inflation and persistent food shortages, the poet found many of his old friends, including Kamensky, Kruchonykh, and Mayakovsky, who helped him find food and clothes. His earlier bouts of typhus had left him in fragile health. "At that time he was quite unlike the former Khlebnikov, the participant in literary uprisings. He was stooped, and his face was buried in a large neglected beard."[87] He stayed at first with Mayakovsky and the Briks on Vodopiany Street.[88] "Vitya Khlebnikov arrived wearing nothing but a shirt," Mayakovsky wrote to Lily Brik. "We got him some clothes and a pair of shoes. He has a long beard, but looks good—except that he looks too much like a bourgeois intellectual."[89] The Poets' Union provided an occasional free dinner at the Domino Cafe.[90]

In spite of his poor health, Khlebnikov was working very hard. Before February he determined the final form of *Zangezi,* a verse drama, drafted the prose piece "At the Sea," and wrote several poems and prose pieces about Stenka Razin. In response to requests from the journal *Makovets,* he contributed poems based on his recent experiences in Persia and Piatigorsk.[91] He also seemed ready to resume his former social life, appearing at public and private gatherings "pale and gaunt . . . in a soldier's coat, a Persian lambskin hat and heavy army shoes. He carried an unwieldy case, chock-full of manuscripts."[92] He was often cheerful:

87. Memoir of Nikolai Nikolaevich Bariutin (Amfian Reshetov), "My Meetings with Khlebnikov," TsGALI, f. 2283, op. 1, ed. khr. 6. Bariutin was the head of the literary section of the journal *Makovets,* which published two issues in 1922. In the second issue, on press just at the time of Khlebnikov's death, an article on Khlebnikov by Reshetov was announced for the next issue. The manuscript "My Meetings with Khlebnikov" is probably a draft of this article.

88. Letter 114, January 14, 1922. In 1972 this street was incorporated into Turgenev Square.

89. Quoted in Katanian, p. 160; see letter 114, January 14, 1922. See also "Pis'ma k L. Iu. Brik (1917–1930)," in *Literaturnoe nasledstvo* 65 (Moscow, 1958), 126.

90. Bariutin memoirs, 1.5, 10.

91. "Noch' v Persii" (Night in Persia) and "Segodnia Mashuk kak borzaia" (Today Mount Mashuk is a hound dog) appeared in the first issue of *Makovets.* The second (and last) issue carried his poem "Kak vody dalekikh ozer" (Like the waters of distant lakes). Bariutin gives an account of the solicitation of these manuscripts in his memoir.

92. Memoir of B. P. Denike, as quoted by Khardzhiev in "Novoe," *Den' poezii,* p. 202.

You hotshot young hustlers,
you air-brains, look out!
There's a new man in Moscow
in an old country coat.[93]

One of the most important tasks for Khlebnikov at this time was
the compilation and publication of *The Tables of Destiny*, a work he
hoped would be the definitive version of the mathematical relationships
he had finally perfected a year earlier. Now that he was back in Moscow,
publishing his discovery was uppermost in his mind. "I hope to have
the Law of Time printed and then I'll be free," he wrote to Pyotr Miturich, an artist who greatly admired Khlebnikov.[94] But in devastated
Moscow the poet also was constantly in need of food and a place to
stay. From Vodopiany Street he moved to a series of temporary lodgings that friends found for him; as had often been the case, he was aided
most by artists. Nikolai Bariutin of *Makovets* remembers meeting
Khlebnikov and the art student Fyodor Bogorodsky one gloomy afternoon on the Arbat:

> Bogorodsky [was] arranging a place for Khlebnikov to stay
> for the night, taking him to a room belonging to some friend who
> had left on a trip out of Moscow.
>
> We go into the house. We go along a long corridor in an
> apartment that at one time had been grand and comfortable, but
> that now was crammed with household junk.
>
> "There's a little stove in here," Bogorodsky says, entering a
> dark room and lighting a match. "Now we'll get it started."
>
> In a few minutes a cheerful fire played in the little wood stove.
>
> "Well, Velimir, here you are. Take off your shoes, take off your
> things, dry out your leggings," Bogorodsky says soothingly. "Lie
> down, get some rest, the owner's away, there is no one here to
> disturb you. There's only one drawback: no night-cap."
>
> Khlebnikov rejoices silently at this place to spend the night.
> He pulls off his wet boots.[95]

Eventually Khlebnikov found a relatively permanent corner of living space in a student room at Vkhutemas, the old Moscow School of

93. "Ei, molodichki-kupchiki," published in *Izvestiia*, March 5, 1922.
94. Letter 115, March 14, 1922.
95. Bariutin memoir, 1.11 reverse, 12.

Painting, Sculpture, and Architecture which Burliuk and Mayakovsky had attended ten years previously. The artist Alexander Labas remembers Khlebnikov's stay:

> Alexei Kruchonykh was a frequent visitor to the Vkhutemas dormitory at 21 Miasnitskaia St. One day Velemir Khlebnikov came with him to see us . . . S. Telingater, then a student, also lived in our apartment and knew Khlebnikov from Baku, from which both had come to Moscow. I remember somewhat earlier Kruchonykh had said that Khlebnikov lived for some time with Mayakovsky. Soon Khlebnikov settled in our apartment, in the first room on the left, where Telingater, Plaksin, and Tomas lived. Everyone related warmly to Khlebnikov and was happy to have him. When I went into that room to see my roommates I would see Khlebnikov; he often sat near the bed, on which lay his notebooks. I remember my first impression of him: first of all huge gray and blue eyes, and a strangely alienated oblong face—he reminded me of a solitary crag.[96]

In spite of the problem of living quarters and illness—which toward spring seems to have become increasingly debilitating—Khlebnikov succeeded in publishing the first section of his *Tables of Destiny*, and two more were in preparation. Bariutin, in search of material for the second issue of *Makovets*, found him one spring day working with a young man who was checking the poet's mathematical calculations:

> When he finished the calculations, the young man proposed they go out to the country. April had been sunny. Khlebnikov was delighted and began to gather his things.
>
> "We can take the trolley from here to Yaroslav station. Then a train to Losipoostrovsky or Perlovka . . . We'll go out into the fields where we can see the whole horizon."
>
> "Wonderful!" said the young man, his eyes shining with anticipation.
>
> "Are you coming with us?" Khlebnikov asked me happily.
>
> I decided not to go. Khlebnikov remembers that I live in a cell in the Simonov monastery, where he has never been. He in-

96. A. Labas, "Razmyshleniia i vospominaniia: Stranitsy iz dnevnikov," in E. I. Butorina, *Aleksandr Labas* (Moscow, 1979), p. 67.

tends to visit me soon. Tomorrow! I say goodbye. We walk together to the exit.

But . . . Khlebnikov, as always, has no money. The young man checks his wallet in alarm. There is enough for one ticket, but for two . . . . . Sadly he looks at those around him, at me. I slap my pockets in embarrassment.

Khlebnikov was much distressed by this failed excursion; he grew morose and withdrew into himself.[97]

But another trip promised to be more successful. He decided to return for a visit to his parents in Astrakhan. Before setting out on the trip south, however, Khlebnikov went first for a few weeks' rest with his friend Pyotr Miturich to the village of Santalovo, near Novgorod, where Miturich's wife was teaching school. Khlebnikov and Miturich left Moscow on May 12 and arrived three days later, after a difficult journey. Almost immediately Khlebnikov became extremely ill and lost the use of his legs. Miturich brought him to a hospital in a neighboring town at the beginning of June, but the doctors there could do nothing to help his paralysis or stop the spread of gangrene in his legs. After three weeks, and now certain of death, the poet returned to the Miturich home and was settled in a small adjacent bathhouse. There he died five days later, on June 28, 1922.[98]

On the 29th we buried him in a corner of the cemetery in Ruchiakh.

The priest there didn't allow him inside the fence of the cemetery, since we were having a civil burial.

But since there isn't another cemetery here, the executive committee ordered him put inside the fence and they gave him a place in the very end with the Old Believers. On the lid of his coffin there is depicted a blue planet earth and the title:

The President of Planet Earth

Velemir I

We put the coffin in the pit and smoked a "peace pipe," and I

97. Bariutin memoir, 1.14, 14 reverse.
98. The account of these last days is from "O smerti Khlebnikova" (On Khlebnikov's death), an unpublished manuscript by Vasily A. Katanian. There has been no medical diagnosis made of Khlebnikov's last illness. Biographical data compiled by E. F. Nikitina indicate that Khlebnikov died of *zarazheniia krovi* (blood poisoning or toxemia); TsGALI, f. 341, op. 1, no. 292. After his hospitalization in Kharkov in 1920, he seems never to have fully recovered the use of his legs.

told the peasant workers about Hiawatha, Velemir's friend, who also cared about half the people of the world, and about Velemir, who cared about the whole world; that is the difference.

And we covered up the coffin and on a nearby pine we wrote his name and the date.[99]

Khlebnikov was just thirty-six years old. *Zangezi*, the poetic summation of his life's work, had been printed in Moscow only a few days earlier.

C. D.

99. In a letter from Miturich to Nikolai Punin, published in Konstantin K. Kuzminsky and Gregory L. Kovalev, eds., *The Blue Lagoon Anthology of Modern Russian Poetry*, vol. 2A (Newtonville, Mass., 1983), p. 42. Miturich uses the spelling "Velemir" throughout.

LETTERS

1 To His Parents

Kazan, Detention Facility
December 3, 1903

Dear Mama and Papa,

I didn't write because I thought one of you would be coming to see me.

I only have a little time left to do[1]—about five days—and maybe even less, and the time passes quickly. We are all in good health. The other day they released one student—Kibardin—who had tuberculosis, and we gave him a noisy send-off. I started drawing on the walls recently and drew a [illegible] portrait from "life" and two other heads, but drawing turns out to be against prison regulations so I washed them off. I have one piece of news, which I will tell you later. I have been studying physics the last few days and I have gotten through more than 100 pages; today I am reading Minto. One of the students here, an upperclassman, a math major, wrote Vasilev[2] a letter asking about the qualifying exams. Vasilev wrote back that the last one would be on December 18th, so there's still time to prepare for it. I've done half the analyses. A few of the people here have good voices and a sense of pitch, and we listen to them sing before the evening lockup, and sometimes we all sing in chorus. Did the art school burn down? There was a rumor here about a fire, but nobody knows anything about how bad it was. Anyone could have predicted a fire there, though; the place was full of flammable materials, and even worse, kerosene lamps with paper lampshades.

Love to everybody, Katya, Shura, Vera, we'll be together soon.

Vitya

1. Khlebnikov entered the University of Kazan as a mathematics major in September 1903. At the beginning of November he took part in anti-tsarist demonstrations sparked by the death of a young Social Democrat who had been confined to a psychiatric

hospital. Khlebnikov was one of thirty-five students arrested and sentenced to a month in prison.

2. Khlebnikov's first professor of mathematics was the great Lobachevsky scholar, Alexander V. Vasilev.

2   To His Parents

Moscow
1904(?)[1]

Dear Mama and Papa,

Love and kisses to everybody. You are probably waiting impatiently for a letter from me. I am writing on my second day here. The train trip turned out comparatively all right, but for two whole days I got only two or three hours sleep, that's all; and all I had to eat the whole time was a couple of piroshki and two glasses of tea, so that when I got to Moscow I was very tired and my legs hurt a lot, because most of the time I slept standing up. I didn't stay at the hotel, I just left my bags with the doorman and went out and found a little room for rent for 6 rubles and after I moved my bags in the same day I went around almost the whole of Moscow. I saw the Tretiakov Gallery,[2] the Museum of History and also the Turgenev reading room, and since I had been on my feet for almost forty-eight hours, and then got to Moscow at 6 in the morning and walked around town until 8 that night, I got very tired and a few times I just had to stop to give my legs a rest. But today it's all cleared up, I feel completely rested. And yesterday I looked so awful (maybe I looked really exhausted) that people turned around in the street to stare. Today I went sightseeing again and saw the Rumiantsev Museum[3] and the Museum of History. Also today I tried to work out a realistic idea of what it would cost to live in Moscow; I figure if you're a vegetarian you can definitely live on ten kopeks a day.

That's a detailed account of my activities. What I liked best at the Tretiakov Gallery were the paintings of Vereshchagin.[4] A few things though were a disappointment. At the Rumiantsev Museum there is a wonderful statue of Victory by Canova, and busts of Pushkin and Gogol. I'll write more details later, love and kisses to everybody: Papa, Mama, Katya, Shura, Vera.

Vitya

1. It is unclear exactly when Khlebnikov made his first trip to Moscow.

2. Now the State Tretiakov Gallery. The gallery is named after its founder, Pavel Mikhailovich Tretiakov, who commissioned and collected the progressive realism of the Wanderers school and portraits of contemporary Russian writers, artists, and scientists. Tretiakov gave his unique collection in 1892 to the city of Moscow; it was nationalized by Lenin in the summer of 1918. From the Tretiakov Gallery by way of the Museum of History on Red Square to the Turgenev reading room is a distance of about two miles.

3. The Rumiantsev Museum was located in the Pashkov mansion at Znamenka and Okhotnyi roads (now Frunze Street and Marx Prospect). From 1861 to 1925 it maintained collections of Russian and Western European art, ethnographical materials, and a famous library. It is now part of the Lenin Library.

4. Vasily Vasilevich Vereshchagin, a painter of historical and military scenes, was very popular in the late nineteenth century. Khlebnikov was probably especially attracted to Vereshchagin's detailed ethnographical studies, the result of travels in India, Syria, Palestine, and Central Asia. Vereshchagin maintained studios in Munich and Paris and exhibited widely in Europe and the United States as well as at home. He was a casualty of the Russo-Japanese War when the battleship on which he was sketching was sunk at Port Arthur.

3 To His Parents

Moscow

1904(?)

Dear Papa and dear Mama,

I'm writing on the third day of my stay in Moscow. Moscow has become so familiar already that I can't imagine myself any place but Moscow. Yesterday I gave you the wrong address. It's: c/o Glazunov, Dominkansky Street, Meshchanskaia district. So my street isn't Ulansky, but Dominkansky. Today I went walking again and went to the Historical Museum a second time and to the Igumnov house.[1] The Igumnov house is built in the style of a boyar terem[2] and is very artistic with potbellied columns, ceramic tiles, and a scaly roof. I asked a cabdriver where the house was—he told me, and added "a wonderful house." Since ordinary people don't really appreciate architecture, that evidently means this style feels closer and more accessible to Russians, otherwise the cabdriver wouldn't have singled it out. And if that's the case, it means this is the only style that can be called a Russian National style. I would make them teach architectural history in the seminaries, because the local clergy has no idea at all how to preserve the monuments of the past. There are a lot of old churches here; at one time they must have been very beautiful and distinctive, but now thanks to the negligence of the priests they all look like ordinary churches, painted yellow with green metal trim. Sometimes you even see wonderful old moldings covered with rough plasterwork, and in fact in the Historical Museum I saw an old icon with a depiction of Assumption Cathedral; at one time it evidently had a great deal in common architecturally with St. Basil's Cathedral, but now there is not the slightest resemblance.

1. The mansion of N. V. Igumnov is at 43 Dmitrov Street. Built by the architect N. I. Pozdeev in the "Russian revival" style and completed in 1893, it now houses the French Embassy. In the late nineteenth century this style of architecture was associated with Pan-Slavic political sentiments.

2. The tower in old Russian mansions where women were secluded.

4 *To Viacheslav Ivanov*[1]

Kazan
March 31, 1908

While reading these poems I kept remembering your "Pan-Slavic" language, whose shoots are meant to grow through the thickets of contemporary Russian. Which is why it is your opinion of my poems I value and consider important, and why it is you I have decided to turn to. If you find you are able, please let me know your opinion of the enclosed lines, at this address: V. V. Khlebnikov, c/o Ulianov, 2 gora, Kazan.

I will be most deeply grateful to you.

V. Khlebnikov

1. Viacheslav Ivanovich Ivanov was one of the leaders of the Symbolist movement in Russia. Petersburg poets and artists who attended his "Wednesdays" often remarked on Ivanov's talent for drawing out and encouraging others. This letter from Khlebnikov included fourteen poems written early in 1908, all marked by neologisms based on Slavic roots. The idea of a Pan-Slavic language is discussed by Ivanov in his essay, "A Joyous Craft and an Intellectual Joy" ("O veselom remesle i umnom veselii," 1907): "Through the thickets of contemporary speech the language of poetry, our language, must grow— and grows already—from the underground roots of folk speech in order to sound forth like the vocal forest of the Pan-Slavic word."

5 *To His Sister Vera*

Postmark: Petersburg[1]
September 23, 1908

And how are We feeling? Have We by any chance left the Caucasus and migrated to Australia?

I haven't had a single letter from you, not a single line—and in the meantime on Sept. 22nd I was at Aunt Sonya's and saw Uncle Sasha and grandmother Olga P. and Sofia N.(?) They asked me to convey warm family greetings. I liked Uncle Sasha best. O. P. (grandmother) hasn't got a single gray hair. Aunt Sonya lives with a black poodle named Heather who didn't like me at all. She doesn't look very much like the pictures of her we have at home, but sometimes her smile, her laughing eyes and her tone of voice give the impression of splitting in two and you start thinking she's Aunt Sonya and Aunt Varya. So far I haven't been to see Uncle Petya.[2]

I send my most affectionate regards.

My address: 19 Maly Prospect, apt. 20, Vasilevsky Island.

1. Khlebnikov enrolled at St. Petersburg University on September 18, 1908, as a third-year student in the Natural Sciences Department.

2. The relatives mentioned here are from his mother's side of the family: Uncle Sasha is Alexander Nikolaevich Verbitsky, his mother's older brother; Aunt Sonya is Sofia Nikolaevna Verbitskaia, his mother's sister. Aunt Varya is Varvara Nikolaevna Riabchevskaia, his mother's other sister, who lived in Odessa. Uncle Petya is Lieutenant General Peter Nikolaevich Verbitsky, his mother's second brother.

6 *To His Father*

Postmark: Petersburg
October 13, 1908

Your Excellency!

I humbly beg you most respectfully to please send me my *Zoology*— I forget the author's name. Sometime in the near future could you wire some money and send me a winter coat. I got 30 + 25 rubles already. Vital statistics: I live on Vasilevsky Island about 15–20 minutes from the University. I pay 10 rubles for a single room, I eat at the dining hall for 10 to 50 kopeks—the food is always terrible. I could eat at the landlady's for 11 rubles, but that's for when times get better. The distances are killing me. The trolleys too. I've seen the relatives, except for Uncle Petya. I also got *Golden Fleece*,[1] one or two issues. Not long ago I went to "An Evening with the Northern Panpipe"[2] and saw them all: Sologub, Gorodetsky, and the rest of the zoo . . . . .[3]

In Petersburg the distances are so enormous that you spend almost all your time walking . . . . .

1. *The Golden Fleece* (*Zolotoe runo*) was an elegant Symbolist journal founded in 1906 by the financier Nikolai Riabushinsky. It was published in French and Russian and continued until spring 1910.

2. "Artistic evenings" of poetry, music, and theatrical presentations were a popular form of entertainment in Russian cities. The poet Alexander Blok was present at this one and wrote: "'An Evening with the Northern Panpipe' distinguished itself by its vulgarity and its fundamental monstrosity; there was something in it that demanded, cried out for, literary castigation; but that's a topic I'll discuss at length somewhere else. For the most part this evening was no better and no worse than all such evenings, past or yet to come; some very bad actors performed a very bad play; Remizov read, two poets read—Gorodetsky and Roslavlev—a singer sang. Why all of this had to go on in front of a fence surmounted by a steamship funnel is unclear to me still."

3. Fyodor Sologub, poet and novelist, one of the older generation of Symbolists. His prose had some influence on Khlebnikov's (see notes to letter 11). Sergei Mitrofanovich Gorodetsky was a poet (and in this period, an artist) whose work the young Khlebnikov admired and whose archaizing may have served as an early model for his own (see notes to letter 18). Gorodetsky's brother Alexander also painted and wrote poetry; he contributed a poem to *A Jam for Judges* (see letter 27).

7 *To His Sister Vera*[1]

October 18, 1908

This is a letter about me; yesterday I had the pleasure of seeing a piece of mine, "A Sinner's Seduction,"[2] in print, in the magazine *Spring*. My fishing expedition to the land of gloryhood will be smooth sailing, as long as I have the desire to do it.

1. This excerpt is the only text available for this letter.
2. Khlebnikov's first literary publication.

8   To His Father

Petersburg
November 25, 1908

I am living temporarily with—guess who? With Grigory Sudeikin![1] They moved to Lesnoi and I've moved in with them, since I was
thrown out of my apartment on the 21st. I borrowed 20 rubles from
them. I left the letters in Kharkov care of General Delivery.[2] For the
sake of "the unification of the church" I am willing to join you in
Odessa as soon as I have finished up my literary affairs. Uncle Sasha
was retired without a pension; the matter is under investigation by the
State Duma. I saw Uncle Petya and Aunt Masha[3] again. I don't have
any address for the moment, since I'll be moving again soon and I don't
know where. Grigory Sudeikin's address: 4 Institute Lane, apt. 2, Lesnoi. They send their regards. I feel there is something I ought to be
writing you about, but I can't remember what it is. How is Katya feeling? And what's her address?

Love and kisses. It would be nice to come south to see you all,
wherever.

1. Grigory Semyonovich Sudeikin was a friend of the Khlebnikov family and taught
at the Forestry Institute in Petersburg.
2. Khlebnikov's father was now working in Kharkov.
3. Aunt Masha is Maria Konstantinovna Timofeeva, the wife of Peter Verbitsky.

9   To His Mother

Petersburg
November 28, 1908

28 November. It's been a long time since I've had any word from
you, or from Kharkov. Nor have I gotten the "tribute" the older generation is supposed to be paying the younger, at least not so far. Which
is why I have spent about a week with Grigory Semyonovich Sudeikin.
They live at 4 Institute Lane, apt. 2, Lesnoi. They send their warmest
regards. Tomorrow I am moving to my own room, 2 Guliarnaia St.,
apt. 2, Petersburg Side. A few more days of fussing with literary affairs.
I lead a "bohemian" life. Petersburg can be like a good stiff breeze; it

has a chilling effect. My Slavic feelings are frozen as well. Once I finish things up here, I wouldn't mind coming to see you.

Grigory Semyonovich is trying to get me to finish my notes on the Pavdinsk region.[1] I still have a few things on my mind, but once they are taken care of I am ready to flee the city and head for the bottom of the sea. In this chorus of grasshoppers my note is distinct, but it isn't strong enough, and I don't think it can be sustained through to the end. Love to you all, and say hello to the Riabchevskys, to Aunt Varya and Kolya and Marusya.[2] How is Katya? Is she getting better? Tell Vera I'll write her about the exhibit.[3] I'm sending new offprints.

Is Shura continuing with natural history?

1. Khlebnikov eventually sent his notes from the 1905 field trip to his brother Alexander, who encorporated them into "Ornithological Observations in the Pavdinsk Preserve."

2. The Riabchevskys are the Odessa relatives of the Khlebnikov family. Aunt Varya is Varvara, the sister of Khlebnikov's mother. She was married to Nikolai Riabchevsky; Kolya and Marusya are their children.

3. Khlebnikov probably plans to write to Vera about the large Salon exhibit that was being organized by Sergei Makovsky. The exhibition opened in Petersburg in December 1908. Makovsky was trying to offer a comprehensive view of contemporary Russian art, and so in addition to painters closer to the critic's taste such as Vrubel, Serov, and the World of Art painters, Khlebnikov probably saw works by the more radical Javlensky, Kandinsky, and David Burliuk.

10 *To His Mother*

Postmark: Moscow
December 28, 1908

Through the combined forces of evil fates, mine and others', I never left for Odessa. My coming to visit you was an inner necessity, but to tell you the truth, I got into a kind of impasse about it and couldn't figure a way out. I arrived at the train station in a kind of intoxication just at feeling myself already on the way to Odessa. But it had never dawned on me to tell the cabdriver to hurry. The cabdriver pulled up to the entrance exactly as the clock was striking three. I ran to the track and got there just as the guard was locking the gate. So I have experienced the power of retribution, mockery of some kind, and I don't know the reason for it. Now I'm in Moscow. Today I went to explore the Kremlin. Tomorrow the Tretiakov Gallery and lots more.

We found a free place to stay, a bed (in student dormitory no. 3) and have been met generally by the usual Moscow hospitality. I was surprised to discover the worth and nobility of the ordinary Moscow character. Moscow was the first city that conquered and won me. It has changed for the better since I was last here.

Happy New Year!

11   *To Vasily Kamensky*[1]

Sviatoshino
January 10, 1909

Dear Vasily Vasilevich,

I am sending you three pieces ("A Scythian Story," "The Crimead," "The Burial Mound of Sviatagor"). Can you find a place for them? That would encourage me. I am planning a big novel whose prototype is Savinov's *Bathers*[2]—freedom from time, from space; the coexistence of the act of desiring and the thing desired. The life of our own time fused with the era of Vladimir the Shining Sun[3] (Vladimir's daughter, wedded to the Danube River) as it might be imagined by the composers of byliny[4] and their audience. Some chapters will (will?) be written very realistically, others rhythmic, measured, some will be dramatic pieces (dramatic in the sense of differentially analytic), others will be narrative. And all linked by a unity of time, piled into a single current at one and the same time. In addition, retired officers, pacificationists, maximalists, and so forth, in the spirit of *Dead Men's Magic*.[5] But I need an editor's blessing. Will you give it to me? Of course that's a secret.

What does Remizov say about my *Snow White*?[6] If you see him, please don't hesitate, Vasily Vasilevich, ask him.

What is the first issue of the paper like? Would you send me a copy, if it isn't too much trouble? I'm very sorry I wasn't able to write something from Old Russian life. But I've got so many things going that the whole Russian feeling has fallen off. I've been shunted off to Sviatoshino—

Viktor Vladimirovich Khlebnikov
53 Severnaia St.
Sviatoshino
Kiev District, Kiev Province

Do you know how many cities you've destroyed, you red raven? In your veins flows the blood of your ancestors the Novgorod river pirates, and your whole publication seems to me the work of young men speeding their boats down the Volga, searching for new freedom and new shores.

If you can use the enclosed, let me know right away, if you can't, send them back. These pages mean a lot to me.

All the same, editors are a major evil.

The Word-Wooer

P.S. Six pages enclosed.

1. Kamensky was a prolific writer and memoirist; two of his works from this period are *Mud Hut* (*Zemlianka*), a novel, and *Tango with Cows* (*Tango s korovami*), a concrete poem. As editor of *Spring*, he had been responsible for publishing Khlebnikov's "A Sinner's Seduction" in October 1908. By January 1909 Kamensky was working on the short-lived literary magazine *Light Ray* (*Luch sveta*), for which Khlebnikov sent him the selections mentioned in this letter. *Light Ray* folded before Khlebnikov's contributions were published, but the first issue did contain Nikolai Kulbin's (see letter 77) debut as an art critic, his review of Makovsky's Salon exhibition (letter 9).

2. A painting by Alexander Ivanovich Savinov, known for his portraits and genre scenes. Actually called *Bathing* (*Kupanie*), it was shown at Petersburg's Academy of Arts in 1908, the year Savinov left that institution.

3. Vladimir I, Grand Prince of Kiev (978–1015). He figures under this epithet in folk tales and epic poems.

4. These Russian epic oral poems, going back to the Middle Ages, were still being recited by rural singers in the early part of this century.

5. *Navi chary,* a three-part novel by Fyodor Sologub, published in 1907–1909, is known in English under the title of the first book, *The Created Legend*. Its elements of eroticism and black magic elicited widespread criticism. One critic called it "a strange novel, an attempt at depicting a bloody nightmare of recent times combined with mysticism, pure fantasy, and lyricism." Other critics considered it one of the most significant works of its time.

6. Khlebnikov's play *Snezhimochka* was not published until 1940. Alexei Mikhailovich Remizov was a writer much admired by Khlebnikov.

12   *To His Mother*

Postmark: Petersburg
May 22, 1909

I still haven't the slightest idea what's happened to my things. This is the fourth night I haven't slept at all, and I am discovering it's good for you as long as you keep eating well. Since I am in Petersburg incognito, I haven't gone to see anyone and I don't intend to. I have become a child of the streets, but of course please don't believe any of this is true. At the University (for some reason I haven't been expelled yet) some people are organizing a trip to the Caucasus—hunters, philologists, on foot through Svanetia. Wouldn't Shura like to join them in Tsaritsyn? Today is a beautiful sunny day.

13 *To His Father*

Postmark: Petersburg
May 31, 1909

Greetings from 1000 versts away.[1] I would be very obliged if I could hear from you *immediately*, with some exact indication of what your plans are for June 2nd. That would spare me any unnecessary ordeals and deliver me from this uncertainty, which is the worst thing. I met with Ivanov. He was extremely sympathetic to my literary efforts. Love and kisses to everybody. Did the Odessites[2] arrive? If so, give them my regards. 5 Guliarnaia St., apt. 2.

I'll see you soon, I hope [illegible].

1. A verst is about two-thirds of a mile.
2. Khlebnikov's Aunt Varvara and her family.

14 *To His Sister Ekaterina*

Postmark: Petersburg
June 8, 1909

I will be seeing you all soon. Wouldn't Shura like to join the hiking tour (university students, zoologists, photographers) to Svanetia (N. Caucasus)? He could join them and they would greet him with outstretched arms (they already left Petersburg on May 30th). I had my picture taken recently with a skull and when I get home I'll show it to you.

This fall in Petersburg they are organizing a group, where my stuff will be read.

15 *To Viacheslav Ivanov*

Petersburg
June 10, 1909

Know that I write for one reason, to convey to you that at this moment, four hours after leaving you, I am for some reason full of sadness, sad without knowing why, and I regret very concretely that I did not succeed in extending my hand, in saying goodbye—bidding farewell—to Vera Konstantinovna[1] and the other members of your circle, whose acquaintance I hold most dear and value very highly.

I am being carried along by some power on a course I cannot and do not want to see, but my glance is turned back toward you and your hospitality.

I know I will die within these 100 years, but if it is true that we die continually beginning from birth, then I have never died so *starkly* as I have these last days. A whirlwind seems to have washed my roots free from the soil they were born in and need. That is why the feeling I have—that death is not the last act but an event attendant on life, part of the *whole* of life—is stronger now and more palpable than it was.

What have I been doing these last few days? I went to the zoo, where I had the strangest vision of some kind of connection between Buddhism and a camel, and between Islam and a tiger. After a brief reflection I arrived at a formula: natural species are the offspring of belief, and religions are infantile species. One and the same rock has split humanity into two currents, which has given us Buddhism and Islam, and also split the unbroken core of animal nature, giving birth to the tiger and the ship of the desert.

In the camel's calm visage I read the open book of Buddhism. On the face of the tiger certain slashes proclaim the law of Mohammed. From such perceptions it is not difficult to affirm that species are species because the animals that comprise each of them have a specific vision of the Godhead. The religious beliefs that agitate us are merely pale impressions of forces at work eons ago, forces that at some point created the species. There you have my somewhat exalted view of the matter. I think it can be appreciated only by one who has ascended mountaintops himself.

Here are a few lines on the subject, of my own odd composition.

O Garden of Animals!

Where iron bars seem like a father who stops a bloody fight to remind his sons they are brothers.

Where eagles perch like eternity, crowned by a day that has yet to see its evening.

Where a swan is like winter all over, but its beak is like autumn leaves.

Where deer are startled again and again, beneath their branching stone.

Where a clean-shaven soldier throws dirt at a tiger, all because the tiger is greater.

Where a peacock drops its tail, and it looks like Siberia seen from the height of a rock on a day of early frost, when the golden forest fire of leaf-fall enamels the green and the mottled blue of pine groves, when over it all move shadows of racing clouds, and the rock itself seems like the body of the bird.

Where fishwingers sit comically grooming each other, and display the touching compassion of Old World landowners.

Where man and dog are strangely joined, in a baboon.

Where a camel knows the essence of Buddhism, and suppresses a Chinese smile.

Where a snow-white beard surrounds the face of a tiger, surrounds its venerable Moslem eyes, and we honor the first Mohammedan and drink in the beauty of Islam.

Where a humble bird drags behind itself a golden flattering sunset, to which it has learned to pray.

Where lions get up and glance with weary faces at the sky.

Where at last we grow ashamed of ourselves, and begin to think we are older, more worn than we once imagined.

Where elephants sway like mountains during an earthquake, and stick out their trunks for handouts from a small boy, saying "Feed me! Feed me!", echoing that ancient refrain. And they wheeze like pine trees in autumn, and move their wise eyes and their undulating ears.

Where the polar bear hunts like an osprey, tracking his nonexistent prey.

Where we watch in a seal the torments of a sinner, as it cuts the water and wails its unrelenting wail.

Where the beasts have learned to sleep while we gawk.

Where the bat hangs sleeping, and its capsized body resembles a Russian's heart.

Where a sable displays two delicate ears, like a pair of nights in springtime.

Where I search for new poetic rhythms, whose beats are animals and men.

Where the animals in their cages glow, as meaning glows in language.

O Garden of Animals![2]

I saw Remizov today. The attacks in the press seem to be depressing him.[3]

Farewell! In the sense of until we meet again!

Allow me to say farewell on paper to those I didn't see when I left. Please convey my warmth and devotion.

> Velimir Khlebnikov
> 9 o'clock, June 10
> Tsarskoselsky Station

1. Ivanov's stepdaughter, Vera Konstantinovna Shvarsalon.
2. This is the first version of "O Garden of Animals!" It was considerably expanded and first printed in *A Jam for Judges* in 1910.
3. See the following letter to Kamensky, where these attacks are discussed at length.

16 To Vasily Kamensky[1]

Sviatoshino
August 8, 1909

1. I write in the hope of seeing you soon in person.

2. I have been languishing this summer in a "moorish captivity"; I didn't get done what I intended to do.

3. I finished *Malusha's Granddaughter*,[2] but it's not much to brag about.

4. My mood at the beginning of the summer might have been described as a mood of "undisguised malevolence" toward this world and this century, into which I have been cast through the kindness of a benign Providence. But now I'm calmer and look upon creation with tranquil eyes. I've thought up a complicated piece, *Time Transversal*,[3] where the logical rules of time and space are broken as many times as a drunkard in an hour raises a glass to his mouth. No chapter will have any connection whatsoever to the next. I intend, with a beggar's prodigality, to cast upon my palette all the colors and discoveries I have, and they are to have each one authority over only a single chapter: differential dramatic writing, dramatic writing using a method of the thing in itself; included is the right to use newly created words, a kind of writing based on words from a single root, use of epithets, universal phenomena, painting with sound. If it were published, this piece would seem as unsuccessful as it would remarkable. The final chapter will present my prospectus for the future of humanity.

My jolly Vasily, my fiery fellow—I must ask you about an offense that weighs upon me, one that breaks all rules of friendship, sympathy, and all emotional ties. I may nevertheless turn out to be less of a monster than I seem. Our dear Ati Nezhit Mokhoelich[4] asked me to send him clippings from the Kiev newspapers with his pieces, which he needed. Of course I went right away to the editorial offices to look up the issues he wanted. Despite their unfriendly attitude, I got into their files two times, and a third time at another paper, but couldn't find his pieces, even though I went through every issue. That was still nothing serious. But at *Kiev Thought* I turned up a reprint of an article from the *Stock Exchange News* entitled "A Writer Plagiarizes," which describes in insulting language an alleged plagiarism in his story "The Little Mouse" in the collection *Italy*. To accuse the creator of *Clockwise* of robbery is to perpetrate an unconscionable act, malicious and unconvincing, and I reacted to it with disgust and contempt. But I was astonished to find that people around me who think of themselves as progressive and intelligent have blindly accepted this vile article as the truth. It's true another article appeared later on, but still: a Russian writer has been publicly slapped in the face. A cheap rag has made a noisy accusation of plagiarism against a writer, all our writers mill about like sheep at the crack of a whip, and the writer in question practically falls to his knees and in that position begs them not to hit him again. That's a disgrace! How can it not be? I cannot allow someone I call my friend to let himself be insulted with impunity.

His honor must be wiped clean. If Alexei Mikhailovich will not proudly seek satisfaction, then he must allow his friends to seek that satisfaction. We must step forward like Haydamaks, weapons in hand, to defend with our very blood the honor of a Russian writer (that temple, farmed out for revenue). To hell with arbitration boards—this calls for abandon and a few flames. Alexei Mikhailovich should demand satisfaction of Propper, the editor of the paper. I imagine he won't feel like doing it himself, nor will his friends let him, so he must grant his friends the right to seek that satisfaction. This is the only proper behavior for a writer who holds his head high—for a high priest of the truth. We must stand close to Alexei Mikhailovich; we are his friends. Alexei Mikhailovich should remember that each of his friends will accept a duel proudly to defend his honor and the honor of Russian writers in general, just as the Haydamaks once defended their country's honor. But that same friend may not want to lend a hand, if he sees him endure such an insult and then refuse the honorable offices of a friend.

So, once again: I would be proud to accept a duel to defend Alexei Mikhailovich and the honor of writers in general. All of this I cannot convey to Alexei Mikhailovich, so I am writing you, confident that you will make him acquainted with the substance of the above.

1. This letter has been published in Russian in two versions; one by Kamensky in his *Way of an Enthusiast* (*Put' entuziasta*, 1931), a second, fuller, by Khardzhiev in his edition of Khlebnikov's unpublished works. The version we translate here is from Khardzhiev.

2. *Vnuchka Malushi*, a long poem, first published in 1913 in the collection *Rotten Moon* (*Dokhlaia luna*).

3. This piece has not been identified, but the description bears a certain resemblance to his supersaga *Otter's Children*.

4. Alexei Mikhailovich Remizov.

17 To His Father

Postmark: Petersburg

September 29, 1909

My address: 48, Line II, apt. 18, Vasilevsky Island. I changed my major to history and philology[1] and won't have to pay a fee. In order to get credit for this year, I have to pay the university 25 rubles owing from last year before October 10. Also I didn't buy galoshes and boots. So much for my financial affairs. The weather has been good mostly, except for a few rainy days. My room gets a lot of light and is very comfortable. I get my tea in a tiny little samovar. I have seen most of my friends. People here in Petersburg are used to cholera, and it doesn't worry them any more than other diseases like typhus and so forth. Regards to everybody.

1. In October 1909 Khlebnikov was registered in the Department of Russian and Slavic Languages in the School of History and Philology.

18 To His Mother

Postmark: Petersburg

October 16, 1909

This is already the second time I've written: I didn't leave the book at home, it's the librarian who made the mistake.

I have met almost all the young writers in Petersburg—Gumilyov, Auslander, Kuzmin, Hofman, Count Tolstoy, and others including Guenther.[1]

My poem[2] will probably be included in *Apollo,* a new Petersburg journal that will be published here in town.

Dealing with the University wears me out, it takes up so much of my time. I am an apprentice and my teacher is Kuzmin (the author of *Alexander the Great,* etc.). Gumilyov is getting ready to go to Africa.

Guenther wants Kuzmin to marry his cousin. Count Tolstoy wants to write [illegible] and to free himself from outside influences. Gumilyov has strange pale-blue eyes with black pupils. Tolstoy has the look of a contemporary of Pushkin.

Some people are predicting a big success for me. But I feel worn out, and very much older. (Guenther is the hope of German literature.) Love and kisses to all the Lubny and Odessa people.

1. Nikolai Stepanovich Gumilyov was a poet who in 1910 married Anna Akhmatova; they divorced in 1918. His second book of poems, *Romantic Flowers* (*Romanticheskie tsvety*), had been published in Paris the previous year. Gumilyov and Sergei Gorodetsky founded the Acmeist movement in 1912, which, in opposition to Symbolism, advocated concrete referents and logical clarity in poetic language. He was shot for counterrevolutionary activity by the Soviet authorities in 1921.

Sergei Abramovich Auslander, a writer of prose and poetry, Kuzmin's nephew.

Mikhail Alexeevich Kuzmin, a talented novelist and poet. By the time of Khlebnikov's letter, Kuzmin was well known for his novel *Wings* (*Krylia,* 1906), the cycle *Alexandrian Songs* (*Aleksandrinskie pesni,* 1907) and *Nets* (*Seti,* 1908), a book of verse. Kuzmin was especially supportive of Khlebnikov when he first came to Petersburg.

Viktor Viktorovich Hofman, a poet.

Alexei Nikolaevich Tolstoy, a novelist and poet, distant relative of Leo Tolstoy. He became a well-known Soviet writer.

Johannes von Guenther, German poet and translator of Russian, went to Russia in 1906 and frequented Symbolist literary circles in Petersburg; from 1909 to 1913 he was a contributing editor of *Apollo.* His memoir *Ein Leben im Ostwind* (Munich, 1969) describes this circle of young writers and says of Khlebnikov (p. 275): "The highly talented Khlebnikov also seemed eager to join us. With his obsessive interest in the root formations of the Russian word, he was accepted by us as closely related, since we also stood by the motto, 'In the beginning was the Word,' and for us too were the words of Paul to the Corinthians set down, 'For now we see through a glass, darkly; but then face to face'; the sentence may be considered as a motto for Symbolism as a whole, but it characterized Khlebnikov's endeavors as well. He got along with me and Kuzmin; he considered us old acquaintances. He did not get along with Gumilyov, perhaps for political reasons, since he leaned toward the left and had already collided with the secret police years before. Khlebnikov sought my company at every opportunity; we dined together a few times and read each other our poems. He admired my poems, but unfortunately didn't know enough German to perceive their defects. I regret that this connection with us was of such short duration; mutual arrogance—for even the quiet and almost humble-seeming Khlebnikov was possessed of a fantastic spiritual haughtiness—was a firm barrier between him and my friends. I regret it, but I realize that his development would surely have distanced him from us in a few years anyway. And yet Khlebnikov's poetry, with its search for roots and construction of a new vocabulary from those roots, might well have meant something for the Academy, which was founded concurrently with *Apollo* and met in its offices.

2. Certainly "O Garden of Animals!", included in letter 15 to Ivanov—which never appeared in *Apollo* and was first printed in *A Jam for Judges* (1910).

19 *To His Brother Alexander*

Postmark: Petersburg
October 23, 1909

Dear Shura,

How are things in Odessa?

I'm writing this letter in a hurry. I am going to be a member of an "Academy" of poets.[1] V. Ivanov, M. Kuzmin, Briusov, Makovsky, are the leaders of the group.[2] I have met Guenther, whom I like a lot, Gumilyov, Tolstoy.

I've gotten better. And I look good. Gumilyov wrote the poem "Dante"[3] that I remember you liked so much. Write me and give me your ideas about poetry. I value them for their depth and sincerity and originality, which I don't have much of. My prose poem will be published in *Apollo*. I pretend to be very excited, although I'm not.

I'll send you a copy.

I am an apprentice of the famous Kuzmin. He is my magister. He wrote *The Triumphs of Alexander the Great*.

I am keeping a journal of my meetings with the poets.

Regards to G. V. and everyone.

1. The first meeting of the reorganized academy, known also as the Academy of Poets, the Poetic Academy, and the Society of Lovers of the Artistic Word, took place in the editorial offices of *Apollo*. Ivanov served as chairman, and the remaining members of the board were Makovsky, Innokenty Annensky (who died on November 30, 1909), Briusov, Kuzmin, and Blok. Blok read his *Italian Verses* and was a huge success. During the winter of 1909–10 the academy presented a broad program of readings and lectures.

2. Valery Yakovlevich Briusov, a noted Symbolist poet, critic, and translator, founded the journal *Libra* in 1904. Sergei Konstantinovich Makovsky, a conservatively inclined art critic, organized the Salon exhibit of 1908 (see notes to letter 9).

3. Gumilyov's poem about Dante, entitled "Beatrice," was published in the anthology *Pearls* (*Zhemchuga*) in the spring of 1910.

20 *To His Father*

Postmark: Petersburg
November 13, 1909

I got the 30 rubles.

Winter started exactly on November 1st.

If you don't need the winter coat, then I very much hope a flying carpet can transport it to me here in Petersburg, together with a pillow, a hood (if you have one), a warm winter hat (if you have one), and a warm quilt. If the hat is a comfortable fit, that would be wonderful. I am a member of the Academy of Verse, where I have made quite a fool of myself and read my poems twice at meetings. One of my pieces is going to be published in the February issue of *Apollo,* another play may be performed.[1]

How is Vera's painting? I saw Chernov-Plessky.[2] He told me to give you all his regards. I also saw Grigorev.[3]

Shura asked me to send him my notes on Pavdinsk. I'll do it as soon as I can. Unfortunately I don't know his address. The list of birds is in *The Zoological Museum of Kazan University,* Lavrov's article. You've got the book in your library.

1. Nothing by Khlebnikov ever appeared in *Apollo.* The play he speaks of here was probably *The Little Devil* (*Chortik*), which bears the subtitle "A Petersburg Entertainment to Celebrate the Birth of *Apollo.*" The play was not performed and was first published only in 1914 in *Works.*

2. L. M. Chernov-Plessky had taught drawing in Kazan to the Khlebnikov children.

3. Boris Dmitrevich Grigorev was a well-known artist whom Khlebnikov had met in Kazan. Once, while they both were visiting the writer Kornei Chukovsky, Grigorev had occasion to sketch Khlebnikov. The drawing appears on page 129 of *Chukokkala: Rukopisnyi al'manakh Korneia Chukovskogo* (Moscow, 1979).

21   *To Mikhail Kuzmin*

Petersburg
1909

Mikhail Alexeevich,

The ambiguous ventriloquy of the doorman has cast me into depths of despair. I sit here biting my lip and don't know what I should do: divide my wealth equally between poison and paper for a suicide note, or send someone a terrifying challenge, a fearsome declaration of war to the death. I imagine this nail-biting of mine will continue beyond the grave, if only I pretend to be dead and people believe me! But I suspect you don't believe a word of all this, and will write me a nice consoling letter that will dispel my doubts. In case you don't—*persae ex omnibus populis antiquis bellicosi erant.*[1]

Not upon my shield, but not behind it either.[2]

1. The Latin line—"The Persians were the most warlike of all ancient peoples"—reveals, albeit jokingly, Khlebnikov's early identification with the East.

2. The mothers of Sparta were reported to have sent their sons into battle with the phrase "With it or upon it" (carry your shield back, or let them carry you back upon it, dead).

22 *To His Sister Vera*

Postmark: Petersburg
December 28, 1909

Dear Vera,

I hope you'll come around January 1st. At that time we'll work things out together somehow. My enterprising imagination has dreamed up the idea of a trip to Montenegro in the company of a certain artist. I am proceeding under full sail, hoping to make it through the boring holidays and into January. I already moved to a new apartment: 11 Donskaia St., apt. 10, Vasilevsky Island, (next to Line 15, the entrance is on Maly St.). I've been bored lately and feel a bit tired. How are my things? I still haven't picked them up yet. Love to my stormy, unruly, free-love sister

23 *To His Family*

Postmark: Petersburg
December 30, 1909

Happy New Year Katya, Mama, Papa. What did the old year bring me? Weariness, recklessness, thoughtlessness. One person told me that I've written a couple of lines of genius, another (Viacheslav Ivanov) said the heart of a lion beats in my breast. Just call me Richard the Lionhearted. Here everybody calls me Lubek or Velimir.[1]

I had my picture taken and I came out looking like Mlle. Adrienne. Someone here thinks I look like the young Turgenev and refers to me as Monsieur Tourgeneff. I'm sending you my card, with Viktor scratched out and Velimir written in. I'm in a better mood again, feeling reckless and jolly. Love to everybody.

Yesterday the 29th the weather was like spring. It rained, and some colonel's funeral procession went by, with a band, on its way to Smolny cemetery. I am spending the holidays eating, like a goose preparing for the sacrificial knife. What my fatal knife is, you'll know soon enough. The last half a year I have almost gotten into a duel every month. I go around wearing a bowler-hat and everyone thinks I'm in hiding and living under an assumed name. Gumilyov is in Africa, hunting hyenas.

1. Khlebnikov used many pseudonyms, but the only one that remained constant, and became the name by which he was best known, was the south Slavic "Velimir." The choice of a name proper to Bulgaria and Yugoslavia was undoubtedly associated with Khlebnikov's Pan-Slavism; he was also pleased with its etymological derivations, "great world" and "world-commander." It is likely that the name came to his attention when an unknown poet used it in the same issue of *Spring* in which Khlebnikov made his literary debut. See A. E. Parnis, *Pamiatnie knizhnie daty* (Moscow, 1985), p. 166.

24 To His Brother Alexander

Postmark: Petersburg
January 16, 1910

Happy New Year, dear Shura! I apologize in all languages living and dead for still not having sent the birds. The only excuse I have is that my things were stuck in the baggage check at the train station for over a month. We keep putting off what we mean to do, and since a single grain of sand won't make the difference between a hill and a handful, we tend to ignore a single day, and we end up being late. There's a sermon for you. I wish you would do something with the birds. I've given up on them. Perhaps you could add a tail-end to your article, something to express my ideas on the origin of the species? I did think I had something new and profound to say on the subject.

Say Happy New Year to Maria Nikolaevna, Aunt Varya, Kolya Sr. and Kolya Jr., if they don't all seem too stuck up.

Your brother while these earthly errors endure, whether near or far away,

Velimir (Viktor)

25 *To His Sister Ekaterina*

Postmark: Petersburg
February 1, 1910

I wrote two letters not very long ago, but I don't know whether you got them since I wasn't quite sure of your address. I got a letter from Vera, it was pretty illegible, but she seemed clearly very depressed. It must be really cold in Moscow, because she writes "we'll revive come spring" when it's "warm." Also in the letter she writes about a little rusalka who climbed up into an oak tree, and lost her grip and fell to the ground. I haven't been to see Aunt Sonya and the others for quite a while. Everyone liked the doll very much, and if you can, please send me two more like it, or just one. I'll give one away, to Remizov I imagine, and keep the other one for myself. It will make me think of the Ukraine. At the moment I'm alive and well and feeling good. I have a brand-new address: c/o Mikhailov, 54 Volkovsky Prospect, Volkov Village, St. P. I got a job tutoring. What are Shura's plans for the summer? I wish he would go spend some time at Ascania Nova, the Pfalz-Fein estate in Tavrida province, on the Black Sea coast near the Dnieper. There are zebras there, buffalo, bison, wild horses. It's a wild animal preserve known all over the world except in Russia, and it's located right here within our borders. And he could get permission to spend some time observing them. I don't know what I'll be doing or where. For a while I was thinking of taking a trip to Montenegro. Now I don't know. I'm still a member of the Academy of Verse. Tell Shura to write and let me know what he'll be doing with the birds and does he still need them.

26 *To His Father*

Petersburg
Early 1910(?)

I moved to the outskirts of St. Petersburg. c/o Mikhailov, 54 Volkovsky Prospect, Volkov Village.

Please send me as much as you can right away. I'm well. I sent Shura the birds. I got my things. I haven't heard from Vera in a long time. I went to a [illegible] lecture on being a student. I haven't gone to see the Sudeikins in a long time. Or to see Aunt Sonya. I stay at home. One time I had a fight with everybody. I'll see Briusov soon. The weather today is marvelous.

I'm doing some tutoring.

I. I. I.

I haven't been to the Academy of Verse for two weeks. I am preparing to rise from my ashes.

27 *To His Father*

Petersburg
December 1910

Thanks. I went to see Aunt Sonya and got my "tribute"—surprised that I still continue to get it. I really want to quit school, I've been feeling awful, but seem to be getting better now, although I'm still not sure. I'm going to Moscow in a couple of days. Can you let me know where Shura lives? St. Petersburg bores me to death. Best to everyone. I see Vera a lot. After Christmas I'm publishing a book of my own. *A Jam for Judges* did get reviewed—sarcastically.[1] Weather report: rain, slush, melting snow.

1. *A Jam for Judges,* the small collection edited by Kamensky, Mikhail Matiushin, and David Burliuk and published by Matiushin in April 1910, is considered in retrospect to have been the first Russian Cubo-Futurist book. Khlebnikov published here the satiric play *Marquise Des S.,* an expanded version of "O Garden of Animals!", and part of his long poem *The Crane-Beast (Zhuravl').*

In this letter to his father, Khlebnikov probably refers to the mocking quotations from *Jam* that were printed in *Apollo's* "Bees and Wasps" column in the December issue. Later the collection was reviewed by Valery Briusov for *Russian Thought (Russkaia mysl')* and by Gumilyov for *Apollo*. Briusov called it "full of schoolboy tricks in poor taste" and "outside the limits of literature," but he did praise a few lines by Kamensky and Burliuk. Gumilyov thought Kamensky and Khlebnikov the only poets in *Jam* who were not "simply helpless." Matiushin recounts the uproar of *Jam's* first planning meeting: "How many smart remarks, how many wisecracks about the people who would be stumped by the look of the book alone, printed on wallpaper and with its strange verse and prose! Vladimir Burliuk drew the pictures of the participants right then. And right then the witticisms began and brought on more than laughter—hilarity." But "the bomb," Matiushin remembers sadly, was taken for "an ordinary children's firecracker."

28 To Mikhail Matiushin

Alferovo
December 29, 1910

The village of Alferovo,[1] Ardatovsk district, in Simbirsk province—the exact spot on Planet Earth I inhabit. A lazy place, with a
distant awareness that somewhere there's a city called Petersburg or, as
they say around here, the capital that ends in "-burkh." There you have
a few of the wild local notions.

Wild New Year's greetings to Elena Genrikhovna and yourself!

V.

1. Alferovo is about 100 miles northwest of the present city of Ulianovsk.

29 To His Brother Alexander

Postmark: Tyoply Stan
February 25, 1911

Dear Shura,

It was Ostwald[1] I was talking about and I think they sent it. Katya
will be leaving any day now; I'm totally bored and would love to leave
myself, but they won't let me yet. I am making a diligent study of dates
and numbers and have discovered quite a few regularities. I intend to
keep going and work it all out completely, though, until I get some
answers as to why things happen the way they do.

1. Friederich Wilhelm Ostwald, the scientist and educator who in 1909 received a
Nobel Prize for his work in chemistry. Ostwald's socially oriented theories of energetics
and evolutionary monism may have been an important impetus to Khlebnikov's lifelong
study of numbers.

30   *To Mikhail Matiushin*

Alferovo, Tyoply Stan
Ardatovsk district, Simbirsk prov.
April 1911

Dear Mikhail Alexeevich,[1]

If you haven't changed your minds—you, Elena Genrikhovna and the rest of you nasty-minded individuals—about exposing the monstrosities I sent you to public disgrace, if I haven't broken all the rules— the result of my sloth and laziness—then start printing! I've been plunged into the kind of mood where nothing means a thing, where you look at everything without caring, but now I'm thawing out in the spring sunshine. If nothing stands in the way, if you have no heartfelt aversion to printing immediately, send me a telegram with the secret word: yes!—which will rile up the suspicions of the village police and the local authorities.

All letters here are given an acid test and kept for a while before they're delivered. It doesn't incline you to correspondence.

I spend all my time working on dates and on the fates of nations as dependent variables of numbers, and I have made a little progress.

You were probably surprised that I hadn't written, and then probably stopped being surprised. But as you see, I am armed with extenuating circumstances.

I enclose 4 pieces—"High Holy Day," *Asparux,* "The Death of Palivoda," *The Girl-God.*

I purposely did not send any poems or *Snow White,* in order to give some unity to the collection.

As a title I can see *Grandfather's House, The Black Tree,* or *Black Hill,* especially the last. If you have no objections, flaunt it right on the cover.[2]

I'm sending a few drawings, so that Elena Genrikhovna with her natural taste and knowledge of these things can choose 2 or 3; I'd like to see the bird hut on the 2nd page, and also one of the feminine images—the drawings are by Vera Khlebnikova but I don't know whether it's necessary to include her name. Let me know very soon if you will publish the book or not.

My warmest regards to Elena Genrikhovna and the whole circle of artlovers. How is Kamensky?

And the young artist you were so concerned about?[3]

By the way, my stay in this town, this most sordid of towns, has cost you considerably. While I'm in no hurry to total up my account, I hasten to assure you that you will be most carefully and precisely repaid.

Now start the presses!

Very best,
V. Khlebnikov

The manuscripts will get to Petersburg by a fellow traveler. The cover should be as simple as possible, no drawing, just a garland.

1. Khlebnikov gets the patronymic wrong.

2. The proposed volume of Khlebnikov's writings under discussion here was never published.

3. Probably Boris Vladimirovich Ender. Ender was a great admirer of Khlebnikov, and he spoke of Elena Guro as his "spiritual mother"; she in turn saw in him the figure of her "poor knight" of *Autumnal Dream* (*Osennii son,* 1913). In the 1920s the four Ender siblings worked very closely with Matiushin on his studies of color perception.

31 *To His Sister Vera*

April 1911

Vera. I may be printing two of your drawings together with some things of mine (the little hut). How is art? Have you ever run into any of my old friends? I'd like to look at the drawings, but it's so far away. I'm working on numbers and dates. They keep fascinating me all over again. If the collection comes out, it will be called *Black Hill.* Is there any way I can be of assistance? Warmest regards to Aunt Sonya, Uncle Sasha, and everybody. I am printing *The Girl-God, Asparux,* "The Death of Palivoda," "High Holy Day." The population of our barns and chicken coops grows fewer; some of them are on their way to visit you, roasted. Very best to everybody.

32   *To Elena Guro*

Alferovo, Tyoply Stan
Ardatovsk district, Simbirsk prov.
April 1911

Dear Elena Genrikhovna,

I got your letter. I wanted to let you know right away that as far as I am concerned nothing stands in the way of printing our book this summer.[1] On the contrary, I would be delighted to see it appear. I'm sorry you didn't let me know what you thought about the things which I guess you were reading for the first time, nor whether you think the book is overly thin or fat. In either case there's still time to make changes, whatever, depending on your impressions and instructions. I have enough pieces in reserve for two or three more books—does that scare you? Probably. I don't feel very well—kind of like a dying bonfire when somebody takes a stick and pokes at the coals. By the way, I sent you some drawings; I did it on impulse but the way I feel now it would be better not to include them. Let the book be transparent as a drop of water, as an Oriental would say. This autumn I may be in your part of the country.

As far as my secret acquaintance the number 365 is concerned—I did a part of the work and had to lay it aside since there were a few books I didn't have with me.

In some newspaper I saw a report that someone named Vasilev-Kamensky crashed his plane. Is that poor Vasya K? "Ring out the day," indeed! I'd like to have his address. If, which I firmly doubt, you decide not to answer this, it's all right. I'm a patient person, I forgive you, but if you do write and you know his address, please send it.

Were you—I imagine you were—at the exhibit where the Burliuks ruled the roost? I gather that a painting there of an old lemon with green spots was intended to portray me. Artistic impulse in that kind of painting is partly the victim of overintellectualization, and partly just gets torn to bits, like a deer attacked by a bobcat.[3]

Is Miasoedov writing anything at all? On his Bleiana Land there is an absolute swoop of stars, and he could achieve something great and beautiful.[4] The wonderful thing is, his writing is a land that recognizes no influences. I'd be extremely interested in knowing his opinion of my work, *Asparux,* for example. Is that wild German lady with the black sheepskin hair still on the attack the way she was?

Has Mikhail Vasilevich finished his *Don Quixote?* "What a mad thought, to sing the mad hidalgo's praises in the age of Sancho Panza!" I send him my best, send regards to Tamara Johansson and salute you all in general.[5] The patron of your circle doubtless *is* Don Quixote and not the worthy squire, and that is its justification. Hasn't anybody heard anything about *A Jam for Judges?* The slab of silence seems to have been laid upon it, although I would have thought *Apollo* at least might have given it a write-up with a smile of noncomprehension or something.

Today it's windy and cold. I brought home a black hamster, a little animal about the size of a kitten, gentle and tame. In the evenings he runs around the table and reads what I've written. He seems to understand it.

V. Khlebnikov

In the event some baleful stars appear in the firmament of our book, make sure a tiny epistle makes its way to me here! Otherwise I'll go along thinking it's in the budding stage, and it won't ever appear!

1. Still the proposed *Black Hill.*

2. Kamensky, who flew a plane, did have a minor crash. A year later he had a serious accident while giving a one-man show in Czestochowa, Poland. "Ring out the day" is the title of one of Kamensky's poems in *A Jam for Judges.*

3. Vladimir Burliuk showed his *Portrait of the Poet Khlebnikov* at the third exhibition of the Union of Youth, which opened in Petersburg on April 13, 1911. Neither Guro nor Matiushin participated.

4. Sergei Miasoedov, a mathematics teacher, was represented in *A Jam for Judges* by the story "On Route" ("V doroge"), in which people on their way to a fantastic land are described.

5. *Don Quixote* is a piano suite by Matiushin, published in 1915. In response to Khlebnikov's observation Guro wrote: "Our age is not the age of Sancho Panza, who at least had his own conscience and loyalties. Ours is simply the age of the stockbroker who sees only the deal and doesn't go beyond it." Tamara Johansson was a music student of Matiushin's.

33 To His Family

Volga
September 1911

I'm writing on board the riverboat under way. The weather's cold. Gorsky is working on the boat. I'm reading Keller's *Seven Legends* (wonderful book).

Vera is as stubborn as a balky jackass and won't take care of herself. But anyway, health is such a bore. You can get healthy anywhere.

We'll be in Samara soon. I'll mail my letter there. All the best for now, all the pleasures and concerns of autumn. Goodbye to Shura (I forgot to say goodbye to him). He should get the article published— the main body of it about fish, with the Pavdinskian birdtails appended. Remember to send me his address in your first letter to Astrakhan.

Yesterday I had sturgeon for dinner, which I invite you all to share with me in your imaginations.

I remain, and so forth,

The Simbirskian

We reach the Zhiguli Gates soon.[1] There's nothing to do on a riverboat except write hate letters to family and familiars.

I took the blue bag from the box at Pchelovod's!!!?

Kazan is the same as ever, but the people are worse: The young ones have the nasty faces of people over forty.

1. The loop in the Volga that begins north of Kuibyshev.

34 To His Mother

Postmark: Astrakhan
September 5, 1911

Here I am in Astrakhan. I saw Boris and Zinaida Semyonovna.[1] I went right from the boat to the horse races. Boris and Zinaida Semyonovna send love and kisses, regards from each separately and from both together to a whole list of people. They have treated me really delightfully and given me a corner to myself just like one of the family. Details in another letter. The Kalmyks love to race horses and have a great feeling for it.

1. Boris Lavrentevich Khlebnikov, a doctor and a cousin of the poet, and his wife. Khlebnikov's brother Alexander wrote to his mother later: "Vitya came with me when I left Astrakhan. He is in good shape and treated me quite nicely. He told me all about his stay in Astrakhan. He got a wonderful reception at Borya's. Borya was very moved to see him, full of memories of Podluzhnoe, and told Vitya to make himself at home. Zinaida Semyonovna let Vitya stay in her boudoir. But his 'Bohemian practices,' as Vitya puts it, soon upset this idyllic state of affairs . . . Borya gave Vitya a present, a gold watch that his grandfather had left him, and begged him never to sell it or pawn it. Vitya loves the

watch, calls it his 'timepiece' and is thinking of attaching a blackjack to the other end of the chain." (This letter was made available through the courtesy of Mai Petrovich Miturich, Khlebnikov's nephew.)

35   To His Father

Petersburg
October 26, 1911

My address is: 63, Line 12, apt. 153, Vasilevsky Island. I still owe the university 50 rubles.

I may switch over to the Archeology Institute. I'm still thinking it over.

36   To His Sister Ekaterina

Postmark: Kherson
April 23, 1912

This is to say hello and let you know that I will send you soon a new piece I've just thrown together: it's called *A Conversation between Teacher and Student*. I'm publishing it at my own expense (15 rubles).[1] Generally speaking you can publish a book here for about 10 rubles. And at the end of the summer I will bring forth into the world yet another book.[2] Regards to dear Malania Yakimovna and Elizaveta Grigorevna and all the young fry. I already think of myself as growing old and I expect gray hairs any minute. Is Kazan flourishing? I'm sure I'll be able to visit for a while somehow. Too bad I can't hope for an answer to this, since I don't have an address. When the book is out, I'll send you a copy. I expect it will call forth an outburst of dissatisfaction, or be ignored. That's the fate of all books. It must be wonderful in Kazan.

I'll send—well, I don't know what yet. Be well. Regards.

c/o Volokhin, Bogoroditskaia St., Kherson.

I'm leaving soon, but I don't know where to.

1. *Teacher and Student: A Conversation (on words, cities, and nations)* was published in May 1912. Khlebnikov was in Kherson visiting David Burliuk and his family at Chernianka, the estate managed by Burliuk's father.

2. Probably his "Two Individuals: A Conversation."

37 To His Father

Postmark: Odessa
June 5, 1912

I was truly glad to get your letter (I am writing meanwhile to Katya and Shura). It made me glad because of its genuine current of sincerity. But in response I have to be equally and fully sincere: it was saturated with cowardice, and with attempts at subterfuge—things I try to avoid.

I assure you there is nothing in it that might give you cause to shake like a rabbit for the honor of the family name. On the contrary, I am convinced the day will come when you will be proud of me, for I will have spread out a magic tablecloth upon which will appear a spiritual feast for the whole of humanity. But still it's very nice that you liked the middle and the ending.[1]

I didn't borrow any money from Ivan Stepanovich Rozhdestvensky!! I am happy to make you happy. I am reading Schiller while I'm here, and the *Decameron*, Byron and Miatlev.[2] But contrary to my desires I am doing nothing myself. Every day I go swimming in the ocean and I am becoming amphibian since I travel as far by sea as I do by land. I am touched that Vera did not join in the family outcry at the shaking of its foundations, and I thank you for your letter, even though dropped in the box by a rabbity hand.

I like to think you are all well. Marusya has gone to Sviatoshino. Kolya has finished his exams, he has gotten thinner and a lot taller.[3] I'm sending another *Conversation*.

1. This letter appears to be Khlebnikov's response to his father's embarrassment at the publication of *Teacher and Student*.
2. Ivan Miatlev, a minor Russian poet popular in the 1840s.
3. Khlebnikov is staying in Odessa with the Riabchevskys, his aunt's family. Marusya and Kolya are her children.

38 To Andrei Biely

Summer 1912

The Silver Dove has conquered me, and I am sending you a gift from my homeland.[1]

From the encampment of the besiegers to the encampment of the besieged fly not only poisoned arrows, but also tokens of affection and respect.

Khlebnikov

1. Biely, the great Symbolist writer, planned his novel *The Silver Dove* (1910) as the first part of a trilogy entitled *East or West,* depicting Russia as caught between irreconcilable historical currents. This note to Biely appeared as a dedication on the cover of Khlebnikov's booklet *Teacher and Student* (see letter 36). Khlebnikov probably hoped that Biely, the son of a well-known mathematician (Nikolai Bugaev), would be sympathetic to the essay, since it explored topics of mutual interest: the meaning of sounds and letters, history, and the possibilities of mathematical analysis.

39 *To Mikhail Matiushin*

Moscow
October 5, 1912

I beg of you, I entreat you by all that's holy to include these two poems. I know there's a strong current of opposition to their inclusion (D. D. and V. V.). But I know you will honor my request. If you need any extra material, drop me a postcard: 11 Novo-Vasilevsky, apt. 3, and I'll send something right away (a play in verse). My respects to Elena Genrikhovna.

Best regards,
V. Khlebnikov

P.S. The first poem is remarkable for the way in which the image of death enters a child's mind. The second reveals how strongly the image of the Maid of Orleans appeals to a child of our own era. Four years from now this generation will reach maturity. What will it have to tell us? These poems from a child's heart may well give us some idea of what the youth of 1917–1919 will be like. They describe a touching resolution to lay down life itself for freedom of speech and the commonweal and are full of nervous apprehension that those rights may be snatched away. It's important that such apprehension existed. Whether it was justified or not only the future will tell.[1]

1. In the fall of 1912 Khlebnikov settled in Moscow, where he was near David Burliuk, Alexei Kruchonykh, and Vladimir Mayakovsky. This group began work on two publications simultaneously: a second edition of *A Jam for Judges,* to be published by Guro and Matiushin in St. Petersburg, and the collection *A Slap in the Face of Public Taste,* to be published in Moscow by the group Jack of Diamonds. Here and in the next letter,

Khlebnikov is writing to Matiushin about *A Jam for Judges II*. In spite of the opposition of Burliuk ("D. D.") and Kamensky ("V. V."), its editors, *Jam* was published (February 1913) with two poems by a young girl Khlebnikov had met. She was identified as "Militsa, a thirteen-year-old Ukrainian."

40 To His Own Shadow[1]

Postmark: Moscow
November 19, 1912

I hasten to inform my lady shadow of her proprietor's arrival in this honored town. How is she feeling? Is she still squabbling with the natives in imitation of her lord? etc.

Lord of the Shadow

1. Khlebnikov mailed this note to himself.

41 To His Cousin Boris

Postmark: December 13, 1912

Let me give you a few particulars about the matter, dear Boris Lavrentevich, which clearly deserve consideration. Here is the address for the watch: David Davidovich Burliuk, c/o David Fyodorovich Burliuk, Chernianka, Malaia Maiachka P.O., Tavrida Province. I owe 20 rubles on it, plus two rubles expenses.[1] I have just finished 100 pages, written to astonish the world. My book is already in press, and I'll have something to send soon. It's called *A Slap in the Face of Public Opinion*. I'm getting a job with a magazine for 40–50 rubles and so I'll be in better financial shape.

Seryozha Maslovsky[2] sends his regards to Ekaterina Nikolaevna and to Vladimir Alexeevich Khlebnikov.

I went to see Zinaida Semyonovna, but she already left two weeks ago.

Cordially and sincerely yours.

I saw Tiger.[3]

1. Boris Khlebnikov had given him a gold watch, which he subsequently pawned against his cousin's specific request (see note 1 to letter 34).

2. A friend of Khlebnikov's from his schooldays in Simbirsk.

3. According to Nikolai Stepanov, editor of the Soviet edition of Khlebnikov's *Collected Works,* this is "evidently Tigran, a boy Boris Lavrentevich knew."

42 To Viacheslav Ivanov[1]

1912(?)

Dear Viacheslav Ivanovich,

I asked myself if perhaps it wasn't time to give you an account of my work, whose variety and incoherence wears me out. I have sometimes thought that if the souls of the great departed were condemned to wander about the world, they would find themselves wearied by the nothingness of most of the people in it, and would be forced to choose the soul of one man as an island, a place of rest and reincarnation. And in this way the soul of one individual might become an entire assembly of great spirits. But if that island among the waves were a bit crowded, it wouldn't surprise me if one of those immortals occasionally got tossed overboard. In which case the crew of the great would be constantly changing. Well, down to business.

Bismarck and Ostwald were themselves part Russian. We are living through a time of "Strife *und Drang*." European science strictly defined is turning into a *continental science.* A person who inhabits the interior of a continent is superior to one who inhabits the shore, and sees more. Which is why the growth of science anticipates an Asiatic component that even now can just barely be perceived. It would be desirable if some of the hammerblows in this forge of the New Age were made by Russians. But Russians are somewhat cold when it comes to the heroic exploits of their compatriots, and they never seem to care about being in first place. I generally doubt whether we Russians can publish anything except translations or imitations . . .

1. This excerpt from a letter to Ivanov was printed by David Burliuk in the collection *Mares' Milk (Moloko kobylits)* in February 1914.

43   *To Mikhail Matiushin*

Moscow

December 1912–January 1913

Dear Mikhail Vasilevich,

Just in case the problem was merely a matter of content, I'm sending you a new poem by my *protégé*(?). I'm sure you can always find a place for it if you leave out one or two of my short poems.

Your consent is of course required, and it has been given already. So what is the source of the hesitation? This is not fair. If you hadn't already promised, then things might be straightened out, but now of course she (El. Al.) is waiting anxiously for her first poems to appear in print, because she trusted me, just as I trusted *you*. Grant me this one pleasure, I don't seem to have many anymore. You see how upsetting the whole matter is! If the book were not to appear at all, I'd only feel bad for a half hour. But the exclusion of these childlike endeavors wounds me much more deeply. Of course it's a small miracle, the idea of these poems appearing in a big book, but art and miracles are closely related, aren't they? Don't prevent that miracle, Mikhail Vasilevich! Don't be cruel to me, or else you'll practice a cheap deception on a young girl's hopes; don't let there be a fly in the ointment where this book is concerned. One page is all, and nothing about a children's section, just the signature "Militsa, 13 years old," Moscow.

Let me add that I will be very, very obliged to you, if the bloody intent to murder these two poems is abandoned, or even if you replace them with the enclosed poem. I will make it up to you some way later on. Otherwise, all my delight at the beautiful appearance of *A Jam for Judges,* and now suddenly this "terrifying leap, hot breath, and a fiery face."[1] You are waving a bloody knife over this child's poems, and the ferocious expression on your face doesn't suit you. In Moscow you were happy and more warmhearted.

Thank you for your good opinion of the pieces I sent, and even warmer gratitude, if you print the enclosed instead of them. I forget what she said exactly, but I think Elena Genrikhovna too will speak in favor of including these poems. Just one little page is all, and you can sign it "A Ukrainian girl, 13 years old."

My respects, and I think during carnival week I may get to visit you.

Yours in hope, and I think there has merely been a correctable mistake made, not a fatal one.

V. Khlebnikov

(Perhaps this is a case of outside influences.)
11 Novo-Vasilevsky, apt. 3.

Once again: No need for a children's section (this isn't a kindergarten). And you will have room if you take out one or another of my poems. Will you write me and allay my fears?

I'm sending *Teacher and Student* to Elena Genrikhovna also by parcel post.

1. The line is from Khlebnikov's long poem "I and E," which was printed in *A Slap the Face of Public Taste* in December.

44   *To Alexei Kruchonykh*[1]

Early in 1913

Thank you for your letter and the book; its cover and general appearance are very clever.[2] I'm really sorry I haven't replied, I couldn't help it. I'm glad in any case you haven't made a *casus belli* of it. I've been a prey to melancholy lately, a pardonable offense, but it has stretched *everything* out, and now here is the answer to your letter, a month later.

I can't say I approve of your poem "Rattletrap roof-ends, a mishmash."[3] You seem to be throwing out the baby with the bathwater, as the Germans say, though I do get the feeling of something sharp that isn't fully expressed. The long poem reads like an amalgam of unsuccessful lines with a passionate, precise understanding of present-day reality.[4] To be able to say "Old Believers beat / From within / With fire with brand" you must be able to see the true state of Russian affairs and give a true description of them. The same youthful attack and youthful extravagance are audible in "Make a laugh / Light a fire," that is, the extravagance of youth carelessly flinging the required sense and meaning in concise words, and disinterestedly serving destiny by propagating its commands, combined with a cool indifference to the fate of that propagation. True, I'm afraid that Old Believers here refers not only to the class of people who follow the old ways, but also to upholders of oldfashioned taste in general, but I think that in this case too you were writing under the pressure of two minds: the conscious and the subconscious; and consequently with the single point of a double pen you were referring to the original Old Believers. These two places, as long as they are correctly understood, are valuable for an understanding of Russia in general; an understanding which the Russians themselves (it is their tribal characteristic) do not in fact possess. And so the meaning of Russia consists in this: "Old Believers beat / From within / With fire with brand," with a heat accumulated by their ancestors, while their children the Lauflings have lit the fires of laughter, the sources of joy and happiness. Whence the view of Russian happiness as an ancient wine in the skins of Old Belief. And alongside are the Whiners whose tears freeze and turn to icicles and so have overgrown the Russian hut. These latter, obviously, are the offspring of the believers in "isms" who yearly chill the Russian abode. They pass their lives like warriors of rain and autumn. The duty of personifying these forces they fulfill with rare integrity. Also good: "Make a big fat fist / Forge a big black sword / Break a bone / Join a horde." There are deficiencies in other lines: they preserve the strength and the lack of order which is appropriate here, but the angularity of their images leaves the mind unaffected and they pass on by. By the way, here are some thought-provoking projects:

1. To put together a book of ballads (many contributors or only one). Subjects? Russia's past, the Sulims, Yermaks, Svatoslavs, Minins, etc. Vishnevetsky.

2. The glorification of Rus beyond the Danube. The Balkans.

3. A ramble through India, where people and divinities walk side by side.

4. A look at the world of the Mongols.

5. At Poland.

6. The glorification of plants. These are all steps forward.

7. Japanese poetry. It has musicality, but no sound patterning. Each poem has four lines. It consists of an idea, a kind of kernel, and a vision

of the world that surrounds the kernel like wings or down. I am sure that the secret aversion to sound patterning and the demand for content which is everywhere evident are harbingers of a rain that the laws of Japanese literature will soon pour down on our land. Sound patterning is of Arab origin. But here objects are seen at a distance, the way a ship going down in a storm can be seen from a distant cliff.

8. To look into the vocabulary of the Slavs, the Montenegrins, and others (the Russian language has not yet been completely collected), and select many beautiful words—precisely the ones that are beautiful. One of the secrets of creation is to be able to see before you the people you are writing for, and to seek out a place for your words on the life-axis of that people, the extreme points of their height and their extent. Thus, by erecting such a life-axis, Goethe became a forerunner of the unification of Germany around that axis, while the flight—almost the cascade—of Byron from the steep heights of England celebrated the approaching acquisition of India.

I enclose a piece I haven't yet finished, "Nymph and Gnome."[5] Feel free to mark up and cross out, and if any corrections occur to you, make them. It's fragmentary, written grudgingly, but it has something in it, especially the ending.

Yours,

V. K.

1. Alexei Eliseevich Kruchonykh, an artist and poet, was a major theorist of Russian Cubo-Futurism. He shared Khlebnikov's interest in linguistic innovation, and the two poets collaborated frequently in 1912 and 1913. Kruchonykh is responsible for the Cubo-Futurists' principal theoretical statements, and with the artists Mikhail Larionov, Natalia Goncharova, Kazimir Malevich, and others, he produced the most visually successful of the early avant-garde brochures. Later, from 1924 to 1933, Kruchonykh and a group of fellow writers and artists brought out "The Unpublished Khlebnikov," a series of twenty-four booklets devoted to Khlebnikov's work.

2. Between mid-1912 and February 1913 Kruchonykh published six small books: *Old-fashioned Love* (*Starinnaia liubov*), *A Game in Hell* (*Igra v adu*, with Khlebnikov), *The World in Reverse* (*Mirskontsa*, with Khlebnikov), *Hermits* (*Pustynniki*), *Pomade* (*Pomada*), and *Half-Alive* (*Poluzhivoi*). In this letter Khlebnikov is probably thanking Kruchonykh for a copy of *The World in Reverse*, a collection of poems by both of them, with illustrations by Larionov, Goncharova, Malevich, and I. Rogovin. The cover by Goncharova has a pasted-on paperfoil flower.

3. The poem ("Starye shchiptsy zakata zaplaty") appeared in *A Slap in the Face of Public Taste* (December 1912).

4. Khlebnikov is discussing Kruchonykh's poem "Make a big fat fist, forge a big black sword" ("Kuiut khvachi chernye mechi"), published in *The World in Reverse*. Here is a translation of the poem (set in two columns here only for appearance):

Make a big fat fist
Forge a big black sword
Break a bone
Join a horde
Pick a hand-picked fight.
It's a dark road
A long road
A hard road
To the stronghold.
Their sword don't fear
No fire no pyre
No sheepskin pelt
No thick mesh net.
Make a big fat laugh
Light a real bright fire
Be a beast join the band

Grow a claw on your hand
Be a beast made of steel
You don't have to feel.
Cut hack rip skin.
See the Old Believers beat
From within
With fire with brand
Out of hand.
And the man in the hack
Turns back
He goes right goes left
Hits a post has a wreck
On the roof.
Drive stink
Raise hell
Beat bell.

5. "Vila i leshii" eventually appeared in the collection *Roar! Gauntlets!* (December 1913).

44a To Alexei Kruchonykh[1]

1913

There is a theory about a single law that embraces all of life (the so-called Kant–Laplace mind). If we insert negative values into this expression, then everything begins to flow in reverse order: first people die, then they live and are born; at first they have grown-up children, then they get married and fall in love. I don't know whether you share this opinion, but for a Futurian *The World in Reverse* is like an idea suggested by life for someone with a sense of humor, since first of all the frequently comic aspect of the fates can never be understood unless you look at them from the way they end, and secondly, people so far have looked at them only from the way they begin. And so, take an absurd view of the difference between your desired ideal and things as they are, look at all things in terms of their return unto dust, and everything will be fine, I think.

1. This piece of a letter was first printed in the new Soviet editon of Khlebnikov's selected writings, *Tvoreniia* (Moscow, 1987).

45 To Elena Guro

Moscow
January 12, 1913

Dear Elena Genrikhovna,

I'll send you a cleaner copy of the book later.[1] This one was left in the bottom of the basket by some miracle. It is one of the many books that have suffered in their times, witness its cover with the dark stripe and the faded binding that older books have. *Autumnal Dream* sounds a familiar note, numerous baby camels, long-legged eccentrics, Don Quixote, Tamara, Assyrian wisemen, it all recalls Litseiskaia Street and the little yellow window.[2] In "Grasshoppers" I hear a faint snicker at the other, fleeting life, but that very snicker provides a key to understanding it, and absolves its mistakes and obstinacies. In M.V.'s violin pieces is "livelier" meant as a replacement (for *fortissimo*)? A real contribution, and a place to begin. Allusions to the past are scattered throughout, and its waves pour from the pages of the book, while in the lexicon of tropes and words there is "They think the true knightly word," and certain reasons for considering that very important. The drawing of the ghostly young man, slender as a whip, is an ornament to the book. Do I belong to the number of those who understand it and do not have to guess? It is valuable to those who will see in it a floodtide of life that innundates mere literature, and who can read the signs of what's valuable. I was also very taken with the comparison of a German with a fat boar.

Regards to Mikhail Vasilevich. Thank him for understanding me.

V. Khlebnikov, Warrior of the Future
Moscow, 1/12/13

Desperate fights are imminent. Pro and Con. Perhaps today.

I'm tired of waiting for *A Jam for Judges*.[3]

"Venus and the Shaman" came out vulgar and superficial. What saved it in manuscript form was my beautiful handwriting. Two or three lines are out of place.[4]

---

1. Khlebnikov had evidently sent Guro a copy of *Teacher and Student* (see letter 36). Two months later that essay was printed again, along with "Two Individuals" and the poem "War—Death," in the third issue of *Union of Youth*. Guro and Matiushin also contributed to this issue.

2. Guro had sent Khlebnikov a copy of her book *Osennii son* (1912). It contained a

play of that name and some poems and other pieces, including violin music for the play by her husband. In Petersburg Matiushin and Guro lived on Litseiskaia Street.

3. The second edition appeared in February (see letter 39).

4. Khlebnikov's poem "Shaman i Venera" was about to appear in *A Jam for Judges II*. He had seen galley proofs.

46   To Mikhail Matiushin[1]

Astrakhan

June 18, 1913

Your grief and your loss are echoed in me; the image of Elena Genrikhovna is bound to me by many ties. I remember as if it were this very moment the courageous things she said during my last visit; in Elena Genrikhovna's opinion, the too obstinate obsession of one individual with a particular notion can cause the death of another. She seemed untroubled, and all things seemed to be a part of her, except her disease. My first impression was how radically she had changed during that time. But then she had always seemed to me under the influence of forces that had no effect on the majority of people, that were indeed foreign to them. But painful feelings can be allayed by rational reflection, which seems to say "Be in no hurry to mourn; no one who has not died can know what death is. It may be a joy, it may be a sorrow, or something else again."

That belief was no stranger to Elena Genrikhovna, as witness those signs of the lack of coincidence of meetings, found on the trunks of birch trees. Her last things are powerful because of their elevated moral teaching, the strength and sincerity of the convictions they express. In them, a cloak of mercy falls upon the entire sentient world, and people deserve the same compassion as the little baby camels of the sky, as young animals who perish "all fluffy and golden." Russians tend to lack a good or appropriate sense of rationality rather than an appropriate sense of emotion. These pages, with their strong, severe style, with their Hafiz-like affirmation of life, are especially wonderful because they are inspired by elevated thought and the imprint of the spirit. They also signify that the sea of lies and viciousness that now inundates the writings of our Bayans and Father Petrovs is drying up. There are always certain words we are afraid to pronounce when they have an objective content. I believe that death is such a word, when it catches you un-

awares. You feel like a man who owes a debt—and upon whose neighbor his creditor has just paid a call. Death indeed is one of the aspects
of the plague, and it follows that any life, always and everywhere, is a
Feast during the Plague. For which reason, remembering Pushkin's
Mary, should we not raise a cup of kindness in her honor?[2]

Or rather, let us rise to meet death like a rebel who feels his bodily
chains, but is already freed from them in spirit. And let us mount the
platform of defiance like a high priest and confront the abductor; I
know abstractly that I will die, but I don't feel the fact. If gravity is so
all-powerful, then aeronautics and relative immortality are closely connected. These days I feel I am somehow like a rock sinking to the bottom, that I no longer incline toward my birth but toward my death.
What will be will be. Elena Genrikhovna had a face as white as chalk,
eyes black as birchwood coals, almost mad, hastily combed golden hair.
Now she waits to meet us where we will some day join her. How stupid
that people die, which means that we'll die too, and still we go on
writing and publishing. And I am dying spiritually. Some sort of
change; a disenchantment; a failure of belief, coldness, callousness. I
know only that I intend to greet death calmly.

Mikhail Vasilevich, farewell.

I'll see you this winter. If I have the right to instruct you: be easy,
be joyful, be good, and everything will be all right.

I am not afraid of feeling prematurely old. Should the dead mourn
the living or the living mourn the dead?

Although I couldn't altogether believe what I read in your letter
from Uusikirkko, my hands were somehow paralyzed, and I couldn't
write you. I felt I should write, and at the same time felt I wasn't able.
I share your sorrow, in friendship, and I love you.

V. Khlebnikov

But in general words are somehow irrelevant.

I am sending a few things for you and Kruchonykh care of General
Delivery.

1. Written to Matiushin on the death of his wife. Elena Guro, thirty-five years old,
died of tuberculosis at their summer house in Uusikirkko, Finland, on April 24, 1913.

2. Bayan, a contemporary journalist; Father Petrov, a contemporary publicist and
writer on spiritual concerns.

3. In Pushkin's play *A Feast during the Plague*, Mary sings of the death of her beloved and the devastation of the plague; Khlebnikov returns to the connection between
Mary and death in his short essay "A Second Language" in 1916.

47　To Mikhail Matiushin

Astrakhan

July 1913

Dear Mikhail Vasilevich,

I'm coming! Expect me and send me 18–20 rubles, those earthly wings, so I can fly to you from Astrakhan.[1] I have tried in vain to get something done here, and something has been doggedly hindering my work. I've tried to get the freshness back, but it's been the same failure wherever I turn, and still I love Astrakhan and I forgive her indifference to me, and the heat, and the fact that everything here revolves around fish and everybody pretends to read books and think about things. Besides that, intermittent fevers, sultry nights, and as a special touch, there's always the local press. And so I'm coming. Perhaps autumn will grant my wishes, and I'll write something to spite summer.

Goodbye for now and I plan to see you soon, also Kruchonykh, all perhaps a week from now. It means a lot to be understood. Goodbye, Mikhail Vasilevich.

I'll see you soon.

1. On July 18–19, 1913, Matiushin, Malevich, and Kruchonykh met at Matiushin's home in Uusikirkko. They gave their meeting the rather grand name, "First All-Russian Congress of Poets of the Future (the Poet-Futurists)," and laid ambitious plans for literary and theatrical activities during the coming season.

48　To Mikhail Matiushin

Astrakhan

July 1913

Dear Mikhail Vasilevich,

Let me tell you briefly what happened. Two or three days after I got your letter and the money order, I went swimming and dropped my wallet in the pond. This absolutely improbable occurrence is all the more remarkable since I have dropped nothing this entire summer, although I have gone swimming lots of times. I'd be willing to swear there were devils involved, if I believed in devils. The wallet slipped from my fingers as if it were something alive, and then disappeared. This is an evil omen, and so I've postponed my trip till autumn.

I know you'll believe me when I say that it all happened exactly as I've written, and that I'm not to blame.

Astrakhan is a bore, since I don't belong here.

Velimir Chlebnikoff

P.S. After it happened, I organized a frog-wallet fishing expedition, with nets and hooks and everything, but no luck.

49　To Alexei Kruchonykh[1]

Postmark: Astrakhan
August 19, 1913

Author: Word-doer, sometimes word-worker.

Literature: Word-work. Letterature.

Comedy: Jesture, Love-laugh, Bye-bye-sigh-cry.

Performance: Contemplay. "I went to a contemplay."

Cast of characters: Play-persons.

Theater: Play-place, hear-house, see-site. Contemple, from contemplate.

Farce: Gut-buster.

Slice-of-life play: Life-loaf.

Chorus: Sing-songers. Who arranges the stage?

Critic: Arty-smarty.

Act: Dream-dram. Dream-dram One, Dream-dram Two; sometimes the whole play is a dream-dram.

Tragedy: Fatalization, Fatalation. Fatalaction.

Musical: Hippity-happity.

Opera: Sing-thing (tinkle-toy). Songation, songala, singsation, big-singsation, songsation.

Hum-strum: Musical accompaniment.

Drama: Do, ado, deed-do. An act-out. Conversignation. Maybe sometimes talkarama.

Actor: Play-person, charactor. Facer, face-factor.

Spectator: Eyer, contemplor.

Spectacle: Contemple.

Company of actors: Play-people.
Director: Dynamor, energizer, imager.
Poet: Cloud-climber, cloud-claimer, dreamore. Skyscratcher. Sky King.

Sorry my handwriting is such a mess. I'll write everybody a letter in a few days. Pick out the terms here you think will work.

1. In this letter and the next one, Khlebnikov drafts lists of possible new theatrical terms. Khlebnikov wrote the prologue to Kruchonykh's opera *Victory over the Sun* (*Pobeda nad solntsem*), which was performed in December in Petersburg. Matiushin wrote the music; sets and costumes were designed by Malevich. The final version of Khlebnikov's prologue considerably expands the possibilities of these lists.

50 To Alexei Kruchonykh

Postmark: Astrakhan
August 22, 1913

Imagician: Actor.
Wordorderer: Author.
Judge-mentor: Critic.
Drampers: The cast, dramatis personae.
Peoplay: The company, who play the meaning of the whole.
Clearing: Backstage.
Cloudbanks: Balcony seats.
Treetops: Box seats.
Action: Showantell.
The Lowlands: Orchestra seats.
Playpause: Time-out-of-play, intermission.
Songiver: Poet, lyricist. Singster, dreamster.
Sound-stirrer: Composer. Praise-singer.
Theater: Show-place, show-playce. Contemple, contemplace, contem-
    palace.
Actor: Imaginator. Face-changer, look-changer, clothes-changer.
Prompter: Wait-whisper, line-loan.
Dram-drum: The signal that the play is about to begin.
Bedram: A play out of time.

Dodram: A play set in the present time.
Diddram: A play set in the past. Oldram (Tantalus).
Willdodram: A play set in the future.
Singsign: Melody.
Play based on factual knowledge: A drama.
Play based on the imagination: A dreama (*The Girl-God, Earth*).
Vast-voicer: Opera. Voicysteria.
Rector: Director. Cor-rector.
Role: A share.
Look-see: Rehearsal.
Spectators: Row-rats.
Sufferation, painplay: Tragedy. Grimgroan, diredram, fate-fight.
Box office: Play-pay.

V. K.

51 *To Alexei Kruchonykh*

Astrakhan
August 31, 1913

I'll come.[1] It's wonderful, and very clever. I didn't read *Russian Riches*,[2] haven't heard anything from Chernianka, I'm thinking of writing them. *Trio* is a bad name all around, even worse coming after *Trio Tract*.[3] It seems to me that it, this collection, will be just as pale as *Trio Tract*, and if it turns out to be a funeral wreath, then it's all the sorrier.

I'm afraid of abstract arguments about art. Much better if an artist's work (his do-ing) affirms this or that; he shouldn't do it himself. Look around you and write: if youth follows age, then what comes later might have come earlier. First you have the old men, then the young ones. I agree that the sequence *aio, yeyeye* has a certain meaning and content, and that in skillful hands it might become the basis for a universal language. EUY accords with a flower.[4] The rapid shift of sounds conveys the tight petals (of a curved flower). Impassioned words in defense of Adam make you and Gorodetsky a pair. There's some sense to it: we are writing after Tsushima. But one must *be* Adam, and makeup will never help those who try to fake it. Severe? It is the young man who is the father of his people. To be that is to perform a great service—let him perform it who can. *Lyki-myki* is a Moslem notion: they also have *shurum-burum* and *pivo-mivo, sharo-vary;* that is, they ornament the word by adding an almost identical component that has nothing to do with the sense. *Dyr bul shchyl* seems to soothe the most conflicting passions.

For me, the important thing is to remember that the elements of poetry are elemental forces. They are an angry sun that strikes with a sword or a flyswatter at the waves of human beings. In general lightning (the discharge itself) can strike in any direction, but in fact it strikes the point where two elements are joined. Such discharges sliced open the Russian language when it was centered on peasant-village life. The life of Pushkin's time and circle thought and spoke a foreign tongue, translating into Russian. As a result lots of words are missing. Others languish in the captivity of Slavic dialects.

Thanks for your letters.

I am studying mountains and their placement on the Earth's crust.

1. Kruchonykh, Matiushin, and Malevich planned a series of meetings and performances for the fall and winter of 1913 in Petersburg. This letter is Khlebnikov's reply to Kruchonykh's invitation to attend.

2. An article in the magazine *Russkoe bogatstvo* by A. Redko had confused Ego-Futurism and Cubo-Futurism. Vladimir Markov, *Russian Futurism* (Berkeley, 1968), p.84.

3. *Trio (Troe)*, published by Matiushin in September 1913, contained writings by Khlebnikov, Kruchonykh, and Elena Guro and was dedicated to her memory; Malevich did the cover and illustrations. *Trio Tract (Trebnikh troikh)* had been published in March by Kuzmin and Dolinsky in Moscow (see letter 66). It contained verse by Khlebnikov, David and Nikolai Burliuk, and Mayakovsky, and was illustrated by David, Vladimir, and Nadezhda Burliuk, Vladimir Tatlin, and Mayakovsky.

4. EUY became the name of Kruchonykh's new publishing house. All these remarks about poetic language are in response to Kruchonykh's *Declaration of the Word as Such (Deklaratsiia slova, kak takovogo,* 1913), an explication of beyonsense language, printed during the summer. About a month after this letter, he and Kruchonykh published a booklet with a similar title and subject: *The Word as Such (Slovo kak takovoe,* 1913), illustrated by Malevich and Olga Rozanova.

52 To Mikhail Matiushin

Astrakhan
September 15, 1913

Dear Mikhail Vasilevich,

I sent you a telegram to let you know I wanted to come visit you, either in Moscow or Petersburg. Hoped to be an onlooker at the congress and what went on there. But now the congress is over, and you and I are still on different seashores; nevertheless I am coming, as soon as I can muster the energy. I do intend to come; I repeat that here in case you don't get my telegram. Right now I am preoccupied with numbers. I do calculations from morning to night, as long as it's quiet, and I've made a few small discoveries.

Love, Velimir

My units are 2^{64}, 2^{21}.
Best regards to all our comrades-in-arms.

53 To Alexei Kruchonykh

Postmark: Petersburg
October 14, 1913

Dear Alexei,

Dostoevsky was born into a family with close ties to the Russian military circles of those years. The Russian army (and the Russians) had returned home after their march against the Gallic capital in 1813, and with the candor of the victorious they saw at home only brute force, while in the living spirit of Gallia they saw the "measure and restraint" (taste, intelligence, elegant manners) that were lacking at home.

Since official Russia at that period had embraced German principles, those elements of society in contact with the military saw in Gallic "manners" a release from an oppressive state system. For this reason, that part of unofficial Russia of the period which had lived beneath the banner of freedom was uniformly colored by French influence, just as the state system (performance of duty) was by German (Teutonic). According to a law of physics—the angle of incidence is equal to the angle of reflection—they sought and found in France identical principles, only in reverse, i.e., they sought only values opposed to the German principles of the state system. They found Proudhon, St.-Simon, Fourier. Petrashevsky was their fervent and erudite teacher and the channel through which French negative values (− −) and Teutonic quantities (+ +) flowed into Russia.

Dostoevsky in the Petrashevsky years was a ray of light directed toward *l'ésprit français*. But exile deflected that ray and turned it homeward, toward Russia. Russia was revealed to him through her laws. The Petrashevsky circle made him an extreme Gallicist, and exile placed him in the position of a foreigner who discovers a new land called Russia.

Because the tribunal of official Russia removed the noose and pardoned Dostoevsky, the tribunal of free public opinion pardoned Russia, just as [illegible] and removed the spiritual noose from her neck.

Dostoevsky's entire opus is a work of mercy, a repayment for the mercy shown him by the tribunal of official Russia.

54   To Alexei Kruchonykh

Postmark: Petersburg
October 16, 1913

It is extremely important to note the unmistakable geneological relationships between *bes* [demon] and *belyi* [white], and *chert* [devil] and *chernyi* [black].[1]

Chert, precisely, with his little goat horns, is the passive object acted upon by the *chernyi* forces of vice, forces hurled by powerful, imperious Cherun. *Cherti* [devils] are *cheliad* [henchmen] of Cherun (cf. Perun[2] and *priperty* [those he op-presses]): he is more their victim than their creator. Hence his acting out of fear, not in accord with his conscience, the fact that he performs petty services; he is Cherun's lay brother, with his doleful Lenten countenance and frequently punished paw.

The *ch* sound signifies the dependence, the subordination, of his existence. He is a pathetic little *cherviak* [worm], *chasto* [often] crushed by a *chernyi* foot.

Vchera [yesterday] (cf. *v starye gody* [yesteryear]) shows that *-chera* has acquired the meaning of something like nonexistence. So it is precisely a *nichtozhnyi* [insignificant] and repellent creature that we call *cherviak*.

(*Vera* [religion, that which ties together] and *vervie* [rope]. Also *bolezn* [illness] and *volezn* [willness].)

While the *ch* sound accompanies a sense of life subsiding, *ischezanie* [dying out]: *pochit'* [to pass away], the shadow-side of existence, then the *B* sound represents the apex of existence—*bit'* [to beat], *burlo* [alarm bell], *berdysh* [poleax]. Consequently *bes* [demon] occupies the realm of *buistvo* [riot], *bitvy* [battles], *hedy* [misfortunes], and other manifestations of a life of extremes.

Get a Czech dictionary, also Polish, Serbian, and a few others and pick out words you can understand just by looking at them, for instance the Czech word *zhas* compared to the Russian *uzhas*.

Write: we have destroyed the Slavic dialects, laid them up like little lambs on the altar of the Russian language, and what remains are Russian languages (i.e., we have preserved them).

1. This letter should be read in conjunction with such essays as "Let us consider two words" and "Here is the way the syllable *so* is a field." Here Khlebnikov is beginning to work out possible semantic values for individual sounds of language.

2. Perun is the major deity of the old Slavic pantheon, a thunder god similar to Zeus. Khlebnikov invents a new deity by analogy, Cherun, a god of darkness and evil.

55 An Open Letter[1]

February 1, 1914

In the collections *Poems of V. Khlebnikov: Volume I, Stop-Gap,* and *Journal of the Russian Futurists,* David and Nikolai Burliuk persist in printing pieces bearing my name that are total rubbish and that have been deliberately garbled in the bargain.

The Burliuks managed—by deceit—to get hold of a lot of worthless scrap paper that I never for a moment intended to print, and now, without even asking my permission, they publish it as my work.

Handwriting does not automatically imply a signature. In the event that the publishers at any future date make so free with my signature, I hereby remind them of due process and the prisoner's dock, since I have entrusted the defense of my rights to a legally responsible agent, and for the above reasons I now demand: first, that they destroy the page in *Stop-Gap* that contains my poem "Endlessness"; second, that they print nothing that bears the mark of my creativity without my permission, and in my right as author I hereby forbid them to publish Volume I of my poems, since they do not have that permission.

Viktor Vladimir Khlebnikov

1. This letter was written during Khlebnikov's great upset over Marinetti's visit to Russia. He regarded the Burliuks' acceptance of the Italian poet as traitorous to the cause of Russian Cubo-Futurism (see letters 56 and 57). The letter was never sent and was published by Kruchonykh only after Khlebnikov's death.

56   To Nikolai Burliuk[1]

Petersburg
February 2, 1914

Let's forget about Dr. Kulbin's beastly behavior. That lamebrained idiot, that absolute Licharda, that convinced fool, hoped his obstinate abuse would sully someone's good name. But in the aforementioned doctor's beastly behavior I hear an Italian voice, an Italian who runs a puppet show, and therefore with a certain repugnance for the whole filthy business I give you back Kulbin's own words: coward, villain. He is your bondslave (the Slav has found a master with a whip). Stand up for your servant as someone stronger and more my equal, and since you bear the responsibility for his behavior, bear also the weight of those words *coward, villain,* and accept a slap in the face meant for Marinetti, that Italian fruit.

Understand this letter however you like—you and your three friends together or separately—but the East hereby hurls a challenge at the arrogant West, stepping with scorn over the bodies of the carrion eaters.

Your Italian Marinetti (the exchange in *Stock Exchange News* No. 13984) astounds us with his pleasant familiarity. We have no need to accept these views from the outside, because we launched ourselves into the future in 1905. The fact that the Burliuks and Kulbins never noticed this lie proves that they were only pretenders, not true believers.

P.S. Seeing that your friend has rejected any responsibility for his words, I am quite convinced that your behavior will correspond to his, and have decided not to bother you with any requests whatsoever, since I consider the incident closed.

Cowardice is a national trait of the Italians; they are mercantile-minded and master swindlers.

My letter will not be kept a secret. From now on I no longer have anything in common with the Hyleans.[2]

1. The flamboyant Italian Futurist, Filippo Tommaso Marinetti, made his only visit to Russia in 1914. On the evening of February 1, Khlebnikov appeared at Marinetti's first Petersburg lecture to distribute a leaflet, signed by himself and the poet Benedikt Livshits:

> "Today, because of personal considerations, the Italian colony on the Neva and a few locals are falling at the feet of Marinetti. They are traitors to Russian art in its first steps along the path toward freedom and honor, and they place the noble name of Asia beneath a European yoke.
>
> Let those individuals who refuse to wear a horse collar around their necks remain impassive observers of this dark victory, as they did in the shameful days of Verhaeren and Max Linder.
>
> Individuals of strong willpower will stand to one side. They are aware of the laws of hospitality, but their bow is drawn, and their brows burn with anger.
>
> Foreigner, remember what country you are in!
>
> Sheep of hospitality, wearing the lace collars of servility."

Khlebnikov probably wrote this letter to Nikolai Burliuk on the following day, when his leaflet was reprinted with editorial comment in the *Stock Exchange News*.

2. An early name of the Russian Cubo-Futurists.

57 *To Filippo Marinetti*[1]

Petersburg
February 2, 1914

You untalented loudmouth.

Your exchange in No. 13984, by the way, is a monologue from Griboedov ("The French Fop from Bordeaux"). You came a little late to Russia, friend; you should have come in 1814. The man of the future, born a hundred years too late. There is more purpose to the mad rush of life than having a French Fop from Bordeaux hop from century to century. Therefore, to use the same language your bondslave Kulbin used, you are a coward and a villain. Thus does a Futurian honor the French Fop from Bordeaux. Farewell, you fruit.

I am convinced that we will meet one day to the sound of cannons, in a duel between the Italo-German coalition and the Slavs, on the Dalmatian coast. I suggest Dubrovnik as the place for our seconds to meet.

1. Part of a letter to Marinetti, probably written at the same time as the previous letter to Nikolai Burliuk. Another extant fragment by Khlebnikov on the same subject repeats the title of the Russian manifesto, *A Slap in the Face of Public Taste:* "Public taste nowadays wears a Gothic moustache. Marinetti! Show us your public taste, so I can give you a slap in the face of your public taste!" For a detailed account of Marinetti's visit to Russia, see N. I. Khardzhiev, "Veselyi god Maiakovskogo," in *Vladimir Majakovskij: Memoirs and Essays,* Bengt Jangfeldt and Nils Åke Nilsson, eds. (Stockholm, 1975), pp. 108–151.

58 To Alexei Kruchonykh

March-April 1914

Lunev or Kruchonykh. I got *Selected Poems.* Say hello to Filonov. Thank him for the wonderful drawings.[1]

1. This note is on the reverse of the manuscript of "!Futurian." Khlebnikov probably means that, because of its polemical nature, the essay should be signed with one of his pseudonyms, "Lunev," or ascribed entirely to Kruchonykh. *Selected Poems,* with Filonov's drawings, appeared in March 1914.

59 To Alexei Kruchonykh

Astrakhan
April-May 1914

Alexei Eliseevich,

If there is no conflict where the Crane publishers are concerned (M. V. Matiushin; ask him), then publish *The Girl-God* or *Otter's Children* as you wanted to do earlier, for the sake of Filonov's drawings and his debut as an illustrator. For which purpose both you and he have the right to change the text as you like, make cuts or changes, improve the dull parts.

I insist: a whole lot of drawings.

Half of the profits from *Otter's Children* for Filonov, half for you.[1]

1. Khlebnikov greatly admired the work of the artist Pavel Filonov. Late in 1913 they became especially close, and Filonov's drawings appeared as illustrations in the collection *Roaring Parnassus (Rykaiushchii parnas)*, published by Matiushin and Boguslavskaia in January 1914, and in Khlebnikov's *Selected Poems* the following March. Filonov also wrote poetry; his poem-play *Prophesalvos of a Branching Universe (Propeven' o porosli mirovoi)*, which was influenced by Khlebnikov, appeared in 1915. Khlebnikov here proposes to reissue his supersaga *Otter's Children*, published earlier in *Roaring Parnassus*, or his play *The Girl-God* from *A Slap in the Face of Public Taste*.

60   *To Vasily Kamensky*

Astrakhan
May 1914

Dear Vasya,

Rejoice desperately. I write and stretch both hands across the Urals: you are out there somewhere and my blessing will find you.[1] I envy you: even the nightingale's song is a blur to me. When I decide to marry, I shall seek a blessing from you in return. My dear, dear V! And I got a letter from Nikolaeva (Maximovich died, I wanted to go but couldn't).[2] She's probably angry. I got a letter recently from my "thirteen-year-old" from *A Jam for Judges II*.[3] But I answered so stupidly that I'm afraid she won't like it. Your "Spring Field" I know and love already from your letter. Wish me a Spring Field too, and you will be like a white-bearded high priest, sending me a blessing from afar.

What can I say? Live in peace, be afraid of me? Preserve your feelings of Futurist fear. This verse becomes the property of your Spring Field for all eternity: what more can a solitary Shepherd wish you?

I'd thought we might see each other this summer, but that's no longer possible. Unfortunately. I have a business proposition for you: describe the days and hours of your feelings as if they moved the way the stars do. Yours and hers. The angles, turning points, high points. And I'll work out the equation! I've put together the beginnings of a general law. (For example, the connection between our feelings and the summer and winter solstices.) You have to discover what relates to the moon and what to the sun. The equinoxes, sunsets, new moons, half-moons. That way it's possible to work out our stellar dispositions. Work out the exact curve of feelings in waves, rings, spirals, rotations, circles, declinations. I guarantee when it is all worked out MES will explain it—Moon, Earth, Sun. It will be a tale told without a single word. Newton's law will peep out between I and E,[4] and so far it's still breathing.

Love,
Your Vitya

I don't have Vol. II of the journal.[5] Nor *Tango with Cows*. Send them. Wonderful to hole up with a Spring Field!

I live here next door to a criminal investigation detachment. What a dirty petty business. And their hordes keep passing my windows. That's what your Commandant is doing, he's being bored. In captivity at home. Where are you living, by the way? Do you have your own place? Do you know anybody thereabouts? My folks never let me go anywhere. I raise a goblet of muddy Volga water and drink a toast to your Spring Field. Hip-hip-hooray! Wish me two things: let me love somebody and write something.

So far neither is possible. By the way: *molniia* and *molodets, solntse, solniia,* and *solodka* (a Ugrorussian Russian word) are related.[6]

The beast in the yellow shirt (i.e., V. Mayakovsky) hates the sun: "Your souls are his slaves, his kisses have killed them." "Souls with sounds that burn like streetlights" is written in praise of lightning; so is "pat black cats" (to get sparks of lightning). Victory over the Sun with the help of Lightning?[7] Tell your Spring Field that she is my friend already, the friend of a friend. My very dear Suncatcher and his Spring Field!

Goodbye. Love.

I'm stuck here between four walls, sick of Astrakhan, I don't go out anywhere. I'm sorry I came. I'm writing some semiscientific articles, but I'm not happy with them.

May a rainbow unite you both, with a cocky sparrow perched upon it.

All the best. Yours!

I shall dedicate to you both anything you like—things I've written or have yet to write.

1. Khlebnikov is replying to a letter from Kamensky announcing his marriage to Avgusta Viktorovna Yugova, whom he called his "Spring Field."

2. Nadezhda Vasilevna Nikolaeva, a dancer, was a friend of the Cubo-Futurists. In the spring of 1914 she performed with Mayakovsky and Burliuk on the Futurist "tour." The artist V. N. Maximovich commited suicide in April.

3. See letters 39 and 43.

4. I and E are characters in a poem of Khlebnikov's.

5. He is probably referring to *The Futurists: The First Journal of the Russian Futurists* (*Futuristy: Pervyi zhurnal russikh futuristov*). The first issue (called No. 1–2), with illustrations by Alexandra Exter and David and Vladimir Burliuk, was published at the end of February or early in March 1914. The next issue, supposed to appear two weeks later, was never published. *Tango with Cows: Ferro-Concrete Poems* (*Tango s korovami: Zheleznobetonnye poemy*), a collection of Kamensky's graphic poems, was published in March, illustrated by the Burliuks.

6. Khlebnikov here relates *molniia* (lightning) and *molodets* (good fellow, also congratulations) and *solntse* (sun), *solniia* (a made-up word by analogy with *molniia*), and *solodka* (sweetroot) on the basis of the imagined roots *mol-* and *sol-*. These comparisons serve as a departure for the involved compliments of the paragraphs that follow.

7. Khlebnikov is quoting from Mayakovsky's play *Tragedy*. In *Victory over the Sun*, the Cubo-Futurist opera, the central image is the capture of the sun.

61   To Nadezhda Nikolaeva[1]

Astrakhan

August 26, 1914

I am sending you: myself, some kittens, and some question marks???

The picture was taken in Petrograd, with some people I didn't know. I'd been reading over old letters. And regretting the past. I'll be passing through Moscow.

Your Velimir

1. See note 2 to preceding letter. Khlebnikov enclosed a photo of himself and a postcard reproduction of a painting entitled *Kittens* by A. Weczerzick.

62   To Nadezhda Nikolaeva

Astrakhan

August 29, 1914

How are you doing?

Here. N. V.? . . .

Did you take part in the controversies on "Soldiers' Day"?

My future isn't clear yet, but it does look like I'll soon be living more northerly than I am now.

Your Khlebnikov

63   To Nadezhda Nikolaeva

Petrograd
October 7, 1914

Nadezhda Vasilevna,

I hope October 13th will bring you joy, tranquillity and all good things, and heal all your ills.
I'm still here.
I'm finishing an essay.
I don't go anywhere.
I'm sending two books.[1]

1. Nikolaeva's birthday was October 13th. Khlebnikov sent her copies of *Roar! Gauntlets!* and his *Works, 1906–1908.*

64   To Nadezhda Nikolaeva

Petrograd
October 11, 1914

Dear Nadezhda Vasilevna,

I've settled down—rather badly—in Shuvalovo, near Petersburg, where I have the pleasure of seeing Kruchonykh every day. I like the quiet and the lake near the cottage; I'm working at finishing an essay and getting it printed; I am now firmly convinced that there isn't a single person around here who's capable of understanding me.

Off to war: (1) Vasilisk Gnedov; (2) Gumilyov; (3) Yakulov.[1] Don't have any news; the Stray Dog is dead.[2] I almost never see anyone I know.

I send you my very best wishes and greetings for the 13th; we haven't been able to get *Roaring Parnassus;* it's locked up at City Hall.[3] What I'll be doing in the future I have no idea; whatever, I must break with the past and find something new for myself.

I'm sending a couple of little books that came out a while ago; I think they're repulsive.

All the best for October 13th!

Devotedly,
V. Khl.

1. Vasily Ivanovich Gnedov, a poet whose work is marked by neologisms and sound play, earlier considered himself an Ego-Futurist; with the disintegration of that school before World War I, he moved closer to the Cubo-Futurists. For Nikolai Gumilyov, see note 1 to letter 18. Georgy Bogdanovich Yakulov was an artist known for his interest in light and cosmic theories; he was tangentially associated with the Russian avant-garde at this time.

2. The Stray Dog Cabaret had been started in a cellar on Mikhailovsky Square in Petersburg by Boris Pronin, Nikolai Kulbin, and Nikolai Evreinov. From its opening on the last night of December 1911 until its closing in 1915, it was a center of artistic and literary nightlife. Its main habitués were from theatrical circles or from the Acmeist and Symbolist schools of poetry. The Futurists had of course "crashed" the place and were tolerated. As Viktor Shklovsky put it, talking about the Futurists: "We weren't the ones who did the drinking at the Dog. We were the other ones."

3. The anthology published by Matiushin in January 1914 was confiscated by the police because of objections to some of Filonov's drawings.

65   *To Mikhail Matiushin*

Astrakhan
November(?) 1914

Dear Mikhail Vasilevich,

As you recall—partly with regret, partly with satisfaction—I left Nevsk on a cold, gloomy day, trying to escape the cold and freezing weather. As the train began to move off, you waved a very friendly goodbye. I found myself in gloomy company; I left on Tuesday and arrived on Saturday, a total of five days on the road; I'd added one extra day for myself. After we crossed the Volga I turned into a block of ice and began looking at the world from the Kingdom of the Shades. I wandered up and down the train in that condition, visiting horror upon the living; so sailors reef in their sails and head for shore when they see the icy figure of the Flying Dutchman. My fellow travelers scrambled aside when I approached; children stopped crying and old ladies stopped their gossip. But eventually the snow vanished from the fields and we approached the capital of Go-Aspa.[1]

I grab a cab, tip the porter and rush off home; I get an enchanting reception, a couple of rams are roasted in my honor, candles are lit, incense is burned. A swarm of familiar figures, all swearing up a storm; I stand there with my head in a whirl; everything grows dim; I look at myself in the mirror; instead of eyes bright with inspiration, I see the dull eyesockets of a corpse. In some existence I can't fathom I feel myself already punished. All the better. Here I am condemned to watch as a German doctor rips away the veil from the secret of death. He leans his wise skull against his hand and turns the hollow of his eyes upon a woman's golden-haired corpse. I swarm through the Brockhaus encyclopedia, that multitomed opus on humanity, but I breathe upon a candle flame and never notice that it moves.

I'm waiting for my little booklet *A New Theory of War*.[2]

As it turns out, if it hadn't been for the cold, I might not have left; they had worked out a kind of salary for me (40 rubles) starting on the 28th.

For the time being (this week) all I do is dream of thawing out after my surprising journey. It's not snowing at the moment, raining a little; sometimes it's sunny in the afternoon but I can't get rid of this feeling of cold.

Regards to Alexei Eliseevich, Vasily Kamensky, Burliuk.

If there's enough room, Mikhail Vasilevich, please print the following notes at the end:

Notes

1. It should be noted that 317×4 years before the Code Napoleon we have the Codex Justinian; to be precise, the first 5 books of the Napoleon were published in 1801, 317×4 years after 533, when on Dec. 30th the compilation of Belenissa's son acquired force of law; the struggle between the Jacobins and the Royalists took place 317×4 years after the rioting between the Blues and Greens in 532. 317×10 years before the worship of the goddess Reason in France, the son of Tiy, Amenhotep IV, changed his name to Akhnaton (1378 B.C. and A.D. 1792). He was the Pharaoh who changed the letter *m* in Amen's name to *t* and introduced the worship of the Sun god into Egypt. So we see that the worship of the Sun and the worship of Reason existed on this Planet Earth 317×10 years apart. Akhnaton had poor health and a narrow chest.

2. 365 ± 48 may be understood generally as $365 \pm (\sqrt{365} + 28)$; $19^2 = 361$; the period of 28 years is connected with the lunar month of 28 days.

3. Ptolemy was born $365 + (2 \times 48)$ or 461 years after Aristotle.

4. Years of invention and scientific discovery sometimes fall into very regular patterns, like waves. Take for instance 1542, the date of Copernicus' Laws:

after 28 × 3 years,
    1626: Willebrord Snell's laws of the refraction of light.
after 28 × 2 years,
    1682: Isaac Newton's Laws of Universal Gravity.
after 28 × 2 years,
    1738: Laws of the Speed of Sound. The Academy.
after 28 × 4 years,
    1850: Joule's mechanical equivalent of heat.

The invention of the percussion gun in 1807 occurred 28 × 2 years after the invention of the breech-loading gun (Chaumette and Forsyth), in 1751.

The production of beet sugar in 1801 began 27 × 2 years after the discovery of beet sugar in 1747 by Marggraf and Achard.

Production of aluminum was begun in 1854 by Sainte-Claire Deville, 27 years after the discovery of aluminum by Wöhler in 1827.

Soemmering's electric telegraph, 1809, was invented 28 years before Steinheil's needle telegraph in 1837.

1662: Boyle's law
1690: Huyghen's wave theory of light
1802: Romagno's electromagnetism
1886: Hertz's theory of light

The progression of dates here is 1, 4, and 3 (a total of 8) times 28 years. Thus Hertz's theory came 28 × 7 years after Huyghen's theory.

1775: Lavoisier's theory of combustion
1803: Popov's light ray
1831: Faraday's induction currents
1859: Bunsen's spectrum analysis

1. Go Aspa was the name of the Volga Khanate under the Tatars, from which the Caspian Sea gets its name; Astrakhan was its capital.

2. Matiushin published Khlebnikov's pamphlet *A New Theory of War, Battles 1915–1917* in November 1914. The notes that Khlebnikov attached to this letter arrived too late to be included in the printed text.

66   *To Mikhail Matiushin*

Astrakhan
December 16, 1914

Dear Mikhail Vasilevich,

Thanks for the letter and the books.[1] I'm so unscrewed it was very hard to get myself together for the rare moment I can write a letter. These are very crucial days for me, since according to my calculations on December 15 and December 20 there are to be sea battles, on a massive scale. I wrote about it a long time ago to Georgy Kuzmin[2] (his address: 1st Aviation Company, Polytechnic Institute, Petrograd), and now today the 16th in the papers there are "rumors of a great naval battle." Tomorrow I'll find out for sure if it took place or not. If it did, then I can accurately predict the dates of the major sea battles of the entire war and their outcomes. The day or the twenty-four-hour period of the crisis point! I picked this date as a test. If it turns out I was wrong, then I'll give up these wearisome computations, calculating all these regularities. And for a whole month I've been living for nothing but this. Adams and Leverrier! The second discovery of Neptune![3] Or . . . . . Or . . . . . Or a laughable mess of ineffectual calculations. Neither exceeds the possibilities of human nature, and I am almost indifferent to either outcome.

I am in a much reconciled mood; best regards to everybody.

Special thanks to Kruchonykh for his efforts in looking over my little booklet. It's a little immature, and gives the impression that the bluebird flew away while they were getting the cage ready. So perhaps it would be better for us Suncatchers to say that the sun has gone behind a cloud. But I shall come back to this question again—to scratch it to death with my claws, if they don't fall out by then from old age.

You won't judge this simpleminded nonsense too harshly, I know, Mikhail Vasilevich, since you spoil me as always and encourage my feeble efforts with great words like "genius." This year I have been aware of a reverse connection to the past, i.e., days that were dark for me last year have been bright for me this year.

I wanted to spend some time studying *Pushkin's Works and Days* by Lerner, to grasp a human life measured out exactly in time. But not now. So please buy it and save it for me just in case.

If there existed a chronology, but a really detailed one, of all ages and nations, it would be extremely useful, or even just a history of naval battles.

Bekhterev wrote about three dimensions, but he knew nothing of the form and meaning of the fourth dimension, whose origins lie in the assumption that there is nothing inherent in the nature of space that limits it to three powers only, that it is similar to numbers, which can be raised to powers ad infinitum; so therefore he concluded that the three semicircular canals in the human ear were the most immediate cause for man's perception of three-dimensional space; to which Poincaré replied in his book *Science and Hypothesis* or in *Mathematics in the Natural Sciences* that we would then have to concede to rats only two-dimensional space, since they have two canals in their inner ear, and doves (it appears) one-dimensional space. He accused Bekhterev of not understanding the true meaning of four dimensions and called this an unsuccessful attempt to build a bridge between the natural sciences and numbers.[4]

The best on the fourth dimension is in the Lobachevsky Jubilee collection of essays, published by the Mathematical Society of Kazan.[5]

1. *A New Theory of War,* published the previous month. Kruchonykh wrote the preface and did the proofreading.

2. Kuzmin and Sergei Dolinsky supported the publication of seven of Kruchonykh's books.

3. In the mid-nineteenth century, J. C. Adams and U. J. J. Leverrier both calculated, independently, the existence of the planet Neptune.

4. Khlebnikov's discussion of spatial dimensions was probably in direct response to Matiushin's inquiry. Questions about the nature of the fourth dimension occupied many artists at this time, and Matiushin had discussed it in his presentation of excerpts from Gleizes and Metzinger's *Du cubisme* and P. D. Uspensky's *Tertium Organum* in the third issue of the Union of Youth journal (March 1913).

In addition to his other major contributions to psychoneurology, V. M. Bekhterev established the physiological and anatomical basis of equilibrium and spatial orientation. His work directly influenced Kulbin and thus Cubo-Futurist aesthetics. Henri Poincaré discusses the role of the senses and the body in the generation of notions of space in several publications, including *Science and Hypothesis* (1902) and *The Value of Science* (1904). In the latter work he examines the opposing views of Mach-Dalange and M. de Cyon. According to Poincaré, Cyon cites the behavior of lampreys and Japanese mice (which have, respectively, one and two pairs of ear canals) in defense of the theory that ear canals produce the sense of spatial dimension—a theory that Poincaré found altogether inadmissable.

5. *Prazdnovanie imperatorskim Kazanskim universetetom stoletnei godovshchiny so dnya rozhdeniia N. I. Lobachevskogo* (Kazan, 1894).

67　To Mikhail Matiushin

Astrakhan

December 17, 1914

Dear Mikhail Vasilevich,

I commence the account of my errors. I thought there would be a naval battle on the 15th. There wasn't. My error consists of several parts:

1. The assumption that one war recapitulates the eras that preceded it; the way a dying man's entire life, according to the widespread belief, flashes before his eyes. (I can't say, I've never died.)

2. The assumption that for naval warfare in 1914 I had to take the era of the struggle between Islam and the West beginning with the Crusades—1095.

3. The assumption that if a particular correspondence was discovered, it would repeat itself further on.

Numbers	Corresponding Events	
1	1095. Beginning of Crusades.	19 July. Beginning of the war.
5	1099. Conquest of Jerusalem.	23. Sinking of the *Amphion*.
93	1187. Jerusalem captured by Saladin.	19 October. Battle of Chile. Sinking of the *Monmouth* and *Hodgon*.
89	1183. Saladin conquers Mesopotamia.	15 October. Battle with the *Pearl*. Sinking of the *Itaro* and *Katashiko*.
	1147. Destruction of Edessa by Nur al-Din.	9 September. Sinking of the *Cressy, Hogue,* and *Aboukir*.
The same series		
1	1099. The Christians capture Jerusalem.	23. Sinking of the *Amphion*.
	1187. Jerusalem captured by Saladin.	19 October. Battle of Chile.

1180. The Portuguese defeat the Moors.	12 October. 2 German cruisers.
1110. Capture of Sidon.	3 August. The *Zrinya*.
1189. Conquest of Safed.	21 October. Sinking of the *Yorck*.
1196. German crusade in Palestine.	28 October. Sinking of the *Emden*.
1183. Mesopotamia conquered by Saladin.	15 October. Battles with the *Pearl, Itaro, Katashiko*.
1147. Destruction of Edessa by Nur al-Din.	9 September. *Aboukir, Cressy, Hogue*.
1118. Conquest of Aragon.	11 August. The *Zenta*.

Based on this series, where Islamic victories correspond to German victories on October 19, October 15, September 9, I figured there would be naval battles on the day corresponding to the taking of Jerusalem in 1244, i.e., on December 15. Then it would be possible to predict a great battle on the day corresponding to the year 1453, the great year of Islam. But there was no battle on the 15th. Consequently the path I have followed is mistaken, and one would do well to avoid it.

There's the history of my defeat. Personally I'm quite happy about it, because it seems to have taken a load off my mind. Now that I have understood my mistakes, I'm free.

Fondly,
V. Khlebnikov

Wouldn't it be wonderful if we published something for the benefit of the wounded? A collection or notebook. "A Futurite Anthology." Although I don't have anything for it.

After I understood the mistakes I'd made, I felt as if I'd just floated free of a sandbar.[1]

1. Khlebnikov wrote a poem about these particular calculations; he called it "The Story of a Mistake," although it celebrates the correspondences of his figures. The poem is undated, but we may presume it was written at about the time he made the calculations.

68   To Mikhail Matiushin

Astrakhan
January 18, 1915

Dear Mikhail Vasilevich,

The recent battle in the North Sea with the disabling of the *Lion* and the sinking of the *Blucher* on January 11 and the *Gazelle* at Rügen takes upon its giant's shoulders the weight of my theory that the naval battles of 1914 are repeating the struggle between Europe and Astsu (Islam) beginning with the year 1095—that is, the battle between the *Blucher* and the *Lion* on January 11 corresponds to the years 1271 and 1270 of the last crusade; one is therefore emboldened once again to expect a great naval battle 20 days after January 11, on January 30 or February 1, with a successful outcome for the Germans. In 1291 Acre fell, the last Christian stronghold in Palestine; the corresponding day turns out to be January 31. A *very* great battle 162 days after January 31; a major one 95 days after January 31 and several in between.

If there is a major battle on January 31 or 30, then the course of the war at sea will be rather clearly indicated by my theory. If this prediction comes true on January 31, then it is important to *publish at once* my timetable for naval battles with the outcomes for the opposed forces.

2 pages.

I am studying [illegible].

V. Khlebnikov

I am sending you a lotus from the Caspian.

This summer it would be nice to organize an expedition on a special barge; Argonauts to Astrakhan, sailing from Perm in search of lotuses.

69 To Alexander Belenson[1]

Astrakhan
Spring 1915

Dear Alexei Emmanuelovich,

Here's the complete story; I couldn't send the other one, another I haven't copied out yet. I am very anxious to hear from you.

I remain yours truly,
V. Khlebnikov

1. Belenson, editor of *Sagittarius,* a miscellany first published in Petersburg in 1915, had written to ask for a contribution. Khlebnikov proposed his story "Dream" and wrote this note on the last page of the story, but he seems never to have sent it.

70 To Mikhail Matiushin

Astrakhan
April 1915

Dear Mikhail Vasilevich,

The book is the most beautiful thing Crane has ever published. I like the fact that there are no extra pages and that the cover doesn't have any advertisements—that always spoils a book.[1] That's what spoiled *A New Theory of War,* for instance. I expect good things from Filonov as a writer; and there are lines in this book as good as anything ever written about war. In a word, what I liked so much about the book was the absence of cheap commercialism. "Universal Flowering" also sounds very good.[2]

I like very much the drawing of the cave archer, the deer, the dogs torn to pieces by their own madness and looking as if they were still unborn, and the nervous, apprehensive deer.

I am going ahead with my calculations, but so far nothing new, only a greater elegance when you examine events in terms of 317 year intervals. That precision has enabled me to devise a very concise layout, so that I only have a step to go and the first draft will be ready.

I'm studing Marie Bashkirtseff's *Diary* again.[3] It provides keys to the interpretation of dreams.

I'm looking forward to May. If you want to print before May a mimeograph edition of 4–5 pages of my tables with the invasions every

317 years, write me and I'll send them. If you can't for some reason, don't bother.

By the way, who has been spreading the rumor that Alexei Kruchonykh has a contract to sell my work? That's a very gross error.

Yours,

V. Khlebnikov

For me, only three things exist: (1) Myself. (2) The War. (3) Igor Severianin?!!!⁴

I spent a miserable winter, surrounded by crowds but totally alone. This is a petty, money-grubbing town.

1. Matiushin had just published Filonov's *Prophesalvos of a Branching Universe,* with illustrations by the author.

2. This was the name Matiushin used as publisher of the book—also the name of the group of artists, Matiushin among them, gathered around Filonov at this time.

3. Maria Konstantinovna Bashkirtseva was a painter and writer. A Russian, she lived in Paris and wrote in French. Her journal, published in Paris in 1887 and in Russia in 1893, was a source for Khlebnikov's discussion of the perturbations of the human psyche in *Time Is the Measure of the Universe* (1916).

4. Pseudonym of Igor Vasilevich Lotarev, creator of the Ego-Futurist school of poetry. Early in 1914 Severianin began to publish with the Cubo-Futurists under the general designation "Futurists." Khlebnikov always speaks of him with amused contempt.

71 *To Mikhail Matiushin*

Tsaritsyn
June 8, 1915

Dear Mikhail Alexeevich,

I am in Tsaritsyn; I'll be in Moscow in two days, without much money. Are you by any chance headed there? Meanwhile here's my address: Gen'l Del. Moscow, Central P.O. I've made three minor discoveries, that's all. I'll be seeing the Burliuks and Co. I've misplaced Aseev's address. It would be wonderful if by some chance he came to Moscow and began publishing. I want to work with him.¹

1. Nikolai Nikolaevich Aseev had a long and brilliant career as a Soviet poet, which began with his admiration for—and frequent imitation of—Khlebnikov.

72 *To His Sister Ekaterina*

Postmark: Moscow
June 11, 1915

Hello from a distance, in ink.

My address: c/o Ignaty Shimanov, village of Akulova Gora, Railway line North, Pushkino Station, Moscow. It's very nice here and a two-week vacation doesn't cost anything; I came from Tsaritsyn by railway.

Best to everybody. I haven't seen anyone, including Shura.

73 *To the Khlebnikov Family*

Kuokkala
August 21, 1915

Dear Everybody, and anybody else around.

I'm in Kuokkala,[1] I got the money, and spread it around, for which many thanks. I go swimming in the ocean—went swimming, I should say, as long as it was warm. What else? I visit the local representatives of the arts, and keep expecting what? The Army reserve, I suppose.

I'm staying here until September 6th, then I'm going to Moscow. Haven't had any great adventures. Everything has been peaceful, monotonous and boring. I'll soon be seeing a lot of Shura as a result. I hope that in the future also you will remain faithful to obligations you undertook of your own free will.

September sixth or first

I still haven't gotten the photograph. The things I wrote this winter are being published. I have a great number of rather shallow, superficial acquaintances. I have indicated directions for further study in the experimental (through experience, not merely speculation) investigation of time. That is how I will go down in history—as the discoverer of the Laws of Time. Until then don't forget to send me what you said you would on the first of each month. So much for my entreaties.

I value very much my friendship with the family of the writer Lazarevsky. An old sea wolf with the blood of Zaporozhian cossacks in his veins.[2] The Evreinovs, Chukovskys, and Repins are all somehow counterfeits as people, when it comes right down to it.[3]

My theory of war has changed into a theory about the conditions necessary for the similarity of two points in time.

I find a feeling of freedom here, and I have enough room to spread my wings like a Caspian osprey, and I scoop up my prey from the sea of numbers. Behold how the whitetail falcon flies, from the Volga over Beloostrov. Thus spake Zarathustra.

What is Militsa doing? [4]

Anna Pavlovna?

Nina Pavlovna?

Zinaida Semyonovna?

Lavr. Lavr.?

Pavel Alex.?

Pavel . . . . .

N . . . . .

Profoundest respects to one and all—whose names, oh God, alone thou knowest.

Me

1. A resort on the Finnish coast where many Russian artists and intellectuals spent the summer.

2. Boris Alexandrovich Lazarevsky, a minor writer.

3. Nikolai Evreinov, playwright and theater director. Kornei Ivanovich Chukovsky, critic and author of children's books, was an early supporter of the Cubo-Futurists. Ilya Repin, the painter, was the leading figure in the Realist school of the late nineteenth century.

4. Militsa, the young girl from *A Jam for Judges II* (see letters 39 and 43). The other names on this list are relatives.

74 *To Vasily Kamensky*

Petrograd
September 1915

Dear Vasya,

I was in very bad shape, practically crawling on my hands and knees, and I missed the train. I didn't have a watch! I got distracted. And now this stupid breach of the laws of friendship and everything. Forgive this rotten mess in the wilds of Petrograd. It's half past seven and I'm a wreck.

What's happening to my story "Ka"? Did you get it?
Geisha? [1]
Say hello to everyone for me.
And Samuel Matveevich. [2]
Nikolaeva?
Tomorrow I am doing a prose portrait of myself.
400 lines of verse, from ten to a hundred rubles??!!
Please send back any unpublished manuscripts within the month.

1. Presumably Nadezhda Nikolaeva, who was interested in oriental art.
2. Samuel Matveevich Vermeil was the editor of the Futurist collections *The Muses' Springtime Delivery Service* (*Vesennee kontragentsvo muz*, 1915) and *Moscow Masters* (*Moskovskie mastera*, 1916).

75 *To Nikolai Aseev*

Petrograd
December 1915(?)

I'm in Petrograd.

I Took It has been in print since Saturday.[1] I got on the 11 o'clock Kursk train but changed over to the Nikolaev since I didn't want to pay for the express and left at 12; the trip wasn't bad. Mikhail Matiushin is writing a curious new piece; Mayakovsky is happy, busy handwriting a tiny little book with red capital letters;[2] today I'll be running around on business. Still haven't found anything out. The room was empty the whole time, which was a nuisance. I'm delighted with *I Took It*. The second collection will be called *I Took Another One*(!) I saw Shimann[3] (he's an old friend of Matiushin's).

Best regards to everyone. I'm rushing back with books for a final blow (the coup de grâce) that will break the neck of the old way of thinking.

Velimir

1. *I Took It* (*Vzial*), subtitled *The Futurists' Drum*, was an antiwar collection published in Petrograd, containing pieces by Khlebnikov, Mayakovsky, Aseev, and others.
2. Mayakovsky's first major long poem, *A Cloud in Trousers* (*Oblako v shtanakh*).
3. Eduard Gusmanovich Shimann was an artist, a friend of Evreinov and Pasternak; he took part in the Jack of Diamonds exhibit in 1917.

76 To Dmitry Petrovsky[1]

Postcard: end of April 1916

The King is out of luck;
The King is under lock
  and key.
Infantry Regiment Ninety-Three
Will be the death of the child in me.

Address: V. V. Khlebnikov
        Co. 2, 93 Inf. Reg. (Res.)
        Tsaritsyn

1. Khlebnikov went home for Easter, was drafted on April 8, 1916, in Astrakhan, and sent to Tsaritsyn for training. Dmitry Vasilevich Petrovsky, a poet and writer, had met Khlebnikov in Moscow in January 1916 at Vermeil's house. Petrovsky's memoirs of Khlebnikov were published in *LEF*, no. 1, 1923.

77 To Nikolai Kulbin[1]

Between late April and May 17, 1916

Dear Nikolai Ivanovich,

I am writing you from the hospital—"the itch detachment," where for the time being I've been relieved from military duties, which I am so unsuited for that they seem like punishment, a refined torment, but I am still in a difficult and uncertain situation. I won't even mention the fact that in this detachment I am surrounded by 100 men suffering from skin diseases, whom nobody looks after properly, so I could catch any one of them including even leprosy. That's the way it goes. But that's not all; again the hell of trying to turn a poet into a mindless animal who gets talked at in gutter language, and their idea of coaxing is to put a knee in your stomach and pull your belt so tight it takes your breath away, where they hit us—me and my fellow soldiers—in the chin to make us hold our heads up higher and look happier, where I am becoming the focus of rays of hate because I am different, not part of a crowd or a herd, where there is only one answer to all arguments: I am still alive, while whole generations have been exterminated in the war. But is one evil a justification for another evil and their chains? All I can do is get court-martialed and wind up in the stockade. Marching, orders, it's murdering my sense of rhythm, and makes me crazy by the end of the evening detail, and I can never remember which is my right foot and which is my left. Besides which because I am so preoccupied I am completely incapable of obeying orders fast enough, or precisely enough.

As a soldier I am a complete nothing. Outside the military establishment I am something. And even though there's some question about it, that something is exactly what Russia lacks now. She had a lot of good soldiers at the beginning of the war (strong, hardy animals who obeyed without reasoning why, who parted with their reason when they shaved off their whiskers). And she has few, far too few others left. I'd make a lousy second lieutenant.

And what am I to do about my oath of allegiance, when I've already given my allegiance to Poetry? What if Poetry prompts me to make a joke of my oath? And what about my absentmindedness? There's only one kind of military duty I'd be good for, and that's if they assigned me to a noncombat outfit to do farmwork (fishing or gardening) or to a responsible and challenging job on the airship *Muromets*.[2] But the latter is impossible. And while the first would be completely bearable, it would be stupid. A poet has his own complex rhythm, and that's why military service is so oppressive; it makes him endure the yoke of a different and discontinuous rhythmic pattern, one that derives from the nature of the majority—i.e., a lot of farmers. Thus, defeated by war, I will be forced to smash my rhythm (the fate of Shevchenko[3] and others) and fall silent as a poet. The idea does not attract me in the least, and I will continue shouting to a stranger on the steamship to throw me a lifesaver.

Thanks to the continual monotonous cursing and swearing, my feeling for language is dying within me. What place has the Eternal Feminine in a barrage of heavy-artillery curse words? I feel as if the gardens and castles of my soul have been rooted out, leveled and destroyed. Furthermore I am obliged to claim the path of special rights and privileges, which calls forth hostility from my fellow soldiers because they don't recognize as legitimate any excuses except a missing leg or a stomachache. I have been snatched away from the very front lines of the fight for the future.

Now I haven't the slightest idea what lies ahead of me. And since I am of use to everyone in the realm of peaceful labor but am nothing in the service, they even call me a "physically underdeveloped individual." For a long time now they've been referring to me as "it" instead of him.

I am a dervish, a Yogi, a Martian, anything you want, but I am *not* a private in a reserve infantry regiment.

My address: Pvt. V. K.

"Itch Detachment"

Military Hospital 93rd Res. Inf. Reg.

Tsaritsyn

I'll be in this hospital for two weeks. The head doctor, Shapiro, is fairly good-natured, but strict.

Sincerely yours, who has saved me once already (a reminder).

Velimir Khlebnikov

On February 29th in Moscow a society of "317 members" was founded. Do you want to be a member? There are no rules, just a common cause.[4]

1. Nikolai Ivanovich Kulbin was a physician, a painter, and a patron of the Russian Futurists. Khlebnikov appeals to him here in his position as professor at the Military Medical Academy in St. Petersburg and a doctor attached to the general staff of the Russian army.

2. The *Ilya Muromets* was a large four-engine aircraft desiged by Igor Sikorsky and built in St. Petersburg. Late in 1913 and early 1914 Futurist performances shared the pages of the evening papers with descriptions of test flights of the *Muromets;* possibly it was the immediate source for the airplane in the opera *Victory over the Sun* (December 1913). During World War I the *Muromets* was one of the most effective heavy bombers.

3. The Ukrainian poet Taras Shevchenko was arrested in March 1847 and drafted into the Russian army as a private in an infantry regiment, where he was kept for ten years under specific orders (from Tsar Nicholas personally) that he be forbidden to write.

4. Khlebnikov's Society of 317 became better known as the Presidents of Planet Earth. In addition to Kulbin, Khlebnikov's early projected members included Viacheslav Ivanov, the religious philosopher and mathematician Pavel Florensky, and H. G. Wells. The phrase "common cause" may be a reference to Nikolai Fyodorov and his idealistic philosophy.

78   To Nikolai Kulbin

Tsaritsyn

May 1916

Please, Nikolai Ivanovich, please do whatever you can to keep them from turning a poet and a thinker into a soldier. It amazes me that in Germany Goethe and Kant remained untouched by the Napoleonic hurricane; the laws of their world allowed them to be merely poets.

The fact is, in peacetime they used to call you and me crazy, mentally ill; as a result most government jobs were closed to us; but now in wartime, when every action is especially crucial, I become a full-fledged citizen. Equal rights = equal duty. Besides, poets are members of a theocratic union—should they be subject to the military draft?

Here I will never be anything but court-martialed, I hate the drill and movements so much. There I can be a creator.

Where am I supposed to be?

You saved me already from one disaster. Whatever, I beg of you: write to the medical board by registered mail; of course your opinion will carry enormous weight with them. And the board are the ones able to alleviate my situation.

If it was hard for Pushkin to be a gentleman-in-waiting,[1] it's worse for me to be a draftee at the age of thirty, in filthy messy Co. 6, where I remain,

Your devoted,
V. Khlebnikov

Send your diagnosis.

1. In 1831 Pushkin married the beautiful Natalia Goncharova. Tsar Nicholas was much taken with her and, in order to increase her attendance at court, appointed the thirty-five-year-old Pushkin a gentleman-in-waiting in 1834; it was a trivial position, usually given to teen-aged sons of the nobility. The tsar's reasons were insultingly obvious, and Pushkin was in a rage of humiliation.

79   *To His Mother*

Postmark: Tsaritsyn
May 17, 1916

I went up before a board and am to be sent on to Kazan to the infirmary or the military hospital(?) there to be examined by a new board. Also I got the 20 rubles from the company. That's all the news. I'll be leaving Tsaritsyn for a while, going by steamboat third class, the government pays for it, when I don't know.

80　To His Mother

Postmark: Tsaritsyn
June 4, 1916

Greetings and sincere admiration for the speed and energy of the letters that have so beneficially influenced my life. Stetsenko talked about the letter you sent him. I've been taken down from the cross of military service for two weeks + two weeks, and my position as first King of the Government of Time on Planet Earth has taken a decided turn for the better. I am being held in easy captivity by savages from centuries past. I haven't gotten any letters for quite a while. I got a package and the 20 rubles. After that, nothing. There was a board meeting on May 15th and through the good offices of Captain Suprotivny, they ordered me on to Kazan for an examination. "Kazan Military Hospital." But so far they haven't sent me. I keep asking myself, will they or won't they manage to murder a poet—more, a King of Poets—with this Arakcheevism?[1] It's all totally boring and stupid. Almost everything I hear about Kazan is very depressing. I have no idea what will happen after that. On May 25 a new recruit died while standing in formation; he was from Astrakhan. Please send me 10 rubles by telegraph right away c/o Sylvia Tatlin, 7 Petrovskaia St., corner of Predtechenskaia; I haven't got any money, it's being held up at regimental headquarters.

1. Alexei Arakcheev was a close friend of Tsar Alexander 1 and an all-powerful minister without portfolio. His harsh administration, especially of the notorious "military colonies," and his own sadistic personality gave rise to the term Arakcheevism for the period of his influence.

81　To Mikhail Matiushin

Early August 1916

Dear Mikhail Vasilevich,

What are you up to? I'm free until the 15th of September, on leave. I'll be in Astrakhan until the 15th of Aug. Lengthy researches on language and on numbers. *P, L, Sh, Ch, Shch* are done. Do you need any word chunks? I strongly suggest a general anthology to include us all: Kruchonykh, Mayakovsky, [illegible], Burliuk, and myself.

The letters didn't get here (they got held up). Ten books did arrive,[1] and thank you. A barrage of publications this fall. Will you publish anything? Should I send you something for publication?

A syndicate of publishers for the daily paper.

Peace to anyone I got mad at—otherwise everything would be a mess.

I'll be in Astrakhan until August 15th.

1. Khlebnikov's pamphlet *Time Is the Measure of the Universe,* which Matiushin published in March 1916.

82　*To Grigory Petnikov[1] and Nikolai Aseev*

Postmark: Astrakhan
September 19, 1916

Dear Nikolai Nikolaevich and Grigory Nikolaevich,

I've gone up before one board, and they ordered me sent on to the provincial zemstvo hospital. But so far I haven't gotten there. That's all the news. I've gotten together for *Chronicle:* (1) "Mud and Willow," (2) "5 + p," (3) "The Treaty," (4) "List of Consonants," (5) "Order to Planet Earth," (6) "Poems," (7) "Letter," (8) "About ASTSU," (9) "Gazelle," (10) "Joining the Martians," (11) "Drawing of Miss Death," (12) "Seven Things with Wings."

The essay is almost completed. "*Ka*" *is not. Please* print the essay. It has some terribly important things in it and N. N. Aseev, for instance, approves. Even though it's badly written. But there's a lot of content. If they are all to be published, I'll keep sending you the things for *Chronicle* periodically, in little spurts. If not, then I'll set my writing aside for the time being.

That way *Chronicle* will become a court circular for the three of us and will grow and flower, while I will always know where to send my little pieces to get them published right away.

"The Trumpet of the Martians" is very successful in terms of speed.[2]

All the best.

Astrakhan.

Yours,
Velimir

1. Grigory Nikolaevich Petnikov was from Kharkov in the Ukraine and began writing poetry about 1913. He and Aseev founded the publishing house Lyroon (Liren') and published many of Khlebnikov's works. Of the titles Khlebnikov proposes here, only "5 + p" (under the title "A Second Language"), four poems, and "Letter" ("A Letter to Two Japanese") were actually published in Petnikov's journal *Chronicle* (1916).

2. Lyroon had just published the essay, written earlier that summer.

83   To Grigory Petnikov

September 23, 1916

Today the 23rd I'm going into the zemstvo hospital to be "examined." Goodnight! So far I haven't copied out anything.

84   To Grigory Petnikov

Postmark: Astrakhan
September 30, 1916

Today is September 28th.

I'm still left hanging between my first and second board hearings.

A well, a camel, crocodile, mice.

A cloudy situation. But I've copied out everything and sent them except for my story "Ka²."

I keep you in mind.

I'm content with myself and still at liberty. I very much hope the collection will see the light of day. I'm sending an essay, "The Tree of Wars."

"Myself and Planet Earth"—"va + v"—12 pgs, "ASTSU"—4 pgs. "Mud and Willow," "List of Consonants," "5m + p." "Gazelle." Critical Essay. Poems. "Letter to Two Japanese."

I'm sending the drafts separately.

V. Khlebnikov

85 To Mikhail Matiushin

Astrakhan
September 30, 1916

Dear Mikhail Vasilevich,

Petnikov wants to have your stuff, and Guro's. He asked me to write you about it before I leave.
I'm still free for a while. After that I don't know.
It's still warm here.
Best regards to you and everybody.

V. Khlebnikov

86 To Grigory Petnikov and Nikolai Aseev

Postmark: Astrakhan
November 2, 1916

Gr. Nik. and Nik. Nik,
Nik. Nik. and Grig. Nik,

I'm in the hospital today. I think because of the campaigns of the future that it's imperative to print much of what I sent. If the essay on numbers is printed, that will give me the strength to move ahead on the path marked out there, a path already clear. The summit—all knowledge in one equation with the value of $\sqrt{-1}$.
Our glorious goal is to find the living (animal) number.
I didn't have enough time or strength to copy out my story "Ka."
I'll send it to you, but I don't know when. If it matures well, it will be a good piece. You can find out Wells's address at the office of Mr. Williams, 9 Admiralteiskaia Naberezhnaia, Petrograd.[1]
[In the margins of the postcard:] A stock of anti-money. New models. For information call 365–365. Advertisement: our firm produces great quantities of $+\sqrt{-1}$ people, call n^n.

V. K.

1. Probably Harold Williams, a British journalist who with Hugh Walpole ran the British propaganda bureau in Petrograd. Williams married Ariadna Tyrkova, a member of the central committee of the Cadet Party.

87 *To Grigory Petnikov*

Tsaritsyn
Between November 24 and early December 1916

I'm in a rotten mood. Three weeks in the company of madmen, and again a board hearing ahead of me, and nothing to indicate that I'll be set free. They have me completely in their clutches. And they haven't let up on me so far.

The short essays can be laid out with number headings, this way:

1

(essay)

2

(essay)

3

Zirin. The Ball of Asia. Instead of Velimir Khlebnikov you can put Hiawatha's Unsuri.

That's why you should put the anthology together yourself. Or rather if I get to Petrograd then I'll get a copy of my pieces. It's very important for me to have "The Tree of Wars" printed, also "Myself and Planet Earth," "A Checklist of the Alphabet," and the little essays on numbers. If things get speeded up you can send "A Checklist of the Alphabet" to *The Enchanted Wanderer.*

Title the first anthology "Bend of the Bug" or "A Shaft of Lightning" and the second "Witch on a Swan," if you have no intention of using that combination of words. Or perhaps call the first one "Lalia Rides a Tiger."

That, I think, is all I had in mind.

Can we use drawings?

It looks as if I'll soon be back in the infantry again . . . . .

Goodbye!

88 *To Grigory Petnikov*

Stamp: 90th Inf. Regiment
Postmark: Saratov
December 22, 1916

I am a private in the 90th Inf. Regiment, Reserve Co. 7, 1st Platoon. I live 2 versts from Saratov behind a cemetery, in the gloomy surround of a camp. I'm being paid back for *Chronicle* and Petrograd. I didn't make use of the summer for my own affairs and now I'm suffering for it. Couldn't we declare that *Chronicle* is a business venture vitally concerned with national defense?

Goddam everything to hell and I will write you a letter about that.

V. Khleb.

89 *To His Family*

Saratov

December 25, 1916

Dear next-of-kin,

Holiday greetings! I hereby exhort you: Live in peace, be not angry, love and comfort one another, above all remember to keep honorable the Khlebnikov family name.

I am supposed to hop and skip and celebrate the first day of Christmas, and I got so depressed at the thought that I started writing letters and preachments. I wasn't allowed to go into Saratov: it seems I don't know how to salute. I'm afraid they're right—it's true, true, true. What happened was I saluted with my hand in my pocket and the lieutenant jumped on me: "Your hand, your hand, where's your hand?" The night before Christmas we conducted a search for enemy infiltrators. Beyond the stand of birch trees the thousand lights of Saratov glow; our barn is covered with the icy hair of melting icicles and looks almost alive, with yellow rabbit eyes. It breathes, craftily. I won't write you any more because you don't write me.

I foresee the weeping of tears, familial horrors, and a war of two. For shame, children!

It's too bad I have to write on such a sloppy piece of paper. Write Shura and let him know I'm trapped again. Behave yourselves, children, keep calm and quiet until the war is over. Which will be only 1½ years until the war without is transformed into the ground swell of a war within.

. . . and the printed symbol for peace and love

I only got one letter from Vera.

Send me "The Trumpet of the Martians" and "Miss Death."

I wept with emotion today. They gave us all a Christmas present: a French roll and a piece of salami, just as though we were dogs.

"Special Greetings" to Shura the Pavdinian.

90 *To Grigory Petnikov*

Postmark: Saratov
January 4, 1917

!... ....!

I got a copy of *Will* from an unidentified correspondent with a barely noticeable handwritten remark: "Send your correct address."

On the assumption that it was you who wrote it, I hereby fulfill your request. Letters: 1st Platoon, 7th Company, 90th Res. Inf. Regiment, Saratov. Books: c/o N. N. Gorsky, 89 Kirpichnaia St. (corner of Kirpichnaia and Nikolskaia), Saratov.

If you come *in person:* Saratov Station, corner of University. Trolley #1 marked Cemetery, takes you to the cemetery, and a cab from there to camp #1 costs 2 rubles.

I can't be any more exact than that. Thanks for "Miss D." It's beautifully published, but I'm extremely sorry that the essays weren't included, only her. You lightfoot, you! I'd love to see you.

....!

91 *To the Commanding Officer, Training Detachment*

Saratov
February 17, 1917

I am desirous of being transferred to active service, and hereby request your assistance in arranging such a transfer with the next returning reinforcements.

Pvt. Viktor Khlebnikov

92 *To His Mother*

Saratov

February 19, 1917

Hello. I send you my precipitous prattle(!) External Affairs: I've been transferred to a training detachment and I keep expecting letters from you: I got your most recent ones two weeks ago c/o Gorsky, also the money order; I have sent you "Lion" and the Japanese poems. I don't know what's going on there at home. What's Shura doing? I keep expecting letters either c/o Gorsky (the money order) or to me at this address: Training Detachment, 90th Reg., Saratov.

Maybe everything will work itself out without great shocks and shakeups. There have been occasions here when letters took eleven days to get from Saratov to here (that's 3 days per verst). Lt. Col. Dombrovsky from our regiment has moved to Astrakhan. Spring was in the air for a moment today, it was the first break in the season. But there's a lot of snow, and winter still. Time hangs heavy, and the only distractions are squabbles with my new unit. I send you my cheerfulest best wishes. I'll be writing you. I'm just not sure you're getting my letters.

Veli Mir

93 *To His Mother*

Saratov

Between February 19 and 28, 1917

General attention!

Prick up your ears! Gorsky has left, so send the copy of my diploma, plus the telegram from High School No. 3 certifying that I finished high school, not to him, but *to me* at the regiment. There's no longer any reason to be especially worried: I went to see the adjutant's aide and showed him my papers (hippity-hop); he said he'd put me on the list and that with papers like that I could have been at military school long ago. That's wonderful. The whole day before that I was singing "Malbrouk" and "O clair de la lune, mon ami Pierrot" and for the first moment in all this time I felt in a military mood.

So: 1. Please ask them to send me here at the regiment, by telegram, notification that I graduated from Kazan High School No. 3 in

1903—that's the first urgent matter. 2. Please ask them to send me here at the regiment a copy of my diploma—that's the second, less urgent, matter. As is my birth certificate.

Meanwhile I'll take my own measures and steps to get my name on the list. Goodbye for now. I apologize for this business letter. I haven't washed once since I've been here. They may not send me back to the 93rd and I may not have to go.

94 To Grigory Petnikov[1]

Soon after March 1, 1917

Dear Petnikov,

You know that our goal, a goal we have attained already, solving with the sound of strings what is usually solved by cannon fire, is to grant power over humanity to the world of the stars, by eliminating unnecessary intermediaries between them and us.

Into streets torn by the lion's jaws of revolt we go like a martyr unwavering in her faith and the meekness of her upraised eyes (eyes that direct lightning flashes on the sea of terrestrial stars).

The worldwide thundering of revolt—can it terrify us, if we ourselves are a revolt more terrifying still? You remember that a government of poets has been founded and encompasses Planet Earth. You remember that the sounding string of tribes has united Tokyo, Moscow, and Singapore.

We imitate the waves of the sea, white-capped by the storm, now uniting and rising up, now subsiding into multitudinous distances. You remember that we have succeeded in discovering the harmony of our destinies, which enables us to hold humanity in the palm of our thoughts and raise it to the next stage of existence.

Still it moves, this wanderer of the centuries.

How the harmonies we found have tied the letter U into the thundering of the A string, into the foot soldier's march and beats of the heart, the thunder of the waves, the harmonies of births—these are all similar points of the ray of destiny.

Remember how a foundation was built, solid enough to let us speak of rays of people, or people light, on a line with the black, cold, and burning ray, and the resinous ray of furious lightning. This was done in order to transfer lawmaking power to the scientist's desk, and to exchange the arrogant Roman law, based on word definitions, for the approaching law of the Futurians, which consists of equal signs, multiplication and division signs, signs of the square roots of 1 and n, imaginary quantities brought to bear on the substance of humanity. How we dream of constructing viewing glasses and magnifying lenses for people rays in the elemental agitation of their wars, and of replacing with scientific waves the ordinary barbarous ray of human nature and its blindfolded progressions. All inventions for lesser rays, all the laws of Balmer, Fresnel, Fraunhofer, and Planck, all the art of reflecting, directing, distancing, bringing closer—we swear, we young people, to employ them upon the rays of the human race. Thus will victory be accomplished over space, while victory over time will be attained by means of a movement and transmission of consciousness during a second rebirth. We are determined to die knowing the instant of our second birth, vowing to complete the poem of ourselves.

This is the action of fate's sewing machine—the point of birth is a needle, and in obedience to a law it sews a knot onto the canvas of the human race.

Aryabhatta and Kepler! We see again the year of the ancient gods, great sacred events repeating themselves after 365 years. That is so far the supreme string in the Futurian's scale, and are we not rapt in admiration, seeing that at the end of this growing advance of the laws of origin we find an oscillation of vocalic U and the waves of the A string, the main axis of the sounding world. This is the first section of our pact with heaven for the human race, signed in the blood of the great war.

As far as the second barrier on our path is concerned—multilanguage—remember that an overview of the fundamentals of languages has already been accomplished, and a discovery made: that the alphabet is the sound machine of languages, and each of its sounds hides a fully exact and spatial word image. This knowledge is essential in order to transport man to the next stage—a single common language, and that we will do next year.

Entirely yours,
Velimir Khlebnikov

1. This letter to Petnikov exists only in this version as printed in the collection *Beyonsensicals* (*Zaumniki*, Moscow, 1922). The dating is uncertain, but the euphoric tone and the references to "revolt" indicate that it was written soon after the February revo-

lution. It is the first working out of a grand design for his theories; the ideas and images it contains are presented more thoroughly in the final section of "Our Fundamentals."

95 To Mikhail Matiushin

Tver
May 13, 1917

I'm writing at the table in the guardhouse. Arrested yesterday and taken off the train. I'm in a stupid predicament. I have a feeling it's going to go on being stupid. Had a five-month leave of absence, was on my way to Petrograd, but was taken off the train at the station in Tver on May 12 and wound up in the guardhouse of the local military command, even though my papers said I had five months' leave.

V. Khlebnikov

What's with Petnikov?

96 To Mikhail Matiushin

Kiev
June 11, 1917

Dear Mikhail Vasilevich,

I'm in Kiev.

On the way the train axle began to heat up, it started to sputter and smoke, they poured water on it, which didn't do any good. That was in Kursk. From Kursk on, we had to ride on the roof.

P.S. In the list of dramatic works I forgot about *The Little Devil* and *Hooder* (from *Works*).[1]

1. Khlebnikov had asked Matiushin to bring out a collection of his plays. He adds here two titles, one of which, *Hooder* (*Khovun*), is a prose piece and was printed not in *Works* (1914) but in *A Jam for Judges II* (1913).

97 To Mikhail Matiushin

Astrakhan
August 8, 1917

Dear Mikhail Vasilevich,

I've been in Kiev, Kharkov, Taganrog, Tsaritsyn. I swam in the Sea of Azov, and now I am in the never-sufficiently-to-be-reviled city of my great(?) ancestors (i.e., Astrakhan). I'm taking a trip tomorrow with a child of the sun, to bask in the sun like a lizard and drink watermelon and kumiss.

It's all old stuff here. I had visions of going to the Caucasus, but never made it. I'll be here two weeks.

In the list of dramatic works is *The Little Devil* which I forgot to note (from *Works*).

What is Kruchonykh doing? What about publishing a collective anthology (Burliuk, Kamensky, me, Kruchonykh)? *A Tent for Two.*[1]

1. The proposed collection of plays was never published; neither was the anthology *A Tent for Two* (*Tabor dvukh*).

98 To Grigory Petnikov[1]

Krasnaia Poliana
Spring 1919(?)

The garden is in flower. Haven't the strength to leave—what a crime. I'll be arriving on Tuesday.

Vel. Khlebnikov

[A drawing of a wheel appears here, with the inscription: Mailed at Krasnaia Poliana.]

1. The dating of this letter is uncertain. Khlebnikov visited Krasnaia Poliana, the Siniakov family's country house, many times, as did Petnikov and Aseev. Aseev married one of the beautiful Siniakova sisters, Oksana, and Petnikov another, Vera. Khlebnikov was also captivated and wrote his long poem "Three Sisters" about them.

98a To E. G. Shableev[1]

Kharkov
June 1919

I have absolutely no money, but am enjoying myself anyway. [. . .]
Love,
Velimir

A wonderful spring.

1. This piece of a letter was first printed in the new Soviet edition of Khlebnikov's selected writings, *Tvoreniia* (Moscow, 1987).

99 To Grigory Petnikov[1]

Kharkov
Around October 21, 1919

Dear Grigory Nikolaevich,

I'll be here until next Tuesday. So come earlier, before October 28th![2] The bearer of this letter will be either my friend the artist Subbotin or someone who works here. Hunger like a crosswind unites the Saburov Home and Old Moscow Street. Please make use of this rare occasion and send envelopes, paper, something to smoke, and bread and potatoes. And may you be blest, and may your years be long upon the earth! *Allah verdy.* It would be tactful if you were to think up a few other things too. If there is anything to read (Jerome Jerome),[3] then that too.

We

[Attached on two scraps of paper:]

> Drelin-dron!
> Lirum-larum!
> Drelin-dron.
> Lirum-larum
> Larum-lirum.

A poem out of Myself and Planet Earth.
The surface of my red corpuscle is $\frac{1}{365}$[110] part of the surface of the entire Planet Earth. The mark of this hand and the inscription "signed by hand" I have seen on all things, in a thousand mirrors.

1. This letter is written on the back of a cartridge box. Khlebnikov spent several months in the Saburov Home, the psychiatric ward of Kharkov Hospital, under observation to determine his fitness for further military service. Dr. V. Anfimov, the psychiatrist who examined him, later published an interesting record of Khlebnikov in the hospital, as well as the texts of several poems written there.
2. The date of Khlebnikov's thirty-fourth birthday.
3. Jerome K. Jerome was an English humorist whose books were translated into Russian and became immensely popular. Khlebnikov may have been particularly interested in Jerome's account of his visit to Russia in 1899–1900, which appeared in Russian as *Liudi budushchego* (The People of the Future, 1906).

100   *To Osip Brik*[1]

Kharkov
February 23, 1920

Dear Osip Maximovich,

We were cut off from Moscow all summer, and now everything there seems very mysterious to me. But the biggest mystery, the one that shines like the North Star, is—have my works come out or not? I'm very worried they haven't! It'll be the same thing as "The Internationale of the Arts." One day very soon won't you send me a big, thick Pushkinian tome? With corrections to be made and the ink not yet dry? Won't you? Wouldn't that be wonderful?

When judging the language in this letter, remember I just got out of bed after two bouts of typhus. I absolutely must get some money. Won't IMO send some?[2] To: Vikt. Vlad. Khlebnikov, apt. 2, 16 Cher nishevskaia St., Kharkov.

What is the fate of my epistle, good or bad?

All told, trying to avoid being drafted by the Whites and being sick with typhus, I've spent four months on my back in military hospitals. Awful! Now I'm always dizzy and my legs hurt.

Yours, Khlebnikov

P.S. I was hoping to receive 10 thousand, or 5—but that's already no good.

1. A philologist and Formalist critic, friend of Mayakovsky.

2. A complete edition of Khlebnikov's writings had been planned since 1918, to be published by the new Soviet Education Commission in Petrograd and by IMO, a Futurist publishing group. Mayakovsky was instrumental in arranging the venture and managed to secure Khlebnikov an advance of 1150 rubles before Khlebnikov left Moscow for Kharkov and the south in April 1919. These publication plans were never realized. In the spring of 1919 an anthology called "The Internationale of the Arts" was planned, for which Khlebnikov wrote "Artists of the World," but this book never came out either.

101 To Osip Brik

Kharkov

April 30, 1920

Dear Osip Maximovich,

I'm sorry the collected works hasn't been published, but I'm getting used to the fact.

Since Esenin[1] and some others have made me a few offers, I would like to know if a time has been set for the complete works to come out within the next two months?

It's impossible to put it off any longer—that is the source of my earnest desire to have you take upon yourself the task of arranging a timetable for the edition, to be definitely no more than two months.

I regret very much I can't be in Moscow to oversee things myself. G. Petnikov might undertake to begin negotiations in this matter. I would very much like to see my things printed.

Regards from the far-off southland to Lydia Yurevna and to Vladimir Vladimirovich.[2]

I am beginning to work once again, which for a long time I simply could not do.

V. Khlebnikov

1. Sergei Esenin, poet and sometime husband of Isadora Duncan, was associated with the Imagist group. On April 19 Esenin and his friend, the poet Anatoly Mariengof, had come to Kharkov and arranged an evening at the Civic Theater, where the two Imagists inaugurated Khlebnikov as President of Planet Earth—in a mock ceremony that Khlebnikov took very seriously. Khlebnikov's poem "A Wagon from Moscow" ("Moskvy kolymaga") was written about the encounter.

2. "Lydia" Yurevna is Lily, Osip Brik's wife (Khlebnikov consistently mistook her name). Vladimir Vladimirovich is Mayakovsky, who was living with the Briks.

102 To His Sister Vera

Baku
January 2, 1921

Dear Vera-bunny, yoo-hoo!

Fly little letters, like little birch leaves, over the russet head of the ones I love, fall upon the enchanted dwellers-by-the-Volga! It is time to begin disillusioning the serpents, so there will be much hissing in the snake kingdom. This year will be the year of a great and final battle with the serpent. Everything my consciousness contains: black nighttime windows, the hissing of the breathless firewood as it hastens to ashes—I raise it all to salute my victory over the serpent. These past days I have forged a spear for my combat with him—it is a vision of the future: I possess equations for the stars, equations for voices, equations for thoughts, equations of birth and death. I am the first to set foot on a new continent: a place that commands Time. I was the first to appear upon it, intoxicated with joy, but people remain people—and I returned in chains from my first encounter with the serpent: all my thoughts abandoned me, and my enchanted world vanished just as if I had betrayed it. All visions of the future suddenly abandoned me the way a flock of doves, having rested, abandons the tree they no longer need.

All this happened after I trusted people for the last time in my life and read a report at a scholarly meeting at Red Star University. It's true I put them through the most exquisite torments: I announced to the Marxists that I represented Marx squared, and to those who preferred Mohammed I announced that I was the continuation of the teachings of Mohammed, who was henceforth silenced since the Number had now replaced the Word. I called my report the Koran of Numbers.[1]

Which is why those whose self-esteem goes no further than getting a pair of boots as a reward for good behavior and loyal thoughts have drawn away from me, and now watch me with terrified eyes. But all the same the die is cast, and the serpent will be thrust through the very belly. Until that moment, though, life is caught in the coils of his slimy body and its baleful patterns of the death of body and soul.

And yet! The duel will take place!

My witness is what's left of my smoke, my only friend at the moment. Oh, by the way, I've been using paper gunpowder cartridges to roll my smoke and then using the sticks of gunpowder to write with.

But I'm so scatterbrained I put the lighted butt down on the powder and it ignited and caught fire, so I put it out with my hands. In fact it wasn't so dangerous, gunpowder burns very slowly, and from the long black cartridges you slip out terrific powdersticks, perfect for Futurites (Future-wrights) to write with, only it makes a really loud bang.

I have been pursuing my lonely goal in a bitter depression, but your letter with its visions of spring has warmed me up and I feel talkative. I assure you that I have been thawing out, and drip-drip.

All this dark depressing truth, that we live in a world of death, that death has not yet been bound and cast down a captive, that our enemy is not yet overcome—it makes my warrior blood stir. I mean that seriously. Because now it's important to be a warrior. Now I no longer say, as I did recently, that I refuse to "dance around with a gun," to condone by my presence that foul and ancient ritual. I can't forgive myself for not being in Kiev.

I would have found myself able to do that.

I am writing so freely and openly today only because my word hoard has been stirred by the rays of your letter. Let's make a pact together to pick branches of blueberries by the noise of mountain streams, and to steal quietly upon sleeping tortoises. What more do we need?

I have forgotten the world of poetry and sound, I have cast them as sacrifices into the bonfire of numbers. But a little while longer and the sacred gift of speech will return to me.

That's the extent of my rambling . . . . . A letter is not a ledger, and there's nothing more boring than detailed accounts.

Best to everyone.

I wanted to go to Persia, but I may go to Vladikavkaz or Derbent.

Love and kisses. I think of you. Until spring.

Perhaps this spring we can find common contentment at the seashore, in the Caucasus, but for that we will need a breakthrough(?) and decide upon a flight out of Egypt.

1. On December 17, 1920, Khlebnikov read a report at the recently organized proletarian university in Baku. The paper's title involves a play on the Russian word for root (*koren'*) and was a major attempt to work out significant correspondences between numbers and historical events. The paper seems to have been the first public disclosure of his Laws of Time and was evidently received with considerable derision.

103 To V. D. Ermilov[1]

Baku
January 3, 1921

Dear Vasya Ermusha!

Please pardon the salutation, but that's how it came out.

I'm in Baku (Bailovskaia Street Dormitory, Naval Prolitprosvet).

I have discovered the fundamental Laws of Time, and I believe that now it will be as easy to predict events as to count to three. If people don't want to learn my art of predicting the future (and that has already happened in Baku, among local thinkers), I shall teach it to horses. A government of horses may turn out more gifted scientists than a government of men. Horses will be grateful to me. They will have, besides riding, another supplementary source of income: they will be able to predict the fate of human beings and to aid governments that still have ears to hear. Schleimann is here from Kharkov, he's sick. Also Mané-Katz.[2]

In the mountains, where I was living before I came to Baku, it was wonderful.

We have the sea here, and the Bibi-Aybata Valley, which looks like a mouth puffing at a whole lot of cigarettes.

Happy New Year (New Fear?), Year or Fear, that's the question!

ME

1. Vasily Dmitrievich Ermilov, a painter Khlebnikov had known in Kharkov, was a leading member of the Ukrainian avant-garde and printed Khlebnikov's long poem *Ladomir* there in June 1920.
2. Pavel Sergeevich Schleimann was a poet and translator Khlebnikov had met in Kharkov. Mané-Katz (M. L. Mane), a well-known painter, emigrated to Paris shortly after this letter was written.

104 To Vladimir Mayakovsky

Baku
February 18, 1921

ROSTA.[1] To: Vladimir Vladimirovich Mayakovsky

I am thinking of writing something that the whole of humanity, all 3 billion of them, could take part in—and participation would be required. But for something like that, ordinary language won't do, so I have to invent a new one, little by little.

This is to introduce you to Comrade Solnyshkin, a good friend of mine.[2] Besides Kruchonykh—who's getting ready to come visit you—Samorodov is here, also Loskutov and Solnyshkin. All of whom you will see in good time. When the printing presses stop, I'm dead.

Here's to the resurrection of print from the dead!

1. During the winter Khlebnikov worked for ROSTA (the Russian telegraph agency), which was turning out propaganda for the new Soviet government. Mayakovsky worked in their Moscow office, where he produced rhymed slogans and drawings for posters. Khlebnikov in Baku was writing similar verse.

2. Solnyshkin was a sailor Khlebnikov had met in Baku. This letter and the following one were written on the same piece of paper and were presumably to have been delivered by Solnyshkin. But they were found among Khlebnikov's papers.

105 To Vladimir Mayakovsky

Baku
February 18, 1921

Dear Volodya!

The writer's inkwell is dry, and the fly was *not* amused when it dove in for a swim.

That is the truth of the new constellation that rules our times, the new Ursa Major.

I am living on the border between Russia and Persia, which is a place I am really drawn to.

The Caucasus this summer will be wonderful and I have no intention of leaving it.

I doff the turban of Elbruz and venerate the relics of Moscow.

I have studied much and become a master of numbers. I could create a springtime of numbers, if only the presses were working.

But instead of a heart I seem to have something resembling a chunk of wood or a kippered herring. I don't know. No more songs.

That's the reason for these lovely cries of Evoë! and for letting my hair down.

Yours,
V. Khlebnikov

106   *To Vsevolod Meyerhold*[1]

Baku

February 18, 1921

Dear Vsevolod Emilevich,

Allow me to introduce my dear friend Comrade Solnyshkin, so he can bring to your northern capital a little, just a clutch, of the eternal fire of Baku. If gloom now rules the universe of your stage, then hang him way up near the top of the proscenium as a little artificial sun. That's my advice. He has the ability—in his own time and at his own pace, be patient with him—to cast a ray of warm sunlight wherever there is gloom and dampness, if it's really wanted. You'll be convinced of that yourself after a while. Besides many various talents that the world unfortunately does not yet appreciate, he is drawn to the world of your art, that is to those transfigurations and disguises of the spirit of man whose tailor and fitter is man himself. That desire to share in the plurality of an existence that beats in a thousand waves against the rock of his individuality, against the chain of singularity, seeks a natural outlet in your domain, the art of the theater. I am of no high opinion concerning a country that forces a man like Comrade Solnyshkin, while he is trying to gain experience in lighting, to resort to pieces of incandescent sulphur, as he had to do when he was young. As for my own concerns: I have reached the promised breakthrough in my understanding of time, which involves work in several sciences, and I absolutely must have an authorization for getting my books printed. What if one could be sent to me here in Baku? That would be the best way out of the situation. The book is all ready and written in the language of equations. It is a canvas painted only in numbers.

Let's hope by the time we meet again it will already have appeared. I remain,

Yours truly,

V. Khlebnikov

1. Vsevolod Emilevich Meyerhold, the brilliant stage director, enthusiastically greeted the revolution and was now head of the Theatrical Section of the People's Commissariat of Education, officially in charge of all theaters in the Soviet Union. This letter, like those to Mayakovsky, was never delivered.

107 To Vasily Ermilov

Baku
April 7, 1921

Hugs to you and Katiusha.[1]
Foreknowledge of the future *exists,* protected by the trustworthy wall of my silence. Which will come to an end this autumn.
You must come down here, it's wonderful.

V. K.

1. Ekaterina Karlovna Neimaer, poet and ballet dancer.

108 To His Mother

Baku
April 9, 1921

Hugs and Kisses.
I couldn't find out anything about Shura, where he was stationed. The 9th Army is now on the Kuban.
Alive and well. You should all move here. This place is wonderful! I intend to spend my whole life in the Caucasus.

V. K.

109 To His Sister Vera

Enzeli[1]
April 14, 1921

Bold as a lion I take pen in hand.
The banner of the Presidents of Planet Earth follows me wherever I go, and waves now over Persia. I got my exit permit on April 13th; on April 14th with the weather calm, as if heaven were smiling on all humanity, I set sail on the *Kursk,* south toward the blue shores of Persia.
The mountains, their peaks covered with snowy silver, looked like the eyes of the Prophet, hidden in brows of clouds. The snowy pattern of the peaks looked like the work of austere thought deep in the eyes of God, like the austere eyes of majestic contemplation. The blue mir-

acle of Persia rose out of the sea, above the endless silk of reddish-yellow waves; it called to mind the eyes of destiny of a different world.

The streaming golden south is like the finest silks spread beneath the feet of the Mohammed of the north, and to the north beyond the stern of the *Kursk* they turned a twilight color, silver, lusterless blue, where the transparent surface of the turning waves grew green, brighter than fields of grass, and snowy snakes of foam wriggled and bit themselves in torturous convulsions. The *Kursk* moved noisily southward, her shiny white paint clashing with the plumage of the gulls.

She was a word uttered by human reason in the ear of the majestic sea.

Boar hunters stood on deck; they talked about hunting. They bathed me in warm sea water, dressed me up in white and fed me, and addressed me affectionately as "little brother." I am an old hunter after foreknowledge of the future, so I proudly accept the title—"little brother" of the warship *Kursk;* it was my sea-christening.

After a winter in Baku that was like being in the Nerchinsk mines, where I nevertheless attained my goal: I discovered the great Law of Time, which I subscribe to with all my past and future—and to do that I reckoned up all the wars of Planet Earth—in which I believe and will make others believe.

April 14th was the day of Festive Rites of Spring, a day of Rebirth and a salute to myself (the impulse to self-esteem).

As I was leaving Baku I began a study of Mirza-Bab, the Persian prophet, and I intend to lecture here for the Persians and Russians on "Mirza-Bab and Jesus."[2]

Enzeli greeted me like the miraculous high noon of Italy. The mountains were silver visions high above the clouds, sky-blue specters in snowy crowns. Black sea ravens with humped necks rose in a black chain out of the sea. River and sea come together here, and the water is yellow-green.

After a meal of wild boar, sobza, and rice, we hurried off to take a look at the narrow Japanese streets of Enzeli, the green-tiled baths, the mosques, the round towers of a previous century covered with green moss, and wrinkled golden apples in sky-blue foliage. The golden drops of autumn glitter on the skin of these little golden suns of Persia, whose heaven is a green tree. These garden-skies have hundreds of golden suns for eyes and appear above the stone walls of every garden here, while near them stroll chadors with deep dark eyes.

I raced toward the sea to listen to its holy speech. I sang, dismaying the Persians, then for an hour and a half I wrestled and splashed about with my water-brothers, until my chattering teeth reminded me it was time to dress and take on human shape once more—to return to the dungeon where man is locked away from sun and wind and sea.

Kropotkin's book *Bread and Will* was my companion on the crossing.[3]

Vera! Come to Enzeli! If you don't have a permit I'll try to get one for you. I went wild boar hunting.

This day, April 14th, is the birthday of "Kurskism," a new religion to honor the meeting of the sea and the Future.

I told the Persians I was a Russian prophet.

1. The Red Army moved into Persia in the spring of 1921, by treaty. Khlebnikov accompanied the army as a lecturer and a journalist for the newspaper *Red Iran*. Enzeli, now called Bandar-e Anzali, is located on the Caspian shore.

2. Khlebnikov had been lecturing for about a year. He began in Kharkov in the spring of 1920, receiving small sums and a food allotment for lecturing to soldiers about his social projects and the Laws of Time. He continued as a civilian volunteer lecturer when he moved to Baku early in October. Among the lectures delivered at the garrison club in Resht were "The Truth about Time" and "Destiny in a Mousetrap." There is no record of "Mirza-Bab and Jesus."

3. Published in English as *The Conquest of Bread,* this is a description of Peter Kropotkin's anarchist society.

110   *To His Mother and Sister Vera*

Enzeli

May 1921

Dear Mama, Dear Vera,

I am sending you some leaves from a quinine tree, I picked them in a garden in Enzeli. Which is where I am. I'm in Persia. I have seen the sky-blue specters of the Persian mountains, the yellow stream of the river Iran on whose banks grow broomstalks of sedge, swaying like the spears of an army that has fallen asleep.

I shot at spawning *sudaki* in the water, in the evenings I scared flocks of white herons, whose S of snow is a finial on thick gazebos of water-drowned trees. The banks of the Iran are thick with rotting *sudaki* and *somi*.[1]

Enzeli is made up of a great number of little brick houses, all covered with carpets of green moss and pretty little red flowers. Golden *narynchi* and *partakhalari* cover the branches of the trees.[2] Dervishes have knotty staffs that look like writhing serpents, and the stern faces of prophets, and they fill the streets with their chanting.

Faces of Persian women behind black veils, wrinkled like the faces of the dead; the soft faces of the merchants; all of Persia drawn toward France—they have two capitals, Paris and Teheran; and the magic song of jackals, sometimes like babies crying, sometimes a loud and mocking laughter at people—who call them redheads —a thousand voices, like people wrapped in foxskins, imitating all the twists and turns of the human heart. A pheasant flying straight up into the sky like a column, its slick plumage shimmering. These are my impressions. My hands are all cut up from a big sudak, I tried to grab it from the river bank.

Love to Borya, Katya, Papa.

Vera, come for a visit. It's wonderful here.

Iranian Com. Party (Adalet), Politburo of the Caspian Fleet, Enzeli.

All of you come to Persia, or Dagestan (but not Baku, which is awful). Write me. Come out here with me. There's room here and everything you need. Persia is wonderful, especially the snowy mountains, only the people themselves are kind of a mess.

Oranges are called *partakhalari*. The word for "month" in Persian is *ay*. In July the lotuses are in flower here, we can pick them together! People here have christened me a dervish because of my long hair.

1. *Sudaki* are pike-perch; *somi* are sheat-fishes, a large European river fish.
2. Seville oranges and sweet oranges.

III   *To the Khlebnikov Family*

Shahsevar
July 1921

Dear Astrakhanites,

I am in far-off Persia on the seacoast in the port of Shahsevar, with a Russian detachment. Life here is very boring, there's nothing to do, society here consists of adventurers, soldiers of fortune like Amerigo Vespucci and Fernando Cortez. On the other hand there are no difficulties about getting provisions. If only Vera would come visit! It would be good for her, and she and I could have a good time. I am on the staff of a Russian weekly here on the barren shores of Persia. You can get here through the Propaganda section.

Love and kisses to everybody,

Yours,
Vitya

112 To His Father

Piatigorsk
October 1921

Dear Father,

I got your letter today and was greatly pleased to hear that by and large, except for Shura, everything is, if not good, at least not too bad. About Shura, there's a possibility that he was captured with Gay's army at the siege of Warsaw and is a prisoner in Germany; the 33rd division was there.[1]

Things are hard for you in Astrakhan; so why don't you leave? Here in Piatigorsk, or in Grozny, or Derbent or Vladikavkaz, life would be a lot easier. I advise against Baku—it has all the expense and difficulties of a big city. Piatigorsk is convenient because in case you become ill you can always take a cure at one of the sanitoriums. Zheleznovodsk is beautiful in the summertime. Besides, there's a constant stream back and forth to Moscow and Petersburg, and it's easy to get there. Since Vera's an artist she could always get a job with ROSTA in Piatigorsk or in wonderful Zheleznovodsk with its surround of snowy mountains. Summers you could travel, go to the mountains or the coast, Derbent is nice. Generally speaking you're too sedentary and don't have enough interest in things.

If Vera felt like it, I could send her a prepaid travel authorization. It's true right now that traveling conditions are awful. It took me seven days to get from Baku to Piatigorsk and I was half dead for a month afterwards. Of course I was broke, which didn't help. My situation is different now; I was completely barefoot when I got here, bought some wooden clogs, of course they wouldn't work and there I was, going around rattling and clattering like a convict, stopping in the streets to get them to stay on. But today TERROSTA where I work (as a night watchman!!) presented me with some terrific American boots, black and well-made—and aren't I the sporty one, as people used to say. Now I just sit and admire them.

Working conditions in TERROSTA (Terek Rosta) are excellent, really comradely relations; all I do is sit in this room every night, also I print poems and essays and I get around 300,000 rubles; I could do more (but laziness has reared its ugly head) and that's enough for me. You can eat as much as you want here for 10,000 rubles a day, even better for 20. Black bread 3 thou, white 4 thou, grapes 5 thou, dinner 5 thou.

I got the night-watchman job as a joke, after I had to spend a couple of nights sleeping on a table in another outfit, where they were very hospitable. The head of ROSTA is Dmitry Sergeevich Kozlov, they call him the American—he spent several years in America—and he likes me very much. We got to be very good friends and I am very fond of him. I will soon be going maybe for a short while to Moscow and then back to ROSTA in Piatigorsk. I don't have the nerve to advise you to come to the Caucasus at the moment because of the traveling conditions, but this summer I really will insist that you come; many of the shore towns, the mountains villages, Derbent on the seacoast, are really wonderful (an absolute paradise) and it's easy to find a place. Next summer in all likelihood I will go back to Persia, and if Vera wants we can go there together.

My trials seem to be over now; one time I got so weak I could scarcely cross the street; I used to sway when I walked and was pale as a corpse. Now I've gotten better, I'll soon be strong again, and active, and I intend to shake up the universe. But seriously, Vera could come here now. I could help her arrange it through ROSTA, which is easy.

1. Khlebnikov's brother Alexander, drafted into the army before the revolution, was reported missing in action; later it was learned that he had been killed.

113 To Lily Brik

Moscow
January 1922

Dear Lydia Yurevna,

This little note is proof that I'm in Moscow and staying with my very dear friends on Miasnitskaia Street.

In Baku I discovered the fundamental Laws of Time. That is, I put a ring through the nose of the Bear of Planet Earth—a cruel thing to do—with the help of which we can give public performances with Mishka, our new dancing bear.

It will be very amusing and lots of fun. It will be a game in a crazy house, trying to tell who's crazy—him or us.

Vel. Khlebnikov

114 To His Mother and His Sister Vera

Moscow
January 14, 1922

Hugs and kisses! Happy New Year.

I'm in Moscow. Everything in Moscow is expensive. It is also the turning point of the past and the future, split down the middle. Black bread costs 11,000, an average gambling loss runs into six figures, sometimes nine.

There has never been such a display of Slavic merry-making as this holiday season. Moscow is standing firmly on its own two feet and there is no devastation, death, and savagery as in other cities.

I'll drop by to visit you this spring.

Love to you all once again.

Vitya

So far I've got clothing and food. When I arrived in Moscow all I had on was a shirt; I lost my last stitch of clothing in the south, but my Moscow friends gave me a fur coat and a gray suit. I look like a crane when I walk from Arbat to Miasnitskaia. I made the trip here in a heated hospital train, took a whole month.

c/o Osip Brik, 3 Vodopiany Street, apt. 43, Miasnitskaia P.O.

115 *To Pyotr Miturich*[1]

Moscow
March 14, 1922

Dear Pyotr Vasilevich Miturich,

I've been in Moscow two months already. I have read your letter and with all my heart sympathize in the subjugation of the heavens, although the configuration of force and mass along the axes of the flying body[2]—that's an area where my brain has not yet set foot, I am only a pagan at the threshold of that particular temple. I am constructing an edifice out of threes and twos only, and I have many notes and many separate pieces.

My fundamental Law of Time is this: there occurs in time a negative shift after 3^n days and a positive one after 2^n days; events, the soul of time, become retrograde after 3^n days and strengthen their numbers after 2^n; between the Moscow uprising of December 22, 1905, and March 13, 1917, 2^{12} days elapsed; between the conquest of Siberia in 1581 and the retreat of the Russians at Mukden in 1905 on February 25, $3^{10} + 3^{10}$ days elapsed. When the future becomes clear thanks to these computations, the feeling of time disappears; it's as if you were standing motionless on the deck of foreknowledge of the future. The feeling of time vanishes, and it begins to resemble a field in front of you and a field behind; it becomes a kind of space.

We are organizing a publishing house abroad, Kamensky has published *My Journal,* Aseev is arriving soon. I am bringing out the *Velimir Khlebnikov Bulletin.* I hope to have the Law of Time printed and then I'll be free.[3] I am sending you incantations of friendship, and mentally call up wind and storm from the quarter which will help you most in your undertaking. In your imagination strap on the timepiece of humanity, my work, and lend me the wings of your work; the heavy tread of my present existence is boring.

So: let us agree to trust one another at a distance and also when we meet.

V. Khlebnikov

1. Pyotr Vasilevich Miturich, an artist, was not yet a close friend, but he became very important in the last months of Khlebnikov's life. Since 1916 Miturich had been part of a group of Khlebnikov's admirers in St Petersburg; after the poet's death he married Vera Khlebnikova.
2. Miturich was working on a wave-motion airplane, one of many such inventions that occupied him throughout his life.

3. Two issues of *My Journal* were published, both in 1922. There were two lithograph issues of the *Velimir Khlebnikov Bulletin*, the first almost entirely devoted to "Order from the Presidents of Planet Earth." Part of Khlebnikov's final version of his Laws of Time, *An Excerpt from the Tables of Destiny*, was printed before his death.

116 To His Mother

Moscow
April 1922

Dear Mama,

I'm once again in Moscow getting a book ready;[1] I don't know if it will appear or not; as soon as it's printed I will be traveling through Astrakhan on my way to the Caspian; maybe everything will turn out differently, but that's what I'm hoping.

You wouldn't recognize Moscow, the city seems to have suffered a painful illness, Zamoskvarechie[2] no longer exists, and the teas and samovars are gone and the stodginess and rich pastryness of the past! It seems to have lived through a "cosmopolitan fever" and the people now are always in a hurry; their faces and movements remind you of a city in the New World.

My life is not so good, but generally I have enough to eat and shoes on my feet, even though I don't have a job. My book is my main concern, but it's bogged down on the first sheet and isn't getting any farther. There have been articles about me in *Revolution and the Press, Red Virgin Soil,* and *Beginnings.* Jakobson has published a paper about me.[3]

Every once in a while I run into Tarasov-Rodionov and Denike.[4] Tarasov has become part of the history of our time, as an expert Nat Pinkerton. He was responsible for the arrest of Purishkevich, Komissarov, and Gen. Krasnov, and has served at the front.

I'm visiting in the country at the moment. I see Kruchonykh, Kamensky, Mayakovsky, Evreinov. Time hangs a bit heavy, spring was very lovely, a few clear sunny days. Abikh is here too. I'm sharing a single room with the painter Spassky. 21 Miasnitskaia, apt. 39.[5]

I hope to see everyone soon and say hello to everyone after such a long absence.

Around Christmastime they figured that an average income for a working Muscovite was 30–40 billion; heavy gambling losses were 7 billion; a wedding costs 4 billion. Now everything costs ten times more; a prewar ruble equals 2 million, a taxi ride costs 5 million an hour.

1. Probably *Zangezi*.

2. The south embankment of the Moscow River, an old section of the city across from the Kremlin and Red Square. Before the revolution it was the center of merchant society and the sentimental locus of "Old Moscow."

3. The journal articles Khlebnikov mentions are *Pechat' i revolutsiia* 3 (1921): I. Aksyonov, "K likvidatsii futurizma"; *Krasnaia nov'* 2 (1922): A. Voronsky, "Literaturnye otkliki," which contained quotations from Khlebnikov's poems; and *Nachala* 1 (1922), which contained a review by Zhirmunsky of Roman Jakobson's monograph on Khlebnikov, published in Prague (1921).

4. Tarasov-Rodionov was a writer Khlebnikov had known in Astrakhan. Denike, later an art historian, had met Khlebnikov at Kazan University and wrote a short memoir about Khlebnikov.

5. This is a dormitory room at Vkhutemas, the former Moscow School of Painting, Sculpture, and Architecture.

117 To Dr. Alexander Petrovich Davydov

Korostets
June(?) 1922

Dear Alexander Petrovich,

I here recount my medical woes, to you as a doctor: I'm in the country in a village called Santalovo (40 versts from it, actually), Borovenka Sta., Novgorod Prov. I walked here, I slept on the ground and I've lost the use of my legs. They don't work. An upset [illegible] from work. They put me in Korostets "hospital," 40 versts from the railroad, Novgorod Prov.

I want to get better and be able to walk again, and to go to Moscow and back home. How do I do that?

BIOGRAPHICAL WRITINGS

Questionnaire

[A form used by S. A. Vengerov for his unfinished *Critical and Biblio-graphical Dictionary of Russian Writers.*]

Biography

1. Q. Name and patronymic?
   A. Viktor Vladimirovich.
2. Q. Year, month, and day of birth?
   A. 1885, October 28 [November 9 N.S.].
3. Q. Place of birth?
   A. The Astrakhan Steppe. Khanate Headquarters.
4. Q. Who were your parents?
   A. Ekaterina Nikolaevna Verbitskaia and Vladimir Alexeev-ich Khlebnikov.
5. Q. Religion?
   A. Russian Orthodox.
6. Q. A brief history of your family. Specifically, were any members of your family outstanding or well known for any reason?
   A. The first Khlebnikov is said to have been governor of Rostov in central Russia.
7. Q. Educational history. Indicate any intellectual and social in-fluences.
   A. High School (began in sophomore year).
   University (never graduated).
   My father is an admirer of Darwin and Tolstoy. He is a great expert on the bird kingdom and studied birds all his life. Many of his friends were widely traveled. One brother went

to New Zealand and never returned; one of the Khlebnikovs was a member of the State Council.

My grandfather died on a pilgrimage to Jerusalem.

One of his sons is a professor (physics) at the Military Medical Academy.

Many of the Khlebnikovs are famous for being petty and tyrannical.

8. Q. Outline of your literary activities from their inception.

   A. First published in Shebuev's *Spring;* a blatant appeal to the Slavs in the newspaper *Evening.* Reviewed by Chukovsky in *Hedgerose.* Wrote two dramatic pieces, *The Girl-God* and *Otter's Children*—appeared in *A Slap in the Face of Public Taste* and *Roaring Parnassus.*

9. Q. Name the outstanding events of your life.

   A. In *Teacher and Student,* a scientific work, I arrived at the notion that similar events in history occur every 365 ± 48 years (the bridge to the stars).

V. Khlebnikov

[On a separate page]

   During my student days I imagined a rebirth of language and wrote the poems "Incantation by Laughter" and *A Game in Hell.*

   Being much concerned with the *mollification* of human behavior, there is a great deal I have not accomplished.

August 5, 1914

Bibliography (a complete list of all your writings or translations):
[This section was written several years later, around 1920.]

'I was born on October 28 O.S., 1885, in an isolated area, at the Khanate Headquarters of the Kalmyk steppe, or on the seacoast of Russia not far from the mouth of the Volga.

   Publications: 1. An appeal to the Slavs in the newspaper *Evening,* articles in *Slavianin,* a description of a trip through the Pavdinsk region in *Nature and Hunting,* the poem "Incantation by Laughter" in *The*

Impressionists' Studio, one piece in *Spring, Marquise Des S.* in *Jam for Judges I, Maria Vetsera* in *Jam for Judges II, Teacher and Student* (a conversation that predicted the fall of Russia in 1917) in *Union of Youth* in 1913 and in a separate edition in 1911, *The Girl-God* in *A Slap in the Face of Public Taste, Otter's Children* in *Roaring Parnassus.* Published in *Sagittarius, Futurists, Mares' Milk, Rotten Moon, Anthology, Roar, Works, Miss Death Makes a Mistake.* In *Chronicle* published by Lyroon in Kharkov, five issues, in the newspaper *Freedom Bonds* in 1917, in the newspaper *Red Soldier,* Astrakhan 1918, the journal *Paths of Creativity,* Kharkov 1919, in the anthologies *Dawnlight Diner, We, Rye Word, I Took It, Centrifuge, Trio, Trio Tract, A Game in Hell, The World in Reverse.* In separate editions: *Time Is the Measure of the World, Battles of 1917–1918, Teacher and Student.* In the publications of the Kazan Society of Natural Scientists a 1905 article on the cuckoo *Cuculus miporus.*

There has been no Collected Works.

My "Trumpet of the Martians" was published in 1916 and, in 1917 in *Chronicle,* "An Appeal by the Presidents of Planet Earth," also by me.

V. Khlebnikov

[V.279–280]

Autobiographical Note

I was born on October 28, 1885, in the camp of Mongolian Buddhist nomads—Khanate Headquarters in the steppe—the dried bottom of a vanished part of the Caspian (the sea of 40 names). During Peter the Great's travels on the Volga, an ancestor of mine presented him with a goblet of coins gotten by brigandage. I have Armenian blood in my veins (the Alabors), also Cossack blood (the Verbitskys), whose special nature is evident in the fact that Przhewalski, Miklukha-Maklai and other explorers were descendants of the children of the Sech.

I belong to the place where the Volga meets the Caspian Sea (Sigai). More than once during the course of centuries that area has held the balance of Russian history and shaken the scales.

I have made a contract of matrimony with Death, and I am therefore married. I have lived on the Volga, the Dnieper, the Neva, the Moscow, the Gorynia.

Crossing the isthmus that joins the reservoirs of the Volga and the Lena, I made a few handfuls of water flow into the Arctic Ocean instead of into the Caspian Sea.

I have swum across the Gulf of Sudak (3 versts) and the Volga at Enotaevka. I have ridden unbridled horses from other people's stables.

I have demanded in public that the Russian language be cleaned of the litter of foreign words, and accomplished all one could expect in 10 pages.

I published "Incantation by Laughter"; in 365 ± 48 I gave people the means to see into the future, I discovered the law of generations; I wrote *The Girl-God,* where I peopled Russia's past with bright shadows, and *A Country Friendship;* I hacked a window to the stars right through the everyday laws of people's lives.

Once I made a public appeal to the Serbs and Montenegrins on the occasion of the theft of Bosnia and Herzogovina, an appeal vindicated in part a few years later in the Balkan War, and in defense of the

Ugrorussians, whom the Germans relegate to the ranks of the vegetable kingdom.

The continent, waking from its slumber, extends its staff to the people who live beside the sea.

In 1913 I was named the great genius of modern times, which title I possess even now.

I have never been in the army.

[ca. 1914: NP 352–353]

Self-Statement

In *The Girl-God* I wanted the pure Slavic element in all its golden linden-light, in threads that stretched from the Volga to Greece. I used Slavic Polabian words, like *Leuna*. Valery Briusov was wrong when he said I invented those words.

In *Otter's Children* I touched the strings of Asia, its swarthy cast-iron wing, and told the different fates of two beings over the course of centuries, and then, using the legends of the Orochs—the oldest legends in the world—about the fiery nature of the earth, I made Son of Otter attack the sun with a spear and destroy two of the three suns—the red one and the black one. And so, the cast-iron wings of Son of Otter from the East, golden linden light from the West. The separate planes make up a complicated structure and tell of the Volga as an Indo-Russian river, and treat Persia as the angle where two straight lines—the Russian and the Macedonian—meet. The sayings of the Orochs, that ancient Amur tride, had a profound influence on me, and I conceived the idea of creating a pan-Asian consciousness in my poems.

In "Ka" I offered an echo to "Egyptian Nights," the attraction of northern snowstorms to the heat of the Nile. I have taken for the Egyptian period the year 1378 B.C., when Egypt smashed its beliefs like a handful of rotten sticks, and individual deities were replaced by the hand-rayed Sun, shining with multitudes. The Unclothed Sun, The Naked Sun-Disk, became for a while, through the will of Egypt's Mohammed, Amenhotpe IV, the sole divinity of the ancient shrines.

If we want to make the distinction in terms of elements, then "Ka" has a silver sound, *The Girl-God* a golden sound, while the sound of *Otter's Children* is brazen, iron: The voice of Asia in *Otter's Children*; the voice of the Slavs in *The Girl-God*; the voice of Africa in "Ka."

"Nymph and Gnome" mixes Balkan and Sarmatian images. The city is treated in *Marquise Des S.* and *The Little Devil*.

In certain essays I have tried to give a rational justification for prophecy, by offering a true view of the laws of time, while in my studies on language I engage in frequent dialogue with Leibniz's $\sqrt{-1}$.

"The Crimead" was written in free verse.

Little things are significant when they mark the start of the future, the way a falling star leaves a strip of fire behind it; they have to be going fast enough to pierce through the present. So far we haven't figured out where they get that speed. But we know a thing is right when it sets the present on fire, like a flint of the future. There were nodes of the future in "The Grasshopper," in "BO BEH O BEE," in "Incantation by Laughter"—a brief appearance by the fire god and his joyful gleam. Whenever I saw old lines of writing suddenly grow dim, and their hidden content become the present day, then I understood. The future is creation's homeland, and from it blows the word god's wind.

I wrote "Turnabout" in a state of pure irrationality. Only after I had lived through on my own its lines *Chin zvan . . . mechom navznich* (the war) and had experienced for myself how they turned empty afterwards—*Pal a norov khud i dukh vorona lap*—did I realize what they were: reflected rays of the future cast by a subconscious "I" upon the sky of the rational mind. Thongs cut from the shadow of fate remain, and the soul remains entangled in them, until the moment when the future becomes the present, when the waters of the future, where reason bathed, dry up and only the bottom remains.

To find—without breaking the circle of roots—the magic touchstone of all Slavic words, the magic that transforms one into another, and so freely to fuse all Slavic words together: this was my first approach to language. This self-sufficient language stands outside historical fact and everyday utility. I observed that the roots of words are only phantoms behind which stand the strings of the alphabet, and so my second approach to language was to find the unity of the world's languages in general, built from units of the alphabet. A path to a universal beyonsense language.

When I was writing the beyonsense words of the dying Akhenaton in "Ka"—"Manch, Manch"—they almost hurt to look at; I couldn't read them, I kept seeing lightning bolts between them and myself. But now they don't move me at all. And I don't know why that is.

David Burliuk was right when he painted a heart with the uncompromising cannon of the future passing through it. He was showing us how inspiration works: the heart is a highway for the hooves of the future, its horseshoes of iron.

"Ka" took a week to write, *Otter's Children* took more than a year, *The Girl-God* was written in twelve hours straight, without a single correction, from morning to evening. I smoked and drank strong tea the whole time. I note these facts in order to show how varied are the circumstances of creation. "Zoo" was written in the Moscow zoo. In *Mrs. Laneen* I wanted to discover the "infinitesimals" of artistic language. *Otter's Children* conceals a complex study of magnitudes—the play of quantities beyond the predawn of qualities. *The Girl-God* came out as suddenly and as casually as a wave, without the slightest correction, like a bullet of creativitity, and so it may serve as a study of irrationality. *The Little Devil* was written just as fast, a sudden conflagration of layers of silence. Any desire to understand the "sense"—and not the beyonsense—of language destroyed all artistic involvement in language. I mention this as a warning.

I swore to discover the Laws of Time and carved that promise on a birch tree (in the village of Burmakino, Yaroslavl) when I heard about the battle of Tsushima. I've been working at them for the last ten years. One brilliant result of my research was the prediction of the fall of the government in 1917, which I made a few years before it happened. Of course that's not enough to convince science. I solemnly urge all artists of the future to keep exact spiritual records, to think of themselves as the sky and to keep exact notes on the rising and setting of their spiritual stars. In this area of endeavor, humanity possesses the diary of Marie Bashkirtseff and that's all. Such spiritual poverty, such lack of knowledge of the soul's sky, is the most glaring black Fraunhofer line in contemporary humanity. It is possible to devise a law of multiple proportions in time on the string of humanity where wars are concerned, but there is no way to devise such a law for the brief streams of an individual life—the foundations aren't there. We don't have the diaries.

Recently I have begun writing with numbers, as Number-Artist of the eternal head of the universe, how I see it and where I see it from. This art form is now being developed out of bits and pieces of modern science, just like contemporary painting; it is accessible to all and is destined to swallow up the natural sciences. I am clearly aware of the spokes of a wheel turning within me, and I work at my diaries in order to grasp the law of those spokes' return. This desire to bring beyonsense language into the realm of sense is, I see, the advent of an old spoke in my wheel. How I regret that I can talk of these spokes, of life's recurrences, only with words, allusive words!

But my situation may soon change.

[1919: II.7]

From Journals

November 28, 1913. Gumilyov told about how in Abyssinia cats are not treated very well, and they never purr, and that his cat only purred after he had stroked her very gently for over an hour: all the Abyssinians came running and saw an extraordinary event: sounds they'd never heard before. . .

December 19, 1913. Matiushin was here and calmed me down . . . turn to strictly pure behavior.

November 30 or 31, 1913. Went to bed at six o'clock, got up at two; dream: flying from Astrakhan to Petersburg. The Stray Dog, gave a reading. Mandelstam announced that it had something to do with him (not true) and that he didn't know me (good riddance). Shklovsky: I cannot kill you in a duel, they killed Pushkin, they killed Lermontov, people will say it must be a Russian custom . . . I cannot be another Dantès. Filonov kept uttering dark remarks, offensive, they were so vulgar and obvious. So much for "and they tear in disgust from their lofty brows wreaths of fame, made of bathhouse brushes."

December 9, 1913. Dec. 7, the shortest day. I spent it in Kuokkala at Puni's house. The day was cheerless and . . . (my Sweetroot) was in an angry mood. 1st fight. Fight, and angry at me. Will the days grow longer? Fight or make up. Didn't leave my room for three days. Autumn solstice, dismal mood.

[Note added subsequently by Khlebnikov: September 2, 1915. Two times 317, when I spent those nights at Puni's in 1913. I found out that a dog bays at the moon as if it were his distant master, and that the force of gravity and tears are identical.]

Extremely important, I got a letter from Thirteen Springs written in

Moscow on May 4, 1914, where she writes: I'm bored, I am proud, very proud. The first in all this time. Raskolnikov has the mouth of Demon . . . and on that same day May 4th I asked Z.S.K. for the right to be in love with her, and the answer was, suppose I did fall in love with her, she would burst out laughing, and marry me. And so on the same day the 1st letter from L. Dzel. and the first direct question and proposal to Z.S.K. and almost [illegible] and a foreknowledge of time.

On May 17, 1914, I experienced clear weather in my heart . . . equilibrium, disappearance of storms . . . a calm spirit. On the 20th I started growing a beard for the first time . . . That day P. D. Sviatopolk-Mirsky died, he was born 28 years before me, a contemporary of Papa's. I tried to find a secret reason for the change of mood; that day (17th–20th) for the first time I felt compassion for my father and began to see things from the family's point of view.

We have locked up a contemporary, he moans and tosses in his cage and we . . . throw him . . . meat . . .

The division is between fighting men and guppies; we are the fighting men, and the guppies are the ones who nibble our leftovers; among the most notable of the guppies are Kuprin and Sologub.

June 12, 1914, my mind is working wonderfully, it's coming up with results.

June 7th (?)—went, did I make it up?

May 10th—letter from Kamensky.

The 8th I had a fight with . . . Demidovskaia, or actually on the 11th, the 8th I was at . . .

1914, June 9–10, a change, the calm weather of happiness.

June 10, 1914, autumnal calm.

July 7th a dismal day . . . paint it black.

July 8th. 1000 Chinamen *bride money* for a wife. 77 years in nature. 365 + 48 in nature. One event:

1837
1914

Water in the Chusovaia River on May 17, 1914. The Kama is six and a half meters higher than its usual natural level.

June 14, 1914, contemplating myself at a distance. News flash: In a fit of inexorable self-loathing Khlebnikov threw himself for the 101st time onto a burning pyre and wept as he stood at a distance.
The destinies of feelings and a year.

Feelings, as well as our emotional destinies, are tied to the sun: feelings have their cycles and can dry up instantly according to their own particular laws.

I left Petersburg on the first day of Spring. In Moscow 10 days—about to die of boredom.

If I am Parsifal, then the moment of atonement came on Sept. 19, 1914, in a Finnish shoe store, where a Finnish girl with blue eyes got right down on her knees and took off my shoes in a swift, sure movement and her dark forehead begged for a kiss. Just as if I were Jesus Christ. She looked me straight in the eyes—and all of her own volition, and with a rush of ineffable delight.

I bought a pair of high-top boots with double soles . . .

Letters to me from Belenson, written February 11, 1915, and Aseev written December 29, 1914.

From Kuzmin.

August 21, 1915, Burliuk.

November 21, 1914, Nikolaeva.

Too bad I don't have a diary.
A letter from Viacheslav Ivanov.

A real seven-day rhythm on August 24, 1914, a day everything coincided: 1. A letter from Vera . . . 2. A letter from Zinaida Semyonovna. Tonya stopped by. Nightingale—August 31. Zinaida Semyonovna arrived seven days later. I have quit the ancestral home. Driven out by my parents . . .

September 7th. "Dear Vitechka, don't forget me, please write. Nadochka and I are now on familiar terms."

September 23, 1914, a wonderful day, sunny, warm . . .

A fight with Repin because of Lukomsky (angle, affectation).

"I can no longer remain in the company of people who live in the past, I must leave." Repin: "As you wish, we won't go after you." Shebuev ran out in a fright—Bergson's coachman; everybody. Lukomsky asked: Do Ts. D. artists ever come here? Do they stand in one of the corners? No!!

This is an affectation of the artists or something. Segantini . . . Repin was protecting himself with a club of painters. "Insignificance, imbecility, poverty, crazy people!" But how insignificant must a country be, to pay so much attention to such an insignificant phenomenon.

Year and date of birth
The Turkovskys
The Lishnevskys
Puni
Boguslavskaia
Lazarevskaia
Budberg

March 9–10, 1915. Recopied "Ka." The fall of Przemysl.
January 7, 1915. Lishnevsky's wedding. Turkovsk.
August 21, 1915. I spent the night at Puni's.
K. Chukovsky March 19, 1883.
Khlebnikov October 28, 1885
or $731 + 223 = 954 = (317 + 1) \times 3!!!$ Very nice.
Friendship; the laws of friendship
sendship lendship
service; the laws of service

O. Puni January 24, 1892 = a.
Ivan Andreevich February 22, 1890 = b.
Between me and Ivan Andr.
$(317 \times 1) 5 - 1$ days or simply $(317 - 1)5$.
$a + b = 365 + 48 \times 7 = 701$ days.
$1 =$ the occasion of marriage.

August 21, 1915, at Lazarevskys, told fortunes with cards that belonged to Oleg Konstantinovich who is dead; results:

1. emotional difficulties
2. didn't know
3. a flatterer (twice)
4. a widow, no longer young, kind, affectionate, but not very accommodating. (Aseev)
   5. an unexpected sum of money
6. an invitation
7. great happiness

Sept. 19, 1915. Tripped and fell on Brik's threshold.
Sept. 22. Saw Glebova. A corrupt Eastern beauty.

Sept. 14, 1915. Fight for a bench by Pushkin's statue because of Nikolai Kudel.
A 22-yr-old soldier in the reserves. A pogrom against Germans.
Visit to Budbergs September 18, 1915. Gave a reading, bored them.

And September 12, 1915, for the first time Vera.

September 17 meeting on the beach September 24, 1915. Jumped around the cliffs, started throwing rocks; felt like a falcon. August 16, 1915, I have met V. Lazarevskaia 5 times. 5 meetings; a lost bracelet.

1. On the beach—4 in the morning
2. Train station—5
3. Restaurant—7
4. At the movies—8
5. On the beach at 11:30 at night

August 16, 1915	August 16, 1915
August 11, 1913	317
June 24, 1914	September 28,1914
May 7, 1913	November 15, 1913
March 29, 1912	December 29, 1912
	January 15, 1912

August 16, 1915
Saw the lovers 5 times: the happy little couple, Vera Lazarevskaia and Adam Adamovich.

Two times 317.
November 20, 1913. What was it?
Candle end—B.
Kerchief—Gr.
Tie—Evr.
Shirt—Chuk.
A penny.

2 times 317 will be September 14, 1915 2 times 316 is September 12, i.e., my first meeting with the Budbergs, friends of Matiushin; very respectable family. Vera Al. astonished me with the beauty of her cool, restrained movements and the beautiful quality of her blue-gray eyes. Will the prophetic series continue further? Cool gray-blue eyes . . .

October 19, 1915 I sat next to Vera. "It's lucky, sitting next to someone who's engaged; it means you'll get married soon yourself." Andreev and I were on either side of Vera. I was in tears inside, but I cheered up when I thought that at least Vera wasn't married yet . . . Her black knitting on her knees. She is sorrowful and austere. She sat opposite me, with her legs crossed and she seemed awkward, she kept very deliberately showing the bottom of her skirt, and her stocking feet under it . . . Her knees seem a little awkwardly shaped. Irina had a red flower on her bosom, she's sort of dumb, funny and very nice.

1915 went to Budbergs with Andreev on October 19. We sat like this:

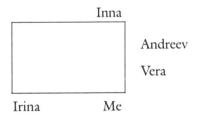

Andreev asked a vulgar question: "And where did you latch onto your fiancé?" Vera blushed and said, "That's a difficult question, but—" Irina frowned; somebody at the table said: "Vera is engaged to Behr" (he works in a bank). I wept inside; Vera poured wine and said: "Smoking is a sign of masculinity, hurray, let's smoke!" Vera is beautiful. She sat there in silence and smoked with concentration, asked an occasional question. Inna was sad. Vera was happy, that's the way it was meant to be. Vera said, "I wonder if perhaps I'll go to war too?"

October 26, 1915. Mayakovsky couldn't come, "Say I'm sorry; I'm working, writing." Inna started to laugh. When I finished reading my poems, Vera lit a cigarette and said (with a smile) "What a shame!" and poured some wine, and asked me "May I pour you some?" I got all red, thanked her and looked . . . It turns out we both like goats. She was telling hunting stories, how a rabbit would scream when you hit its head against the rifle butt . . . Inna . . . a helmet and they all decided I was handsome and looked like a heroic knight. Vera said "yes." They decided I was a warrior. ". . . I took a shot at the rabbit and hit it, only I got it in the hind legs. And I really don't know—I grabbed it by the head and started banging it on the gun butt. And it screamed and screamed—I really don't know. I felt very sorry (a drag on her cigarette) for that rabbit . . ." The rabbit story at Budbergs' on October 23, 1915.

October 14, 1915, evening K.R.; spent 10 rubles; shaved; ran into Urvantsev, who said he had a feeling he was going to meet me.
　　　Lensky—Grushnitsky. Onegin—Pechorin. I don't want to be Pechorin and I'm afraid of being Grushnitsky.
　　　Vera Lazarevskaia—Tolstoy's Natasha Rostov. Vera Budberg . . . someone out of Lermontov, but no Russian writer has yet created a character to equal her. On the 26th I looked at her rings and I was delighted to realize they were engagement rings (gold and heavy). Is it possible this is my last dream and my last ordeal? I will never love again!

October 14, 1915, I broke a glass with lump marks in it; that means a change of life.

October 13 I remember Brik, he got so young-looking you couldn't recognize him.

November 25, 1915, I burned the pack of cigarettes from Kuokkala, I had a sense of a weight being lifted from my shoulders.

November 23, 1915, I wrote *Miss Death Makes a Mistake*—a victory over death.

October 23, 1915, at Mayakovsky's and at Francesco's. The Lishnevskys. That night at 10 o'clock at Evreinov's, at Zheversheev's from 12 until 5 a.m. 24th at Briks. The Mikado's coronation and Mayakovsky called me the King of Russian poetry.

October 24, 1915. Party. Mayakovsky named me King of Russian poetry, read "A Cloud in Trousers" worse than usual. Pasternak. Shklovsky said "You've gotten better looking." Kriven said "He amazes me" and Vera agreed with him.

October 30, 1915, Maria Mikhailovna Urechina arrived.

October 22, 1915, went to see the Lishnevskys. Got into a fight, won't go there anymore.

December 20, 1915, was elected King of Time.

December 31, 1915, Osip Brik proposed a toast to the King of Time, Velimir Khlebnikov.

January 5, 1916, this evening none of the girls said anything; "what's your name?" came out sounding stupid; this one officer gave me a salute and said now they're all in love . . .

(1915) notes from October 27: Lily Brik gave me a coin for good luck (half a kopek). Mayakovsky insisted I bring *Roaring Parnassus,* otherwise I'm going to get mad at you.
Shklovsky's coldness. Tried unsuccessfully to find Evreinov. Went to visit Belenson. The 28th my birthday.
    Made up my mind not to go to the Briks'. Had two ounces of meat concentrate for breakfast, then went to watch a fire, in the evening went to see Evreinov and Etter. My money ran out that evening, down to the last kopek. A fire was in one of the government buildings, in the late afternoon (firemen in the smoke, torches, people hurt, hanging lamps). Medicine—for scabies. Kissed Evreinov, congratulated Mileev. Decided to visit only Evreinov and Etter; saw Pavlusha. Evreinov said: Vera Alexandrovna Khlebnikova [illegible] Vera Alexandrovna Behr—try to keep seeing her, paying attention to her; he said anything's possible, just don't rush matters. When I was leaving I said, "So this makes

us conspirators." "Yes," he said, "now don't rush things. You have to break a girl down, subdue her; remember you've only known each other a few days, keep her apart from the other sisters, take any opportunity to call her, or stop by at 6 in the evening." [. . .]

A conspiracy on my birthday! I told him I didn't believe any of it, but that I would be a very happy conspirator. At Evreinov's, the 28th; I swear I'll play Antichrist, if that's the way it has to be. Was I not too much the Grushnitsky. I kissed (licked) Evreinov, he looked like a page boy with his medieval face, he said: "And when it happens I'll be your best man." A courageous, uncompromising man, warm and good-hearted. I really love him.

February 27, 1916, Shura left.
February 30, 1916, have discovered that men have 317 × 2 muscles.
March 5th saw Picheta.
March 12th went to a meeting of etheromaniacs: black sand.
March 17th saw Nadezhda Vasilevna's mother.
March 19th saw Zinaida Semyonovna.
Found a comb.
July 6, 1917, wrote *The Scythian Headdress*.
August 10, 1916, discovered 861 = 317 *e*.
Telegram about Vera's return to Russia.
August 19th spent some time reading the Persian girls' letters.
August 20, 1916, went off to visit the Urechins.

Dream, September 13, 1916. Zheverzheev, nighttime, infirmary. I smashed two light fixtures (fight, an official complaint), then took off my boots and ran barefoot around Petrograd all night. On the 20th dreamed about Budberg laughing.

September 26th, dream: Vermeil and the crazy wife he deserted in church.

September 23, 1916. Copied over the whole article for "Alloo" on the floor. A Greek sage.

December 10, 1917. Kamensky's Polish girl.

December 14th. Gypsy girl.

1915 summer solstice June 10th and December 10th on the solstice a reawakening of healthy feelings.

Searching, wanting, dreaming, calm. October 29, 1915, the landlady had a dream that I was in the hospital and a nurse came up all dressed in black and said "We're going to have to disinfect you." I was sick with scarlet fever or diptheria. I had three beds in my room (my wife, my son, myself) . . . G. L. Kuzmin says that he has rarely dreamed, perhaps 5 times in all, but that he remembers them all well and almost all of them were clairvoyant except the first one and the funny one. Dream #1. He dreamed he killed some girl, which by his own admission he was incapable of doing. Dream #2. He saw a dead man lying there, an officer, and a revolver. In the morning when he woke up he said to himself, I think that was B. D. (someone he didn't know very well, the brother of a friend). After lunch S. D. showed up in a hurry and said, you know, something awful happened, my brother shot himself in Vladivostok, I just got a telegram. #3. He dreamed about a lot of stars, a glow, flames, sparks and the face of Makarov with a black beard. In the morning a telegram arrived about the sinking of the *Petropavlovsk*. #4. He dreamed about a man in a heavy cloak and a hat standing by the door; he got out his gun, half-awake, and opened the door and saw the man. He tried to shoot—the gun wasn't loaded. He threw the gun at him, then went back to sleep. Next morning he told everybody, they all laughed, found the gun. Then the doorman came up and said they'd captured an escaped convict in a heavy cloak and a hat. #5. He dreamed about a dog who could talk and bow.

December 31, 1914, Kamensky told fortunes . . . my good genius . . . the two of hearts.
    The 30th 1915 went to see the Budbergs. No one there. Inna Alex. sat knitting a stocking, then her mother came in . . . then Vera Alex., very sad, weary. Inna A. kept on: "Now that you're a king, do you want me to be your queen?" I didn't say anything; just turned pale. She showed me to the door and then when she saw my worn-out old galoshes she said: "Don't you have any galoshes?" Whenever I'm sitting there, sometimes Vera and Irina go off and write something.

Cervantes and Shakespeare both died on April 10, 1616.

[V.327–335]

From Notes from the Past

October 19, 1915. Went to see Vera B. again. I sit next to her. What happiness. Also Gernov. "It's lucky, sitting next to someone who's engaged; it means you'll get married soon yourself," Mrs. B. told us. What? Vera is engaged. And I didn't even know. New sorrow.

Tears rose in my throat, I admit it, I felt the scalding tears in my throat. Surrounded by studious, attentive people. But maybe it's good she's still single. Vera is sorrowful and austere. Her black knitting lay in her lap—a sign of sorrow. For whom? She sat opposite me with her legs crossed, awkward, smoking. She wore a yellow ski sweater, she was totally fragile, sorrowful, weary. She kept smoking and a certain awkwardness in her hands touched me. I kept looking at her too persistently and she awkwardly rearranged the bottom of her skirt.

We talked about the pogroms. "They'll be rioting against us soon," she said, as she smoked. Her northern delicacy and her blue eyes, and she was sorrowful, and weary, almost doomed, and her direct looks, and her fatigue after tending the wounded—I'd forgotten she was working as a nurse. Vera engaged—I wept inwardly, like a hurt kitten; Vera said "Maybe I should go to war"; she poured me some wine. "May I?" she asked. "Go ahead and smoke, smoking is very masculine," she remarked. She has a lot of simplicity in her and a touch of austerity. She is somewhat cold and cruel; she told some hunting stories.

October 26th. Went to visit again; I stared at the northern delicacy of her hair, a cloud combed above her face, at her enormous blue eyes, like a blue pearl on its austere string about her shoulders, and I listened. Rapture, there was still no gold ring on her hand.

Here's a fragment of a conversation: "I took a shot at the rabbit and hit it, only I got it in the hind legs. And I really don't know how I did it, I grabbed it by the head and started doing . . . you know, beating it against the gun butt. And of course it kept screaming and screaming,

I really don't know—I felt very sorry (she took a drag on her cigarette) for that rabbit." She gave a barely perceptible laugh.

Inna picked up a blue-gray helmet; I put it on and began pretending I was a medieval warrior. "You look just like a warrior!" She doesn't say much, but what she does say is exactly right and appropriate.

The 28th—my birthday and a first-rate fire at one of the government buildings on Liteiny Prospect. Coincidence. The firemen, red figures in the wavering gray smoke, the wounded, indifferent, in rooms untouched by the fire. Moans, cries, the glow of brass on the galloping fire engines, horses' hooves raised suddenly into the air in a wild song-like rapture, in a rage of impulse—they were like warriors from centuries past, there's a reason their helmets are made of brass—they call upon humanity to moderate the blaze of the sun and to abandon these boring stupid wars. Beyond us, beyond us somewhere a wild howl, the noise of the fire engines, their path made bright by gallopers . . . . . oily smoke and the leaping brightness of a horseman, the sharp sound of trumpets. I stood opposite and watched, enjoying the terror of some and the delight of others. That morning I drank some meat concentrate for breakfast.

I went to see my friend; I told him excitedly all the things that had been happening to me. He gave me advice as a friend, a man of experience: "Try to keep seeing her, paying attention to her; remember you've only known each other a few days; call me if anything happens. Keep on seeing her, remember, you have to subdue her. My father spent ten years courting a woman."

"We're conspirators!" I exclaimed, giving him a kiss. I solemnly swore to play it through to the end, if that's the way it has to be. I love him, a courageous, uncompromising man with a warm heart. That evening I drank to the realization of my boldest and most passionate hopes. A seven-year-old boy, the son of friends, read my poem "Incantation by Laughter." I talked a lot with him and we felt like a pair of conspirators among those grown-ups.

Surely this won't turn out to be only a dream?

The boy was only just out of his perambulator. He looked at me with delighted eyes, childlike, alive, ardent and bright; he read my poem and afterwards he kept on snitching bites of some kind of pudding, laughing and turning around to watch the grown-ups.

For beyond this Vera, just as beyond Vera Lazarevskaia, there gleams the lance of my first Vera from Kazan, who achieved death, dying among flowers, smiling, surrounded by friends who clutched at her hand as if to awaken her. But the poppy kills like a bullet.

Yes, more and more often these last days I have felt the gleam of the lance of that first Vera, the suicide, who flew to her ancestors on beautiful virginal wings, seventeen years old.

But her pearl-gray eyes, her restrained northern gestures, the stories about wild goats in her homeland—all this during a stormy time of war, whose horses' hooves and heavy gun carriages had passed like apparitions through my heart two years before the actual real war, and I, who had furled up in my heart the banner of my nation's wild freedom, and she, who spoke the language of my enemies and whose blood was the blood of my enemies, but who was taking care of the wounded on our side and it made her so sad, so thoughtful—who are we? No, we are the first to escape from the storm of war and seek refuge on the dry land of a deeper humanity, and we understood that only together.

[IV.321–323]

The Khlebnikov family, probably in Malye Derbety, ca. spring 1886. Vladimir (father) in window; Ekaterina (mother) in dark dress; E. P. Levitova (grandmother) seated center; V. N. Riabchevskaia (Aunt Varya) standing right; Viktor on nurse's lap at right

The Khlebnikov family, probably in Kazan, ca. 1900. From left: unknown; Ekaterina (sister); Vera (sister); Ekaterina (mother); Viktor; Vladimir

Pyotr Miturich, drawing of Vera Khlebnikova, dated August 1924

Pyotr Miturich, drawing of Vladimir Khlebnikov, dated September 23, 1926

Studio portrait of Viktor, ca. 1890s

Viktor, 1908–09

Vera Khlebnikova, drawing of Velimir in a Mordavian hat, ca. 1910

Khlebnikov, ca. 1912

Vladimir Mayakovsky, drawing of Khlebnikov, 1916

Khlebnikov in army uniform, 1916

Ivan Puni (Jean Pougny), "Khlebnikov reading his poems to Xana" (Puni's wife Xenia Boguslavskaia), Petrograd, 1917

Mechislav Dobrokovsky, drawing of Khlebnikov, ca. 1920–21

Porfiry Krylov, drawing of Khlebnikov, ca. spring 1922

Porfiry Krylov, drawing of Khlebnikov, 1922.

Pyotr Miturich, Khlebnikov in the hospital (from memory), 1923

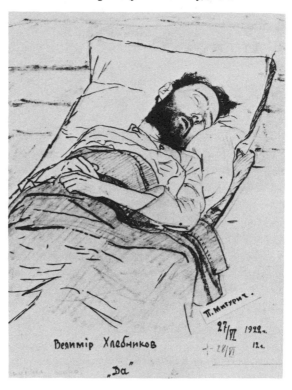

Велимір Хлебников

„Da"

Pyotr Miturich, Khlebnikov, "Da," June 27, 1922

Maria Siniakova, portrait of Khlebnikov, n.d

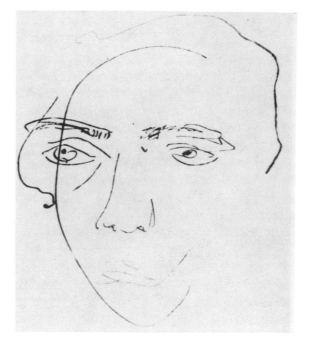

Khlebnikov, self-portrait, n.d

Vladimir Tatlin, drawing of Khlebnikov (from memory), 1939

Khlebnikov (front left) with Nikolai Burliuk, David Burliuk, Vladimir Mayakovsky, Georgy Kuzmin, and Sergei Dolinsky, ca. 1912

Khlebnikov with Sergei Esenin (left) and Anatoly Mariengof, Kharkov, 1920

Khlebnikov with students at Vkhutemas, Moscow, between December 1921 and March 1922. K. at top, third from left

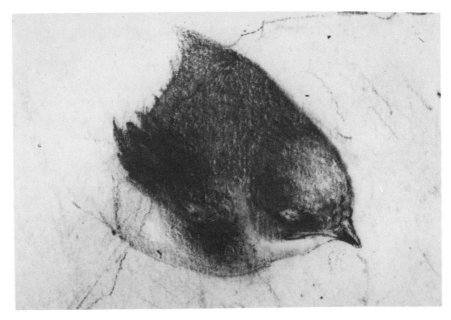

Khlebnikov, drawing of a bird, ca. 1900

Khlebnikov, sheet of drawings, dated June 21, 1900

Khlebnikov, drawing of Vladimir Tatlin, ca. 1915

Page of word play from Khlebnikov's notebooks, n.d.

Theoretical Writings

introduction

KINDRED SPIRITS

He was such a child he imagined that six
came after five, and seven after six.
—"Let them read on my gravestone"

"My father was an admirer of Darwin and Tolstoy," Khlebnikov wrote
when asked about his early intellectual influences, and in his own life's
work the son adopted paternal ideals, the vision of a vast synthetic task
formed by the accomplishments of those two great historians of life on
earth. To these models Khlebnikov added some of his own discovering,
men encountered in his studies of the history of science, most especially
the Greek philosopher Pythagoras, the philosopher and logician G. W.
Leibniz, and the non-Euclidean geometer Nikolai Lobachevsky. The
objects of Khlebnikov's esteem tended to be men who combined a revolutionary theoretical understanding of the natural universe with a
solid respect for the concrete physicality of the world and a desire to
improve it morally, practically, and socially. He himself possessed all of
these qualities.

Khlebnikov's vision of reality was based on an unshakable faith in
numbers, but not in numbers for their own sake; he was not at all a
numerologist. Rather, his perceptual understanding of the world was
in mathematical terms; numbers enabled him to see; they serve the human mind, he said, "in the same way that charcoal serves the artist's
hand." Objective reality, for Khlebnikov, was first of all the diverse ma-
terializations of natural law: "I see right through you, Numbers. / I see
you in the skins of animals, / coolly propped against uprooted oaks."[1]
The poet in this respect distinguished himself from Pythagoras, for
whom numbers had a mystical and self-sufficient significance. "Actually
I am the antipode of Pythagoras," he once told a friend. In his view,
"there exist only two trees, three rocks, etc., and not two in general or
three in general. The numbers are abstractions which reflect only relationships between realities, and *outside these realities they don't exist*."[2]
For Khlebnikov, who embraced all of nature with a passion close to

1. *King of Time*, p. 28.
2. A. N. Andrievsky, "Moi nochnye besedy s Khlebnikovym." *Druzhba narodov*, 12
(1985), 240

Walt Whitman's, numbers were an index of the heart of reality, its "supreme arbiter"; they explained the form and the interelationships of its every aspect, even the psychological inner reality. To establish a numerical basis for the tides of human feelings, in his "Self-Statement" the poet urged "all artists of the future to keep exact records, to think of themselves as the sky and to keep exact notes on the rising and setting of their spiritual stars." The empirical determination of the logical and formal bases of the real world motivated virtually every one of his multitude of interests.

Khlebnikov's linguistically oriented poetry and utopian social visions were for him but two aspects of this more general lifelong exploration of the nature of the world and of history—and of time, the continuous creator of the first two. He aspired to nothing less than the discovery of the concrete laws of nature, the equations that ran the world, the stable mathematical patterns concealed beneath the outward clutter of life. His interest in design—of words and houses, railroads and letters of the alphabet—was an expression of an extraordinary search for unifying principles of organization. Khlebnikov was convinced that the world was one, and that language, images, and events were governed not only by the laws specific to them, but also ultimately by a single "general principle" that determined every force in the world. Human language was for him only one way into this natural world; as an organic, evolving part of human nature, language must necessarily also contain keys to the way the universe works, and to understand the one, the poet believed, was also to possess a vital part of the other.

The quest for a holistic universe was not unique to Khlebnikov, of course. At the turn of the century there were many attempts at a "unified theory"; the new progress in science had brought such a vision tantalizingly close. Einstein worked on a general theory all his life, as did Charles Henry, the scientist friend of the neo-Impressionist painters—to take two quite different examples.[3] Progressive literary Symbolism in the second half of the nineteenth century also aspired to a holistic understanding of the aesthetic media; its major theoretical direction was to define and broaden the physical context through which poetry functioned. Mallarmé, for example, tried to associate sounds with colors, and René Ghil wrote "evolutionary" or "scientific" poetry,

3. A bibliography of the many works of Henry may be found in José A. Argüelles, *Charles Henry and the Formation of a Psychophysical Aesthetic* (Chicago, 1972).

in which he identified specific equivalents between the sounds of individual letters or combinations of letters, the notes produced by certain musical instruments, and a variety of sensations and emotions.[4]

What was unique about Khlebnikov's syncretic vision was its breadth—the scope of his ambition. Not only was he interested in the fundamental meanings of letters and sounds and colors,[5] but he saw them as indications of the way the entire universe functioned. He mined a tremendous amount of seemingly unrelated material—from art, mythology, folk tales, geography, daily events, history—in order to collect sufficient data for a model of the mechanisms that determine our life on earth, to "read the writing traced by destiny on the scroll of human affairs." In the course of his life Khlebnikov wrote volumes of verse, long poems, short stories, plays, and essays on politics, language, history, and science, but to his mind the most important of these were the essays in which he made arithmetical connections between all of his interests, in the hope of divining a Pythagorean "measure, order, and harmony" behind the seeming chaos of human events.

Khlebnikov ultimately saw this reach into all disciplines as a method that he called "the new creativity"—a mode of thought in which the "cages and barriers" of the various areas of knowledge were abolished and the artist-scientist roamed the world of ideas freely, in search of evidence of the great natural Law. In this he followed Leibniz's method; he too had worked across disciplines in a quest for the interconnectedness of things. On the personal level, Khlebnikov's interdisciplinary studies were a way of seeing his life whole—a rationale for combining the scientific loves of his early life with poetry and writing. In fact, he may have been attracted to writing partly because of the scientific Symbolist ideas of Ghil and others. Khlebnikov studied French from an early age, and during his years in Kazan he read the French-oriented Symbolist journal *Libra* with great interest.[6] He him-

---

4. René Ghil, *Le traité du verbe,* Stephane Mallarmé, intro. (Paris, 1886), *En méthode à l' oeuvre* (Paris, 1891), *De la poésie scientifique* (Paris, 1909). Mallarmé and especially Ghil were well known to the Russian Symbolists.

5. In "Artists of the World" Khlebnikov attempts to include color concepts within the symbolic meanings of sounds. He mentions the affinity between his color theories and those of Mallarmé and Baudelaire in "From the Notebooks."

6. According to his mother, Khlebnikov read French before he was twelve. On Khlebnikov and *Libra* see the memoirs of B. P. Denike quoted in Nikolai Khardzhiev, "Novoe o Velimire Khlebnikova," *Russian Literature* 9 (1975), 7

self never felt any split between the two areas of endeavor—both science and poetry emerged out of the matrix of his intense curiosity about the nature of the world.

Behind Khlebnikov's investigations is the assumption that if only one collects enough information and studies it fully and arranges it properly, its natural laws will become self-evident. This, after all, was what was commonly understood about the method of Charles Darwin, whose theory of evolution, already the primary model for scientific investigations in many fields for more than a generation, had seemed to emerge out of an analysis of vast quantities of information on an endless variety of flora and fauna.[7] It was Dmitry Mendeleev's method as well; his patterned arrangement of the chemical elements into a periodic table had made the apparent randomness of their physical properties logical and predictable. In these cases at least, basic knowledge about the nature of life and matter had clearly been acquired by finding their proper order.[8]

Khlebnikov had been raised in the lively and inquisitive family of a natural scientist; close observation and classification, and a consequent interest in transformation and evolution, were primary activities of his childhood and adolescence. The poet's father, an ornithologist, was concerned with problems of taxonomy and geographic distribution of species,[9] and Viktor was himself interested in botany and quite actively involved in the visual identification and collection of birds for his father. There exist ornithological observations made by the boy in 1897, when he was twelve years old.[10] In the northern Urals for five months in 1905 with his brother Alexander, he recorded sightings of birds, their habits and calls, and collected specimens; and in 1907, when he was already writing poetry, he published his proposed explanation for an

---

7. In Khlebnikov's time Darwinian evolution and biological thought generally were being applied with some success to mathematics, linguistics, folklore, social theory, and aesthetics.

8. Mendeleev's discoveries were well known in Russia. In addition he had a special connection with the Symbolists; his daughter Liubov married the poet Alexander Blok and was the celebrated object of the affections of Andrei Biely.

9. See e.g. "Spisok ptits Astrakhanskoi gubernii," *Protokoly zasedanii obshchestva estestvoispytatelei pri Kazanskom universitete* 121 (Kazan, 1891), 1–32.

10. Nikolai Khardzhiev, "Novoe o Velimire Khlebnikove," *Den' poezii* (Moscow, 1975), p. 203.

unusual species of cuckoo he had observed in Kazan province.[11] In addition to his study of birds, Khlebnikov had other practical experience in tracing the course of evolution in the natural world: two years before his ornithological expedition to the Urals, he assisted a professor of geology on a expedition to Dagestan to collect Mesozoic fauna from the deposits in that area.[12]

The success of Darwin's theory of evolution in the second half of the nineteenth century had not greatly altered traditional taxonomic work. Even though Darwin described the gradual transformation of species through spontaneous variation and so called into question the very notion of species as stable and distinct categories, he proposed no new mechanisms or methods for classification. At the turn of the century, therefore, taxonomy was still relied upon, as it always had been, to "expose the hidden order of the natural world."[13] Systems of classification were based on field descriptions of external morphological forms, the identification of new forms, and their ordering into a framework of natural relationships. By Khlebnikov's time it was generally accepted that organisms were related through descent, that is, through their diverse development from common prior sources, rather than existing as permanently independent entities, but this did little to diminish interest in gathering and ordering data according to established methods of classification. Khlebnikov's interest in the problems of speciation reflected current scientific and popular discussions of Darwinism. In 1904 he said he had freed himself from the hold of species, and three years later his article on the cuckoo described a "transitional" species, a cross between two formerly distinct types which he believed was spreading across the country in "waves," as one species dispersed into the area of another. In a letter to the poet Viacheslav Ivanov in 1909 he equates animal speciation with the plurality of religions, suggesting that "the religious beliefs that agitate us are merely pale impressions of forces at work eons ago, forces that at some point created the species."

11. "On Finding a Cuckoo Similar to the *Cuculus intermedius Vahl,* in Kazan District, Kazan Province."

12. P. Kazansky, "Predvaritelnyi otchet o geologicheskoi ekskursii v Dagestan letom 1903 goda," *Prilozhenie k protokolam zasedanii obshchestva estestvoispytatelei pri Imperatorskom Kazanskom universitete za 1903–1904gg.* (Kazan, 1904). See also Khardzhiev, "Novoe," *Russian Literature,* pp. 121–123. The date of the trip given in this source is incorrect.

13. John Dean, "Controversy over Classification: A Case Study from the History of Botany," *The Natural Order: Historical Studies of Scientific Culture,* Barry Barnes and Steven Shapin, eds. (Beverly Hills, 1979), p. 214.

His poem "O Garden of Animals!" gives this idea a sharply visual image by associating certain animals with specific religions. Evidently the young poet also formulated his theory of species scientifically; he expressed his desire to publish it early in 1910 in a letter to his brother about their ornithological work: "Perhaps you could add a tail end to your article, something to express my ideas on the origin of the species? I did think I had something new and profound to say on the subject." But unfortunately the poet's concept of the speciating "forces at work eons ago" never saw publication, and so we can only speculate about its details.

Khlebnikov amassed historical and linguistic facts as painstakingly as he did scientific data, and in the same faith that their natural laws would be obtainable from the collection of information. And, as in the world of birds, he believed it was the passage of time operating through the laws of nature that generated the variety observed in the world of language, mythology, religion, and human affairs. The way to understand the natural law, then, would be to understand its effects over time. Khlebnikov worked empirically on time's external products—examining the structure and essence of contemporary words, events, myths, and beliefs—and this massive study acquired an almost metaphysical importance in the poet's life.

Khlebnikov's art also reflects his effort to base his work on mathematical and biological models. In his attempt to discover natural patterns, Khlebnikov found it necessary to search for reverses and in other ways to look backward in time for original forms, the basic units upon which time had acted.[14] In the plays *Miss Death Makes a Mistake* and *Marquise Des S.* time flows backward: the dead come back to life, and clothes turn back into their constituent natural elements.[15] Similarly, *The World in Reverse* gives us a series of vignettes in which the characters become younger as the work progresses. Khlebnikov's format here supposes a Laplacian mechanistic universe. It may also be related to the witty popular woodcuts showing "the world the wrong way around," and mimics the act of reading comic-strip scenes—such as those in the

14. The notion of original forms may be compared to the pre-Darwinian idea of fixed species or to Goethe's concept of archetypal morphological forms. But inherent in this idea is also the atomistic view of naturally existing simple units, a basis of modern cosmology and minimalist and systems art.

15. Khlebnikov thus anticipates the "reverse time" scene in Kurt Vonnegut Jr.'s novel *Slaughterhouse Five*, in which a bomb returns to the innocence of its constituent elements.

woodcuts and in "saint's life" icons—from the end back to beginning. In *Mrs. Laneen* the poet is concerned with isolating small units of perception, "the infinitesimals of the poetic word," in order to construct a poetic calculus in which experience may be precisely differentiated and integrated over time. Tolstoy had suggested this process and its analogy to calculus, a "modern branch of mathematics, unknown to the ancients":

> Only by taking infinitely small units for observation (the differential of history, that is, the individual tendencies of men) and attaining to the art of integrating them (that is, finding the sum of these infinitesimals) can we hope to arrive at the laws of history.[16]

In 1919 Khlebnikov wrote retrospectively about his study of time: "I swore to discover the Laws of Time, and carved that promise on a birch tree (in the village of Burmakino, Yaroslavl) when I heard about the battle of Tsushima." And again early in 1922: "I first resolved to search out the Laws of Time on the day after the battle of Tsushima, when news of the battle reached the Yaroslavl district where I was then living . . . I wanted to discover the reason for all those deaths." But as far as we can discover, at the time of the battle of Tsushima—on May 14–16, 1905—Khlebnikov was actually many hundreds of miles from Yaroslavl. He was in the Pavdinsk region of the northern Urals with his brother observing birds, from May through October of 1905.[17] Either Khlebnikov's brother began the ornithological observations alone, long

16. Leo Tolstoy, *War and Peace,* Norton Critical Edition, George Gibian, ed., Louise and Aylmer Maude, trans. (New York, 1966), p. 918. The status of calculus and the concept of infinitely small units and their relation to the real world remained problematic in Khlebnikov's time. In later work Khlebnikov parted company with Tolstoy's views about the applicability of this model for history. He concluded that the movement of history was not continuous, as was necessary for the applicability of calculus, but discontinuous (see "Trumpet of the Martians"), which accounted for the differences between generations, among other things. This is one reason he avoided calculus in computing the Laws of Time.

17. From 1900 to 1918 the Russian calendar was thirteen days earlier than the Western calendar. According to Western dating, the battle of Tsushima took place on May 27–29, 1905 (May 14–16 by Russian dating). The brothers' first day of observation, as given in the published report of their findings, was in fact May 13, 1905, the day before Tsushima, and the last day of observation was October 25. There are no significant intervals between the recorded days of observation, which means the poet must either have received the news about Tsushima in Pavdinsk or not have heard about it for more than five and a half months—unlikely, since he saw many people during this period. For observation dates, see "Ornithological Observations in the Pavdinsk Preserve."

before the poet reached the Urals, or almost twenty years later he was repeatedly misremembering his location when he heard of Russia's great naval loss to Japan.

But it is also possible that Khlebnikov is speaking more metaphorically than factually when he describes Tsushima as the spur to his numerical research. Khlebnikov apparently turned immediately to his search for laws of time, never for a minute ascribing the Russian defeat to more obvious causes, such as the Russian commanders' ineptitude. It was clearly against Khlebnikov's analytical nature to ascribe the defeat to an act of God or to spiritual or moral deficiency. In spite of his sympathy for other aspects of Slavophilism, Khlebnikov does not seem to have shared in its belief in God or in a mystical hierarchy.[18] In fact, the reason Khlebnikov gives for his search for historical law is strikingly similar to Tolstoy's statement in *War and Peace* about Napoleon's invasion of Russia motivating his own study of history: "Why did millions of people kill one another when it has been known since the world began that it is physically and morally bad to so so?" And his answer is also similar: "Because it was such an inevitable necessity that in doing it men fulfilled the elemental zoological law which bees fulfill when they kill one another in autumn . . . Taking a wide view of history we are indubitably convinced of a sempiternal law by which events occur."[19]

The first specific mention we have from Khlebnikov about his study of numbers and history is in April 1911, when he wrote to a friend in Petersburg from his parents' house: "I spend all my time working on numbers and on the fates of nations as dependent variables of numbers, and I have made a little progress." In fact, Khlebnikov had begun considering questions of space and time the previous year. His theory of metabiosis, published in the university's student journal in 1910, was an attempt to formulate a general description of sequential relationships that occur between organisms existing in the same location. Although the article uses examples drawn from agriculture and the natural sci-

18. His older sister remembers Khlebnikov's inability to profess belief in God, as was required for graduation from the gymnasium. In the end the boy went to a priest who was stone deaf: "[he] said his thing, [Khlebnikov] said his, and everything turned out fine" (Memoirs, 1929).

19. Tolstoy, *War and Peace,* p. 1372. Khlebnikov uses the same image in "Let them read on my gravestone": "He often emphasized that he saw in the concept of worker bees his own personal ideal." This image seems to be a very common one in discussions of scientific history; see e.g. Condorcet's characterization in Isaiah Berlin, *Concepts and Categories: Philosophical Essays* (Middlesex, Eng., 1981), p. 106.

enccs, the structure of the theory itself betrays Khlebnikov's incipient interest in history, as well as his ongoing reflections on the transformation of species and the essential connection between human beings and animals. Between examples drawn from forestry and soil conservation, Khlebnikov suggests that the notion of metabiosis can also describe the relations between the Slavic and German worlds, thus indicating a basis for his pursuit of historical intervals.[20]

The connection between Khlebnikov's Slavophilism, his study of history, and the pursuit of a numerical law is thus visible in his work some time before his involvement with the Cubo-Futurists. Early literary works already address two of Khlebnikov's scientific concerns: time and the fundamental units. His search for elementary, meaningful language sounds was also a quest for primal units, here considered as the original forms that were acted upon by time and the environment and from which all the various species of language descended. As he follows this train of thought into the roots of language in succeeding years, his theories will inform Cubo-Futurist poetry and painting and so become the basis of the first truly modernist movement in Russia.

Khlebnikov, like Tolstoy, looked upon the study of history as more urgently important than creative work. And, ironically, in both cases the historical portions of their oeuvre are now the parts their readers most often choose to ignore. Tolstoy wrote *War and Peace* for the explicit purpose of exploring historical inevitability: "I naturally was unable—when describing the historical events of 1805, 1807, and especially 1812 in which this law of predetermination is most prominently displayed—to attribute importance to the actions of those who thought they controlled the events . . . The activity of these people interested me only as an illustration of the law of predetermination which in my opinion guides history."[21] But instead of Tolstoy's microscopic exami-

20. "An Attempt To Formulate a Concept in the Natural Sciences." Khlebnikov may have been influenced in his choice of land-management examples by his father and by Grigory Sudeikin, a professor at the Forestry Institute with whom he lived briefly late in 1908 and who took an interest in his work.

21. "Some Words about War and Peace," as translated and reprinted in *War and Peace*, p. 1374; originally published in *Russkii arkhiv* (1868). In contrast to the other Cubo-Futurists who regularly vilified Tolstoy and Pushkin, Khlebnikov wrote deferentially about both authors. In "Monuments" (1912–13) his suggestion for the monument to the Russian language includes the representation of only two books, by Pushkin and Tolstoy. In "An Indo-Russian Union" (1918) he treats Tolstoy as the greatest cultural and religious representative of Russia in history, substituting his name for the more obvious one of Christ: "We have dived into the depths of centuries and gathered up the signatures of

nation of people and events, which by his own admission had proved unsatisfactory, Khlebnikov tried to see concrete experience more generally, from a more distant point of view: "I wasn't concerned with the life of individuals; I wanted to be able to see the entire human race from a distance, like a ridge of clouds, like a distant summit, and to find out if measure, order, and harmony were characteristics of the waves of its life" ("Teacher and Student").

Both authors believed in historical determinism, and both undertook to decipher it. In wars and military battles, they saw destiny working itself out especially clearly. For this reason the poet—before 1916—praised the wisdom of Russian folksongs that glorified war and military exploits, and rejected authors who "understand war as useless slaughter." In *Battles 1915–1917: A New Theory of War, Time Is the Measure of the World, The Tables of Destiny,* and numerous other pieces, Khlebnikov worked on algorithms to predict battles and their outcomes. Tolstoy had also given some thought to arithmeticizing military science. "The spirit of an army is the [unknown] factor which multipled by the mass gives the resulting force," he wrote in *War and Peace:*

> Ten men, battalions, or divisions, fighting fifteen men, battalions, or divisions, conquer—that is, kill or take captive—all the others, while themselves losing four, so that on the one side four and on the other fifteen were lost. Consequently $x/y = 15/4$. This equation does not give us the value of the unknown factor but gives us a ratio between two unknowns. And by bringing variously selected historic units (battles, campaigns, periods of war) into such equations, a series of numbers could be obtained in which certain laws should exist and might be discovered.[22]

Military action, both authors believed, graphically marked the periodic movement of ruling nations or civilizations in cyclical fashion from west to east and back again. "The fundamental and essential significance of the European events of the beginning of the nineteenth

---

Buddha, Confucius, and Tolstoy." The apparent exception in "The warrior of the kingdom"—"We demand that the floodgates of Pushkin and the waterlocks of Tolstoy be thrown open"—was written as a piece of Cubo-Futurist polemic and was not intended to be published under his own name. Khlebnikov's participation in S. A. Vengerov's Pushkin seminar at the University of St. Petersburg may have confirmed his love for the poet irreversibly. For Khlebnikov and Pushkin, see also Roman Jakobson, "Igra v adu u Pushkina i Khlebnikova," *Sravnitelnoe izuchenie literatur* (Leningrad, 1976), pp. 35–37.

22. *War and Peace,* p. 1149.

century lies in the movement of the mass of the European peoples from west to east and afterwards from east to west," Tolstoy wrote in *War and Peace*. Napoleon moved eastward across Europe, and then inexorably "an unnumerable sequence of inverse chances occur," leading to the predestined countermovement from east to west.[23] This "law of the see-saw," as Khlebnikov called it, proved to be one of the fundamental tenets in the poet's final formulation of the oscillating Laws of Time: "The staff of victory changes hands, passed from one warrior to another. Waves of two worlds, the alternating spears of East and West, clashing through the centuries."

The nineteenth century was characterized by an enormous interest in finding general laws for history. Like Khlebnikov, many historians—Comte, Taine, Buckle, Marx, and Engels among them—believed general laws existed and attempted to elucidate historical mechanisms. Especially popular were models derived from natural science, which would subject history to the same sort of mathematical analyses as geography, geology, and sociology.

> In regard to nature, events apparently the most irregular and capricious have been explained, and have been shown to be in accordance with certain fixed and universal laws. This has been done because men of ability, and, above all, men of patient, untiring thought, have studied natural events with the view of discovering their regularity: and if human events were subjected to a similar treatment, we have every right to expect similar results.[24]

Khlebnikov, above all a patient and untiring man, took up the search of the century. Although he clearly understood the vitalistic and evolutionary models of growth and change, and frequently based his art and language studies on them, he did not use them in his study of time. The nineteenth-century evolutionary paradigm of modifications resulting from interactions with the environment, which had been a model for the changes described in his article on metabiosis, proved an unsatisfactory model for the motive force of the system as a whole. Among other reasons, he must have found evolutionary concepts concerned too exclusively with the details of surface variety and appear-

---

23. *War and Peace*, pp. 1258, 1261.
24. Henry Thomas Buckle, *History of Civilization in England* (London, 1857), vol. 1, pp. 6–7, as quoted in Berlin, *Concepts and Categories*, p. 106.

ance. For the Laws of Time, physics and mathematics were his conceptual models.

Both Tolstoy and Khlebnikov were certain that a successful science of history would permit the prediction of the future. But Tolstoy's close analysis of concrete events—the painstakingly detailed recreation of what he believed history really consisted of—led ultimately to pessimism about whether historical laws were, in fact, accessible. The more data he accumulated, the clearer the hopelessness of the process seemed to become. The science of history would work in principle, Tolstoy finally concluded, but not in practice.[25] Khlebnikov, by contrast, pursued historical laws more abstractly, by collecting the dates of actual events and, categorizing them conceptually, then seeking mathematical patterns in their apparent randomness. For him, who by nature consistently opposed every kind of pessimism, the more facts one had, the more hope there was of finding the system. (Khlebnikov, like Walt Whitman, was an avid reader of newspapers.) Historical science, Khlebnikov believed, could be made to work in practice. "Destiny is clearly outlined in these numbers," he wrote, "just as perceptible as a body wrapped in a wet sheet" ("Teacher and Student").

The individual, in Tolstoy's view, could have no effect on the working out of historical inevitability; that genius could matter at all to the course of history was for him a great human illusion created by our helplessness in knowing the ultimate purpose of events. Indeed, although internally "we feel ourselves to be free," he thought that from the historical perspective individual freedom did not exist, or existed only to an infinitely small degree. Khlebnikov would have agreed that free will is a subjective illusion and that great men are merely those with great destinies. But, unlike Tolstoy, he argued that although people could not affect what they did not understand, there was no great bar to human comprehension. If people did understand, they *might* alter the laws. In Khlebnikov's view, a conscious understanding of the fixed laws of destiny was humanity's only hope for a truly free will.

Khlebnikov and Tolstoy differ most markedly in their vision of the future. Both agreed that future time is presaged in the present. Khlebnikov calls the hints of the future "nodes" and "reflected rays." He could

25. Isaiah Berlin, *The Hedgehog and the Fox* (New York, 1966), p. 78.

see them in his literary work when he looked back at pieces written in the past, and also in history and in the incidents of daily life.

Little things are significant when they mark the start of the future, the way a falling star leaves a strip of fire behind it; they have to be going fast enough to pierce through the present. So far we haven't figured out where they get that speed. But we know a thing is right when it sets the present on fire, like a flint of the future. ("Self-Statement")

In spite of his own attempt at historical science, Tolstoy did not believe that science, technology, or rationalism in general could be expected to create the conditions for human happiness. But Khlebnikov saw science as the only possible answer to the social havoc wrought by older generations acting out the negative forces of destiny. His most optimistic visions of the future were antidotes to his wretchedness when in 1921 he was confronted with the extreme privation created in Russia by drought and social upheaval. Khlebnikov's "lakes of soup" were invented during the famine in Piatigorsk, as he witnessed the town's starving children. Whereas in the end Tolstoy gave up hope for finding the laws that govern events because he found that minute causes and interrelationships created too much data and were too complex for human beings to manage, Khlebnikov, until the end of his life, believed that discovery of predictable patterns in natural forces was civilization's hope for improvement. Science and technology provided the only practical means by which humanity could ever hope to take destiny into its own hands.

Khlebnikov's understanding of history, although somewhat romantic, was, like Tolstoy's, ultimately rational. His interest in mysticism and Eastern traditions was always conditioned by his effort to find their logical base, and to explore what contribution they might make to his collection of data. In this he undoubtedly had as a model his father's ethnographic studies of the habits and lore of the Kalmyks. And just as outer events for Khlebnikov always gave some indication of the deeper structure of universal forces, mysticism gave prescientific hints at a rational truth. In Khlebnikov's way of thinking about these subjects, we can feel again his urge toward an holistic vision. Unable to split the conceptual world into rational and irrational spheres, he always took up a position calculated to heal the breach. Everything in his universe contrived to form one idea, to make one sense. Khlebnikov was strongly attracted to Eastern thought because his childhood experiences inclined him to feel a truth in it; but he also needed to delve into it, to question it closely, to compare its teachings with other, scientific, ideas and so to find their hidden common root. Mystical ideas, he believed, like fairy tales and folk beliefs, were visionary and so in a sense "true." They constituted an accessible form of something simpler and more essential, but hidden—empirical data for a natural scientist whose realm of study embraced every aspect of the world.

Although Khlebnikov was not a mystic, for him and his colleague Alexei Kruchonykh, Cubo-Futurism was in a important way the art of the transcendent. The theory of writing associated with early Cubo-Futurism, especially as it was developed by Kruchonykh, postulated an evolutionary psychic elevation of human consciousness to a state similar to that achieved through Eastern religious practices, such as the discipline of yoga. In fact, mystical concepts infused all of early Cubo-Futurist theory, motivating its approach not only to poetic language but to art in general. *Zaum,* beyonsense, was a reflection of an expanded sense of logic and reason; yet it was not entirely emotional in concept, nor was it anti-intellectual in intention. Both Khlebnikov and Kruchonykh thought of it as a transcendental "language of the future," the outward manifestation of a change in consciousness as well as a mode of communicating the content of a person's altered perception.

The idea of *zaum* as a higher perceptual plane, one that is beyond reason, is similar in meaning to the samadhi state in yoga, which teaches that "the mind itself has a higher state of existence, beyond reason, a superconscious state, and that when the mind gets to that superconscious state, then this knowledge beyond reasoning comes."[26] Kruchonykh's linguistic model for beyonsense was the ecstatic experience of Russian religious sects, the automatic stream of senseless words emitted at the moment of religious ecstasy, when the sectarians were

26. Swami Vivekananda, *Râja-Yoga* (London, 1896) as quoted by William James in *Varieties of Religious Experience* (New York, 1958), p. 307; this book appeared in Moscow in 1910 as *Mnogoobrazie religioznago opyta.* Vivekananda appeared in Russian as *Filosofiia Ioga: Lektsii o Radzha Ioge, so vkliucheniem aforizmom (sutr) Patandzhali* (Sosnsitsa, 1906). Both Vivekananda and James were well known to the Cubo-Futurists.

thought to be in "a state close to samadhi."[27] This "speaking in tongues" seemed to be early evidence of a new and future clarity for humanity, and in his essays on the new language he quoted and drew parallels taken from recently published transcripts of sectarian glosso-lalia.[28] The Cubo-Futurist painter Kazimir Malevich agreed: "I consider the highest moment in the poet's service to the spirit to be that of his wordless dialect," he wrote, "when demented words rush from his mouth, mad words accessible neither to the mind nor to the reason."[29]

Even though Khlebnikov's approach to the development of beyon-sense was more consciously intellectual and rational than Krucho-nykh's, it included the same idea of unintelligible but significant speech sounds derived from the superconscious: "The speech of higher reason, even when it is not understandable, falls like seed into the fertile soil of the soul and only much later, in mysterious ways, does it bring forth shoots" ("On Poetry"). But Khlebnikov also understood language as having evolved from older root meanings of speech sounds, and it was on the basis of these primary semantic units, which he believed were common to all languages, that he constructed his beyonsense words. Khlebnikov's conception of *zaum* did not exclude Kruchonykh's transcendent aims, but he often approached them with more rational methods and interpretations.

Khlebnikov clearly associated poetry generally and *zaum* in particular with the wide use of irrational words in folk practices and religion: "spells and incantations, what we call magic words, the sacred language of paganism, words like 'shagadam, magadam, vigadam, pitz, patz, patzu'—they are rows of mere syllables that the intellect can make no sense of, and they form a kind of beyonsense language in folk speech" ("On Poetry"). Nevertheless, his scientific inclinations engaged him irresistably in trying to figure out the reason for the power of such words, and in creating his beyonsense through conscious methods of word creation: "Beyonsense language is used in charms and incantations, where it dominates and displaces the language of sense . . . But

27. M. V. Lodyzhensky, *Sverkhsoznanie*, 3rd ed. (St. Petersburg, 1915), p. 225.

28. Vladimir Markov notes Kruchonykh's source in both *Russian Futurism* (Berkeley, 1968), p. 202, and in the notes to texts in *Manifesty i programmy russkikh futuristov* (Munich, 1967).

29. K. S. Malevich, "On Poetry," *Essays on Art, 1915–1933*, Troels Andersen, ed. (London, 1969), I, 81.

there does in fact exist a way to make beyonsense language intelligible to reason" ("Our Fundamentals").

In the course of Khlebnikov's linguistic explorations, beyonsense took on several forms, but it was the quest for exactitude and intelligibility that was the primary motivation of his search for meaning in the sounds signified by the letters of the alphabet. In the haphazard shape of common words Khlebnikov saw "traces of our bondage to birth and death," and he aspired to create a language that more faithfully reflected universal truths, that was, like Lobachevsky's geometry, the "shadow of other worlds" ("The Burial Mound of Sviatagor"). Early in this work he looked for conceptual units beyond individual words, the silent meanings common to words in several languages. Another approach to this problem convinced him that the deep meaning of a word was controlled by its initial consonant, and that the semantic elements common to words beginning with the same letter might indicate a meaning inherent in that language sound. Between about 1913 and 1916 Khlebnikov worked in a concentrated way on deciphering the meanings of letters and developed an "alphabet of the mind." Initially he was concerned with the consonants as units of semantic information—his "simple names"—but as he attempted to generalize meaning from ever greater numbers of words, the idea of purely conceptual abstractions emerged, an alphabet of formal geometric relationships as the deepest meaning of the letter sounds.[30]

Simultaneously, the poet advanced the notion of "number-nouns," whereby numbers assigned to every action and image made possible precise and instantaneous transmission of ideas by means of "radio telegrams" or long-distance light projections. In both its alphabetic and numerical forms, Khlebnikov's linguistic explorations at this time bear a strong resemblance to Leibniz's "alphabet of thought." Leibniz proposed analysing all of human thought into the simplest possible concepts and assigning each a number or other sign. All complex notions might then be represented by combining the signs according to various mathematical systems. Khlebnikov was well aware of Leibniz's work on

---

30. Khlebnikov's term "simple name" is analogous to Leibniz's "simple concept" for units of thought and also to the traditional use—from Aristotle to Mendeleev—of "simple bodies" for the physical elements. There is an early version of the alphabet of the mind in "The warrior of the kingdom" (1913). Later versions seem to have been the result of work done in 1916.

conceptual alphabets and refers to him approvingly: "Leibniz and his exclamation: 'a time will come when people instead of abusive arguments will calculate.'"[31] In attempting to develop a spoken and written language for poetry, Leibniz analyzed actual languages and developed a system of correspondences between concepts, numbers, and letters of the alphabet. He believed his systems of logic had special importance in international affairs, and he compared it particularly to written Chinese, which enabled speakers of various dialects to communicate.[32] The mathematically based logic developed in his thesis "De arte combinatoria" was associated also with the creation of his infinitesimal calculus.[33]

Like Leibniz's alphabet of thought, Khlebnikov's alphabet of the mind was intended to permit extremely concise expression of ideas. "So Mo Ve + Ka" in this system, for example, means "they scattered into numerous bands and settled and remained peacefully on their own lands." Khlebnikov's conceptual units of meaning are spatial and often reflect the graphic shape of the Russian letters that are their signs. The basis of their universality is the abstract relationships that are prior to both sound and letter. In this Khlebnikov is in accord with Leibniz's

31. *Vremia mera mira* (Time Is the Measure of the World), reprinted in Markov, III.446.

32. Leibniz was very knowledgable in Chinese history and culture through reading and contacts with Jesuit missionaries. See David E. Mungello, *Leibniz and Confucianism: The Search for Accord* (Honolulu, 1977).

33. Leibniz and Newton independently developed versions of the calculus. Leibniz's alphabet, which he worked on from the age of eighteen, is one of many such attempts to rationalize language. In his book on universal languages, James Knowlson identifies 65 such alphabets designed in seventeenth- and eighteenth-century England and France. Leibniz's work comes closest to that of John Wilkins and George Dalgarno. See *Universal Language Schemes in England and France, 1600–1800* (Toronto, 1975). In Russia in the twentieth century, Konstantin Tsiolkovsky and Pavel Florensky developed related ideas. Similar interests closer to home may be seen in the work of the American Benjamin Paul Blood (b. 1832), who characterized the semantic meanings conveyed by each letter of the English alphabet, creating a special alphabet for poetry. See his *The Poetical Alphabet* (New York, 1972), which is an excerpt from Blood's large work *Pluriverse* (Boston, 1920).

Like Lobachevsky, Leibniz had a particular connection to Kazan, the home of Khlebnikov's first university. I. I. Iagodinsky, a member of the faculty there, was one of Russia's foremost specialists on Leibniz, the translator of much of his work into Russian and the author of many works about him. His series of articles from the university's *Scholarly Notes* appeared in book form: *Filosofiia Leibnitsa* (Kazan, 1914). For Leibniz's own relationship with Russia, see V. I. Chuchmarev, *G. V. Leibnits i russkaia kul'tura* (Moscow, 1968).

view that a truly scientific language should reproduce the structure and relationships of natural mental discourse. By the time "Artists of the World" was written, he had become somewhat dissatisfied with the ability of the Russian alphabet to satisfy this condition. The new alphabet he urges worldwide artists to design will more faithfully mirror the conceptual elements it signifies, and the simple names will become more exactly their own definitions.[34]

The possibilities that beyonsense, as it was manifested in the abstract alphabet of the mind, had for international communication and understanding were obvious and important for Khlebnikov, as they had been for Leibniz, and the poet began to compile a glossary of universal words. His sketches for it form "A Little Introductory Dictionary of Single-Syllable Words," and "A Checklist: The Alphabet of the Mind." But at the end of 1916 Khlebnikov was forced by war and revolution to postpone the project; he would return to it again only in 1919 in "Artists of the World," when he repeated his list of simple names and called for a single written language that would "prove to be the new vortex that unites us, the new integrator of the human race."[35] Khlebnikov's artistic transformation of the language of the mind formed part of his last publication, when it became the "star language" of *Zangezi*.

Khlebnikov could not have been unaware of another of Leibniz's ideas: that of a Russian-Chinese alliance. In the late seventeenth and early eighteenth centuries, Leibniz maintained a correspondence with Peter the Great and his deputies.[36] In a major letter to Peter urging the founding of a Russian Academy of Science, Leibniz told the emperor that God had "decided to have the sciences of learning extended

34. For Leibniz and the tradition of natural discourse, see William Kneale, "Leibniz and the Picture Theory of Language," *Revue internationale de philosophie*, 20/75 (1966), 204–215.

35. This essay was prepared in April 1919 for "The Internationale of the Arts," a collection of essays to be published by Lunacharsky's Ministry of Enlightenment; it did not appear. Khlebnikov's ideas about the alphabet and his discussion of Malevich's work in the essay both date from 1916. On Khlebnikov's examination of Malevich's paintings, see L. Zhadova, *Malevich* (New York, 1982), p. 123. Khlebnikov's emphasis here on written, rather than spoken, language and his reference to a single written language uniting the "Chinese and Japanese peoples [who] speak hundreds of different languages" echo the ideas of Leibniz and many other seventeenth-century thinkers. Jonathan Cohan, "On the Project of a Universal Character," in *Mind* 63 (January 1954), 51.

36. Leibniz's correspondence relating to Russia is collected in V. Ger'e, *Sbornik pisem i memorialov Leibnitsa otnosiashchikhsia k Rossii i Petru Velikomu* (St. Petersburg, 1873).

throughout the world and that Peter is in an ideal position for being an instrument to that end by drawing knowledge from both Europe and China."[37] Leibniz in fact may have been the immediate inspiration for Khlebnikov's letter to two young Japanese men, written at the time that he was working on his alphabet of the mind; the two Leibnizian ideas— a Russian-Asian cultural alliance and a description of a language of numbers—appear together there.[38] If this is the case, Khlebnikov's proposed "Higher Instruct of the Futurians" is a modern echo of Leibniz's Russian Academy of Sciences. Another of Leibniz's letters ends with an educational and scientific agenda for Russia—seven numbered paragraphs strikingly similar in form to the numbered sections that conclude Khlebnikov's letter.[39] It seems fair to speculate that in the summer of 1916, at home in his father's library, Khlebnikov was reading some of the many Russian publications describing Leibniz's work. The poet may even have read Leibniz's letter with the numbered postscript in the local press; that year, 1916, was its two-hundredth anniversary.

Khlebnikov's conceptual units were manifested first as sounds, and as such they possessed a cyclical nature that related them to the larger concepts of natural vibrations and the Laws of Time. This idea places the poet in close connection also to certain scientific teachings of Indian philosophies.[40] According to the Samkhya and Tantra systems of thought, ideas generally familiar to Khlebnikov and the Cubo-Futurists, the universe repeatedly evolves in stages out of a primal sound vibration; everything within it, material and immaterial, is composed of combinations of wave patterns. It is sound that generates light and space.[41] The repetition of a sound syllable can create patterns of

37. Mungello, *Leibniz and Confucianism*, p. 7.

38. "Letter to Two Japanese," "A Checklist: The Alphabet of the Mind," and "A Second Language" were all published in Kharkov by Petnikov in his magazine *Vremennik* (Chronicle) in November 1916.

39. This page of Leibniz's letter is reproduced in V. I. Chuchmarev, *G. V. Leibnits i russkaia kul'tura* (Moscow, 1968), p. 33.

40. This discussion of Samkhya philosophy is based on several sources, including Ajit Mookerjee and Madhu Khanna, *The Tantric Way: Art, Science, Ritual* (Boston, 1977), Ajit Mookerjee, *Tantra Art: Its Philosophy and Physics* (Basel, 1983), and Philip Rawson, *The Art of Tantra* (New York, 1977).

41. Points of sound at one stage in the manifestation of the world become light, and light in turn creates patterns that enclose and define cosmic space. These ideas are

vibrations specific to any object in the world. Indian thought has developed techniques of intoning sound syllables, or mantras, to activate the psyche and induce the superconscious state. Certain combinations of sounds, seemingly syllables without semantic content, can exercise a particularly powerful force. Such a "seed" syllable may contain in extremely concentrated form the entire nature of a divinity or even an extended text. Such sounds are associated with geometric patterns, and by extension the letters of the Sanskrit alphabet are understood to be the root forms of which the entire cosmos is composed.[42] In the seed mantra SRIM, for example, which represents the "female energy of abundance and multiplicity," the *s* sound refers to the divinity of abundance, *r* to wealth, *i* to fulfilment, and *m* to limitlessness. The combination of the three sounds *a, u,* and *m,* in the syllable OM make it the most powerful of all mantras; it is thought to encompass all knowledge and to be the "key to eternal wisdom and power."[43]

Khlebnikov's treatment of the OOM poem that forms the ninth plane of *Zangezi* is a good example of his double-edged approach to the creation of beyonsense. Built on many repetitions of the word *um* (mind), and so creating an obvious and striking parallel between the sounding of the Russian syllable (*oom*) and the traditional intoning of the mantra sound OM, Khlebnikov goes on to build logically with it, using OOM as the semantic root for meaningful new words by attaching to it a variety of prefixes derived from his alphabet of the mind. He means these newly created words to be precise and includes in his notes for the poem a list of specific definitions.

The permeation of the world with oscillating forces was for Khlebnikov a mechanism that could connect such disparate empirical phenomena as the sounds of letters and words, an individual's oscillations of moods, luck, and personal events, and the rise and fall of great nations. "I am clearly aware of the spokes of a wheel turning within me," he wrote in "Self-Statement," "and I work at my diaries in order to grasp the law of these spokes' return." His interest in time, "which

---

compatible with Khlebnikov's conceptual geometry of the language of the mind, and both are probably the basis of his statements in *Zangezi:* "Alphabet is the echo of space" and "Scrape the surface of language and you will behold interstellar space and the skin that encloses it" (*King of Time,* pp. 205, 199). See also his statement in "Artists of the World": "the sounds of the alphabet . . . are the names of various aspects of space."

42. As with Khlebnikov's simple nouns, the graphic forms of the letters of the mantra are related to the concepts they signify.

43. Mookerjee and Khanna, *Tantric Way,* p. 134.

moves like a piston," drew his attention to turning points, annual natural cycles, palindromes, and the "reverse spirit" of the world running backward.[44] But further than that, the concept of universal vibration gave Khlebnikov a means to explain even those phenomena that do not at first seem dependent upon oscillation or frequency. The interference patterns produced by a vibrating surface, for example, could become a mechanism for transforming time into space. The location of cities could be understood as concentrations of population produced by standing waves, of the sort that appear in a resonant space.[45] In this connection Khlebnikov mentions (in "Proposals") the work of the physicist August Kundt, who used a fine powder or dust inside a glass tube to show the position of the standing waves of sound. It is typical of Khlebnikov's artistic use of scientific ideas that the dust of resonance theory not only explains the actual rising up of cities on the surface of the earth, but also turns into a striking visual image in his poetry. The waves of dust in Kundt's glass tubes are the nature metaphor underlying Khlebnikov's geography lesson:

Pattern the dust into circles, curves
Like the gray insides of a wave,
And let some schoolboy say: that dust
Is Moscow, there, and that's
Peking, or a cowfield near Chicago.
Capital cities have encircled the earth
In the mesh of a fisherman's net.[46]

The concept of universal oscillations also gave Khlebnikov his image of "people rays," the continuous waves of population that move in historical time across the earth and are governed by periodic laws similar to those that govern all oscillating phenomena, that control the increase and decrease and resonance within a certain space. The periods

44. Note also that oscillations and resonances are related to time in Samkhya: they create the breathing of living things, and breath "is the gross form of time (Kali)." Rawson, *Art of Tantra*, p. 204.

45. The German acoustics scientist Ernst Chladni first studied vibrating plates by means of the figures they produce in a fine sand spread on their surface. In Khlebnikov's time Chladni figures were also explained and illustrated by the Theosophists Annie Besant and C. W. Leadbeater in their popular book *Thought-Forms* (1901), a work well known to the Cubo-Futurists.

46. "Let the plowman leave his furrow," *King of Time*, p. 55.

associated with particular nations or other groups of human beings, on the order of thousands or hundreds of thousands of years, would obviously be longer than the rapid frequencies associated with light and sound, but Khlebnikov's imagination possessed a large time scale and he could see the surface of Earth from afar, in constant motion like a greatly speeded-up, stop-time movie, alive with its alternately advancing and receding people rays.[47] The social system that would be logically based on this conception of history and geography Khlebnikov called "political rayism."

Khlebnikov's discussion of waves and his inclination to search for cyclical laws of historical time was clearly a legacy of his scientific training. He was certainly aware that the course of nineteenth- and early twentieth-century physics had repeatedly demonstrated the wave-form proclivities of nature. Indeed for the educated public as well as scientists, the world in Khlebnikov's time seemed to be full of radiation of various types. Only about thirty years before, harmonics and other periodic properties of sound waves had been exhaustively explored in Hermann von Helmholtz's well-known publications. And at just the same time, light was accepted as a form of electromagnetic oscillations and electric "wireless waves" were discovered, which would then make radio possible. The sensational detection of X-rays in the last decade of the nineteenth century, followed shortly by the discovery of radioactivity, inaugurated an exhilarating new era of physics. It should come as no surprise, then, that the poet understood wave-form radiation as the essential form of all force and energy; it was a natural and quite rational idea to hold at the time.

Khlebnikov probably comes closest to ideas we associate especially with some schools of Indian thought in his view of rebirth. "Even if something is dead or seems dead," he asks in an early essay, "must we not begin to perceive its connection with the eternal?" And later he boasts: "We are endowed with reason, and we contemplate death with the same equanimity as a farmer who contemplates replacing one plow with a better one."[48] An important part of Khlebnikov's concept of a unified world and his theory of history is the continuity within the

47. See "Our Fundamentals." Khlebnikov often takes a planetary view of Earth: "We may imagine an observer from another planet who is able to perceive all mankind quite clearly, but who can distinguish neither nations nor states" ("The Wheel of Births").

48. "The Burial Mound of Sviatagor," "An Appeal by the Presidents of Planet Earth." The brain as a plowed field is a favorite image of Khlebnikov's.

natural oscillations of types of individuals. In a theory strongly reminiscent of Hindu and Buddhist concepts of karma, he believed that people with the same "life task," or who "strive for the same life's cause," reappear on earth at predictable intervals. So, for example, he sees Kepler born with the same life task as the Indian Aryabhatta, and Walt Whitman as related in a similar way to Jesus Christ.[49] This "carrying over and transmission of consciousness during a second rebirth," as he writes to Petnikov, is a mechanism that affords a kind of "victory over time," because when the equations of history become understood "we are destined to die knowing the instant of our second birth, leaving the poem of ourselves to be completed." Like other elements in his world view, this notion of present continuity with past lives seems not to have been only theoretical but empirical. Khlebnikov himself experienced sensations similar to reincarnation: "I have [the strong feeling] that death is not the last act, but an event attendant on life, part of the *whole* of life."[50] The poet's view is not necessarily of singular rebirths. In his own case, he seems not only to have been unclear about who his predecessors were but, overwhelmed by the "variety and incoherence" of his researches, he appears to have ascribed his mental state to the presence of so many kindred spirits:

> I have sometimes thought that if the souls of the great departed were condemned to wander about the world; they would find themselves wearied by the nothingness of most of the people in it, and would be forced to choose the soul of one man as an island, a place of rest and reincarnation. And in this way the soul of one individual might become an entire assembly of great spirits. But if that island among the waves were a bit crowded, it wouldn't suprise me if one of those immortals occasionally got tossed overboard. In which case the crew of the great would be constantly changing.[51]

Khlebnikov shared his belief in preexistence and earthly survival with Leibniz and Pythagoras. Leibniz thought that birth and death should

49. "Our Fundamentals"; see also Khlebnikov's earlier connection of Aryabhatta and Kepler in letter 93 to Petnikov, March 1917. "Wheel of Births"; note that the Whitman-Christ connection is also suggested by R. M. Bucke, whose *Cosmic Consciousness* was of primary importance to the Cubo-Futurists.

50. Letter 15, June 10, 1909.

51. Letter 42, 1912(?) Khlebnikov mentions the transmigration of souls again in 1916 in his "Letter to Two Japanese."

be considered merely "growth and development" and "envelopment and diminution,"[52] but Khlebnikov, with his special feeling for animals, probably felt closer to the ideas of Pythagoras, who believed in the transmigration of souls among animals and humans.

Khlebnikov worked diligently for ten years on the periodicity of historical events before he became convinced that he had found a satisfactory solution. He approached his task by looking for algorithms—largely by trial and error—which, when solved for different variables, would produce the dates of occurrence in any class of events—the dates of major sea battles or the founding of major cities. In this laborious search Khlebnikov avoided the use of calculus and decimals, working only with integers.[53] The philosophical attractiveness of such a procedure derived from the idea that integers were a "natural" set of numbers and that mathematics should have to do only with the real world. Nature, after all, did seem to work in integers; it grew, for example, by doubling and doubling again, and it transferred units of energy in integral multiples. Khlebnikov's adherence to a "natural mathematics" underscores his belief that his theories, far from being mystical or purely conceptual, concerned relationships that lay at the heart of a demonstrable physical reality.

Starting about 1912, Khlebnikov thought that the recurring intervals between events were multiples of periods of 365 ± 48 years; that is, events such as the fall of states or military battles occurred at multiples of 317, 365, and 413 years. These intervals were especially satisfying to him because the fundamental unit, derived from empirical fact, coincided with a major natural cycle, the 365 days of the year. He saw

52. *Monadology*, p. 73, as quoted in Berlin, p. 106.

53. In this he adhered to the tenets of a philosophy of mathematics known then as Intuitionism and in its latest version now called Constructivism. Its best-known representative was the German mathematician Leopold Kronecker, a mid-nineteenth-century algebraist. He and his followers sought to admit to mathematics only integers, and they developed various proofs against the notion of infinitesimals, reducing the operations of differential and integral calculus to algebraic solutions. This view of the proper domain of mathematics was quite widespread at the turn of the century. Khlebnikov probably adopted it from his mathematics teacher at Kazan University, Alexander Vasilev. See Alexandr Vasilevich Vasilev, *Iz istorii i filosofii poniatiia o tselom polozhitelnom chisle* (Kazan, 1891), and *Novye idei v matematike*, 10 vols. (St. Petersburg, 1913). Charles Henry (see note 3) adhered to a similar philosophy of whole numbers.

these repetitions as a variety of the natural cycles of a vibrating string, a classical idea, and he could speak therefore of "the vibration of continents" and "the string of mankind," and he imagined these concepts as a part of a "great sonic art of the future."[54]

Late in 1920 Khlebnikov revised his units of time. The new formulation was a further extension of the idea of forward and retrograde cyclical motion; he was sure then that he had at last discovered time's purest and most fundamental laws.[55] This discovery was slightly more sophisticated mathematically than the interval of 365 days. Perhaps stemming from the fact that 365 could be written as the sum of the series $3^5 + 3^4 + 3^3 + 3^2 + 3^1 + 3^0 + 1$, he took the underlying form 3^n as the primary interval; that is, 3^n days after a given event, another event takes place that is opposite in spirit to the first event. "After a lapse of 3^n days the second event moves counter to the first, in reverse, like a train speeding in the opposite direction, threatening to derail the purpose of the first event." Khlebnikov also discovered a secondary effect: reinforcing events, events of the same spirit, occur after an interval of 2^n days. These very simple mathematical expressions, based on aesthetically satisfying small numbers, the poet found to be at the root of all history, of every event, large and small, in the lives of nations, races, and individuals.

If history is governed by natural law, historical events must be considered to happen of necessity; they are determined and predictable. Such theories call into question our most cherished ideas of individual and social free will and seem to pose a threat to ethical and moral values. Both Leibniz and Tolstoy were forced by the logic of their ideas to accept a virtually determined universe— Tolstoy by his belief in scientific history, Leibniz by his belief in a God who refrains from acting counter to natural law. But Khlebnikov found an optimistic solution to

54. "Our Fundamentals." Khlebnikov's choice of the fundamental interval seems to have been complicated by two competing ideas: the necessity to be grounded in physical reality and the attraction of working with integers. In the end he made two parallel sets of computations, on the basis of 365 and 365¼ days. For discussions of this theory, see also "Teacher and Student." In basing his theory on the intervals of natural harmonies, Khlebnikov is following in the tradition of Pythagoras, Newton, and Kepler. He relies for his sound paradigm on harmonic analysis and the physics of the motion of vibrating strings, a subject of mathematical analysis since the seventeenth century. A modern theory of universal harmony was also advanced in the 1930s by Hans Kayser; see his *Akróasis: The Theory of World Harmonics*, Robert Lilienfeld, trans.(Boston, 1964).

55. "Excerpt from The Tables of Destiny"; letter 103, January 2, 1921.

the dilemma of determinism in the application of technology to the most fundamental scientific concepts of the universe, developing the vision of a cosmic science grounded in the laws of physics, an idea unique among philosophers and scientific historians.

The question of human alteration of a preset destiny arose with particular urgency during World War I. Until then Khlebnikov seems to have been satisfied to view military battles as the inevitable product of the Laws of Time. But as the horrors of the Russian front became apparent to the general population, and when even he was drafted into service in 1916, he began to search for some means of avoiding the inevitable. His theoretical writing in 1916 and 1917 emphasizes the elimination of war and the establishment of human harmony on earth. In his letter to Petnikov at this time, he speaks of transferring "lawmaking power to the scientist's desk" and of "replacing with scientific waves the ordinary barbarous ray of human nature and its blindfolded progressions." His "Outline for a Public Lecture and Discussion" from the spring of 1917 includes as a topic: "We are sunburnt hunters, at our belt hangs a trap, and in it Destiny trembles, a terrified mouse darting its black eyes. Destiny defined as mice. Our answer to war—a mousetrap."

But the subjugation of destiny applied not only to the elimination of war. Once we have the measure of the world, Khlebnikov argued, we are forewarned and so will be able to survive all our predestined crises more successfully. Understanding the forces that govern humanity and the natural laws of time will permit the inauguration of an era rational in all respects. We will know the day and hour of our rebirth, for example, and will no longer fear death. People and nations will find themselves bound together by known and exact laws, and therefore legislative power can eventually be transferred to scientists, who would "replace the crumbling planks of the thousand-year-old Roman law with the equations and numerical laws that govern the behavior of rays." Inevitably, nations as we now know them would become anachronistic. And more than that, if the proper lens or mirror can be devised, the rays themselves could be adjusted; like their physical relatives, sound and light, the universal wave-shaped forces would become liable to change and control: "All inventions for lesser rays, all the laws of Balmer, Fresnel, Fraunhofer, and Planck, all the art of reflecting, directing, distancing, bringing closer—we swear, we young people, to employ them upon the rays of the human race" ("Letter to Petnikov").

Now that the great rays of human destiny have been studied, rays whose waves are inhabited by human beings, where a single stroke is of a century's duration, the human mind hopes to apply such mirrored control devices to them as well, to construct a power that consists of double convex and double concave lenses. We may even hope that scientists will be able to manipulate the century-long vibrations of our gigantic ray as easily as they do the infinitely small waves of a ray of light. Then the human beings who populate the ray's wave and the scientists who direct the path of those rays, able to change their direction at will, will be one and the same. ("Our Fundamentals")

In the manipulation of our inherited natural law lay Khlebnikov's hopes for the abolition of war and for an improvement upon individual fate.

Suppose I make a timepiece of humanity,
Demonstrate the movement of the century hand—
Will not war wither like an unused letter, drop
From your alphabet, vanish from our little gap
Of time? Humanity has piles, got by rocking
In armchairs forever and ever, compressing
The mainspring of war. I tell you, the future is
Coming, and upon it my superhuman dreams.
    ("Suppose I make a timepiece")

Perhaps this was the only truly fantastic element of the poet's vision: his belief in our ability not only to find the natural harmonies, to read the laws of the stars, but to render them harmless—even helpful—to humanity. Khlebnikov's hopefulness, to the point of utopianism, is a product of his deep faith in the natural law, the logic of numbers, and the power of analysis.

Khlebnikov's interest in religions had always been motivated by the vestiges of ancient forces he believed they offered for study, rather than by a desire for divine guidance. Even in this connection he did not directly inquire into the origin or purpose of the patterns of time; his primary concern was for the natural rather than the supernatural. Khlebnikov believed, as Tolstoy maintained, that history, having abandoned the concept of intervention by a Deity, had become a rational discipline and therefore must inquire only into the notion of impersonal forces producing historical events. Just as mathematics and the other sciences seek law, "the property common to all unknown, infinitely small elements," rather than cause, history also must concern itself with structure. In general, Khlebnikov appears to have taken the oscillating forces of destiny, to whose mathematical properties he had devoted so much of his life, to be the irreducible element of the universe.

But, inevitably, the concept of a unified theory of human history raised the question of a first cause. Several times, especially toward the end of his short life, Khlebnikov seems tempted to reach beyond the concrete natural world on which he had modeled his search toward some ultimate geometry, the relationships, as a final principle. The consistent basis of his understanding of language and history—and even of his "framework-buildings"—had been a deeply patterned structure, and ultimately it was this that would connect the heavens and humankind, the planets and our bloodcells, in a "beautiful concordance of two worlds." Stripped of its accidental manifestations, perhaps the geometry that connects the individual, the state, and the stars was after all the irreducible core of Khlebnikov's teleology. The bone-revealing X-ray and the arrangement of the constellations, so like the points of an overarching mathematical set, are apt images for this furthest abstraction of the patterns of nature.

> These exact laws pass freely through states without marking them, just as Roentgen rays pass through the muscles and show us the imprint of the bones: they strip away from humanity the ragged garments of the state and provide clothes of a different pattern, cut from the starlit sky.[56]

The starlit sky: the patterns revealed by time are identical with their mysterious first cause, and revelation is to be found within nature, not above it. Even Leibniz, a devout seventeenth-century man, put his faith

---

56. "Our Fundamentals." Khlebnikov also uses the same image in regard to the Laws of Time: "In the equation I distinguished muscular structure from bone" ("Excerpt from The Tables of Destiny").

in a God who did not act against his own natural laws. His view of the world and of the God that determined it, in fact, was strikingly in accord with Khlebnikov's—ultimately both were mathematical:

> I maintain then, to explain myself in algebraic fashion . . . that if we . . . could express by a formula of a higher Characteristic some essential property of the universe, we could read from it all the successive states of every part of the Universe at all assigned times . . . I think I have good reasons for believing that all the different classes of beings whose assemblage forms the universe are, in the ideas of God who knows distinctly their essential gradations, only like so many ordinates of a single curve.[57]

His passionate belief in the sovereignty of a lawful nature gave Khlebnikov great freedom in the pursuit of its boundless variety, in poetry and in the languages he devised for poetry. It removed the constraints of common forms, opening words to the wide prospects enjoyed by natural objects whose behavior obeys general laws; words became subject to the deep scrutiny of analytical dissection and deductive reasoning and, illustrative of the operation of an "essential property of the Universe," could be expected therefore to reveal something about the natural world.

Art was an investigation for Khlebnikov, a creative search for the underlying cosmic order; to find it would be to make life whole. Poetry, more clearly here than is often the case, functioned as a kind of model building, each fragment contributing to the construction of a poetic world that mirrored the tales of harmony told by history. In the end, the new forms that Khlebnikov sought—so consciously and so patiently—emerged from the mythic activity we find common to every artist:

> Man is surrounded by a world full of things which are amazing and powers, of whose laws he has intimations but can never unravel—intimations which reach him only in occasional fragmentary harmonies; while his sensibility is kept in unresolved tension, he conjures up for himself, in play, the perfection which he misses; he builds in miniature a world in which the cosmic laws appear

---

57. Leibniz, letter to Varignon, 1702, as quoted in M. Grene and J. R. Ravetz, "Leibniz's Cosmic Equation: A Reconstruction," *Journal of Philosophy* 59 (1962), 141.

before him . . . self contained and in this respect perfect; in this play he satisfies his cosmic instinct.[58]

Khlebnikov's grand idea, the search for the perfection of the world system, was for him a consuming effort and a constant preoccupation. If he often neglected the ordinary details of life, it was not from indifference or for the sake of some ascetic principle, but out of passion for the means of proof; he stuck to his calculations tirelessly, like a mother whose child's life is in danger. The laws that govern the language of birds, the emergence of species, a universal alphabet, and the cycles of history are also the driving force for his poetry. In his need to comprehend the world, science and art were the same medium; if words were the material of his art, number was always the language of his faith. Khlebnikov saw little distinction between the two: "Words are only the numbers of our existence made audible." He considered it the task of the creative artist as well as the scientist or, even better, the universal "number-artist" to pursue the measured image: to "read the cuneiform of the stars" and to "draw the inspired head of the universe as he sees it turned toward him."

C. D.

58. Gottfried Semper, *Der Stil* I (Munich, 1878–79), as quoted in Michael Podro, *The Critical Historians of Art* (New Haven, 1983), p. 7.

one

NATURE

In Khlebnikov's theoretical and scientific articles written between 1904 and 1910, we find the major patterns of his work strikingly foreshadowed: the syncretic bent of his imagination, the dream of prophesy and of discovering a single principle behind apparent multiplicities—species, the senses, the effects of space and time. The young Khlebnikov's field observations of bird species and their continuous evolutionary changes served as a paradigm for later studies of language and provided material that in the poetry yielded dozens of neologisms personifying abstract qualities as birds. In his article on metabiosis he extends his interest in the effects of time and the environment into political history. In addition to demonstrating the depth of Khlebnikov's scientific interests, these writings allow us to observe the beginning of a system of poetic metaphor rooted in detailed observation of the natural world.

"Let them read on my gravestone"

Let them read on my gravestone: He wrestled with the notion of species and freed himself from its hold. He saw no distinction between human and animal species and stood for the extension to the noble animal species of the commandment and its directive: "Love thy neighbor as thyself." He called the indivisible noble animal species his "neighbors," and would point out the advantage of utilizing experiences from the past life of the most ancient species. So he supposed that it would benefit the human race to introduce into human behavior something like the system of worker bees in a hive, and he often emphasized that he saw in the concept of worker bees his own personal ideal. He raised high the banner of Galilean love, and the shadow of that banner fell on many a noble animal species. The heart, the real meat of the contemporary impulse forward of human societies, he saw not in the princely individual, but in the prince-tissue: the princely lump of human tissue confined in the calcium box of the skull. He was inspired to dream of being a prophet and a great interpreter of the prince-tissue, and of that alone. Divining its will, with a single impulse of his own flesh, blood, and bone, he dreamed of increasing the ratio ε/ρ, where ε equals the mass of prince-tissue and ρ equals the mass of peasant-tissue, as far as he personally was concerned. He dreamed of the distant future, of the earthball of the future, and his dreams were inspired when he compared the earth to a little animal of the steppe, darting from bush to bush. He discovered the true classification of the sciences, he linked time and space, he established a geometry of numbers: He discovered the Slav principle. He founded an institute for the study of the prenatal life of the child. He discovered the microbe that causes progressive paralysis. He linked and explained the fundamentals of chemistry in the natural environment. Enough, let a page be devoted to him, and indeed not one alone.

He was such a child he imagined that six came after five, and seven after six. He used even to dare think that as a general rule wherever we have one and then one more, we also have three, and five, and seven, and infinity—∞.

Of course, he never thrust his opinion on anyone else, he considered it belonged to him personally, and he recognized that the most sacred and holiest of all rights was to be able to hold a contrary opinion.

On the five-and-more senses.

Five aspects, there are five of them, but that's not enough. Why not simply say: there is only one, but a great one?

Pattern of points, when will you fill up the white spaces, when will you populate the vacant slots?

There is a certain muchness, a manifold with an unspecified number of dimensions incessantly altering its shape, which in relation to our five senses stands in the same position as a continuous two-dimensional space stands in relation to a triangle, a circle, an oval, a rectangle.

That is, just as a triangle, a circle, an octagon are parts of a plane, so our senses of hearing, seeing, taste, and smell are parts, accidental lapses of this one great, extended manifold.

It has raised its lion's head and looks at us, but its mouth is sealed.

Furthermore, just as by the continuous alteration of a circle one may obtain a triangle, and the triangle may be continually altered to form an octagon, and just as from a sphere in three-dimensional space through continuous variation one can obtain an egg, an apple, a horn, a barrel, just so there exist certain quantities, independent variables, which as they change transform the senses of the various classes—for example, sound and sight or smell—one into the other.

Thus by changing certain existing values, the blue color of a cornflower (I mean the pure sensation as such) can be continuously varied through areas of disjunction we humans are unaware of and be transformed into the sound of a cuckoo's call or a child's crying; it *becomes* them.

During this process of continuous variation, it forms a certain one-dimensional manifold, all of whose points, except those close to the first and last, belong to a region of unknown sensations, as if they come from another world.

Surely such a manifold has at least once illuminated the mind of a dying man, flashing like a lightning bolt that links two swollen clouds, linking two orders of experience in the inflamed consciousness of a diseased brain.

Perhaps at the moment just before death, when all is haste, when everything in fear and panic abandons itself to flight, rushes headlong, leaps all barriers, abandons hope of saving the whole, the sum total of many personal lives, and is concerned for itself alone, when what happens in a man's head resembles what happens in a city inundated by hungry waves of molten lava, perhaps at that moment just before death in a terrifying rush in every human head there occurs just such a filling up of gaps and ditches, such destruction of forms and fixed boundaries. And perhaps in every human consciousness, in just such a terrifying rush, a sensation that belongs to one order, *A,* is transformed into a sensation of a different order, *B,* and only then, after it has become *B,* does that sensation slow down and become graspable, the way we can distinguish the spokes of a wheel only when the speed of its revolution drops below a certain limit. The speeds at which the sensations move across that unknown space are selected in such a way that the sensations most closely connected, positively or negatively, with the safety of the whole being move most slowly, and may thus be examined with precision, in the greatest detail. Those sensations which have the least to do with matters of survival pass more rapidly and the consciousness is unable to dwell upon them.

[December 7, 1904: NP 318]

"On finding a cuckoo"

The westward migration of eastern species constitutes a fairly wide-spread phenomenon, known, for example, in the case of *Emberiza aureola Pall.*, *Phylloscopus viridanus Blyth*, and several others.

We may now be able to talk about the westward migration of yet another species, namely, *Cuculus intermedius Vahl.*

Reztsov has already noted the presence in the northern portion of Perm Province of a cuckoo that combines the features of *C. canorus* and *C. intermedius Vahl.*[1] A specimen similar to the transitional Perm type (with the voice and a few changes in coloring of the small cuckoo; otherwise with the coloring of the medium and large cuckoos) was evidently obtained May 31, 1906, in the Stolbishchensk Crown Forest, Kazan District. Moreover, that cuckoo's voice has been heard with some frequency elsewhere throughout Kazan District. The assumption that the bird simply had not been sighted before is contradicted by the fact that it does not exist in Moscow Province, for example, which has been studied quite well. Reztsov's observations[2] imply a preponderance in the northern portion of Perm Province of transitional specimens over the pure *C. intermedius Vahl.* If that is so, then the spread of transitional specimens in Kazan and Perm provinces can be seen as proof of the general position which says that, with the spread of a species through an area occupied by a species that is crossing with the former, the appearance in any such locality of the dispersed species is preceded by the appearance of a cross of both species. This "wave of crosses," preceding as it does the spreading species, divides the area of diffusion of both species by a strip of preponderance of transitional specimens, and this strip, in the present instance, passes through Kazan District, Kazan Province. The reason for this new westward migration of *C. intermedius* apparently must be seen in the reduction in area of the habitat occupied by *C. intermedius* (which may have come about through the encroachment on the habitat of *C. intermedius* by other types of habitat, for example, the habitat of *Alauda arvensis L.*). This reduction in area, which must necessarily have provoked attempts on the part of the species to disperse beyond the limits of its occupied habitat, may have been provoked by the construction of the Great Siberian Railway and the accompanying upsurge in migratory movement.

Material: *Cuculus canorus L.* × *C. intermedius Vahl.* May 31, 1906, Stolbishchensk Forest, Kazan District.

Can be distinguished from *C. canorus L.* by the following characteristics: darker coloration of the craw, neck, underbill; heavy tinge of ochre in the coloration of the underside, especially strong in the feathers at the base of the tail; weak development of the white spots on the wing feathers and a supplanting of the white by yellow in the coloration of the outer wing feathers; a light blue-gray, with a slightly darker blue tinge along the lower half of the back and upper tail; a greenish cast to the humeral and upper outer wing feathers.

Length of the wing—8.1 inches; voice—*C. intermedius Vahl.*

Notes

1. S. A. Reztsov, *Birds of Perm Province* (Moscow, 1904), 91 pp.
2. Reztsov draws a different conclusion from the observations he cites, in favor of greater caution on the part of *C. intermedius Vahl.*

[1907: Supplement to the Proceedings of Natural Scientists of
Kazan Imperial University 38.240]

Ornithological Observations in the Pavdinsk Preserve

In the spring of 1905, supported in part by funds from the Kazan Society of Natural Scientists, we were able to go to the Pavdinsk Preserve, situated along the eastern slope of the northern portion of the central Urals at a distance of about 60 versts [40 miles] to the north of the town of Verkhoture. In past years the Pavdinsk Preserve area has been studied by Sabaneev.

This locale is remarkable not only for its virgin taiga, extraordinarily varied (because of the presence of mountains), but also for its huge reservoir, where in the spring and autumn great numbers of migrating water fowl stop. Unfortunately, this reservoir had been drained long before our arrival, and now migrating water fowl stop in relatively insignificant numbers. The topography of the Pavdinsk Preserve is fairly varied: large, low, broad gullies are interspersed with more elevated spots and with an uneven surface of steep slopes and knolls; in several places there are big hills—known locally as rocks. Magdalinsk Rock (height 2340 feet) is situated to the west, as is Lialinsk Rock (2812 feet); Sukhogorsk Rock (39,600 feet) stretches out to the east, as does Konzhakovsk Rock (approximately 5188 feet). Konzhakovsk and Sukhogorsk, especially the former, consist of an entire string of peaks, bare cliffs linked by forested or treeless ridges. Streams and brooks are quite numerous. Like mountain streams, they usually rush noisily over the rocks, splashing foam up onto the banks. In the central stretch of the mountains, there are a great many tiny streams running in and out of the rocks. One only has to listen attentively to hear their melodious rippling here and there. Among the species in the Pavdinsk Preserve one most often encounters pines (about 40 percent), spruce (about 20 percent), firs (about 15 percent), larches and cedars (about 10 percent), and birches (about 5 percent).[1] Although the number of species is not great, the character of the taiga, due to the uneven topography, is extraordinarily diverse. The lowest places, marshy shores of lakes and swamps, often extend for many versts and have a quality similar to the mossy swamps of north central Russia, with the same stunted sparsely growing pines and the thick moss carpet beneath them littered with last year's cranberries; once in a while the presence of stunted cedars and bearded lichens brings the north quickly to mind. These places are very lightly populated. Here and there one runs across the tracks of willow grouse, deer, and bears; very occasionally a nutcracker or a titmouse will fly overhead; and only waxwings regularly fly in to feast on last year's cranberries, while in the spring the black grouse swoop down on them with their mating call. All in all, the bleakness of the swamp is oppressive. It is as if living things stop there only in passing. Somewhat more elevated places are usually taken up by thick mossy stands of cedar and equally thick stands of spruce, fir, or pine, often difficult to penetrate. Like the swamps, they are distinguished by the absence of wildlife, especially in the thickest parts. Seldom does the song of the thrush or mountain finch penetrate; the titmouse and Siberian jay fly right by; and only when the nuts of the cedar tree are ripening does the place burst into life with masses of visiting nutcrackers.

At approximately the same elevation along the river valleys and where there have been big fires, one encounters thick stands of birch. The soil in the birch stands is usually covered with moss, berries, and grasses. These are the liveliest places in the taiga. Here the black grouse and woodcocks prefer to make their nests, and one sees broods of wood grouse and hazel grouse; hordes of finches fill these forests with their singing; especially numerous are buntings, pipits, warblers, and marsh titmice; birds of prey swoop down; there are bluejays and Siberian jays; wherever individual larches tower above the birches, there are a fair number of red-footed falcons. The more elevated spots are usually occupied by branchy, not very dense but often enormous pines, spruce, cedars, firs; sometimes the forest is mixed. But particularly characteristic of this stretch is the coniferous mast forest. This is, so to speak, the most powerful stretch of taiga. Higher up in the mountains the picture begins to repeat itself, but in reverse order: first, not very large but often extraordinarily thick spruce, pines, firs, cedars; then where the forests and the barren spots abut, the character of the vegetation begins to change, becoming more like the vegetation of the swamps, only bearing the traces of a long struggle with the wind—the trees are not only stunted but strangely twisted and often bent low; unbent, rising above all the others, is the larch. In the bare areas between the larches, one often comes across trees with spirally twisted wood. The trees must often lose their bark and perish due to this twisting; at least on the peaks one often comes across such denuded, dead trees. Among them, at the summit of Konzhakovsk Rock, we were fortunate enough to come across a tree of amazing shape: the wood of its trunk was so twisted that the bark had fallen off almost entirely, except for a narrow stripe that spiraled up the trunk. The edges of the stripe gradually closed and merged, as if to form a new trunk, giving life to the branches at the top. The trees on these peaks utilize any available shelter from the prevailing wind, taking on with amazing precision the contours of the cliffs and rocks behind which they hide. Finally, at the peaks of the highest "rocks," there are almost no trees, which thrive only in the holes, cracks, and breaks in the cliffs. The similarity in the distribution of vegetation below and above in the central portion of the mountains, it seems, can be wholly explained by the humidity, since at the peaks there are very frequent rains and heavy dew, and the soil there is as wet as in the swamps: often as we walked over the reindeer moss, water literally sprayed out in all directions, as from a sponge.

According to the local inhabitants, when the skies are cloudy in the valleys, it is already raining in the mountains. The peaks of these mountains, having reached the usual height of low clouds and being cold objects, must cause the fall of precipitation in the form of rain or dew. In the central section of the mountains. the quantity of water is least since it merely flows through, collected into brooks and streams; if one disregards soil conditions, this relatively low humidity does make it possible for trees to grow especially thickly. But it must be noted that changes in the nature of the vegetation in the vertical direction consist not so much in the replacement of one species by another, since it is not rare for a single strain of tree to cover a stretch of the mountains from top to bottom, as in the changes in an individual species of plant: below, the vegetation is weak, branchy, and relatively delicate; toward the middle it becomes more vigorous; and as it reaches the top it once again becomes stunted and coarser, which one must assume is due to the effect of the wind. In particular this is notable in the bearded lichen: below it is delicate, like fleece, and gets as long as 28 inches or more; toward the top it becomes rougher, blunted, and at the uppermost height it is found as a short, dense stubble about 1.75 inches long. Even from this brief sketch one can imagine how extremely varied the taiga can be even given the relatively small number of tree strains. But it should be noted that this variety is greatly enhanced by the presence or absence of undergrowth. Evidently undergrowth has a strong influence on both the makeup and the number of the bird and animal populations of the taiga. In many instances the bird population does not seem to depend on the type of forest in which it finds itself, be it pine, cedar, or spruce; and that is particularly so if the undergrowth consists of strains of larch. There one sees such characteristic forms as warblers and marsh warblers, which one would scarcely expect to see in that type of forest without such an undergrowth. However, the same has been observed in other instances as well, where in a given spot various types of taiga are found at the same time: their populations usually depend very little on one another.

The dispersal of the red-footed falcon over the taiga can serve as a good example. It is found where individual trees, preferably dry and sparsely growing, stick up in the air, regardless of whether these trees are spaced wide apart or stick up over a birch grove or some other type of wood. The altitude of the location and the height of the trees also seem to play an insignificant part; we came across red-footed falcons in varing numbers not only in the valleys but on small trees at the treeline and at the top of Biely Rock. Even local hunters remark that the dispersal of several kinds of animals depends on the presence or absence of undergrowth. Thus they explain the scarcity of hare, fox, and wolves in the Pavdinsk Preserve by the small amount of undergrowth; indeed, 30 versts from Pavdinsk Preserve, near the village of Melekhino, there are forests with undergrowth, and here hare, fox, and wolves are fairly numerous.

Given such diversity in topography and vegetation, one can imagine that the distribution of birds and animals in the taiga is extremely complex. Some places are densely inhabited, others only lightly; in each type of taiga the species of birds and animals are to be found in different combinations; moreover, depending on the season, many birds and animals change habitation periodically in the course of a day. All this is quite striking since the taiga is distinguished by its great differentiation and the large scale upon which each of its types is expressed; even incidental types such as areas of wind-fallen trees stretch out in the taiga sometimes for versts. Nevertheless, the varied birds appear most prone to move about during nesting time; as the fledglings start to grow, the broods start wandering in search of food, and then it is possible to see the same species in diverse types of taiga. Many birds who live on berries visit one or another spot in the taiga with remarkable accuracy according to the ripeness of the berries. Beginning in early spring they feed on last year's red whortleberries and cranberries, then begin flying along the river valleys to feed on honeysuckle; by autumn, having completed the rearing of their fledglings, grain-eating birds like the mountain finch, bullfinch, chaffinch, thrush, and so on, throng in flocks around the mountain berry patches. In fact, these berry patches attract almost the entire population of the taiga, especially bears, who in search of berries in the autumn climb the highest mountains. We came across one knoll covered with berry bushes that had been so trampled by bears that it looked like nothing so much as a popular and much frequented state park. But despite the diversity and changeability of birds' habits in the taiga, one can agree with the local hunters, who distinguish three periods: the spring, when all birds, busy with conjugal affairs, attract our attention by their singing, calling, or movements; the "dead season," when the entire bird population of the taiga, in search of secluded, favored spots, flies all over the area, trying to attract as little attention as possible; and finally the autumn, when once again the birds gather at their feeding places in significant numbers, displaying relatively little fear of man.

The larger animals, at least the "regular" ones such as elk and deer, are remarkably consistent in their preference for one type of taiga over another, depending on season and weather—thanks to which experienced hunters always know where to find them. The most disorganized behavior patterns, according to the hunters, belong to the bear: all summer he roams the taiga haphazardly, and that is doubtless why you can never count on coming across him.

Subfam. Cigninae. Gen. Cygnus. September 26 saw many flocks of swans fly by (sleet). October 6 a flock of swans, about 30 of them, stretched out along Sukhogorsk Ridge.

Subfam. Anserinae. September 26 many geese flew by.

Subfam. Fuligulinae. Gen. Fuligula. Sp. F. fuligula Linn. Many flew by September 26. May 15 killed one of a pair of tufted ducks on Lialinsk Lake.

Gen. Harelda Leoch. Sp. H. glacialis Linn. Sighted many scaup flying by September 26.

Subfam. Accipitrinae. Gen. Accipiter. Sp. A. nisus Linn. The sparrow hawk is rarely encountered in the Pavdinsk Preserve. In the collection, a female.

Subfam. Falconinae. Gen. Lithofalco Hume. Sp. L. Aesalon Briss. A pair of falcons have evidently nested in the pine woods by Lialinsk Lake. Able to observe a falcon chasing waxwings. Since September 24 the falcons have been turning up at the pastures, where the migrating *Otocris alpestris* were stopping. In the stomach of a male killed on September 26, an entire half-digested lark was found (all that was lacking were the wing and tail feathers; in the craw were the heart and bits of breastbone of another). The last falcon was gone from the pasture by October 7.

Gen. Erythropus Brehm. Sp. vesperlinus Linn. In the area of the Pavdinsk Preserve, the red-footed falcon is quite a common bird. It can be found only in those places where individual, preferably dead, trees tower in the air, be it a swamp, covered with grass or bushes, pasturage, mountain tops at the treeline, or dense woods, preferably larch, where large individual trees stick out. In the autumn the red-footed falcons' departure was observed. On the day of departure, from early morning on, the trees at the pasture were scattered with their hunched, motionless figures (up to 11 birds on a single tree). Over the course of several hours the birds sat motionless, precisely as if something kept them there, and only a few of them took wing and made a few circles before coming to land again. At about twelve noon the red-footed falcons took off. We were able to watch those in the front landing on treetops, letting the widely spread-out flock fly by overhead and then catching up with it again.

Killed one October 11 on a steep slope near the village of Melekhino; another October 25 at the top of Pavdinsk Rock.

Subfam. Tetraoninae. Gen. Lagopus. Sp. Lagopus mutus Montin. Gray patridges in the Pavdinsk Preserve area are found only on the treeless summits of the highest mountains. Because of this, their total number is insignificant, despite the fact that in their favorite spots they are rather numerous. We were at the top of Pavdinsk, Sukhogorsk, and Konzhakovsk rocks several times, and each time we managed to see gray partridges.

To this day they are not familiar with man and evidently do not consider him dangerous at all. Just how fearless they are can be demonstrated by citing journal notes from several of our encounters with them.

On June 5 we climbed Novdinsk Rock for the first time. The next day at dawn we were awakened by the cry of a partridge. We separated, and my brother was the first to sight a partridge. This is how he describes it: "That day I was walking along the shoulder of the Rock when suddenly a sound attracted my attention. Dry and crackling, it sounded rather like 'k-r-r . . . a.' The odd thing was that it was very difficult to judge where it was coming from.[2] It was carried to me on the wind and, apparently, died with it. A short time passed, and once again there was a loud, insistent 'kr-rya . . . kraoo' quite nearby. The first syllable comes out softly, the second loudly and carries far and wide. The cry is like the creaking of an old tree or the springtime tapping of the woodpecker on a dry knot. I set down my rifle and see at about 4 yards from me a partridge perched on a broad rock, twitching its tail and quickly contracting its neck. There is something agitated and defiant in its behavior, but it has no intention either of flying away or of hiding. After my shot the wind blows away two winter feathers. By the next day, overnight, the rest of the winter feathers have fallen out."

That same day we saw gray partridges several times. After our excursion through the forest we once again climbed to the summit, and when we had only a little way to go, we suddenly noticed a partridge not 4 yards in front of us. It was lying on a cushion of reindeer moss, stretching its legs out the way dogs do, basking in the sun; it looked at us calmly and it seemed inquisitively, probably taking us for a peculiar species of northern deer or some other friendly beast. Unpleasant as it was to take avantage of its trustfulness, we decided to take aim. The Francot bullet passed on exit through the lower part of the breast. The partridge jumped up, ran a few steps, and sat down in a small hole, closing its eyes. Thinking that it was dying, we wanted to grab it, but no sooner did my hand come close to it than it opened its eyes in alarm and flew away, like a healthy bird.

Evidently to this day the bird still sees no evil intent in us. As the opening of craws has demonstrated, in the summer and spring partridges feed exclusively on the leaves and flowers of alpine plants. Around the time the bog whortleberries are ripening, they visit the various spots where the berry grows and at that time feed, like many herbivores, almost exclusively on the berry. We were not able to find any partridge nests. But one local hunter told us he had found a nest with five eggs on a treeless summit on about May 28. The rather motley coloring of the gray partridges harmonizes exquisitely with the background of moss and gray stone; only when it moves does it ripple somewhat and thereby attract attention. Nonetheless, even if you do spot a bird, you have only to look away and it once again makes itself invisible; only if you first recall its outlines can you spot it again. In the autumn, when at a distance the partridges showed up white on the dull gray background of the cliffs, it was easy to observe their ways—although by that time their habits might have changed somewhat since some of them had suffered gunshot wounds. When they catch sight of a man, the partridges as a flock go into motion: some face front; others, on the contrary, turn in the opposite direction, after which they stretch out their slender white necks very high and freeze, keeping a close eye on the approaching man. The flock remains that immobile until the man gets 2–10 steps away and then bursts straight upward to a height of about 5 yards and races through the air; before landing, the flock tries to fly behind some kind of screen, as hazel grouse do; beyond the screen the flock takes a sharp turn and flies low above the ground for several yards and only then lands. Partridges that have been severely frightened at the summit fly down to the treeline. We never saw them fly into the woods. In extreme circumstances partridges hide by crawling into the spaces between rocks, although of course this tactic works only in defense against predatory birds, and especially when the partridges' coloring, in the spring or autumn, does not coincide with the colors of their surroundings. We did not actually observe this, but these assumptions are indirectly confirmed by the fact that in many empty places between rocks the feathers of partridges can be found, as well as by the statements of local hunters. Thus, according to one hunter, before the snows he managed to hunt and kill 8 newly white partridges: he had gone hunting with a companion; they rolled large rocks down from the top of the mountain and in that way flushed out the partridges, which had been hiding in the cracks. Insofar as could be observed, in the flock one bird takes on the role of leader. When a man approaches, that bird is the first to take alarm and adopts, in contrast to the others, an especially agitated stance, not unlike that of a crowing cock. When that leader cries out, the flock hides. Partridges are rather closely attached to one another. In late autumn, when the partridges had already started to turn white, although no snow had fallen as yet, one partridge from the flock was killed and all of them flew up and started to fly away, but suddenly one separated from the flock, went back, and landed next to the dead bird. As it turned out, after the second shot, this was the female.

In the collection, 2 males, September 15, from Pavdinsk Rock; June 6, male from top of Pavdinsk Rock; male, August 30, Kolpak Rock, Sukhogorsk ridge; June 29, from Sukhogorsk Rock, sex not noted; August 30, female, Kolpak Rock, Sukhogorsk ridge; female, October 6, top of Pavdinsk Rock.

Gen. Tetrao Linn. Sp. Tetrao Tetrix Linn. The black grouse, known locally as the *pal'nushka,* is fairly numerous in the Pavdinsk Preserve area. It is to be found in the greatest quantities in birch groves that have grown up initially on burnt ground. We happened to come across a brood on the crest of Sukhogorsk Rock at the treeline, but failed to obtain one.

Sp. T. urogallus Linn. Locally the wood grouse is called simply a grouse. In the Pavdinsk Preserve area they are found here and there in great numbers. During the nesting period we came across wood grouse as much as a verst from Pavdinsk Preserve. During the dead season, insofar as we could see, wood grouse in seach of sheltered spots scatter across the taiga, preferring at that time coniferous forests; only as autumn approaches do they appear at the berry patches in the birch forests.

In the collection, juv., May 21, pine forest near Pavdinsk Preserve; juv., July 16, Logva River.

Gen. Tetrastes Keys. Sp. T. bonasia Linn. Of all the game birds in the Pavdinsk Preserve, the hazel grouse is found in the greatest numbers. One can estimate their numbers because there are hunters here who hunt hazel grouse exclusively. In the autumn they might bag as many as 70 pair. In the autumn the broods of hazel grouse gather at the berry patches in the birch groves. Hazel grouse gladly settle in the mountains, going as far as the treeline. According to the hunters, mountain hazel grouse get especially large and fetch higher prices from traders.

In the collection, female, October 6, Pavdinsk Rock; male, September; male, October 6; 2 males, June 10.

Subfam. Rhasianinae. Gen. Coturnix Moehring. Sp. C. communis Bonn. In the spring the voice of this quail was heard in the meadows by the Lialia River. Not killed.

Subfam. Charadrunae. Gen. Aegialitis Boie. Sp. A. dubia Scop. July 6, one small plover was caught in the Lialia River valley.

Subfam. Scolopacinae. Gen. Limonites Koup. Sp. L. temmincki Leisl.

Little stints are numerous along the Pavda and Lialia rivers during the spring and autumn migrations. May 19, near the riverbank 3 *L. temm.* were killed, 2 female, 1 male. May 21, one little stint, hiding in mare's tail, was killed.

Gen. Pelidna Cuv. Sp. P. alpina Linn. One specimen was caught; notes were lost.

Gen. Scolopax Linn. Sp. S. rusticula Linn. Woodcocks are very numerous in the Pavdinsk Preserve area, especially since no one hunts them; they are shot only by accident. For the duration of the flight at mating season, a few woodcocks could be seen every evening anywhere in the taiga. We saw woodcocks flying up high mountains to the treeline. When we spent the night at the top of Biely Rock, we were awakened at dawn by the spitting of a woodcock; probably attracted by the smoldering campfire, it hovered about 4 yards above us. They are apparently strongly attracted by fire. On the night of June 10, deep in the taiga, a migrating woodcock flew up to our campfire and perched on a dried-up tree. It was killed, turned out to be a male. The last woodcock was sighted on September 9.

Subfam. Phalaropinae. Gen. Phaloropus Briss. Sp. P. hyperboreus Linn. A phalarope was observed during its autumn migration. In the collection, 2 specimens.

Gen. Cuculus Linn. Sp. C. canorus Linn. The ordinary cuckoo is seen less often than *C. intermedius.* Killed, May 20 on the Pavda River.

C. intermedius Vahl. During the mating season the Siberian cuckoo roams through the forest, and its voice at that time may be heard here and there from morning to evening. The cuckoo does not stay in one place for long, calling out a few times its "tru-tru-tru" in its deep, gutteral, projecting voice; it then gives out a peculiar cry, something like "u-kkha-kkha-kkha," takes off, and flies on farther; during the call its wings trail and its whole body heaves in romantic languor in time to the call. It is rare to get a glimpse of it at this time, since after its call it listens very closely and looks around; at the slightest danger it flies away a few dozen yards farther. It becomes particularly cautious when it sees it is being trailed. But if you approach it as you would a wood grouse uttering a mating call, you can always count on success. Siberian cuckoos prefer coniferous forests; they are most willing to stay in mixed forests and only rarely can be found in pure pine forests. They are relatively few, and only their call draws one's attention to them; ordinarily from any spot you can hear one or two cuckoos; only once in a dying fir grove did we find cuckoos in large numbers. The cuckoo fell silent on June 12. *C. canorus* kept on cuckooing.

In the collection, May 23, male, coniferous forest with undergrowth of pine and larch. Male, June 25. Male, May 31.

Subfam. Picinae. Gen. Dendrocopus Koch. Sp. D. major Linn. On July 5 one large woodpecker was caught near Pavdinsk Preserve. (In 1909, outside Kiev, near Sviatoshina, in the monastery's coniferous forest, I observed a large motley woodpecker pecking open the eggs of a spotted flycatcher. The birds swooped down on the woodpecker, screeching, but each time he fended them off with his beak. When I grabbed the nest, I saw that some of the eggs had already been drained.)

Sp. D. minor Linn. In the collection, a female, coniferous forest with coniferous undergrowth, and a male, July 5.

Gen. Picoides Lacep. Sp. P. tridactylus Linn. Common in the local taiga. In a dense fir grove in a swamp a nest was found with half-grown fledglings. The nest was located in the hollow of a fir at a height of about 5 feet.

Gen. Picus Linn. Sp. P. martius Linn. The black woodpecker, one of the most common and characteristic birds of the local taiga, avoids only very dense fir groves, stunted marshy woods, birch groves, barren places, and the like. It prefers especially to settle in large, not too dense, mixed forests. The black woodpecker raises such a clamor that it always attracts attention. Its springtime call is identical to the call of a bird of prey. During the nesting period, particularly in foggy, overcast weather, the black woodpecker often cries during the day and almost constantly at night. Its cry can be described as "p-ee-ee-t," a sad and drawn-out sound. Hunters are convinced that it is rejoicing in the rain, "asking for a drink" [*peet' proseet*]. We tried counting the number of times per minute the black woodpecker cries; it turned out to be on average about 16 times.

If we take into account that it seems to cry all night long, it would seem unlikely that it does so without cause. Usually the male gives a loud cry and is quiet, then immediately from the nest comes a soft cry in response, audible only at close range, from the female, a cry somewhat similar to the first figure of the hazel grouse: "p-ee-ee-n," and so on endlessly all night long. Recalling that the black woodpecker is not badly armed and possesses great wariness, we can only wonder: Is not this male cry a constant way of luring potential enemies away from the nest; small, predatory, climbing animals who might locate the tree with the nest by smell would be attracted by the cry, and climb after the male and thus give him the opportunity to lure them away from the nest. Adopting that line of reasoning, then the female's cry in response proclaims that everything is all right in the nest; if not, the male goes to the nest and lures the enemy away. We were able to observe this on May 27. Thanks to the chirps of fledglings during feeding, we were able to find a black woodpecker's nest; the next day, when we headed toward the nest with cleated climbing boots, our approach provoked an entire storm of noises: first from various directions the black woodpecker's usual cry started up: "p-ee-ee-t," "p-ee-ee-t"; closer to the nest these noises were superseded by a sharp, loud "teeraan" or "teeran-aan," and the woodpeckers hopped about in the nearest trees. The nest was situated at a height of more than 10 feet in the hollow of a large larch. The length of the hollow was about 18 inches, the diameter of the trough was about 8 inches, the opening was about 6 inches, the height and width were four inches. The young were fully fledged, 2 were taken for the collection. When they were being taken, they let out terrifying cries, just like the meowing of cats. Our attention was drawn to the presence at the bottom of the nest of excrement in unusual solid, leathery coverings. This must be considered an adaptation to nesting in hollows and a defense against predatory animals; if the excrement did not have such covering and were tossed out of the nest, it would attract crawling predatory animals passing below; if it were left in the nest, it would soil the fledglings and there would be an even stronger smell from the nest.

Killed on May 27, Pavdinsk Rock.

Subfam. Alaudinae. Gen. Otocorys Br. Sp. O. alpestris Linn. Observed during the autumn migration. On September 12 and especially September 15 there was a very large migration; during the flight the horned larks stopped on the treeless mountain tops, in pastures, and partly along the treeless banks of mountain streams. Flocks of horned larks readily flew alongside buntings. Killed on September 16, Novda River; and a male, September 26.

Subfam. Fringillinae. Gen. Chloris Cuv. Sp. C. chloris Linn. Killed in a larch wood of the graveyard near Sukhogorsk Preserve, male, June 15; very rare in the area around Pavdinsk Preserve.

Gen. Chrysomitris. Sp. C. spinus Linn. Siskins are found only in small numbers in the area around Pavdinsk Preserve. Killed, male, June 15, in a mossy swamp.

Gen. Carpodacus Kaup. Sp. C. erythrinus Pall. The finch is not uncommon in the pastures and along river valleys. Obtained 1 specimen.

Gen. Pinicola Vieill. Sp. P. enucleator Linn. We observed the pine grosbeak 2 times on June 8, an adult at the treeless summit of Pavdinsk Rock and a young specimen at the treeline on the shoulder of Konzhakovsk Rock.

Gen. Emberiza Briss. Sp. E. rustica Pall. The rustic bunting is a common bird in undersized coniferous forests that grow in marshy soil; it likes a forest with undergrowth. It gladly keeps to thick forest. On May 16 they were still leading a nomadic life and flying in flocks, although they had already grouped into pairs. On August 23 the rustic buntings' departure was observed. Obtained male, May 29, the birch woods near Pavdinsk Preserve; female, June 1, the swamp near Pavdinsk Preserve; juv., July 14, Sukhogorsk Rock; male, June 1, the swamp near Pavdinsk Preserve; male, May 16, a swamp covered with birches; and one with no identification tag.

Sp. E. aureola Pall. In some places the yellow-breasted bunting is very common. It is found in pastures, in clearings, in river valleys, and in the mountains at the treeline; it avoids solid taiga and barren places. June 21, a yellow-breasted bunting nest was found in a marshy spot, at the edge of a small stand of firs; the nest was located on a hummock covered with grass and bushes; there were 5 fledglings, covered with fuzz. Obtained male, May 30, near Pavdinsk Preserve; male, May 17.

E. citrinella Linn. The ordinary bunting is one of the birds most commonly found in the Pavdinsk Preserve area. Unlike the rustic bunting and like the yellow-breasted bunting, it prefers not to settle in solid taiga but only in more or less open places; unlike the yellow-breasted bunting, which prefers damp places with deciduous bushes and particularly meadow with small bushes and trees, it is less fussy and often nests in dry open places. It readily nests at the treeline. On October 18 the bunting migration ended.

E. leucocephala Gm. A female white-capped bunting was obtained July 14 in the dry mowed meadows near Sukhogorsk Preserve; with it was a brood of almost grown fledglings who could fly well.

Subfam. Ampelinae. Gen. Ampelis Linn. Sp. A. garrulus L. In the behavior of the waxwing there is a striking peculiarity: during the dead season, like many other taiga birds, it is distinguished by its amazing caution; a nesting pair usually spots a man in an open area 150–200 paces off and starts circling anxiously with its characteristic whistle, often alighting at the very tops of firs, but even there they never give a man a chance to shoot. Yet when the fledglings have grown up, the waxwings begin to roam in families from berry patch to berry patch, and they become absolutely fearless; as has been observed of the waxwing in the central provinces of Russia, they let men get so close that there is no difficulty getting any bird from the flock. Juv. and a female, July 7, in a clearing of Pavdinsk Preserve.

Subfam. Motacillinae. Gen. Motacilla Linn. Sp. M. melanope Pall. The gray wagtail is common along the banks of rushing mountain streams, regardless of what the banks are like: meadows, covered with bushes, or solid taiga. In the collection, male, by the Pavda River, June 11; 2 males June 17; female May 13.

M. flava Linn. The blue-headed wagtail is not uncommon in the pastures and sometimes can be found in the wet meadows of river valleys. August 23, the last blue-headed wagtail was observed.

Gen. Anthus. Sp. A. arboreus Bechst. The tree pipit is a common bird in the Pavdinsk Preserve. It is not fussy about where it nests. Three nests were found: June 2, with 6 well-fertilized eggs; June 6, with 1 egg; and June 11, with 5 eggs at the base of Pavdinsk Rock. Obtained female, pine forest, June 11; female, June 3; male, June 16; male, mossy swamp, and male, top of Biely Rock, May 26; male, June 26; male, cedar woods, May 20; male, June 18.

A. cervinus Pall. A red-throated pipit was obtained only once, in willow thickets on the banks of a stream near Lialinsk Lake, May 17.

Gen. Parus Linn. Sp. P. major Linn. The great titmouse in the spring and summer is very rare in the local taiga. More often they start turning up in the early autumn. There were many of them on October 3 and especially on October 8.

P. cinctus Bodd. The black-crested titmouse was obtained only once, in the birch woods on the shoulder of Konzhakovsk Rock, a juv., June 17.

P. ater Linn. The Moscow titmouse is seen rarely in the area around Pavdinsk Preserve. Obtained male, the shoulder of Pavdinsk Rock, May 26, and June 23, in the fir woods on the Pavda River.

P. palustris Linn. The titmouse is one of the most ordinary and undemanding birds of the local taiga. It readily stays in the birch groves in swamps.

Gen. Acredula Koch. Sp. A. caudata Linn. The long-tailed titmouse is rarely seen in the local taiga.

Obtained juv., June 13; juv., in the osiers in the Pavda River valley.

Gen. Lanius Linn. L. collurio Linn. The red-backed shrike is seen in the pastures and in unforested river valleys. Obtained female, meadow near Pavdinsk Preserve, June 18.

Gen. Sitta Linn. Sp. S. uralensis Licht. The nuthatch is a fairly common bird. It shuns only the most remote places. On Sukhogorsk Rock we happened to see them flying almost to the very top of the mountain, where only spreading trees grow. In the collction, 4 specimens.

Gen. Accentor Bechst. Sp. A. modularis Linn. The hedge sparrow is very numerous in the mountains at the treeline. Its favorite spot is where the birches still retain their tree character while the firs have turned into low thicket. This thicket or juniper is where the hedge sparrow usually hides. Even when frightened it does not leave but merely flies quietly from one bush to another. It has been noted that in heavy fog it leads a less reclusive life, appearing in open places. In the autumn hedge sparrows were sighted in juniper brakes, in the river valley. In the collection, male from Konzhakovsk Rock.

Gen. Sylvia Scop. Sp. S. hortensis Bechst. One specimen was obtained.

S. curruca Linn. The warbler sparrow avoids solid, dense taiga. It lives in the bushes along the riverbanks, in pastures covered with bushes, and is especially numerous at the treeline in the mountains. It goes very high up: it can be seen where there are only traces of tree growth. But it is especially numerous in the stretch where there are still birches while the other tree strains have formed a thick low carpet beneath them. There one usually sees *S. curruca* with *Acc. modularis*. The bird's springtime dispersal to the nesting ground has several peculiarities which rather clearly indicate the significance for small birds of a habitat as screen. Lakeside willows and other strains of bushes were inhabited by the warbler sparrows only on May 21. The greening of these bushes occurred not gradually but all at once, and the dispersal occurred in exactly the same way, since on May 20 these bushes were deserted and devoid of life. On the other hand, the willows and other bushes along the banks of the Lialia River were inhabited on May 17, since here the bushes leafed out earlier, but even here inhabitation coincided precisely with the greening of the bushes: on May 15, only one warbler was found, hiding at the roots. Before that day, and since the first day of observation (May 13), *S. curruca* kept exclusively to the coniferous brakes of forest cuttings, where it was unusually numerous.

S. curruca Linn. The black-crested warbler is not uncommon in big thick fir, pine, and cedar woods. In the collection, male, cedar woods, on the shoulder of Pavdinsk Rock.

Gen. Phylloscopus Boie. Sp. P. borealis Blas. One specimen was obtained, male, June 10.

Sp. P. viridanus Blyth. The green warbler is a common bird in the sparse vegetation of the taiga and quite readily stays in the birch groves in marshes. In the collection, male, May 15; 3 juvs., July 1; for 3 of them the tags were lost.

P. trochilus Linn. One specimen was obtained in the Pavdinsk Preserve area, a male, June 17.

P. tristis Blyth. The mourning warbler is a very common bird, shunning only the dense taiga. Usually it is found along with *P. viridanus*. We were able to observe a pair of *P. tristis* building a nest starting on the 15th. We saw *P. tristis* for the last time on September 13. In the collection, male, June 17; 3 juvs., Pavda River valley, June 22; 3 juvs., Pavda River valley, June 14.

Gen. Turdus Linn. Sp. T. iliacus Linn. One of the most common and undemanding birds of the local taiga. In the collection, 1 specimen.

Gen. Erithacus Cuv. Sp. E. calliope Pall. A red-throated nightingale was obtained only once, in the thick leafy undergrowth of a group of trees in the meadows near Pavdinsk Preserve, male, August 8.

Gen. Pratincola Koch. Sp. P. rubetra. The meadow chat is a common bird, numerous in some places. It keeps to the open areas of the taiga: pasture, clearings, mountains, river valleys, or lakes. In the collection, 1 specimen by the mossy banks of Lialinsk Lake, May 17.

P. maura Pall. Obtained male, Pavdinsk Preserve meadow, June 15; female June 12.

Subfam. Muscicapinae. Gen. Muscicapa Linn. Sp. M. grisola Linn. The spotted flycatcher is frequently encountered in the local taiga; usually settles in places that have been cleared or denuded by fire; avoids dense virgin taiga. In the collection, 3 specimens, May 19, May 20, May 30.

Gen. Tarsiger Hadgs. Sp. T. cyanurus Pall. During the dead season we saw flycatching warblers only once, although in rather significant numbers, at the treeline on the shoulder of Krest Peak on Konzhakovsk Rock. This locale, because of its vegetation, is quite unique: it is not so high up that the trees have become that much smaller, but the altitude and the stoney soil have had their effect on the cedars that grow here, which are fairly large but stand widely spaced, as in a park. The soil beneath them possesses the same character as that at the treeless summits: covered with berry bushes and a solid carpet of reindeer moss; occasional holes grown over with juniper; cliffs covered with denser forest. The flycatchers we saw here stayed low, for the greater part in the juniper bushes, in the holes: their habits and call are very reminiscent of the robin or the bluethroat.

This is not entirely in accord with Sabaneev's observations. According to him, "In the Urals themselves they are anything but numerous, but even here they inhabit only broad gullies and the bases of mountains, never ascending the latter"; perhaps this contradiction is explained by the fact that Sabaneev almost never explored the tops of mountains. According to him, "They are most numerous of all in the deep fir and pine groves of the Pavdinsk woodlands, where they are seen more often than all the other species of *Sylvia* and *Lusciola*. This is the genuine representative of the northern spruce forests: *Sylvia cyanura* and *Anthus arboreus var.* definitely comprise the chief inhabitants of the latter and moreover are encountered in the densest spots, far from any kind of meadows, glades, or streams." We spent a good deal of time in the deep fir groves during the dead season, and not once did we observe *Sylvia cyanura;* this may have been merely the result of chance, but it does at least indicate that if *Sylvia cyanura* is to be found in the fir groves, it is not generally widespread. According to Sabaneev: "In its habits *Sylvia cyanura* is rather similar to the flycatcher. It is in constant motion as it catches insects; it keeps to the treetops, most of the time of the tallest trees, so that to shoot it is perhaps even harder than *Ficedula borealis*." The flycatching warblers we observed were no different in their fearfulness or desire to keep to the treetops. Maybe these contradictions will become clear if we assume that Sabaneev happened to observe the flycatching warbler at the approach of autumn. During that time they are less particular; and we also came across them in dense coniferous forests, at the base of Pavdinsk Rock; on August 28 we observed flycatching warblers by a stream in a birch grove. There were especially large numbers of migrating flycatching warblers on September 12. Obtained female, Konzhakovsk Rock, July 18; female, Konzhakovsk Rock; juv., Konzhakovsk Rock.

Subfam. Corvinae. Gen. Corvus Linn. Sp. cornix Linn. The hooded crow, common near human habitation. In the autumn, on September 25, on an overcast day we observed a flight of crows. Three flocks flew overhead, stretched out in transverse formation heading southwest; in the smallest flock there were about 78 specimens. Among the crows flew a flock of some sort of small bird.

Gen. Nucifraga Briss. Sp. N. coriocatactes Linn. During the dead season nutcrackers disperse across the taiga and are seldom seen, more of them being found in the cedar woods near barren places.

During this time, like many other taiga birds, they lead an extremely secretive life. The first nutcracker to spot a man usually lets out a short cawing alarm and, without letting itself be spotted, disappears; if followed, it stops cawing and hides. But sometimes, evidently in proximity to the nest, it attempts to lure the man away: to this end it hides behind a tree trunk and cries loudly and insistently; if followed, it flies over unnoticed and again tries to lure him away. As far as we were able to observe, less cautious nutcrackers turn up at barren places, where they go to dig out their last year's reserves of cedar nuts; perhaps this lessened caution can be explained by the distance to their nests. But no sooner have the fledglings been reared than the nutcrackers begin roaming in families across the taiga, and their caution is utterly abandoned. Usually they roam in a file; upon spotting a man, the lead bird flies up close, cawing as a warning several times and flying on; half a minute or a minute passes and a second bird swoops down with the same cry, and a third, and so on. Once again silence reigns, only their voices, calm now, are heard in the distance. But sometimes the nutcrackers take a danger more seriously: should a twig snap underfoot or a rifle clatter, the nutcracker will silently appear on reconnaisance; it flies up, observes, and suddenly the forest is drowned in its constant ear-splitting cry, announcing danger. The nutcracker keeps turning in one direction and then another and cries out long and conscientiously. From all sides its companions come; once convened, they follow the man for a long time, cawing raucously and anxiously.

It is difficult to say whether by chance or not, but we observed this behavior for the most part in early autumn in the cedar groves; perhaps because they rarely remain long in other spots, nutcrackers do not stay long around hostile beings. Here, at their leisure, so to speak, they can deal with them, or perhaps, owing to the presence in early autumn of large reserves of nuts in the cedar groves, they find the presence of outsiders especially undesirable. This is how the local hunters explain it: "Those bums!" they say, "they curse and think we're after their cones."

In the forest they play the same role as lapwings do in the swamp;

with their mobility and curiosity they quickly uncover the hiding places of creatures they consider suspect, their cry being especially bothersome on a hunt. Once we had to spend the night in the cabin of an abandoned mine on the shoulder of Sukhogorsk Rock, but no sooner had day dawned than we were awakened by the frantic, victorious cry of nutcrackers, who had managed to get into the cabin. By their nature nutcrackers are very sociable: we had the occasion to observe nutcrackers who had flown into remote swamps or the treeless heights, cawing long and miserably until they got a reply, after which they usually took off and flew toward the voice or awaited the others' arrival. Nutcrackers are quite raucous. Their cry is unusually rich in intonations: when it sees an enemy it caws menacingly; it moans, cheeps, and mutters as if it were talking with someone. The nutcracker often sits for a while with closed eyes after feeding, ruffling its feathers and evidently reveling in the sound of its voice, as if recounting something of its impressions of the day in its own strange language: "pee-oo, pee-oo, pee-oo," it moans painfully and piteously; "pee-ee, pee-ee, pee-ee," it pipes in a delicate voice, like the cry of the hazel grouse; then insistently and intelligently, "knya, knya, knya"; then switches to muttering, "kya, kya, kya"; then trembling with intensity, almost as if it were angry, and ruffling its feathers, it makes a rude hoarse hiss. Nutcrackers are omnivores, but at least the nutcrackers that inhabit the cedar woods, or so the local hunters assure us, to a significant extent feed year round on cedar nuts. We did not follow up on this systematically, but in fact in early summer the craws of dead nutcrackers were filled almost exclusively with the kernels of cedar nuts. The nutcrackers like especially to hide their stores on the barren treeless heights, probably because in the winter the snow is blown away by the wind and so searching out the reserves is easier; in some spots the soil there is nearly bare. In their favorite places, such as the summit of Biely Rock, we came across many cone-shaped openings made by nutcrackers' beaks and nutshells littered around them. In each hole there are about 10 nuts, sometimes less. The nutcrackers evidently gather their reserves in the summer, guided less by memory than by seeking out the first shoots of germinated nuts; the nutcrackers dig there and find the rest. It is interesting that the nutcrackers do not eat the germinated nuts, but they do dig up the green shoots and throw them away. Hunters say that the nutcrackers do this out of annoyance at not being able to use the nuts. Naturally some shoots survive, and in this way nutcrackers do much to facilitate the spread of the cedar. At the same time, by selecting the best nuts for their stores year in and year out, one can assume they have some influence on the improvement of the nuts themselves. In general they should be thought of as bearing approximately the same relationship to the cedar as humans do to wheat. In the autumn nutcrackers make quick work of the nut harvest, not eating them so much as hiding them all over the forest and dropping them on the ground, to be gathered up by bears, chipmunks, and mice. According to the hunters, the nutcrackers do this by swallowing the nuts and, after collecting a handful or so, spread them all over the forest. Thus, according to the local inhabitants, in 1901 a great many nuts ripened in the Pavdinsk Preserve area, but there was such a horde of nutcrackers that the locals were unable to enjoy the harvest. In the winter, according to the local inhabitants, the nutcrackers get their stores out from under the snow. But when heavy snows fall and a hard frost hits, the nutcrackers do not fare well: many fly one after the other to human habitations at any enticement and are trapped by little boys, or they die of cold and hunger in the taiga.

In the spring, on May 26, at the treeline at the top of Pavdinsk Rock we were observing the nutcrackers unearthing their stores, and we noticed a solitary nutcracker among the rocks; we killed it and found it to be a typical narrow-billed (*macrorhynchos*) nutcracker; its craw was stuffed exclusively with tiny spiders, while at that time the craws of the local (*caryocatactes*) nutcrackers were to a great extent crammed with the kernels of cedar nuts; it is possible that it was unable to find last year's reserves in the ground by their shoots.

In the collection, 3 specimens: 1 from the barrens of Pavdinsk Rock, May 26; Pavdinsk Rock, June 10; and 1 near Pavdinsk Preserve.

Gen. Pica Briss. P. leucoptera. Found quite often near human habitation. On May 21 the nest of a white magpie was found, located in the branches of a spruce. It differed from the nests of the usual magpies seen in the Volga provinces by its rough workmanship, since it was built chiefly from thick and rather large twigs; nonetheless, these traits may have been the result of coincidence. The trough was covered over with clumps of clay. The fledglings were still featherless. In the collection, female, Pavdinsk Preserve area, May 28; juv., pastures near Pavdinsk Preserve, May 27.

Gen. Garrulus Briss. Sp. G. brondti Eversm. The red-crested jay is found only rarely, primarily in coniferous and birch woods. In the collection, male, Pavda River valley, September 24.

Gen. Perisoreus Bp. Sp. P. infaustus Linn. The Siberian jay is encountered only rarely. It prefers staying in the thick and mossy cedar groves. In the collection, male, Sukhogorsk Rock, June 26, and a female.

Subfam. Buboninae. Gen. Glaucidium Boie. Sp. G. passerinum Linn. A pygmy owl was obtained in the remote cedar taiga at the base of Pavdinsk Rock.

Notes

1. The percentages of tree strains in the taiga, and mountain elevations expressed in meters, come from an article by Sidorenko, "Journey to Pavdinsk Preserve."

2. This is probably explained by the fact that, while calling out, the bird twists its head in different directions.

V. V. and A. V. Khlebnikov

[1911: *Priroda i okhota* 12, 1–25]

An Attempt To Formulate a Concept in the Natural Sciences

The concept of *symbiosis*, which arose as an auxiliary means of describing a number of specific phenomena in the vegetable kingdom, was adopted and spread quickly through all areas of the life sciences. It augurs well for the present attempt to formulate the related concept of *metabiosis*. Let us describe it more exactly.

If we use the symbols +, •, and − to designate the consequences that one living organism experiences as a result of its coexistence with another, we obtain the following six relational possibilities:

	1st individual	*2nd individual*
(1)	+	+
(2)	+	•
(3)	+	−
(4)	•	•
(5)	•	−
(6)	−	−

where + indicates benefit, • indicates a neutral condition, and − indicates harm, as a consequence of coexistence. But the nature of these relations is revealed in the following preconditions, which characterize them all: (1) the relations between the two organisms occur at one and the same time; (2) they occur in neighboring but different segments of space.

Such a definition of the circumstances under which these relations develop assumes the possibility of the type of relations that would be possible under the following conditions: (1) the relation between the two organisms occurs in one and the same place; (2) the relation between the two organisms connects two successive intervals of time.

Since a causal connection is operative from the past to the future but not the reverse, it is clear that one of the two subsequently existing organisms will occupy the state we have indicated in our diagram by the period. This reduces the number of possible cases by half, and therefore we have only three of them:

$$
\begin{array}{cc}
\cdot & + \\[6pt]
\cdot & - \\[6pt]
\cdot & \cdot
\end{array}
$$

The first of these cases describes those relations where in any subsequent existence the relationship of one organism to another is advantageous for the former, and it is this phenomenon we may refer to as *metabiosis*.

Thus an exact inquiry into the nature of these and other interrelationships leads us to the following explanatory diagram:

	$=$	x	
symbiosis	t	l	where t indicates time (tempus)
metabiosis	l	t	where l indicates place (locus)

The sign $=$ is understood here as a sign of identity, and the x is the sign of absence of identity.

If we let the sign $\wp$ designate the relations in general between two organisms i_1 and i_2, for symbiosis we get the expression

$$ i_1 \frac{t_n}{l_n} \wp\, i_2 \frac{t_n}{l_{n+k}} $$

and for metabiosis an expression of the type

$$ i_1 \frac{t_n}{l_n} \wp\, i_2 \frac{t_{n+k}}{l_n} $$

where t_n and t_{n+k} are designations of time, and l_n and l_{n+k} are designations of place.

But perhaps this new viewpoint, derived from the earlier one by transposing the characteristic properties of time and space, has too narrow a range to be successfully applied. If so, then the above computations will prove to be of doubtful value. But, as will be seen below, it is possible to find some examples that should demonstrate the breadth of application of the viewpoint here proposed.

The practice of agriculture offers us an especially conclusive example. Properly, every crop rotation, whether simple or involving a number of fields, is based on a relation of metabiosis between grains. We are also familiar with the practice in forestry of preferred growth of certain species in places where another species has vanished.

In the same way, the credo of militaristic Pan-Germanism entails relations of metabiosis between the Slavic and the German worlds.

The activity of soil-altering bacteria connects the world of lower organisms with that of plants by means of metabiosis.

Here we may advance the daring hypothesis that the essence of the replacement of certain realms of animals by others and the various stages of life on earth can also be reduced to metabiosis.

Metabiosis unites the generations of corals within an atoll, and the generations of people within a nation. The death of higher organisms, including even homo sapiens, makes them, through metabiosis, connected with the lower ones.

I here adduce two cases of metabiosis that I was able to observe personally. On May 7, 1902, I was the cause of disturbance in a *Totanus ochropus* that had been sitting motionless on the branch of a fir tree. Parting the branches, I observed the abandoned nest of a thrush, in which the small black bird had settled itself. The bottom of the nest contained fallen fir needles. The clutch of *T. ochropus* consisted of three eggs, their primary color pale green, shaded with brown spots and markings. Without doubt this kind of relationship cannot be classified among those referred to by the term symbiosis; it constitutes a distinct example of metabiosis.

The other example was observed over the course of two years and concerns metabiosis between *Turdus pilaris* and *Muscicapa grisola*. It consists of the fact that the nest used in spring by *T. pilaris* is occupied in the second part of the summer by *M. grisola,* and the two species are thus related by metabiosis.

The examples here adduced give some evidence of the breadth of application of the proposed concept.

[1910: *Vesti studencheskoi zhizni* 1, 11–12]

two

RUSSIA

The pieces in this section, written between 1908 and 1914, illuminate fields of intense concern for the young Khlebnikov prior to World War I. Russia's uneasy position between the cultures of East and West, Asia and Europe, had by then been a matter of public discussion among Russian intellectuals for some seventy years. Khlebnikov, like many others, found a solution to this problem by affirming political and cultural ties to other non-Russian Slavs, and tried to define a common Slavic history, folklore, and social tradition. In the first decade of the twentieth century, such Pan-Slavic sentiments were given added impetus by Austria's annexation of Bosnia and Herzegovina. Khlebnikov's Pan-Slavism and his focus on the cultures of the East—"the continent of Asia"—rather than Europe—"the islands"—were also closely associated with his theories of number and language. In the following writings his attention moves readily from linguistic to numeric to cultural roots. Everywhere he defines a deep connection between a people and its art, and he therefore condemns the narrowness of Russian literature with its Western outlook and pleads for the fusion of "Slavic and Tatar blood."

The tone of some of these pieces is aggressive, polemical, aimed at the established older generation of Symbolist writers—Briusov, Balmont, Merezhkovsky—and their journal Libra. "!Futurian" attacks the wave of European influence that Symbolism represented in Russia. In "The Letter as Such" he praises the Cubo-Futurists' handwritten books and calls attention to the emotion conveyed through the visible gesture of lettering. "The Word as Such" defends Cubo-Futurism from the prior claims of Italian Futurism, distinguishing between the Russian organic treatment of the word and the literariness of the Western movement.

Slavs!

Today Lübeck and Danzig regard us silently, testing us—these cities with German populations and Russian Slavic names. Do your hearts feel nothing for the Polabian Slavs? Have our souls not been mortally wounded by the sight of the iron-clad Reicher, running his spear through Slavic peasant farmers? Your injuries are great, and sufficient to water an entire host of the horses of vengeance. Let us gather them, then, from the Don and the Dnieper, from the Volga and the Vistula. In this host, Montenegro and Belgrade have sworn eternal brotherhood and, with the madness of those whose divine lot is to be victorious, are now prepared to oppose their wills to the will of an incomparably stronger enemy. Will people now say that the spirit of the Hellenes in their struggle against the Persians has revived once again in present-day Slavdom, and Darius Hystaspes and the pass of Thermopylae and King Leonidas with his three hundred will arise soon before our astonished eyes—right now, today even—or must we remain silent? Today do we not observe once more that the man who conquers is the man who loves his native land? Or will we not understand what is really happening—that an inflamed struggle is now in progress between the entire Germanic world and the whole of Slavdom? Will we not respond to the challenge that the German world has hurled at the Slavic world? And will we direct our attack at the armored knights of the Hapsburgs but not the Hohenzollerns?

Our mouths taste vengeance, vengeance drips from our horses' bridles, let us now move our celebration of vengeance, like trade goods, to a place where there is a demand for them—to the banks of the Spree. Russian horses know how to stamp their hooves in the streets of Berlin. We have not forgotten that. We still know what it means to be Russians. The list of Russian nationals includes that inhabitant of Königsberg, Emmanuel Kant. I salute a war for Slavic unity, no matter where it originates, whether in Poznan or in Bosnia! Let it come, the divine dance, with the maiden Slavia as a representative of Montenegro! We will not strike a blow at the Hapsburg stream, we will strike at the Hohenzollern raider. Holy war! Unavoidable, approaching, immediate—war for the trampled rights of the Slavs, I salute you! Down with the Hapsburgs! Hold back the Hohenzollerns!

[pub. 1908: Markov 405]

Who Are the Ugrorussians?

The Ugrorussians, whom the Hungarians call Orochs and who call themselves Russniaks or Russians, comprise a population of 500–700,000 and live in a narrow strip of land between Hungary and Galicia. They are at the moment experiencing simultaneous pressure from the Holy See, desirous of acquiring new spiritual children, and from Budapest and Vienna, attempting to swallow up a group of people who are neither German nor Magyar. Representing the front line of the Slavic floodtide at the foothills of the Magyar lands, immersed in their agricultural labors, the Ugrorussians are not always aware that they are the objects of a brisk trade between the Eternal City and the Hapsburg capital, whose medium of exchange is their ancient Orthodox faith, which they refer to as Russian. Under pressure from Catholicism, propagated now by "civil and military authority," now "quietly and underhandedly" by the distortion of religious texts, the Ugrorussian people are losing defenses that seemed impregnable.

When they looked for support in 1848 to the legitimate Hungarian authorities and put their trust in the Hapsburgs, these authorities replied by sending a Hungarian detachment to execute Miroslav Dobriansky, the son of the leader of the Ugrorussians in 1848; they discovered the "tree of torment," the newest invention of Teutonic-Magyar friendship.

Now this people is beginning to seek help and support from a power as closely related to them as a wave to the sea. Not wanting to be a lifeless pawn or a building block, a peculiar kind of payment for services by certain groups of the Austrian power elite in their betrayal of others, they have attempted to escape from spiritual confinement but are being crushed because Russians know nothing about this other face of the Hapsburg Empire, the face of a torturer of those who are neither Hungarian nor Catholic.

What of their past, these Ugrorussians? Who exactly are they?

Judging by the fact that the local Jews are referred to as Khozars, the Ugrorussians must at some time have been neighbors to the kingdom of the Khazars. A memory that lasts a thousand years cannot be of bookish origin, and since it has passed into human relationships, the Russniaks were quite probably at one time conquered by the Khazar kingdom that was later defeated by Sviatoslav. If the Comte du Chayla's opinion is correct, that the Hungarians borrowed Slavic agricultural terms from the Ruthenians, then their ancestors might be the Duleby, since according to the chronicle the Obry first became acquainted with agriculture during their subjugation of the Duleby. The Obry made use of Slavs instead of cattle for plowing, hitching them in droves to the plow. This is natural enough for a nomadic people who valued horses very highly in their migrations and who considered it humiliating for a horse to be used in agriculture. (Of course the Obry never dreamed of the "tree of torment.") From this it seems clear that the Ugrorussians are emigrants from southeastern Russia carried along in the general flow of migration and are possible descendants of the Duleby of Nestor's chronicle, as evidenced by the words *seno* (hay), *kosa* (scythe), *borona* (harrow), *grabli* (hay rake), *soloma* (straw), and so on, which prove that it was the Slavs who acquainted the Hungarians with agriculture. Today we have discovered the Obry again and find them torturing the contemporary Duleby. The chronicle recorded the connection between the cruelty of the Obry and their final destiny in the proverb, "Ischezosha aki obre" (They vanished like the Obry).

[pub. 1913: *Slavianin* 13/2, 3]

About the Brodniki

The Brodniki are known from the chronicles as a distinct group of nomadic Slavs in southern Russia. The ultimate fate of this tribe from the steppe is unknown. Its name is customarily derived from the verb *brodit'* [to wander, to lead a wandering life]. Nevertheless, if we postulate another derivation for the name, it is possible to conclude that this tribe from the southwestern steppe took part in the conquest of Siberia. Let us suppose that this group of people took its name from the particular kind of footgear they wore. This footgear, as distinct from a boot, had no separate sole and was tightly tied about the ankle with a thong, to prevent the soft leather from slipping down the leg. In ancient times this was the footgear of the inhabitants of Russia's steppe, as evidenced by the plaques and ornaments of burial mounds.

In our own time this footgear is not worn in European Russia; it has been replaced by boots and woven bast shoes. But it is very well known to this day in Siberia, where it is called *brodni* and is preferred to any other footgear by reason of its lightness and the freedom of movement it allows to the foot. A man on foot wearing brodni can go one and a half times farther than a man wearing rigid-soled boots. The insides of brodni are lined with straw to protect the feet from injury, which is exactly what the Scythians did, as can be determined by the swollen depictions of their feet. This Scythian footgear would have been more comfortable than boots for foot soldiers, especially in mountainous country (brodni allow the foot a firm hold on rocky ground).

It is possible to imagine that the Brodniki were Russified descendants of the Scythians, who preserved, along with numerous other traits, the Scythian footgear as well. Hampered by the growing populations of their nomadic habitat, they moved east, took part in the conquest of Siberia, and diffused among the Russian inhabitants of the new region the footgear that gave them their name.

It is not completely impossible either that the leaders of the conquest came from among this tribe: Yermak and Koltso might have been descendants of these leather-stocking-wearers.

Notable, too, is the fact that Khabarov, one of the conquerors of the Amur, was, as his name implies, a descendant of the most valiant [*khrabri*] tribes of the Khazar kingdom, the Khabari. This tribe, oppressed by their fellows, at one point rose in revolt.

[pub. 1913: NP 336–337]

The Burial Mound of Sviatagor

I

The whisper of ocean sea as it ebbs, does it not breathe forth some secret behest to the nation—a behest no other overhears—something the nation has grasped of late through a chink in the burial ground of time, the rising place of a living spirit, a warrior crucified by an iron age? to a nation that has filled with human silt this abandoned bedding ground, losing the body heat of its first warrior, this orphaned, wife-forsaken sea bed?

> Bless or bedew with venom
> But you will remain one,
> Behest of ocean's depths,
> Russia.

Exactly. The Widow's caresses have passed on to us the countenance of her first beloved husband. Her abundant caresses have created a healing idol. We are the inhabitants and inheritors of the northern sea that gives up its bedding ground to us. We are executors of the great sea's will. We are the consolers of the inconsolable Widow. Must we subject our own law to the authority of those who heed the behest of the ancient islands? And the vast extent of our comutual countenance, is it not the lawful inheritor of the vast extent of the ancient sea?

II

Of course truth borrows the voice of the one who said: Words are only the numbers of our existence made audible. Is that not why the supreme arbiter for a wordworker has always been found in the science of numbers? Is it not here that the boundary runs between what has been and what is to come, so that we now desire knowledge even from the "tree of imaginary numbers." We are enamored of expressions of the type $\sqrt{-1}$, which have always repudiated the past, and we thus attain freedom from things. Growing beyond the range of the possible, we now extend our law over the abyss; we no longer distinguish ourselves from God; even the creation of worlds is within our power.

III

The defiant one desires to see himself enrolled among the tribe of the defiant.

The shadow of the northern sea—does it not hang like an evil spell over our wordwork, unable to perceive in the son the visage of the father? unable to acknowledge the son as the son?

And does the land not cry out within us: "Oh, give me a voice! A voice! Give me a voice!" And have we given her one?

How many countless numbers of times has the Widow appeared, clothed in sadness, bodied in rolling plains, to ask: "Behold the body of my beloved husband. But where is his voice? For I see his beloved mouth bewitched by the evil will of neighboring islands. I behold it silent, or hear it repeating the cries of foreign birds, but I do not hear the voice of my beloved." Yes, Russian wordwork echoes voices from foreign places; it has left speechless the mysterious warrior of the north, the nation-sea.

And must we not reproach even the great Pushkin because in his work the sounding numbers of the life of the nation—the sea's inheritor—have been replaced by numbers from the life of nations subservient to the will of ancient islands?

And must we not find someone who will break these evil enchantments—sweet though they may seem—and hail him as "the first Russian who dares to speak Russian," and invoke his coming with cries of "Awake! Awake!"

IV

We know nothing, we predict nothing, we only ask in anguish: Has the time not come? Has *his* time not finally come?

V

Have his branches finally begun to sound, and do we not surround him like a grove of young saplings?

VI

Does not every means desire to become an end as well? Consider the beauty of language set free from its ends. The hedge that forms the hedgerow bears hedgeroses also.

VII

And will we remain deaf to the land as it cries: "A voice! Give me a voice!" Will we forever remain mockingbirds, imitating Western songs?

VIII

And the resourceful Euclids and Lobachevsky—do they not designate the roots of the Russian language as the eleventh of the imperishable truths? In words themselves do they not see traces of our bondage to birth and death? They have called the roots divine, and words merely the work of human hands.

And if the living language that exists in the mouths of a people may be likened to Euclid's geomeasure, can the Russian people not therefore permit themselves a luxury other peoples cannot attain, that of creating a language in the likeness of Lobachevsky's geomeasure, of that shadow of other worlds? Do the Russian people not have a right to this luxury? Russian wisdomry always thirsts after truth—will it refuse something the very will of the people offers it, the right of word creation? Anyone familiar with life in the Russian village is familiar with words made up for a mere occasion, words with the lifespan of a butterfly.

And does it not mean that the gods have been carried out of the temple if those of other faiths mingle fearlessly in the ranks of those who pray and take part in the ceremonies?

> You reject the ancient gesture
> That blessed you in the font;
> And the sacrificial deer still live
> To keep the priest's knife keen.

IX

And does it not behoove us to consider the tree trunk about which a seeming vortex moves the Slavic languages, those beautiful, diversificating leaves, and also consider the common Slavic word, the vortex circle that fuses them all into one single general circle?

X

Of course the Woman, bodied in rolling northern plains, thirsting for the caresses of her first husband, will accept this loving spouse, and for this reason, secretly, with the strength of feminine enchantment, she will reshape his visage into that of her first husband—the ocean sea.

Thus do we change, making ourselves into the likeness of that first husband in order to merit the great favors of the Widow wrapped in plains.

And when those bright mountains born to the second sea pass before our exultant glances, establishing their ice-bound law and its reverberations, is it not fitting to give ourselves over in pure play to the numbers of our existence, enchanting ourselves in discovering a new kind of influence over our lives, and perceiving through them the great primordial numbers of existence, the prototypes? And these wordworkers, proudly floating to take the place of foreign snows—is it not from the abysses of ocean that the greatest icebergs rise, such as do not exist on dry land—do they not fill our soul with trembling and awe?

And will we not then become like a nation of divinities, shining with the light of eternity ourselves and not serving merely to reflect the light of others? Let us consider the rays of earthly wills. If we rest content with a borrowed light, then we consign ourselves to outer darkness, and the good rays will remain forever at the service of neighboring nations. We must not stint in nearness to divinity—even to one whose existence we deny, even to one we ourselves may have willed into existence.

XI

And if mankind is still grass, and not some flower on a mysterious stem, can we not speak prophetically of autumn, tearing itself and its yellow leaves away from the forces of the eternal? Or, hearing a song, do we not look up into the sky to see the first lark? And even if something is dead or seems dead—must we not begin to perceive its connection with the eternal in these latter days?

XII

Let us then be true to the Woman's sea spouse, our prototype, armed like us with the sea as our armor, the millennial roar of the waves as our steeds, and the watery essence of all creation as our shield. He has inspired us with the breath of another age, an age of other mightmakers, rich in muchness. The Widow is forming a countenance for us: we must bend ourselves to her will.

[1908: NP 321]

Monuments

Monuments ought to be erected by the railroad companies, by mine or factory owners, and the government should oversee their operation and help by taking the initiative and providing the brains, milking the great corporations the way a farmer milks his cows.

They will provide a skeleton, a ribcage, and a backbone for the national soul and must be erected by Russians. They must be set up all across the face of the Russian land. They are the fingers of a stone guardian who points the way for young people. Monuments convey to the people that life is an end in itself.

Monuments serve to provide a dialogue between the government and the populace; they are the sounds of a conversation in cast metal between the people and the government. They are easy to read (the eyes of the entire nation focus upon them); they convey ideas; they are storehouses of sense, just like elements of written language and hieroglyphics. So a fitting series of monuments should speak directly to the hearts of the Russian people.

The cast-iron accents of Russian speech should be set up on both banks of the Dnieper, so that steamboats can sail beneath them.

Erect a monument to Ilya Muromets—to the might of the Russian people in his native village of Karacharov. Thus will the government express the hope that Russians will lead their lives on the model of their hero, and mothers will give birth to heros, inspired by the stone erection.

The government intends to erect a monument to Skovoroda in Chernigov. The government thus conveys the message that within its confines one is free to develop all aspects of the Russian soul.

Erect one in Sudak to the first Russian prince, Bravlin.

In Kiev, to the first reigning Russian, Justinian/Upravda.

A monument in Perm to the Stroganovs, pioneers in the conquest of Siberia.

To Peter the Great's mother, Natalia Narishkina, in Petersburg. This will remind the Russian woman of her true role—to be the mother of great sons.

In Kiev, a monument to Herodotus, who first wrote about Russia.

A monument to the Greek sages Plato, Socrates, [illegible], Aristotle, [illegible].

A monument to Lopukhin in the form of the tree beneath which the hero died.

In Kiev, a monument to Nestor, Kotoshikin, Karamzin, Kostomarov, and Kliuchevsky, consisting of a white marble colonnade one and a half times a man's height, with a row of busts.

A monument to the Orel racehorse in Voronezh, with a naked youth beside him.

In Petersburg, to Mendeleev.

A great monument to Ivan the Terrible in Moscow.

In Moscow for the great union of Russians and Georgians, to the great Georgian who defended Russia from the Turks, Bagration. And to the venerable Georgian saint, Nina. In the old days Georgians were no less Russian than the Russians. Let the good old days became a law for the present day.

In Novgorod, erect one to Riurik, the first of the House of Riurik.

A monument to Samko, the first to fight the Germans.

Russians and Armenians may soon become one. We should set up a monument in Moscow to some famous Armenian.

In Astrakhan, erect a monument to Volynsky, Pugachev, Razin—fighters for Russia's freedom.

In Kiev, to Križanić, a Croat worthy of being commemorated in Russia.

[Illegible] to Jan Hus.

To the Boyarina Morozova in Moscow.

In Moscow, a monument to Jan Sobiecki. Thus praising Poland here in the open country.

And to the conqueror of Grunwald, Wladislaw II.

In Moscow, a monument to Gogol, Pushkin, and Mickiewicz—three friends, all beloved by the Muses.

In Moscow or Tsaritsyn or Petersburg, a monument to Sadko the first sailor, the favorite of the King of the Sea.

In Kiev, to the father of aviation, Tugarin-Dragon.

Also in Kiev to old Vainamoinen, in memory of the union of the Russians and the Finns.

A monument to Rublev—to remind Russian art that its roots lie in the distant past.

In Kiev, to Nikita Kozhemiak.

In Moscow and in the Don region—to Platov, Baklanov, Orlov, Dezhnev, the Don Cossack commanders.

In Rostov-on-the-Don, "Glory to the Cossacks," a great iron column with a wreath.

To Vasily Shibanov in Moscow.

On the Volga at Samara (the gateway to Siberia), a monument to Yermak, the tallest monument in the world, like the Statue of Liberty in America, and standing in a boat [illegible] and a colossal statue with a smoking arquebus that glitters with fire.

In Moscow, to Boris and Gleb.

Also to Deshnev and Khabarov in Moscow, and to Afanasy Nikitin there too or in Astrakhan.

On the Volga at Samara, a colossal monument to Planet Earth.

To the Persian princess that Razin threw into the Volga, and to Razin, a sorrowful monument beside the influx of the Volga into the Caspian Sea. To win over the Persians' hearts.

A monument to the Slavophiles, in Moscow.

In Perm, a monument to Kuksha—a torch shining from the top of a mountain.

In the Caucasus, a monument to Prometheus in the form of a statue chained to Mount Kazbek.

In the Crimea, to Diana and Mithradates, and the maiden Iphigenia who was sacrificed there. And to the Roman commander who was sent there. And to Abraham who sacrificed Isaac.

In Kazan, a monument to Okhotin and Kurbsky.

In Pskov, to Ondyn-Nashchokin, prime pillar of the state.

In Samara, a monument to Adam and Eve shaped like a metal palm tree with a tall carved trunk and leaves and white marble statues of our first parents sitting under it, with a lion and a gazelle.

We have to ornament the Volga and the Don—it marks a frontier for the West.

A monument to Riabov in Moscow.

In Kiev, a monument to the Ukrainian hetman Doroshenko and

others. Let there be at least one among all the rest with a name that ends in *-enko*.

In Kholm, to Roman Galitsky.

In Kiev, to the Russian language in the form of an eagle sitting peacefully beside a nightingale, and beneath them a swan perched on a pedestal of marble carved in the shape of books by Pushkin and Leo Tolstoy.

Thus with beauty and distinction will we decorate and sanctify the Russian land and the Great Russian continent, linking and commemorating those who represent the Russian people.

[1912–13: GPB, f.1087, ed.xr.42, printed in E. Arenzon, "K ponimaniu Khlebnikova: nauka i poezia," *Voprosy literatury* 10 (1985), 187–190]

Roar about the Railroads

Roar! The railroads of Italy follow one fundamental law: the main line coincides with the seacoast, and therefore the shapely foot and leg of the peninsula is encased right now in a solid iron boot. Feature number two: railroad lines in the interior of the peninsula are very sparse. The main line never leaves the sound of the seashore, and the features of Italy are outlined in iron and steel. These coastal lines have brought a commercial flowering to Italy.

In Russia coastal lines are found only in partly non-Russian areas (the Caucasus, Finland), in view of the undoubted profitability of this arrangement.

Afraid of meeting the Volga face to face, the Volga line was never completed as far as the Caspian. The mouths of the Danube and the Don, if they were stitched together along the seacoast, would assure the flowering of the southland.

In northern Russia, the Pechera and the Ob, the Lena and the Yenisei, must be connected without delay; only then will there be any sense to the webs that surround the railroad spiders of Moscow and other cities.

Roar! The point of the North American railway "long way around" is that the steel track intertwines with the great river channels of that land and twists its way alongside them; also the proximity of the two ways is so great that the puffing iron horse can always lend a hand to the waterman, and train and riverboat for long stretches never pass from each other's sight.

East of the Vistula, the channels of the Volga and the Dneiper (their middle courses) might be joined by a single circle of railroad lines, like the tops of two trees. At present, in order to go to Saratov or Kazan, someone from Nizhni Novgorod has to go by way of Moscow. A direct line from the mouth of the Volga to the mouth of the Ob would make life easier on both sides of the Urals. Besides, swift, direct train lines would be a change from our present plodding ones. There is a danger that our railroad lines, like the unknown letters of an unknown language, may simply be spelling out, on familiar, well-known pages, the word "stupidity." Words with other meanings exist: "foresight," for instance, or "forethought."

[pub. 1913: NP 344]

A Friend in the West

Germany is still recognized by many as our friend. Friends have the right to offer advice, and recently such advice, based on good neighborly relations in the past, was hurled across the border, intended and understood as a steel gauntlet thrown in the face of Russian public opinion. It called upon the authorities of a friendly Slavic state to resort to the rhetoric of whips in reply to the Slavic exuberance of its people. And—remarkable coincidence—we hear an echo of this in part of a speech by Bethmann-Hollweg, where he emphasized good relations with the Russian government at the same time that he recognized the possibility and even the probability of a clash between the two worlds. Many people were concerned by this German advice because they recognized in it something they knew from the past, the duet between Biron and Volynsky, and they wondered whether such duets would be encored. In any case the advice was not exactly new, since in his preachments on Pan-Germanism the gray-haired Mommsen has spoken of "clubs" to be used on "thick Slavic skulls," in conjunction with the aggressive verbs "beat" and "smash." What was new was that the commandment "Take up your clubs and smash their thick Slavic skulls" was directed at the government of a nation whose non-German characteristics are beyond dispute.

Much has changed since then. The raven of Austria flaps above the pale head of Slavia, crying "Nevermore." The foreign West has become an anvil upon which the sword of war is being forged in a frenzy.

Nineteen years earlier than Russia, Teutonia celebrated the thousand-year anniversary of its existence with a holiday and a monument. During that period the nature of its friendship with the Slavic state emerged quite clearly. We see that the main occupation of our western neighbor during that thousand-year period has been the extermination of the northwestern Slavic states. Teutonic power, very much alive, stands upon a "city of the dead"—the ruins of Slavic states. Hedged within walls of stone, Wanda guards these walls from the weapon of superstition. The eastern slope of this power can be found in the German settlements in Volynia, and beyond, and the law of double citizenship. Following the example of the Zaporozhian cherry tree [*vishnii*] of Vishnevetsky, the persistent hand of the German gardener in his knit cap plants a tree in his turn, Pan Grushevsky's peartree [*grusha*], trying to graft a German bud onto a Slavic rootstock. But the first tree foiled the plans of the one who planted and watered it.

Our scientific and cultural positions are occupied by pilgrims between two walls. The non-Slav has a secret switch that forces Russia to behave according to his desires, moving from the Slavic to the non-Slavic world every time the Slavic mind desires the opposite. Once again the weight of Russia has been thrown onto the Teutonic side of the scale and inclined the decision of a question in Germany's favor—a weight evidently measured in fractions of an ounce. The string of self-preservation by its very nature resounds more strongly in the heart of the eastern Slavs and sounds a summons to awake and prepare for the mighty clash of the Cimbrians and Teutons promised by Bethmann-Hollweg and others.

Cimbrians—this is a nasal pronunciation of Kiabrians. The Kiaber is a tributary of the Danube. The Kiabry (under the name Kii), together with the Czechs (Shchek) and the Croats (Khoriv), founded Kiev. Cimbrians is thus an old name for Slavs. Who will predict the clash of Cimbrian and Teuton, and how? Even Hegel divided humanity into human beings and Slavs. Everyone knows the infamous remark that Slavs are not people, but dirt—a slogan of Mommsen, that pride of German science. On the other hand we have the struggle of Lomonosov, who was very fortunately protected from the lightning that struck his German comrade Riemann, the death of Skobelev, the warning of Križanić, Yermolov's request, the national movement in Volynia, which pan-German sentiment considers the gateway to the Black Sea, a region with a steadily shrinking Russian population. All these things are signs finally coming to light of a covert underground struggle that can no longer be avoided and must finally be talked about. In the spiritual realm, the saturation of the Russian sea with German salt continues, an insidious struggle with those who refuse to accept for their tribe the position of eternal students and apprentices.

Our friends prepare for war by studying the governing methods of Rome and the doctrine of alliances, thus creating for themselves a secular gospel they follow with the devotion of ascetics. Good students of Rome, they have divided the Slavs in terms of ethnicity and power, frightening some with the specter of revolt, others with the loss of freedom; by creating hostility between one and the other, they solicitously take power and give back something similar, almost the same, but with the same distinction that existed between the *pannenka* and the *vedmochka* in Gogol's *May Nights*, a distinction noted by the perceptive Levko. The white vision shone darkly and later turned itself into a raven. When rotten privilege and arrogation and elite groups come to an end, then there will begin only a century of the "tree of torment" and compulsory estrangement for the nation. The upper classes, whose eyes are finally beginning to open but who are dangling above an abyss, are powerless to help. All the Slavic neighbors of Teutonia have suffered the German disease, and that disease unfailingly ends in the downfall of a Slavic state.

In H. G. Wells's *War of the Worlds,* Germany's borders are imagined as stretching to the Pacific Ocean. But Russianness is only partly subject to the laws of Slavdom. Beginning with the time of the Tatar yoke, she has been part of the sphere of influence of other laws. The names Aksakov, Karamzin, Derzhavin, are all descended from Mongols, and it is this fact that makes them German-resistant. The fusion of Slavic and Tatar blood yields an alloy of some hardness. The Russians are more than mere Slavs. Besides, there are signs to indicate that the German century is ending and the Slavic century is beginning. More and more great men of the West have Slavic connections: Ostwald, Nietzsche, Bismarck. Both Nietzsche and Bismarck are notably non-German. One of them even said "Praise the Lord" on that account. With plantlike regularity, Germany has experienced two flowerings, one intellectual and one military, and is now undergoing an industrial one. In Germany today science is the handmaiden of the state. The calculations of Weyrother's German strategy could be upset by the intellectual flowering of the Slavs.

To the ring of European allies we might reply with a ring of Asian allies—a friendly alliance of Moslems, Chinese and Russians. Calls for a grand titanic clash make us think about the *Titanic,* which clashed with the ice and perished, and about Konstantin Leontiev's iceberg. Perhaps the North Sea is still full of icebergs. Perhaps that is why Konstantin Leontiev called for "the thawing of Russia."

[1913: *Slavianin* 3/35, 2–3]

"We want a word maiden"

We want a word maiden whose eyes set the snow on fire. She sweeps the floor with a broom of blue fieldflowers. She scatters pearls, and a flock of peacocks pecks at them. Oh blue-glinting, blue-eyed, blue-breasted peacocks!

We want literature to follow boldly after painting.

It would be totally senseless to engage in a literary war with people who mass-produce literature. They are traitors and must be picked out with a gloved hand; only then will the wheatfields of Russian literature be free of these spiders.

But, we are told, demands such as ours infringe upon the rights of art for art's sake. To that one could raise two objections:

1. Art is currently the prisoner of cruel influences inimical to Russia; the cruel and icy winds of hatred destroy its growth.

2. The freedom of the art of words has always been limited by certain truths, each of which is an inescapable aspect of life. These limits derive from one fact: the essence from which the art of words shapes its foundations is the soul of the people—and not the people in some abstract sense, but in a very precise one. Art always wants to be identified with a spiritual movement, wants to be able to call it forth. But each individual has only one name. For a child of a given land, no art can seem brilliant if it discredits that land. For a race of warriors, any art that presents the dreamy reminiscences of warriors in the form of a rejection of war would be a false art.

Andrei Biely pines in Pushkin's prison, the Pushkin he praises so highly, but already he begins to mourn the fact. By the waters of Babylon we sat down and wept. What does that prison consist of? It is a prison with its own peculiar design. Its first characteristic: it has two stories; the lower level is capricious rejection of the upper level, which glorifies non-Russians. That is how things stood until the moment the Russian people announced that they controlled the Russian word.

[1912: NP 334]

"We accuse the older generation"

We accuse the older generation of poisoning the cup of existence they now pass to the young.

The older generation, instead of carrying to the younger one a platter raised high above their heads, upon it a sheaf of beautiful flowers and a sharp sword (to serve as a warning to anyone who might try to snatch those flowers)—the older generation brings us a sheaf of thistles and says, "These are the best flowers fate has to offer," and among them, painstakingly concealed, lies a snake whose dark shining body is only occasionally apparent. Yes, this is the sense of life that Andreev, Artzybashev, Sologub, and the rest hold out to us: that we, on the threshold of life, are to drink the poisoned cup of existence and accept it with innocent eyes as wholesome drink, that we are to accept the young snake as a harmless detail, an elegant ribbon that ties up the sheaf of grass. Boborykin, the eternal presider at such affairs, hastily draws up a protocol describing the enigmatic occurrence, enigmatically bites his lip, and sends it off to *The Messenger of Europe*.

Here is our judgment against you. We will not punish you, we want no fines and penalties leveled against the defendants, but we distance ourselves from you supposed leaders of the young. We maintain that we are no longer the same as you. We have looked long and hard at that snake of yours.

Some of you are now beginning to eat carrion; others in the fullness of your "accursed questions" have become chambermaids. For this betrayal of one generation by the next you have invented a whole list of titles, such as "accursed questions," "convolutions of the brain," "progress." We are the Russia of tomorrow, and we say: No more! We've had enough, you depraved children, intellects, you men of other ages. We have drawn our sword to ward off the poison cup.

Youth is in revolt. We are its defense and leader against you old men. You are children because you have not lived, you have been nothing but reed instruments in unscrupulous mouths.

You have heeded the praise of unscrupulous mouths.

[1912: NP 335]

Poems by Thirteen Springs
(a little talk about beauty)

It is wonderful when, after a year of praising the new moon, fate takes her panpipe and puts it to the delicate lips of a child and compels her to summon up courage, to summon uncompromising warrior-benefactors.

We may examine here the essential nature of free verse. Let us consider "A Song to the Wind," octosyllabic lines—eight numbers, clothed in sound. Hear how the uneven syllables resound:

Now beneath your doleful wailing
I too feel my sorrows grow.

Observe the exactness of her contemplation. But in the next sixteen syllables

Wind, you enemy, desist—
I hate the angry way you blow.

the word "enemy" doesn't have two stresses, and this enchanting freedom from stressed syllables activates the shift from the persona of the first sixteen syllables to the persona of the second sixteen. The persona in the first sixteen syllables is severe, sorrowful, afflicted. The next sixteen are marked by an attitude of bright resourceful mockery and a certain exuberance of feeling toward the wind. The persona here is young and able to laugh. And so the abstract task of violations in metrical pattern is defined as follows: metrical patterns become the personae of the poem, each performing a different assignment upon the stage of the word.

Such violations are enchanting, they alone can raise the veil from lines dressed in identical meters, and only then do we recognize that these lines are not a single entity, but several, indeed a crowd, because we see different personae. And let us note that a rational, intentional compression, such as we find in the work of Valery Briusov and Andrei Biely, does not give their inventions the appearance of violations, and so their personae seem unnatural and contrived.

And so this meter is in fact a theater of meters, since the veil of meter is blown aside by the gusting wind, and a living persona looks out. A line of verse is the movement, or dance, of a figure who enters at some doors and exits at others. And so that a strict metrical pattern is merely a mute dance, while freedom from it (not contrived, but instinctive, involuntary) is in fact a language, a feeling conveyed by words. This is a characteristic shared by all makers of the poetry of the future.

> Silence, wind, be silent, silent,
> Think of me and pity me.

The line ends in a touching request.

The use of the expression "in beautiful kremlins" in reference to Roman women and Roman life demonstrates how for this young soul even the most exalted figures from foreign life are no more exalted than figures from Russian life, and her youthful spirit rushes despairingly upon the sword in an attempt to prove it.

And so, we conclude, here is a heart whose emotions outstrip her age. They understand that the "I" of the future is the "I" of today. Here is a description of those emotions:

> He forgot all the charms of night
> And saw a pair of dusky eyes

An extremely subtle brushstroke on the subtle clay of a childish soul.

> He squeezed her tender hand,
> Whispered words of love.
> Upon his leaning shoulder
> In trust she laid her head.
> Tenderly he took her hand
> And with it hushed his mouth.

There is a special beauty in the use of simple words to construct an image: the flower of a heart "has withered, / and death walks back and forth nearby." Simple and elegant. Almost an oath:

> I'll never ever
> Study French!
> I'll never open
> A German book!

Here is glory raised on the shield of a youthful wave. She has nothing to learn from any grown-up. And so that grown-ups might hesitate to give the poisoned cup of existence to children (the Russia of tomorrow) if this bitter determination might result:

> Sooner, sooner
> I would die!
> I'll never ever
> Study French!
> I'll never open
> A German book!

The following lines are beautiful because of the universal mystery that illuminates them, even their childish images that nevertheless touch the heart:

> And in a dark little coffin
> Like a warm little bed
> I will lie in fear,
> I will suffer in pain.
> . . . . . but my pain I'll forget
> As soon as I can
> Say the fatal words,
> And I say so again.

What's beautiful is beautiful, you'll say, ignoring the uneven writing of these lines. Here we can hear the cold rush of truth: patriotism is stronger than death. And that is a magnificent truth when it comes from the mouth of a child.

And so universal grief finds the path to a child's heart through French and German, through belittling the rights of Russians. Why not close off this entrance?

We believe that if this creative intelligence remains true to itself, whatever comes from its pen will be beautiful and melodious.

[January 1913: NP 338]

Expanding the Boundaries of Russian Literature

The terms "Russian" and "rich" are generally paired in characterizing Russian literature. A more focused study, however, reveals a richness of untapped possibilities and a certain narrowness in the way in which that literature is currently outlined and defined. It is possible to list areas that have concerned Russian literature little or not at all. For example, it has only rarely been influenced by Poland. It seems never to have taken a single step across the Austrian frontier. The astonishing life of Dubrovnik (Ragusa) with its ardent passions, with its great flowering, the Medo-Pucići, remains foreign to it. In the same way, Slavic Genoa and Venice remained outside its mainstream.

Rügen with its glowering divinities, the mysterious Pomeranians, and the Slavic Polabians who call the moon Leuna—these are at least touched on in the ballads of Alexei Tolstoy. Samko, the first leader of the Slavs, a contemporary of Mohammed and perhaps a northern glimmer of the same flash of heat lightning, is totally unknown in Russian literature. Vadim was more fortunate, thanks to the poems of Lermontov. Justinian/Upravda, as a Slav or even as a Russian (why not?) on the throne of the second Rome, remains also beyond the confines of the magic circle.

Neither Persian nor Mongol influence is acknowledged, although the Mongolo-Finns preceded the Russians in possession of their land. India remains out of bounds, a kind of sacred grove.

In the intervals between Riurik and Vladimir or Ivan the Terrible and Peter the Great, the Russian people seemed not to exist as far as Russian literature is concerned, and as a result today only a few chapters from the Russian bible have survived ("Vadim," "Ruslan and Ludmilla," "Boyarin Orsha," "Poltava").

Within the borders of Russia itself, the states along the Volga have been neglected—the ancient Bulgars, Kazan, the old routes to India, relations with the Arabs, the kingdom of Biarmia. The appanage system, except for Novgorod, Pskov, and the Cossack states, has remained outside the mainstream. No notice has ever been taken of the lower strata of Cossack gentry, formed by the very spirit of the land, similar to the samurai of Japan. As far as the borderlands are concerned, the Caucasus is celebrated, but not the Urals or Siberia with its Amur River and the most ancient legends of humanity's past (the Oroch tribe). The great turn of the fourteenth and fifteenth centuries, where the battles of Kulikovo, Kossovo, and Grünewald are all close to one another, is still unknown and awaits its Przewalski.

Russian literature is hardly aware that the Jews even exist. Nor is there any creation or achievement that might express the spirit of the land mass and the soul of the conquered aborigines, as in Longfellow's *Hiawatha*. Such a work might serve to convey the breath of life from the conquered to the conqueror. Sviatogor or Ilya Muromets.

The propensity of certain Russian nationalities to disaffection may be explained, perhaps, by this unnatural narrowness in the way Russian literature is defined. The creative mind of the land would be better if it derived from the entire land mass; it cannot be Great Russian alone.

[pub. 1913: T 593]

The Word as Such

In 1908 we were preparing materials for *A Jam for Judges I;* some of it wound up in that book, some of it in *The Impressionists' Studio.* In both books V. Khlebnikov, the Burliuks, S. Miasoedov, and others indicated a new path for art: the word was developed as itself alone.

Henceforth a work of art could consist of a *single word,* and simply by a skillful alteration of that word the fullness and expressivity of artistic form might be attained.

But this is an expressivity of another kind. The work of art was both perceived and criticized (at least they had some premonition of this) merely as a word.

A work of art is the art of the word.

From which it followed automatically that tendentiousness and literary pretensions of any kind were to be expelled from works of art.

Our approximation was the machine—impassive, passionate.

The Italians caught a whiff of these Russian ideas and began to copy from us like schoolboys, making imitation art.

They had absolutely no sense of verbal matters before 1912 (when their big collection came out), and none after.

But of course the Italians had started with tendentiousness. Like Pushkin's little devil, they sang their own praises and claimed responsibility for everything contemporary, when what was called for was not sermonizing about it but to leap onto the back of the contemporary age and ride off full speed, to offer it as the grand summation of all their work.

After all, a sermon that doesn't derive from the art itself is nothing but wood painted to look like metal. And who would trust a weapon like that? These Italians have turned out to be noisy self-promoters, but inarticulate pipsqueaks as artists.

They ask us about our ideal, about emotional content? We rule out both destructiveness and accomplishment, we are neither fanatics nor monks—all Talmuds are equally destructive for the word worker; he remains face to face, always and ultimately, with the word (itself) alone.

A. Kruchonykh

V. Khlebnikov

[1913: V.247]

The Letter as Such

No one argues any more about the word as such, they even agree with us. But their agreement does no good at all, because all those who are so busy talking after the fact about the word say nothing about the letter. They were all born blind!

The word is still not valued, the word is still merely tolerated.

Why don't they just go ahead and dress it up in gray prison clothes? You've seen the letters of their words—strung out in straight lines with shaved heads, resentful, each one just like all the others—gray, colorless—not letters at all, just stamped-out marks. And yet if you ask a write-wright, a real writer, he'll tell you that a word written in one particular handwriting or set in a particular typeface is totally distinct from the same word in different lettering.

You certainly wouldn't dress up all your lady friends in standard-issue overalls! Damn right you wouldn't, they'd spit in your face if you did. But not the word—the word can't say a thing. Because it is dead—martyred like Boris and Gleb. Your words are all born dead. You're worse than Sviatopolk the martyr-maker!

Two circumstances obtain:

1. Our mood alters our handwriting as we write.

2. Our handwriting, distinctively altered by our mood, conveys that mood to the reader independently of the words. We must therefore consider the question of written signs—visible, or simply palpable, that a blind man could touch. It's clearly not necessary that the author himself should be the one who writes a handwritten book; indeed, it would probably be better for him to entrust the task to an artist. But until today there have been no such books. The first ones have now been issued by the Futurians, for example: *Oldfashioned Love*, copied over for printing by Mikhail Larionov; *Blow-Up*, by Nikolai Kulbin and others; *A Duck's Nest*, by Olga Rozanova. About these books it is finally possible to say: every letter is letter perfect.

It's strange that neither Balmont nor Blok—to say nothing of those who would seem to be the most up to date of our contemporaries—has ever thought of giving his offspring to an artist instead of a typesetter.

When a piece is copied over, by someone else or even by the author himself, that person must reexperience himself during the act of recopying; otherwise the piece loses all the rightful magic that was conferred upon it by handwriting at the moment of its creation, in the "wild storm of inspiration."

V. Khlebnikov
A. Kruchonykh
[1913: V.248]

Polemical Remarks of 1913

I

You waves of filth and vice, you storms of spiritual abomination! You Chukovskys, Yablonovskys! Know that we steer by the stars, we have a firm hand on the helm, and our vessel does not fear your assaults and attacks.

The word pirate Chukovsky, waving Whitman's battle-ax, has leapt onto our decks during the storm, trying to seize the helm and capture the prizes of our struggle.

But can't you see his corpse already floating on the waves?

II

Patrolman Chukovsky yesterday proposed that we take a rest, curl up for a nap in a jail cell with Whitman and some -*cracy* or other. But Przewalski's proud horses snorted disdainfully and refused. The Scythian bridle—the one you see on the Chertomlyk vase—remained hanging in the air.

[1913: NP 343]

Futúrian

We rang for room service and the year 1913 answered: it gave Planet Earth a valiant new race of people, the heroic Futurians. The Fathers (Briusov, Baby Balmont, Merezhkovsky, Tolstoy, and the rest), with napkins draped over their arms, served as another Tsushima on a platter.

The youn-n-n-ger generation has smashed the dish; a casual kick sent it flying from the hands of the panicky waiter.

We rang for *fresh* meat! Hungry younglings. Wide-open mouths.

Then while we were *sinking* our honest teeth into new victuals— all the humors of the street gathered together and crowded around to try and spoil our dinner.

And this is the way *matters* stand for us at the moment. We can hear the bold barking of the lap dogs: Izmailov, Filosofov, Yasinsky, and the rest of the ringtails.

Proof, by the way, that man wants to be a quadruped: that's what you get when you put Merezhokovsky together with Filosofov, Balmont with Gorodetsky, Briusov with Ellis.

Now hear this: the future casts its shadow over language.

The essence of Briu-Bal-Merezh: they begged for mercy from the expected conqueror, they had visions of disaster from the East, and in advance they begged the bent-browed samurai, "Spare my life! Oh, have mercy on me among the poor flies of this world!"

Libra is a forward-looking, expedient surrender. Every line in it is afraid of strength and righteous anger, as one would expect of vice and lies. All the strong, robust words in the Russian language have been banished from the pages of *Libra*. Their *Libra* is a little lapdog, doing its tricks and waving its paws at the West, yelping to proclaim its complete innocence in front of the yellow wolfhound.

But every line we write breathes victory and challenge, the bad temper of a conqueror, underground explosions, howls. We are a volcano. We vomit forth black smoke.

The heavens open and out comes an imposing
Pile of garbage; it looks a lot like Leo Tolstoy.

Remember that, you people!

Pushkin is an effete tumbleweed, blown hither and thither and even yon by the winds of indulgence.

Tolstoy's first teacher was that ox who wouldn't resist the butcher, but followed him stupidly to the slaughterhouse.

But our burning eyes see Victory ahead, and we have broken ranks to forge knife blades to replace the flint arrowheads of the year 1914. In 1914 we had to take cover—in 1915 we take over!

Remember the bull of Aragon!

In 1914 we lured out into the arena a bull with a beautiful coat, in 1915 his knees began to buckle and he fell over right in the arena. And from the quivering bull mouth flows a river of saliva (praising the victor).

Meanwhile our own development proceeds along artistic lines, Byron's, for instance (we always use our elders as a model).

Screams of anger from the jurors—from the fifty-kopek-a-line men, the journalistic hawkers and hackmen (there's some justification; after all, they've all got families, and they can never catch up with the shadow of our moving locomotive). A hundred thousand of them from asylums and shelters, from maternity wards, all eating at our expense, and they eat better than usual. The doctors and lawyers hurl their angry thunderbolts.

And still we continue to grow.

We were not joking when we announced ourselves "He Whose Time Has Come," since in plain fact (1) we (2) have come.

All the Izmailovs and Yaskinskys have spilt the milk of their displeasure. Welcome this race of milch cows, they're a better breed than the Holmogorsky. Who are the milch cows? Izmailov, Filosofov, Yasinsky, and the rest, the hawkers and hackmen who "tickle" the readers' armpits. Bye-bye bulls.

The bullfighter raises his hat and disappears.

We have made it very clear that 20th century man is dragging around a thousand-year-old corpse (the past), doubled over like an ant trying to move a log. We alone have given man back his own true stature and tossed away the truss of the past (the Tolstoys, the Homers, the Pushkins).

For those who have died but are still wandering about, we have exclamation marks made of ashwood.

For us, all freedoms have combined to form one fundamental freedom: freedom from the dead, i.e., from all these gentlemen who have lived before us.

The realm of numbers has the signs ∞ and o: everything and nothing. For our enemies everything from Germany eastward was nothing, everything westward was everything. They never lived, they only drooled with envy at those who did live—over there. We have put these signs where they really belong and taught the ruling class (M. et Mme. Corpse) how to live.

Above the dark precipice of our ancestors, beneath looming masses of rock, the entire country picks its way on goat feet down the steep cliff face of the present; it steps surefootedly on ledges in the wall—allusions we have majestically let fall, our three-line Korans (for instance "Incantation by Laughter" and "We want to get close to the stars"), skipping from one foothold in the wall to the next, occasionally stopping to rest, elegant as a mountain goat. Eagles watch over its progress.

[1914: V.193]

On the Usefulness of Studying Fairy Tales

It often happens that a future period of maturity can be perceived in the unformed traits of youth.

A flower has a vague sense of its future glory even at the moment it thrusts a fragile stem through the carpet of last year's leaves. And in the adolescence and even childhood of the race, all people love to dream of themselves grown to manhood, when with a masterful hand they will be able to turn the great wheel of the stars. So in the fairy tale about the flying horse, the people predicted the railroad, and in the tale of the magic carpet they foretold the coming of Farman's plane that now skims the clouds. And on a winter's night an old grandfather will sit weaving an immemorial bast shoe and his tale carries his listener on a magic carpet, flying faster than summer lightning and shouting *stop!* to a falling star.

For centuries, for tens of centuries, the future smouldered in the world of fairy tales, and now suddenly it has become the present and we live in it. The visionary aspect of fairy tales serves as a blind man's cane for mankind.

In the same way the image of al-Masih al-Dajjal, of Saka-Vati-Galagalayam, and of Antichrist has been created by the wise men of different religions to convey the doctrine of a single race of mankind, the joining of all nations into the community of Planet Earth. And since we were able to apply our knowledge of the exact sciences to the problem of flight, and thus solve the mystery of the flying carpet, why can we not, through an application of the same sciences to social problems, invent a new flying carpet to solve the mystery of Saka-Vati-Galagalayam? For so the Hindu sages call him. Thanks to the flying carpet, the ocean-sea that all nations once reached out toward now stretches above every farmhouse, every hut. A great international highway in a straight line now unites every single point on the planet equally with every other point. The goal of the great maritime explorers has been attained.

And so it was that mankind as a seed dimly foresaw itself as a flower. The flying carpet transported people to fairy-tale worlds long before it soared into the darkening twilight sky above Russia in the shape of Farman's ponderous butterfly, borne aloft by the human imagination.

[1915: V.196]

three

LANGUAGE

In the essays included in this section, written between 1912 and 1916, we observe Khlebnikov's attempts to work out correspondences between the sounds of language and the spatial configurations of the letters that indicate them. Although he bases his investigations on the consonants of the Russian alphabet, his intention is to create an international system of communication, to provide humanity with "a single, universal, scientifically constructed language."

Khlebnikov attacks the linguistic assumption of the arbitrariness of the relation between sign and object. The evidence for his argument ranges from ingenious permutations of folk etymology to a theory of internal declension: assigning geometric meanings to the letters associated with Russian case-endings. He then investigates binary oppositions, studying the changes in the meanings of words when one sound is substituted for another. But typically Khlebnikov also drew wider analogies from such observations; letters were like the governments of Planet Earth, in constant collision with one another. If a shift in a consonant is all that distinguishes inventors *from* investors *or* explorers *from* exploiters, *we can conjure up the image of a struggle between N and S, between R and T. The movement of consonants becomes a metaphor for political and economic conflict.*

Khlebnikov's most fully developed language theory is worked out in a series of writings that begin in 1915 with "The warrior of the kingdom." Here he introduces an old Aristotelean idea: behind words there is "a silent language of concepts," which precedes their auditory aspect and does not vary from language to language. He analyzes words beginning with the same consonant to get at "simple names," phonemes or individual letters whose semantic meaning he identifies with generalized geometric concepts. The results allow him to move also in the opposite direction, creating new words and a new poetry from the simple names. Beyonsense becomes a poetic language full of meaning, aligned with the natural universe, and not merely emotionally intuitive non-sense syllables.

"Let us consider two words"

Let us consider two words: *lysina* [bald spot] and *lesina* [tree trunk]. Mountains lacking *les* [forest] are called *lysyi* [bald]; the exact area deprived of *les* is called *lysina* [bald spot]; any individual tree, a part of *les*, can be referred to as *lesina*. Should we not attribute an opposition in meaning to these two words distinguished only by a change of vowel, *y* to *e*? Can we consider that *l* and *s* contain a constant element of identity, while *y* and *e* are markers of disparity?

The meaning of the indivisible entity *l* manifests itself when we compare the words *l'nut'* [to lean toward] and *tianut'* [to attract], also the words *legkost'* [lightness] and *tiazhest'* [gravity], *techenie* [flow], and *tyn* [palisade]. *T* indicates an increased expenditure of force, *l* a decrease in that expenditure. *L* indicates that the distance between the comprehending mind and the object comprehended has decreased: the object leans toward or clings to [*l'net*] the individual. *T*, however, indicates a decrease in the distance between them produced by a force on the part of the comprehending agent: the individual attracts [*tianet*] the object. Whence the idea of *les* [forest] as an entity that grows, spreads, and increases in size by itself, in defiance of *tiazhest'* [gravity]. We may even express the same idea this way: *t* gives sound shape to the motion of one of two approaching points caused by a force exerted by the motionless point, while *l* is the motion of a point that derives from its own force.

This same difference can be seen in the voice distinction in verbs. We observe an opposition in meaning between *on bil* [he beat] and *on bit* [he was beaten]. In the word *bi* + *l* the actor embraces [*l'net*] the action of his own volition; in *bi* + *t* he attracts [*tianet*] the action. In the first case the action is directed from the actor toward the action through his own force; in the second a flow [*techenie*] from the individual toward the action is called forth by forces beyond his control. In the word *bit* [beaten] the actor himself does not begin the action but it is attracted by him [*tianetsia*]: it is the action that attaches itself to him [*l'net*]. The active voice, where the actor embraces [*l'net*] the action, is based on the letter *l* of *let* [lift, flight], while the passive voice, where the action flows down [*s-techenie*] to the actor, is based on the *t* of *tiazhest'* [gravity].

As soon as *les* [forest] falls within the sphere of action of *t*, it becomes *tes* [timber]. So *les*, which reaches for the sky and arbitrarily increases its distance from everything immobile, from the perceiving consciousness, independently of that consciousness, begins with the letter *l*. But the moment it becomes something dead and cannot alter that distance, which results in a loss of force on its own part, it becomes *tes*, material for roofs. So we can establish *l* as a marker for self-instigated motion toward an immobile point, and *t* as motion dependent on an external cause going from the point of origin toward an immobile point, and *t* also as a lessening of the distance from a moving point to a motionless point in the direction of the latter. And in fact a *tiazhelyi* [heavy] object *tianet* [drags] the hand down, while a *legkii* [light] object by contrast seems to embrace [*l'net*] the hand of the person who holds it and is experienced as something lying there, causing no expenditure of force.

Whence *likho* [unrestrained] and *tikho* [calm]: someone unrestrained is, as it were, a maximum point of self-willed behavior, of forces acting on their own initiative; someone calm is someone in whom such forces are absent, who does not strive [*l'net*] toward happiness, does not demand obedience of others but himself obeys, one who responds to external influences. And in fact *likhie* was a term once used to refer to highwaymen, bandits who did not stop at murder and robbery to attain their ends. Unrestrained [*likhie*] people are like spring torrents rushing wildly down a mountainside, while calm [*tikhie*] people are like drying ponds, open to every influence from without. *L'gota* and *l'zia* [privilege and permission] seem to define the contours of this turbulent state, the channel in which it flows, while *tucha* and *tusk* [cloud and tarnish] define the contours of an existence in decay, weakening, and dying.

Len' [laziness], *luch* [ray of light], *otlynivaiu* [I e-lude] are distinguished from *ten'* [shade, tenebrosity], *tucha* [cloud] and *tyn* [palisade] by the same opposition of *l* and *t*. In fact, just like *les* [forest], *luch* [ray of light] stands out in nature by virtue of following its own path into space; the word *len'* [laziness] contains the contradiction of its own force opposed to the notion of work; the same is true of *otlynovanie* [e-luding]. The letter *l* everywhere begins words describing self-initiating actions that cut through what surrounds them.

Just as words and songs are sung [*speto*], so the time when the forest [*les*] reaches up [*l'net*] to the skies is called summer [*leto*].

A ray of light [*luch*] moving past earth and forests, a bow [*luk*] that transfers its own movement to the arrow, languor [*len'*] and e-luding [*otlyvanie*]—the activation of forces that cut through the notion of duty, freedom from necessity—they all begin with the *l* of license. Similarly, a subjective treatment of known fact is called lying [*lganie*]. On the other hand, words that indicate the curtailment of privilege, of freedom and of rays begin with *t*. Take *tiazh* [drawing rod] and *lezhat'* [to lie down]: *tiazh* is the part of a machine that is acted upon by forces directed away from it, that the forces attract [*tianut*]. On the contrary, while we are asleep—during our lying-down time [*lezhka*]—all influences from the outside world diminish. If during the day's responsibilities a man is, in his various relationships, a *tiazh,* then nighttime is his leisure [*l'gotnoe*] time, and we may even say that when he lies down at night he belies the day.

In the adverb *tak* [thus] and the pronouns *tot* and *te* [that and those], feeling seems to surrender to superior knowledge; these expressions represent the personal principle yielding to the universal. Here the submissiveness of feelings to destiny is expressed through an attraction [*tiaga*] going from the feeling to the fact that fetters the feeling. On the contrary, in the particle *li* [whether], the feelings seem to burst into the realm of fact; this particle is the particle of doubt. But is doubt not in fact sedition, uprising, revolt against the universal principle?

In the words *tak* [thus] and *tot* [that], we find the iron immobility of heavy [*tiazhelye*] things; we feel the presence of fettered angles fixed so firmly to the ground that no tremor can shake them, while in the particle of doubt *li* we find the separation of the personal principle itself from the universal, a kind of upward flight on the wings of the wind. It would seem then that fact is the essence of the force of gravity. Freedom from this force is called *li,* while rootedness, submission to it, is expressed by the adverb *tak.*

This conjunction of cognitive forces and the forces of gravity is remarkable. It would seem that the principle we call language knows more about gravity than we do.

In distinction to other movements, water flows [*techet*] because it is drawn by lower-lying areas, obeying the force of gravity. On the contrary a bird flies [*letaet*] in opposition to that force; by tearing itself away from the earth, a bird in its flight casts doubt, as it were, on the force of gravity; its nature is contained in the particle *li* in opposition to the great force of the earth. A bird is the incarnation of the particle *li*, a doubt cast upon the force of gravity. By the same token, flowing water constantly murmurs "tak, tak," obedient to earth and in accord with the force of gravity. Such is the nature of flow. The flying bird is light [*legka*], the flowing element is heavy [*tiazhka*]. These examples convince us of the existence of an *l* of inherent motion and a *t* of dependent motion. The first goes to form the active voice (*bil* [he beat]), the second the passive (*bit* [beaten]).

This *l* in the sense of a striving upward begins two words: *les* [forest] and *lysyi, lysina* [bald, bald spot]. Signifying in part of their meanings either the existence or nonexistence of one and the same element, the two words are distinguished by the alternation of *e* and *y*. *E* marks the presence of longing toward height that defines the nature of a forest; *y*, the absence of that longing. If we understand *e* as the smallest phonetic carrier of the meaning *existence*, we can easily explain these two words if we interpret *ly* and *le* as markers for the genitive and dative cases respectively (by analogy with *ryby* [of a fish] and *rybe* [to a fish]): the action of the genitive case signifies the diminution or subtraction of that which is given—the dative case—by means of syllabic composition. Put that which is substantive together with a striving toward height, and you get a forest [*les*]; subtract it from a striving toward height, and the result is baldness [*lysina*].

We noted above that timber [*tes*] is a forest [*les*] that has been subjected to work by man, and that the words are of opposite derivation: consider *tysiacha* [thousand], such a degree of quantity that it is independent of any external influence. Or consider *ves* [weight] and *vys'* [height]: here the same alternation of the dative *e* and the genitive *y* yields partly opposed meanings. *Viazhu* [I knit], *viazkii* [sticky], *vesit'* [to weigh], *vezu* [I carry], *vit'* [to wind], in the sense of joining together two separate and independent entities, signify binding as a kind of spiral, ringlike process; *s* added to the dative case *ve* yields *ves* [weight], a substantive whose meaning is just such a joining (of things to the earth) and *s* added to the genitive case *vy* yields *vys'* [height], a phonetic form for the direction where this joining of things cannot possibly exist.

The fact is that a stone falls to the ground exactly as if it were attached by a line and will not fly up [*kverkhu*] and off into the distance, and *v* here is the representation of this weak, dissipating force, vanquished by forces that drag it down.

The fact is that *pykh* [puffed up] means pride, arrogance, someone for instance who kicks [*pinaet*] without apologizing.

Peshka [pawn] describes a nonentity and general obedience, someone who expects to be moved from all directions.

Someone who loiters [*meshkaet*] is someone whom everything passes by [*minuet*].

Mys' [mouse] signifies something quick.

Tech' [to flow] means to fall downward from above. But you fill [*nalit'*] something from the bottom upward.

A forest is that part of the visible natural world that leans [*l'net*] toward the sky, in opposition to the forces of gravity [*tiazhest'*] that operate downward.

Finally, note that the same dative *e* and genitive *y* proclaim their presence in *vydra* [otter] and *vedro* [pail]. The otter is a creature of water and comes out of it, shaking itself off. A pail is a receptable containing a volume of water. Water protects and fondles the otter; the pail protects water, holds it, carries it. One can feel some kind of intelligent force here streaming between the words and around them, like a particular instance of the force of gravity. Water [*voda*] is a receptacle for the otter [*vydra*], and a pail [*vedro*] is a receptacle for water—each drop of which is inseparable from all the rest.

Time [*vremia*] is what connects past and future; if I believe [*veruiu*] in something I am connected to it (*vera* [belief]; *vervie* [rope]). I bear [*beru*] a burden [*bremia*], a bundle of wood.

The same with gray [*seryi*] and damp [*syroi*], indicating the presence of water. A gray day is when clouds full of moisture obscure the sun. The dative case of the *s* principle indicates the destruction of the force of radiance and heat coming from without. The genitive case of the *s* principle refers to the dissipation of that force from within; the fact is that wet wood won't burn.

A way of studying the changes in the meanings of words that occur when you substitute one sound for another: consider *edu* [I ride] and *idu* [I walk]. It is the *d* that contains the meaning of separation, the moving away of units. Cf. *deru* [I tear up]. *E* marks the dative case, where moving is added to the notion of the individual, to me. *I* marks the genitive case where moving is subtracted from [*iz*] the notion of the individual. Consequently in the first instance moving is accomplished free of charge, at someone or something else's expense, without any expenditure of force on the part of the individual, while in the second it is somehow purchased by the individual at his own expense. Someone who rides [*edet*] takes no part in the work of moving. Someone who walks [*idet*] must work at getting himself there.

Notes jotted on first page of manuscript

L refers to those motions where the cause of motion is a moving point.

T is a cause of motion.

D is a reduction of distance as the self-generated action of a body in motion.

L is the reduction of distance as an action caused by the force of a motionless body.

The meaning of *lit'* [to pour] can be found in a comparison with *tech'* [to flow]: to move downward as a result of the force of gravity. A river flows in whatever direction the lay of the land requires, while man can pour water in whatever direction he likes. Hence *lug* [water meadow], *luzha* [pool].

[1912: NP 325, 459]

"Here is the way the syllable *so* is a field"

Here is the way the syllable *so* [with] is a field that encompasses *son* [sleep], *solntse* [sun], *sila* [strength], *solod* [malt], *slovo* [word], *sladkii* [sweet], *soi* [clan: Macedonian dial.], *sad* [garden], *selo* [settlement], *sol'* [salt], *slyt'* [to be reputed], *syn* [son].

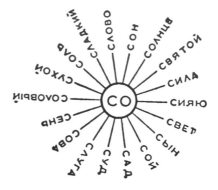

Although the refined tastes of our time distinguish what is *solenyi* [salty] from what is *sladkii* [sweet], back in the days when salt was as valuable as precious stones both salt and salted things were considered sweet; *solod* [malt] and *sol'* [salt] are as close linguistically as *golod* [hunger] and *gol'* [the destitute]. In terms of its sound structure *sol'* [salt] is the reverse of *sor* [litter, in the sense of an extraneous admixture]; consequently it contains the meaning of an intentional admixture, i.e., *posol'stvo* [embassy]. Between *posol* [ambassador] and *sol'* [salt], a substance beloved of animals and ancient man, there is a common ground: both are sent [*poslanyi*], strengthening the bond *so* between something sent (1) by a distant country and (2) as food, that is, between two objects that are unable on their own to come into contact. *Sol'* [salt] activates the taste buds and is called upon to arrange peace and agreement between the mouth and the taste of food. *Sukhoi* [dry] strengthens the bond *so* between parts and particles. Water dissolves, and the liquid mud it contains becomes, as it dries, *susha* [dry land]: the particles have entered into *so,* have become fixed together. *Sliva* [plum] or *sladkaia* [a sweet]. The meaning of *seti* [nets] is clear, as something that closes around the movement of a catch of fish, something that forms a bond *so* between the hunter and his quarry. The common blood of ancestors is *soi* [clan], that is, people of a common tribe are connected by common truth and customs and walk *so. Selo* [settlement] is a place where people are in *so* with the earth, a fixed axis of people, *sad* [garden] is the same thing for plants. *Slovo* [word] is in its own way a kind of *poslannik* [envoy] between people; *slyt'* [to be reputed] means to be sent [*poslanyi*] by word [*slovo*] of mouth; *slavit'* [to praise] means *sozdavat'* [to lay a foundation] for others; *slukh* [hearing] is the receptor of words, and *sluga* [servant] is one who carries out words.

If *sukhoi* [dry] is something drained of water, then *sudno* [vessel, boat] and *posudina* [crock] are things that prevent the flow of water, something water cannot penetrate.

If *griaz'* [mud] is a source of annoyance while traveling, and *kniaz'* [prince] is a source or wellspring of law (of awe), then *svaz'* [strut or brace] describes the environment proper to *sova* [owls or owlets], i.e., the slight, awkward movement of branches; people who are slow-moving and taciturn are sometimes referred to as owls. And we also note that *son* [sleep] is a state of immobility, of *so* with oneself, hence *sova* [owl] is also a *sonnoe* [sleepy] animal. *Solovyi* [sorrel] means heavy-eyed, ready for sleep.

[1912–13: NP 332]

"The ear of the philologist detects"

1. The ear of the philologist detects a family relationship between *pot* [sweat] and *poteiu* [I sweat] and *prakh* [ashes] and *porokh* [powder] or *porosha* [powder, new-fallen snow]. Whence it is not difficult to derive *khoroshii* [good] from *khotet'* [to want]: something good means something we desire.

2. I swear by the whiskers of Vesna [Spring]: you are curious.

3. Consider *o* which, in combination with consonants, yields the prepositions *po* [upon], *so* [with], *ko* [toward], *do* [up to], *vo* [in, into], and the conjunctions *bo* [for], *no* [but], and *to* [then]. It serves a useful purpose; by assuming that *o* here has a single meaning, we are able to examine the nature of these consonants, which are occasionally spelled, in the cases of *so*, *ko*, and *vo*, without the vowel. These parts of speech concern two objects, or, more precisely, they describe five possible relationships between two objects and their respective motions.

A connotation of height is contained, if only partly, in the preposition *po* [upon], and only this preposition can be used to characterize a situation that deals with relationships of relative height and depth. (*Polzat' po potolku mukha mozhet* [a fly can crawl upon the ceiling].) The other prepositions ignore this distinction. Both *po* [upon] and *vo* [into] contain a reference to the reciprocal dimensions of both objects. The indication of motion is an obligatory element of the prepositions *po* [upon], *ko* [toward], and *do* [up to].

So [with] indicates the mutual motion or rest of two objects while the distance between them, factually reduced to a minimum, does not fluctuate. Both objects are exterior to each other; one may be less than or equal to the other.

There is distance between the agents in *do* [up to] and *ko* [toward], none in *vo* [into] and *so* [with] and *po* [upon]. *Po* indicates (invariably) the motion of one body past another with a relatively large surface that remains at rest so that, despite the unilateral motion, the two objects of

274

different orders of magnitude find themselves in proximity. The path of motion is in the plane of this second object. So the direction of motion is more or less printed in the plane of the volume of the second, motionless object, merges with it in such a way that there is no distance between them. Motion is confined to the surface. The second object is larger than the first one.

Vo [into] indicates the enclosure of a smaller volume within the surface of a second. There is no indication of either rest or motion.

So [with] indicates the disappearance of distance between the objects' boundaries and indicates motion that is the same in both speed and direction. Equal dimensions are possible. In the case of shared motion the distance between objects does not fluctuate.

In *ko* [toward] and *do* [up to], one object moves while the other is motionless, and in such a way that the distance diminishes. We have seen that these five prepositions are the names of motions or of the non-existence or decrease of distance between two objects. *Ko* [toward] indicates that the motionless object serves as a terminus for the motion of the other, and as a stopping-point in the given direction. In *do* [up to] the motionless object determines the length of movement. In *do* the object is governed by the motion, while in *ko* the motion is governed by the object.

4. *Ukho* [ear] and *um* [mind]

   glukhoi [deaf] and *glum* [mockery]

   glu + *kh*

   glu + *m*

   kh + *olod* = *kholod* [cold]

   m + *olod* = *molod* [young]

5. *Pech'* [to bake] means to eliminate water in the form of steam by means of heat, to drive water out of a body to make it fit for consumption.

Pit' [to drink] means to add water to oneself, to pour it into oneself.

Zhech' [to burn] means to destroy by fire, to take away existence, life.

Par [steam] is the state of water that has been expelled by means of heat.

Zhar [heat] is radiation from fire.

Zhizn' [life] is the quotient of a number of acts and a quantity of time.

6. The word *saryn'* [riffraff, bullies] is like *sarych'* [buzzard, bird of prey]. "Saryn' na kichku" [bully-boys on deck] means a bird of prey is attacking someone's head, the way river pirates used to attack and board a vessel.

[1912–13: NP 330]

Teacher and Student

A Conversation (on words, cities, and nations)

Teacher: Well, well! So it's true what I hear—you've gotten some work done on your own?

Student: Yes, teacher. That's why I've missed a few of your lectures.

Teacher: What exactly have you been up to? Tell me all about it.

Student: You see, it's a well-known fact that words are declined—they have different endings depending on the case they're in—you have to excuse me, in front of all these bashful young people, if I use Russian examples, it's not a language we have that much regard for. Are you sure this isn't boring you?

Teacher: No, no, not at all. Please go on.

Student: However—have you ever heard of internal declension? Of case endings inside the word? If the genitive case in Russian answers the question *from where,* and the accusative and dative cases the questions *where* and *whither,* then internal declension of a stem according to these cases ought to impart opposite meanings to the resulting words. So words of the same family would have widely disparate meanings. I can prove it. For instance, *bobr* in Russian means beaver, a perfectly harmless rodent, while *babr* is a tiger, a terrifying beast of prey—but each represents a different case—accusative and genitive—of the common stem *bo;* the very structure of the words demonstrates that a beaver is something to be followed, hunted like game, while a tiger is something to be feared, since now a man may become the game and be hunted by the animal. Here a very simple element changes the meaning of a verbal structure by changing its case. The first word makes it apparent that the aggressive act is directed against the animal (accusative case—*bo*—action toward), while in the second word it is clear that the aggressive act proceeds from the animal (genitive case—*ba*—action whence).

Beg [running away] is the result of fear, while *bog* [God] is a being who inspires fear. Also the words *les* [forest] and *lysyi* [bald]—or two even more similar words, *lysina* [bald spot] and *lesina* [tree trunk], which indicate the absence and the presence of some sort of growth. You've heard the phrase Bald Mountain? Bald Mountain is what we call a mountain with no trees growing on its top, on its head, to be precise. So these two words result from a change made in the basic word *la* by means of its declension into the genitive case (*lysyi*) and the dative case (*les*). *Les* is the dative case, *lysyi* is the genitive. Here, as in other examples, the letters *e* and *y* prove the existence of two different cases for an identical stem. A place where the forest no longer grows is called a bald spot. Similarly, *byk* [bull] is an animal from whom we can expect a blow, while *bok* [side or flank] is the place such a blow is usually directed.

Teacher: Are you by any chance making a reference to my bald spot? That joke has gotten a little tired by now.

Student: Not at all! What do we call the period of time when *les* [forest], dead and immobile all winter, grows toward the sky? We call it *leto* [summer]. You see? You're too touchy, teacher. And perhaps I'm being arrogant.

Now suppose we take the pair of words *vol* [ox or bullock] and *val* [wave or billow]. The act of guiding is directed toward the tame bullock, which a man drives, and proceeds from the billow, which drives both man and his boat upon the water. Take two more words opposite in meaning, *ves* [weight] and *vys'* [height]: weight never proceeds naturally toward a height. These words contain the same two letters *y* and *e,* and that is what gives them different meanings. It is the same in the two verb forms *edu* [I ride] and *idu* [I walk]. These words begin with the dative and genitive cases respectively of the stem *ia* [I]: *e* marks the dative case and *i* marks the genitive. They signify that the action proceeds from me (genitive, action from where) when I go somewhere on foot, while the action is within me (dative, action to where) when I am transported by an external force.

Teacher: Aren't the simplest words in Russian to be found in the prepositions?

Student: Of course. And the simplest language perceived only the play of natural forces. Perhaps for the primitive mind these forces simply resounded in the language of consonants. Only the development of science has permitted us to discover the full wisdom of language—which is wise because it was itself a part of nature.

Teacher: Go back a bit—what exactly was it you were trying to say at the beginning of your little speech?

Student: Don't you see, I observed that the interior of a word is also subject to declension. When the silent stem is declined, it sometimes moves the meaning in different directions and yields words that are similar in sound but different in sense.

Teacher: And what other bright ideas have occurred to you?

Student: You really want to know? All right, then, listen: Consider the mysterious causes for the distribution of cities over the face or surface of the Earth. What other issue has been more complicated and entangled in imaginary happenstance and nonsense?

Teacher: Very highfalutin. But not particularly clever.

Student: Perhaps I mispoke myself. No one has yet introduced any general law and order into this intellectual desert. But observe: I now turn the light of observation upon it and provide a rule that allows us to discover the exact spot in any savage, uninhabited land where its capital city will someday spring up.

Teacher: It seems to me your major discovery is an ability to praise yourself in rather grand terms.

Student: Only incidentally. Anyway, what's wrong with doing for others what they are too careless or lazy to do for themselves? Besides, you can judge for yourself: I have discovered that cities spring up according to a law of specific distances from one another, forming the simplest of patterns, so that it is merely the simultaneous existence of several such patterns that creates an apparent confusion and obscurity. Take Kiev. Kiev was the capital of the ancient Russian state. Laid out on a path around Kiev we find: (1) Byzantium, (2) Sofia, (3) Vienna, (4) Petersburg, (5) Tsaritsyn. If we draw a line that connects these cities, then Kiev seems to be set in the center of a spider's web with identical rays to the four other capitals. The measure of distance that separates the center city from the cities on the circumference is quite remarkable: it is equal to the radius of the earth divided by 2π. And Vienna is the same distance from Paris as Paris is from Madrid.

Also, with this distance (suppose we call it the capital measure) the Slavic capitals form two rectangles. Thus the former or present capitals of Kiev—Petersburg–Warsaw–Sofia–Kiev form one equal-sided mesh, while Sofia–Warsaw–Christiania–Prague–Sofia form another Slavic mesh. The perimeters of these two great cells are closed. Thus did the Bulgarians, the Czechs, the Norwegians, and the Poles live and take their place of origin upon a rational pattern of two equal-sided oblique-angled cells with one common side. And at the basis of their existence, their way of life, their governments, there still lies a harmonious pattern. Not savage legends but planetary forces built those cities, raised up those palaces. Should we not therefore seek out new laws for their comprehension? Thus new capitals and cities spring up around an old one, in the arc of a circle with a ray $R/2\pi$, where R equals the radius of the earth. Such exactitude is worthy of the eye of Lobachevsky; it is not characteristic of human order. Supreme forces have called these cities into existence; they branch out to form a polygon of force vectors.

Teacher: And what else have you discovered?

Student: You see, I keep thinking about the action of the future on the past. But given the weight of ancient books that keeps pressing down on humanity, is it even possible to conceive such matters? No, mortal, cast your eyes peacefully downward! Whatever happened to the great destroyers of books? Their waves are as shaky a footing as the dry land of ignorance!

Teacher: Anything else?

Student: Anything else? Yes! You see, what I wanted was to read the writing traced by destiny on the scroll of human affairs.

Teacher: And what exactly is that supposed to mean?

Student: I wasn't concerned with the life of individuals; I wanted to be able to see the entire human race from a distance, like a ridge of clouds, like a distant mountain chain, and to find out if measure, order, and harmony were characteristics of the waves of its life.

Teacher: So what did you discover?

Student: I discovered one or two truths.

Teacher: And what are they?

Student: I was looking for a law that the destinies of all nations obeyed. And I hereby maintain that the number of years between the dates of the establishment of states are multiples of 413. That a period of 1383 years separates the downfalls of states, the destruction of their freedom. That a period of 951 years separates great campaigns repulsed by enemy forces. These are the significant points of my story.

Teacher: And these are indeed significant truths.

Student: That's not all. I have discovered that in general a time period Z separates similar events: $Z = (365 + 48y)x$, where y can have a positive or a negative value. Here are the values of Z that I employ:

$$\text{if } x = 1 \quad \text{and } y = -4 \quad \text{then } Z = 173$$
$$x = 1 \quad y = -1 \quad Z = 317$$
$$x = 1 \quad y = 0 \quad Z = 365$$
$$x = 1 \quad y = 1 \quad Z = 413$$
$$x = 1 \quad y = 2 \quad Z = 461$$
$$x = 3 \quad y = -1 \quad Z = 951$$
$$x = 3 \quad y = 2 \quad Z = 1383$$

A period of 951 years unites the great Islamic campaigns against Poitiers and Vienna, repulsed by the Frank Charles Martel and the Russian Jan Sobieski. These campaigns were in the years 732 and 1683 respectively. Also the terrible attacks of the Hunnic-Tatar hordes in the northwest, the attacks of Attila and Tamerlane, repulsed and met by Aetius and Bayezid occurred in 451 and in 1402, 951 years apart. Charles XII's campaign at Poltava in 1709 occurred 951 years after the unsuccessful sea invasion of China by the Arabs in 758.

It is evident, of course, that 951 is 317 × 3. 1588 was the year of the Armada of the Spaniard Medina-Sidonia against the shores of England. In 1905, the Rozhdestvensky campaign. Between them is a period of 317 years, or one-third of the period between the Mongol-Hun and the Turko-Arab defeats. 317 years before 1588, Louis IX suffered defeat on the shores of Tunis. Does this not show us that in 2222, 317 years after 1905, the ships of some nation will suffer defeat, perhaps near the black island of Madagascar?

Teacher: Wasn't the number 365 considered sacred in ancient Babylon?

Student: It was indeed.

Teacher: What other instances does your law apply to?

Student: Just a moment. I only want to point out first that if you take states belonging to Orthodox Christianity—Bulgaria, Serbia, Russia—and check to see how many years they existed before their first loss of freedom, you come up with a total number of years equal to the existence of Byzantium. Byzantium from 395 to 1453 = 1058 years; Russia from 862 to 1237 = 375; Bulgaria from 679 to 1018 = 339; Serbia from 1050 to 1389 = 339. 375 + 339 + 339 = 1053. This corresponds to the law of conservation of forces. States fall when the force of older states is exhausted. Moving backwards: Spain, from 412 to 711; France, 486–1421; England, 449–1066; the Vandals, 430–534; the Ostrogoths 493–555; the Lombards, 568–774. These existed for 299 + 935 + 617 + 104 + 62 + 206, that is, a total equal to the existence of Rome and Byzantium together.

Teacher: But you promised me a few more discoveries.

Student: If $y = -4$, then $Z = [365 - (48 \times 4)]_1 = 173$. What's remarkable is that 173×14 separates the fall of the kings in Rome in 510 B.C. and in China in 1912. But that's merely incidental.

If $y = 1$, then $Z = (365 + 48)_1 = 413$.

At intervals of 413 years, waves of unification crest among nations. In 827 Egbert united England. 413 years later, in 1240, the German cities united in the Hanseatic League, and 413 years later, in 1653, the endeavors of Khmelnitsky united Greater Russia and the Ukraine. What will happen in 2066, if this wave of unification continues unbroken?

In 1110 the Russians gathered in conference at Vitichev, and 413 years later, in 1523, the last district was incorporated. Russia: In 1380 the various Russian principalities joined together for the battle of Kulikovo, and 413 years later in 1793 came the annexation of Poland.

But as already noted, the time periods separating the origins of states are multiples of 413 years. Varying in extent from 413 to 4130 years, these time periods relate to one another like simple whole numbers 1, 2, 3 . . . 7, 8, 9, 10. The period of 1239 years that stretches from the origin of France in 486 to the origin of Rome in 753 B.C. is 413×3. Between the origin of France and that of Normandy in 899, 413 years passed. Between the origin of Rome in 753 and the origin of Egypt in 3643, there elapsed a period of 2891 years, or 413×7. The date of Egypt's origin is so certain that we find it in dictionaries (see Pavlenko's dictionary). France and Egypt are separated by 413×10 years. The origin of Austria in the year 976 is separated by 413×2 from the origin of the Gothic state in the year 150. 413 years separate Hellas, in the year 776, from the kingdom of the Bosphorus, in 363; Germany, in 843, from the Vandals, in 430; Russia, in 862, from England, in 449. Parker has chanced upon a chronicle which gives the year 2855 B.C. as the date of the founding of China, and we must point out that the year 2855 is separated from the origin of England by 3304 years, or 413×8 and from the founding of Russia by 3717 years, or 413×9.

In the case of nations that arose through revolt against an older power, the time Z that separates them is $[365 + (2 \times 48)]1 = 461$. This is the figure that separates two federated states, Switzerland and America. The first threw off the power of Austria in 1315, the second the power of England in 1776. In the same way Bulgaria freed itself from Byzantium in 679, and Portugal from Spain in 1140. Japan in 660, Korea in 1121. The founding of the Western Roman Empire in 800 is separated by 461 years from the founding of the Eastern Roman Empire in 1261. In 1591 Holland gained its freedom, so we may expect the revolt of a new outlying country in the year 2052.

Teacher: Aren't you really trying to establish an inventory of every event that's going to occur in the course of the next thousand years?

Student: My studies certainly do not exclude the possibility of foretelling the future. Destiny is clearly outlined in these numbers, just as perceptible as a body wrapped in a wet sheet.

Teacher: And do your rules have any other applications beyond these?

Student: They do indeed. If $y = 0$, then $Z = 365 + (48 \times 0) = 365$; if $x = 8$, then $Z = 2920$. That figure is the interval between the founding of Egypt in 3643 and the fall of Israel in 723, as well as the freeing of Egypt from the Hyksos in 1683 and the conquest of Russia by the Mongols in 1237, i.e., events of opposite significance. If Byzantium freed itself from Rome in 393, then the liberation of America occurred $[365 + (48 \times 2)]3 = 1383$ years later, in 1776.

Ah, Destiny! Have I not enfeebled your power over the race of mankind by cracking the secret code of laws by which you govern? What sort of cliff will I be chained to?

Teacher: A pointless bit of boasting. The figure 365 is clear; I recognize the quotient of the year divided by its days. But 48 is unfamiliar. How do you explain the presence of that number in earthly affairs? They would seem to have no connection whatsoever. And yet I must admit—your law does not strike me as hopelessly murky.

Student: Periods of planetary rotation ought to have had an effect on these forces—and we are the offspring of these forces.

Teacher: Very clever.

Student: I agree. The highest source of earth science itself offers an example of exactness. Earth science becomes a chapter of celestial science. But if $y = 2$ and $x = 3$, then $Z = [365 + (48 \times 2)]3 = 1383$. The downfalls of states occur at this interval.

Spain	711	Egypt	672
Russia	1237	Carthage	146
Babylon	587	Avars	796
Jerusalem	70	Byzantium	1453
Samaria	6	Serbia	1389
India	317	England	1066
Israel	723	Korea	660
Rome	476	India	1382
Huns	142	India	1384
Egypt	1517	Judea	134
Persia	226	Korea	1609

The subjugation of Novgorod and Viatka in 1479 and 1489 corresponds to the campaigns in Dacia in 96–106. The conquest of Egypt in 1250 corresponds to the fall of the kingdom of Pergamum in 133. The Polovtsians overran the Russian steppe in 1093, 1383 years after the fall of Samnium in 290. And in 534 the kingdom of the Vandals was subjugated. Should we not therefore expect some state to fall in 1917?

Teacher: You seem to have invented an entire new art form. How did you manage it?

Student: The bright stars of the southland aroused the Chaldean in me. On Midsummer's Eve I found my magic herb—the law of the fall of states. I understand the mind of the continent, so totally different from the mind of the island dweller. No proud son of Asia can ever be reconciled to the peninsular notions of a European.

Teacher: You talk like a child. What else have you dreamed up recently?

Student: I have come to think that Russian art serves either Morana or Vesna. Do you recognize the names of these Slavic goddesses? Look, here are the pages where I jotted down my thoughts as they occurred. Argument: (I) "Russian life is full of beauty"; (II) "Russian life is full of horror."

	I	II
Artsybashev		x
Merezhkovsky		x

	I	II
Andreev		x
Kuprin		x
Remizov (insect)		x
Sologub		x
Folksongs	x	

We see, consequently, that our writers unanimously confirm that Russian life is full of horror. But why do our folksongs disagree with them? Or do the folk who write books and the folk who sing songs belong to two different nations?

Our literature establishes the guilt of: (I) the nobility; (II) the military; (III) bureaucrats; (IV) businessmen; (V) peasants; (VI) young shoemakers; (VII) writers.

	I	II	III	IV	V	VI	VII
A. N. Tolstoy	x						
Kuprin		x					
Shchedrin			x				
Ostrovsky				x			
Bunin					x		
Remizov						x	
Folksongs							x

So folksongs establish that Russian writers are guilty of some crime or other. What crime? Lying? That they are all devious liars? Lately the writers have all started preaching sermons. What are they preaching about?

	Life	Death
Sologub (gravedigger)		x
Artsybashev		x
Andreev		x
Sergeev-Tsensky		x
Folksongs	x	

What concerns Russian writers? They curse:

	The Future	The Present	The Past
Briusov	x		
Andreev		x	
Artsybashev		x	
Merezhkovsky			x

Obviously then, if we ask what concerns a Russian writer, we must answer: Cursing! The past, the present, or the future!

The measure of things:

	Russia	Their latest novel	Everything except Ru⟨
For writers		x	x
For folksongs	x		

Is this not the source of their curses? Merezhkovsky plays the raven's role and prophesies Russia's failure—how does he feel?

"What is to be done?" is the question, and both the country singer and the Russian writer have an answer. But what sort of advice do they give?

	Life	Death
Artsybashev		x
Sologub		x
Andreev		x
Folksongs	x	

Science has made ample means of suicide available. Listen to the advice they give us: "Life isn't worth living." Then why don't the writers set us an example? It would be an entertaining spectacle: (I) those who glorify military exploits and war; (II) those who decry military exploits and see war as useless slaughter.

	I	II
A. N. Tolstoy		x
Merezhkovsky		x
Kuprin		x

	I	II
Andreev		x
Veresaev		x
Folksongs	x	

Why do Russian literature and Russian folksongs occupy separate camps? Is this conflict between Russian writers and Russian folksongs not the same as the conflict between Morana and Vesna? The disinterested folksinger praises Vesna, the Spring, and the Russian writer praises Morana, the goddess of Death. I don't want Russian art to walk at the head of a procession of suicides!

Teacher: What's that book open on your lap?

Student: Križanić. I love to talk with the dead.

[1912: T 584]

Two Individuals

A Conversation

First Individual: Kant set out to define the limits of the human intellect, but all he managed to do was to define the limits of the German intellect. A typical absentminded professor.

Second Individual: I sometimes dream of a great bonfire of books. Yellow sparks, white flames, and transparent ash—an ash so fine that the touch of a finger, a breath even, will cause it to crumble—though even then a few arrogant, boasting lines can still be read upon it. Then the whole mass sinks down and becomes a beautiful black flower, its heart still aglow from the fire, grown from a book written by human beings, just as the flowers of nature grow from the book of Earth—or from lizards' crests and other such fossils. And suppose then, by some chance, there remained on the petals of disintegrating pages a single word, "Kant"—why then someone familiar with Scots dialect could translate the word as "shoemaker." And there you have the entire legacy of our great thinker. He "raised himself a monument not made by human hands" representing the narrowmindedness of his nation. What do you think? Was he really a thinker?

First Individual: There's no need to question everything. He probably was, since so many wise heads and so many voices assure us of the fact. But now I'll open a book containing a different wisdom, although I suppose I shouldn't. But we do a great many things against our will, don't we? Do you recall the seven heavens the ancients wrote of? If we subtract 48 from 365 sequentially, until we reach 29 (29 days is the time it takes for the moon to revolve about the earth), we find we have created seven number-heavens: they surround the number of the moon and are contained within the number of the Earth. Here are the numbers: 29, 77, 125, 173, 221, 269, 317, 365. The first and last of these numbers are the number of days in a month and in a year, and they are no doubt holy. Now, why shouldn't events fly about beneath the firmament of

288

these numbers? Flitting, gamboling about—rather like young cherubs with wings and trumpets intent upon proclaiming their own will.

Second Individual: In our original example thought was treated as an idol; here it has become a toy, a plaything. That is equally dangerous. But are there not, beyond proverbs and the wisdom of everyday speech, grounds for believing that the heavens and the descendant of monkeys (in the opinion of the scholarly Brit) are somehow or other connected?

First Individual: Let me tell you something that happened to me. One time (it was in the autumn of 1912) I found myself deeply troubled, oppressed by something or other, some phenomenon of unknown origin, something undefined, but heavy and painful. This feeling of oppression came to me totally apart from any outside events. But around noon, for some reason I felt it depart, and in the course of the same evening I experienced a new sensation, like a flood of lightness. This increased rapidly until eight o'clock in the evening, like the flame in a vessel being filled with oil. There were no external reasons for it. But that day, I discovered to my great surprise, was the day of the summer solstice—I believe it was the 9th of June—and I thought I had found the reasons for the radical shift in my mood, which seemed otherwise unexplainable. In this case a change in the positions of two heavenly bodies (Earth and Sun) had affected more than just the weather and events; it had had a direct influence on the mood of one particular biped. It may well be that my sensitivity to planetary forces here played a special role—but my depression was definitely of planetary origin. Autumn would cure me of the scorching benefactions of summer.

Second Individual: These seven stages of the moon's ascent to Earth recall the seven heavens, and many other "sevens" as well. But in the names of numbers we recognize the ancient features of mankind. Isn't the number *sem* [seven] simply a truncated version of the word *sem'ia* [family]? In the names of numbers we can find traces of certain activities characteristic of the tribal life of primitive man suitable to a group with that particular number of members.

A group of five young savages and two full-grown men out hunting was denominated by the number seven [*sem*]; the number eight [*vosem*], formed by adding the prefix *vo* [into], indicated that a new entity had joined the group.

Primitive man needed no help from others while eating [*eda*], and the number one [*edinitsa*] correctly signifies precisely that activity. The teeth of that word crunch the shinbones of game, and the bones crack. This tells us that primitive man experienced hunger.

Sto [hundred] indicated a community governed by a *starik* [old man], a blue-eyed elder of the tribe (by analogy: if *ryba* [fish] yields *rybar'* [fisherman], then *sto* yields *starik*).

The number five [*piat'*] may be derived from *pinki* [kicks] via *ras-piat'*, *raspiniat'* [to crucify], and denotes the most scorned members of the family, whose lot in the harsh life of those times was only shouts and kicks; when the group traveled they had to hold on to the garments of their elders.

The single noun *sorok* [forty] was called into being to designate a particular kinship unit. Similar pairs of words exist: consider *toroki* [divine perception] and *tem'* [darkness] or *zorki*, *zorok* [keensighted] and *zemlia* [earth, eye]. As a noun, *sorok* signifies a union of families [*sem'ia*]. Each family is related by marriage to five other families of seven members each; thirty-five people plus five from the first family (I exclude the two elders) comes to forty. Numbers took on the names used to designate the activities of our ancestors in groups of that size.

First Individual: We must remember too that besides *vosem* [eight], we have another form, *osem;* the *v* was added for reasons of euphony.

What a wonderful description, Vintaniuk's comment about Napoleon: "healthy, with a dry face and a not inconsiderable potbelly." An immortal teacher of style. And Romanchenko, a perfect example of the notion: "I see a dark stormy sea and a solitary swimmer in it." I have made a thorough study of samples of self-sufficient language, and I have found the number five quite prevalent in it—as evident there as it is in the number of fingers on the hand. Take my little verse from *A Slap in the Face of Public Taste,* called "Krylyshkuia zolotopis'mom tonchai-shikh zhil" [Glitter-letter wing-winker]. In it, within the first three lines, without any intention on the part of the one who wrote this piece of silliness, the sounds *u, k, l,* and *r* are repeated five times each; *z,* by mistake, is repeated six times. But in the slogan "Bud'te grozny kak Ostranitsa, Platov i Baklanov, polno vam klaniatsa rozhe basurmanov" [Be big, be bold, be like Baklanov, or Platov, or Ostranitsa—stop bending over backwards before Moslem majesty], we no longer observe the same phenomenon. "I and E" (also included in *A Slap in the Face of Public Taste*) has a fivefold structure as well.

For some reason in this connection I also recall "To k svetu solntsa kupal'skogo / ia pel, udariv v struny, / to kak kon' Przheval'skogo / dro-bil peskov buruny" [Now I sang to the light of the midsummer sun, now like a Przewalski horse I broke through breakers of sand].

Second Individual: But do numbers explain anything?

First Individual: Yes. For instance, in A.D. 131 a temple to Jupiter was built on the site of Solomon's temple; 365 years later marked the conversion of Clovis and the Franks to Christianity, in the year 496. After a similar period of time, in 861, Bulgaria was converted; 365 years after the Hegira (622), Russia was converted (988). The conversion of Russia relates to the Moslem groundswell, the conversion of Bulgaria to the groundswell caused by the conversion of Clovis.

Three times 365 years after the conversion of Clovis, in 1589 (this date is off by two years), we have the establishment of the Patriarchy. And three times 365 years after the year 622 is 1717; and in 1721 the Synod was established.

We must also remember that the campaigns of Kublai Khan against Japan (1275) and Hideyoshi against Korea (1592) are exactly 317 years apart, and that a period of 461 years separates the founding of Japan (660 B.C.) and of Korea (1121 B.C.).

But there are many things we should be able to express better than we do.

[pub. 1913: V.183]

"The warrior of the kingdom"

The warrior of the kingdom of the future hereby demands respect and a serious consideration of his beliefs.

1. He is armed like a hunter of wild beasts, with a net to trap ideas and a harpoon to defend them. He is naked and powerful. Who are we? We will continue raging like new-begotten wasps, until you resemble us like two peas in a pod. Then we will disappear.

We are the mouthpiece of fate. We have come from the bowels of the Russian sea. We are warriors, and in our persons we initiate a new estate in the social order.

2. We say that there exists a conceptual framework at the heart of self-sufficient speech, like a hand with five fingers, that is constructed upon five rays of sound, vocalic or consonantal, and can be perceived through the word like the bones of someone's hand. That is the principle of five rays, the elegant five-pointed structure of speech. So "Krylyshkuia zolotopis'mom tonchaishikh zhil" [Glitter-letter wing-winker] from *A Slap in the Face of Public Taste* comprises an even number of lines, the first of which are built upon five occurrences each of the letters *k, l, r,* and *u* (the structure of honeycombs). "My, ne umiraiushchie, smotrim na vas, umiraiushchikh" [We who do not die stand watching you, who do] is built upon five repetitions of the letter *m*. Enough examples of the five-pointed, starfish structure of our speech.

3. We demand that the floodgates of Pushkin and the waterlocks of Tolstoy be thrown open, to let loose the floods and waterfalls of the Montenegrin current in the proud *Russian language*. Example: They ask you, "Kogovich?" [whose son are you?]. You answer, "Ia soia nebes" [I am of the race of heaven].

Once they smash the glass chains on their claws, the eagles will fly ominously over the gulf between us and Montenegro, there to master the scream of new achievements (in the young Ignatov's phrase). Despite the howls of so many throats, we say that the sea is one, whether there or here.

4. I summon you to behold the face of one who stands upon a hill, and whose name is He Whose Time Has Come.

5. We are insulted at the distortion of Russian verbs by imported meanings. We are indignant and we protest loudly—the whole process is torture for us.

6. We teach that the word controls the brain, the brain controls the hands, and the hands control kingdoms. Self-sufficient speech is the bridge to a self-sufficient kingdom.

7. We counsel you to be fishers for pearls in the Russian sea, divers after pearls in grotesque dark shells.

8. We remind you in passing that besides the language of words there is the silent language of concepts formed by mental units (the tissue of concepts that controls the language of words). Thus the words Italia, Taurida, Volynia (all of which mean "the land of the bulls"), which have separate verbal existences, are one and the same thing—a rational existence that casts its shadows upon the surface of verbal expressions and political entities.

9. We remind you that in the land called "Germany" *G/H* and *SH* are the initial sounds in the names of close to two dozen of the greatest writers and thinkers that nation has produced (Schiller, Schlegel, Schopenhauer, Schelling, Goethe, Heine, Heise, Hegel), we remind you of the belligerent *B* in Russian art and of *KH*, which protects freedom and pride of independence in its life, we reveal and affirm the special nature of the initial sound of a word, a sound-noun independent of the word's meaning that appropriates to itself the title of conductor of destiny. In the initial consonant we see the bearer of destiny and the path of forces that give it a fateful significance. This force sign is sometimes common to different name-nouns: Anglia and Albion, Iberia, Ispania. Like the threads of destiny, the initial sound accompanies these states from the cradle to their decline. Consequently, a word has a three-fold nature: it is sound, concept, and a path for fate.

Ruling families often share a common fate sign (a sonic frontal bone) with the country they rule, the initial sound of their shared nature. Germany: Hapsburgs, Hohenzollerns. This is no mere trick of coincidence. It is apparent in language when we think of "fate" in its double meaning, as destiny and as that-which-is-spoken (*fatum*). Like a stroke of destiny, *G* unites Germany and Greece, *R* unites Russia and Rome. The thread of fate twists its way (by means of the initial sound) through the sound leaves and concept roots of words, and consequently it has a tubiform shape.

There is no need for you to greet what we have been saying with superstitious horror. Comparative linguists may have fits? Let them.

10. We maintain that an understanding of tribal life is revealed in numerals, and that it is thus possible to reconstruct the contours of primitive life. The number seven [*sem'*] shows that in ancestral Russia a family [*sem'ia*] was composed of seven [*sem'*] members; both words are linguistically related. The word eight [*vosem'*] indicates the entrance of a new member into [*vo*] the family. Equally distinctive in this respect are ten [*desiat'*] and a hundred [*sto*] and the word forty [*sorok*].

11. We state that:

M [*m*] contains within it the disintegration of a whole into parts (a large entity into smaller ones).

Λ [*l*]—the uncontrolled movement of a great force of freedom (time past).

K [*k*]—the conversion of a force of movement into a force of enduring stasis (from rush to rest).

T [*t*]—the subordination of movement to a greater force, a goal.

C [*s*]—the assembly of parts into a whole (a return).

H [*n*]—the conversion of something ponderable into nothing.

Б [*b*]—growth into something greater, the greatest point of the force of motion.

П [*p*]—lightweight bodies, the filling of an empty space by a supposedly empty body.

P [*r*]—unruly movement, insubordinate to the whole.

B [*v*]—the penetration of a large body by a smaller one.

Ж [*zh*]—increase caused by excess of force (*obzhog* [burned], *zhech* [to burn up]).

3 [*z*]

Γ [*g*]—too little as a result of a situation of insufficient force, hunger.

i—unites
a—against
o—increases size
e—decline, decay
u—submissiveness

Thus a poem can be full of meaning from its vowels alone.

son [dream]—where nothingness penetrates a body.

nos [nose]—where a body penetrates nothingness.

kom [lump]—where a soft entity collects into a hard entity.

mok [wet]—where a hard entity becomes a soft entity (by means of water).

koty [fur slippers]—the movement of feet in shoe housings. Foot covering softens the impact of the feet, so *kot* [cat, the tame animal] means soft-footed.

toki [currents, also threshing-floor] movement [illegible] (water, threshing).

nora [burrow]—a winding hollow.

rot [mouth].

Notes from a notebook: The words *neliubimyi* [unloved] and *neliudimyi* [unsociable] reveal the relationship between love [*liubov'*] and people [*liudi*]. The connections between *sviatost'* [holiness] and *svet* [light] and between *grekh* [sin] and *goret'* [to burn], show that our ancestors distinguished *dusha* [in the sense of stifling heat] and *dusha* [in the sense of soul, spirit, something dear]. The word *teplyi* [hot] can have a pejorative meaning, *svetik* [dear, light of my life] an affectionate one.

[1913: V.187]

Oleg and Kazimir

A Conversation

Oleg: Except in cases of deformity, a hand has five fingers. Does it not therefore follow that self-sufficient language as well would have five rays to its sound structure, like the mane of Przewalski's horse?

Kazimir: Let's look and see.

Oleg: Here's a copy of *A Slap in the Face of Public Taste*. On page 8 we find:

> Krylyshkuia zolotopis'mom tonchaishikh zhil,
> kuznechik v kuzov puza ulozhil
> pribrezhnykh mnogo trav i ver.
> Pin'-pin' tararakhnul zinziver—
> o lebedivo—
> o ozari!

> [Glitter-letter wing-winker,
> Gossamer grasshopper
> Packs his belly-basket
> With water-meadow grass.
> Ping, ping, ping! throstle-whistle
> Sing-song.
> Swan-wing wonder!
> Nightlessness! Brightness!]

I ascertain the fact that this poem contains, from the beginning to the first full stop, five *k*'s, five *r*'s, five *l*'s, and five *u*'s. This is a law of free-flowing, self-sufficient speech. On page 52, "Shopot, ropot, negi ston" [Rustle, rumble, pleasure moan] is based on five *o*'s; on page 31, "My, ne umiraiushchie, smotrim na vas umiraiushchikh" [We who do not die stand watching you, who do] is based on five *m*'s. And there are lots of other examples. And so self-sufficient language has a five-rayed structure where sound arranges itself upon the framework of the concept, between its five points, just like a hand or a starfish (some kinds).

Kazimir: A word generally is a face with a hat pulled down over its eyes. The conceptual part precedes the verbal, auditory part. Which means that the words Beotia, Italia, Taurida, and Volynia are shadows cast upon sound by the concept "land of bulls."

Oleg: It's important to note that the sounds found throughout the extent of a word have unequal destinies and that the initial sound possesses a special nature, different from those that accompany it. Here are some examples of the way the initial sound persists while the rest shift: Anglia and Albion; Iberia and Ispania. *SH* and *G/H* occur regularly as the initial sounds in the names of German thinkers: Schiller, Schopenhauer, Schlegel, Goethe, Heine, Heise, Hegel, Hauptmann. In Russia revolt for the sake of revolt begins with *B*. Sometimes the name of a country and the name of its rulers begin with the same initial letter. Germany: Hohenzollerns and Hapsburgs; Russia: the Riuriks. Duality, the division of the ancient world into G and R (Greece and Rome) is matched in the new era by Russians and Germans. In this case the G–R opposition is older than the countries involved. And this is no mere trick of coincidence. "Fate" has the double meaning of destiny and that-which-is-spoken [*fatum*]. The initial sound in a word, unlike the subsequent ones, is a wire, a conductor for the current of destiny.

Kazimir: And it has a tubiform structure, and makes use of sound in order to overhear the future in the confusion of everyday speech.

Oleg: Yes, we may even say it is the spinal column of the word. The conceptual configuration of language is more ancient than the sound configuration; it does not change when language does, but repeats itself in subsequent locutions. For instance, *teplyi* [warm, hot] even today can have an abusive sense (*teplye liudi* [rogues]), while *svet, svetik* [light] has a loving, affable one (*svetik iasnyi* [light of my life]). And this, of course, is the ancient dichotomy between the principle of sin [*grekh*] from the word *gret'* [to give heat] and the principle of holiness [*sviatoe*] derived from the word *svet, svetit'* [light]. For the primitive mind, material forces were clearly apparent behind the moral order.

Kazimir: What a wonderful description, Vintaniuk's comment about the conqueror: "healthy, with a dry face and a not inconsiderable potbelly."

Oleg: Oh, he is an immortal teacher of style, a model of rhetoric, a centennial judge. That is the century's verdict. And Romanchenko is a teacher of the notion: "I see a dark stormy sea, hackles of lightning and a solitary swimmer." See how the letter *R*, just like the edge of a cloud lit up by destiny, accompanies one pair of nations from the cradle to the present day, while the letter *G* accompanies another. And so the nature of the initial sound is different from the others. The sound *A* stands consistently at the head of the names of the continents—Asia, Africa, America, Australia, although these names are derived from different languages. Perhaps in these words the *A* sound rises up and breaks through the contemporary surface, signifying dry land in some proto-language.

[1913–14: V.191]

On the Simple Names of Language

The names of Dalton, Planck, Weiss, and others remind us that every field of knowledge passes through an age marked by a law of multiple proportions. Philology has not yet attained this age, but now the light of numbers begins to fall upon it as well. Exact concepts will help us approach a solution to the problem of the simple names of language. A language has as many simple names as it has units in its alphabet—some 28 or 29 in all. In what follows, a few consonantal sounds (*m, v, s, k*) will be analyzed as simple names.

M

With *m* begin names signifying the very smallest members of several sets of things.

The plant world: *mokh* [moss] (a toy forest), *murava* [grass] (compared to a tree).

The insect world: *moshka* [midge], *mukha* [fly], *mol'* [clothes moth], *muravei* [ant] (cf. the size of beetles and birds), *motylek* [moth].

The animal world: *mys'* [squirrel], *mysh'* [mouse] (in relation to elephants, elks). Among fishes there is the little fish called *men'* [minnow].

The world of grains: *zerna maka* [poppy seed].

The world of fingers: the smallest, *mizinets* [the little finger].

The world of time: *mig* [instant]—the smallest time division—and *makh* [in a trice].

The world of words about words: *molvit'* [to utter] (to say something once).

In the set of abstract quantities: *malyi* [small], *makhon'kii* [wee], *men'shii* [least] (from the word *men'*), *melochi* [trivia], *melkii* [petty].

In these 19 words that begin with *m*, we see the shifting play of one and the same concept—the quantitatively smallest member of a given category. Any further diminuition would mean loss of the distinctive features of its category.

1. Words from the set of ages (of time): *maliutka* [baby], *mladenets* [infant], *molod'* [young people], *mal'ki* [young boy], *mal'chik* [boy]—all related, even apart from the basic name.

2. Further, *m* begins the names of things that divide other things into pieces: *molot* [hammer], *motyga* [hoe], *mel'nitsa* [mill], *mol* [pier], *molniia* [lightning], *mech* [sword], *molotilka* [threshing machine], *mlin* [mill: dial.], *mel'* [shoal], *mysh'* [mouse], and *mol'* [moth] (that destroys clothes), *mot* [spendthrift] (one who divides his substance), *mys* [promontory], land dividing the space of a gulf, *mezha* [boundary line], dividing a field, *mol* [pier], a structure dividing the sea, *most* [bridge], dividing a river. From the category of abstract concepts: *mera* [measure] dividing things into a certain number of equal parts, *mena* [exchange] (cf. the verb *razmeniat'* [to change]), turning a whole into parts. In division, the divisor is responsible for this process.

3. In the sciences the concept "posterity" is close to the concept "division."

The following words begin with *m*: *mogu* [I can], *moguchii* [powerful], *muzh* [husband], *molodoi* [young], *moshchnyi* [mighty], *moloko* [milk] (infant's food), *molodye* [young], *molod'* [young people], *med* [honey]—these are words of reproduction, fractions, families, and self-division into parts in time (ancestors into descendants). Here we have, beginning with *m*, both the numerator and the denominator of a fraction, whose basis is division.

The stem *-met* (*pomet* [litter] and *namet* [catch]) belongs to this category. Also *medlennyi* [slow] is implied by *khmelnyi* [tipsy].

4. Words indicating objects consisting of a very large number of parts or particles. The corresponding element in division is the quotient. *Musor* [rubbish], *muka* [flour], *maz'* [grease], *-mada(po)* [pomade], *-melo(po)* [mo-p], *mel* [chalk], *mekh* [fur], *mak* [poppy seed]; the abstract notion "a large quantity." Flour and chalk consist of an almost infinite number of particles. Also *maslo* [oil], *omut* [whirlpool], *mut'* [lees], *smuty* [disturbances].

5. Abstract concepts: *molitva* [prayer]—the act of entreaty, to break up the anger of another or the forces of nature; *miagkii* [soft] means easily dividable or separable; (*miakish* [the soft inside of a loaf]), *mylo* [soap] is an instrument for easily separating one thing from another

(division into two). The edge of *mol* [a pier] is the splitting edge of the land; *moika* [washer] is a separator.

Myslit' [to think], *pomnit'* [to recall], *pominki* [wake], *pomin* [prayers for the dead]. Our memory of the deceased is his ultimate division, his final part, still present among those taking part in his memorial service: a thought about the deceased is an atom of his life; *m, i, n,* all belong to section 1 of the *m* words. The root *mnit'* proves that the image of memory is the smallest particle of a life.

Mir [peace] means a limit or end to division by the sword; *mor* [slaughter] means unlimited division, hence annihilation. $1/\infty = o$; *r* has the inherent meaning of the destruction of boundaries; *o* preserves the meaning of *r*, while *i* changes it to its opposite.

The first meaning of the word *my* [we] is a party undergoing attack, being divided; *vy* [you] is the attacking party, the intruder.

If we reduce the content of the *m* word to a single image, then the concept will be an act of division. Sometimes *m* occurs as the prefix *mo-* in the sense of small, insignificant (*mo-rosit'* [to drizzle]).

V

The *v* name expresses an act of subtraction. *V* begins the names of animals that meant danger in the rural life of our ancestors: *volk* [wolf], *vepr'* [boar], *voron* [raven], *vorobei* [sparrow], *vor* [thief], *voina* [war], *voisko* [soldiery], *vozhd'* [commander], *von* [get out!], *vynut'* [to drag out], *vragi* [enemies]; in the realm of private life, *vrun* [liar], *vroz'* [separated, in the sense of breaking faith], *vinovatye* [guilty ones]. Whatever was protected from the first or the second of these categories (the minuend) begins with the *v* name as well: *ovoshchi* [vegetables], *ovin* [barn], *ovny* [rams], *oves* [oats], *voly* [oxen], were protected from the first category; *vladenie* [property], *vlast'* [authority], *volia* [will], *velichie* [greatness], from the second. In the area of human customs: *vera* [religion] (a means of protecting oneself from *vragi* [enemies]), *vorota* [gate], *vino* [wine].

K

K begins either words that deal with death: *kolot'* [to stab], *(po)-koinik* [deceased], *koika* [hospital bed], *konets* [end], *kukla* [doll] (lifeless as a doll); or else words designating lack of freedom: *kovat'* [to chain], *kuznia* [forge], *kliuch* [key], *kol* [stake], *kol'tsa* [rings], *koren'* [root], *zakon* [law], *kniaz'* [prince], *krug* [circle]; or immobile objects: *kost'* [bone], *klad'* [stack], *koloda* [well], *kol* [stake], *kamen'* [stone], *kot* [cat] (who is accustomed to one place).

Zakon [law] and its *kniga* [book] bring peace to a country, as does *kniaz'* [prince], the source of law and order.

Kon' [horse] brings peace to a horseman; *kel'ia* [cell] brings peace to a monk; *konets* [end] of the workday brings peace to a worker. The particles in *kamen'* [stone] are immobile. Absence of motion is the content of the *k* name; it is rather close to the operation of addition.

A border that limits an area gives it beauty, *krov'* [blood] (beneath the skin); *krysa* [rat], (an animal that hides [*kroiushcheesia*]).

S

The operation of multiplication is characteristic of *s*. It begins the most powerful bodies: *slon* [elephant], *solntse* [sun], *som* [large catfish], *sam* [boss], *sila* [strength], *sobranie* [assembly], *soi* [tribe], *selo* [village], *sem'ia* [family], *stado* [herd], *stanitsa* [flock], *staia* [pack], *sto* [hundred], *sad* [garden] (a unification of things).

Multiples (unifiers): *soiuz* [union], *sol'* [salt], *sladost'* [sweetening], *sud* [court], *(po)sol* [envoy], *slava* [fame], *slovo* [word], *slukh* [hearing], *semia* [seed], *syn* [son], *son* [sleep]. The axis of unification of a tribe: *sud* [court], *starets* [elder], *sivii* [graying], *sizii* [dove-gray], *sedoi* [gray], *sam* [male]. *Soi* [tribe] and *sivii* [graybeard] (the source of the tribe) are related in the same way as *boi* [battle] and *ubivets* [killer] and *biven'* [tusk]. If *ded* [grandfather] is someone who in time past was *dei* [doer], and now represents the working principle in retirement (*daiu* [I give], *dadeno* [given]), then *sedoi* [gray] is related to *sei* [sow] (*seiatel'* [sower], *sem'ianin* [family man, in retirement]). Spring occurs before things multiply, *osen'* [autumn] afterwards. Thanks to *slava* [fame], *slovo* [word] and *slukhi* [sounds], a preconceived image can be made accessible to a multitude of people (multiplication), may be repeated among them, and thanks to *slava* [fame] the number of viewers of any phenomenon increases infinitely. *Osen'* [autumn] and *osel* [ass], by the way, are related in the same way as *vesna* [spring] and *veselyi* [jolly]; *osel* [ass] is *oslukh* [unhearing], *neposlushnyi* [disobedient]; *vecher* [evening] is the gateway to darkness (blackness); *veselyi* [jolly] is like *soglasnyi* [in agreement], *poslushnyi* [obedient]; *vesna* [spring] opens the gateway to something and *osen'* [autumn] brings it to a close. *Tyn* [palisade] and *temia* [crown] (of the head) are related like *syn* [son] and *semena* [seeds]. In our opinion, the *s* name hides an abstract image of the act of multiplication.

[1915: V.203]

Z and Its Environs

(from a projected book *On the Simple Names of Language*)

Let us suppose that *z* means the equality of the angle of a falling ray to the angle of a reflected ray AOV/SOD. In that case *z* should begin words referring to: (1) all kinds of reflecting surfaces; (2) all kinds of reflected rays.

Kinds of reflectors: *zerkalo* [mirror], *zrenie* [vision].

Names for eyes, as reflecting structures: *zen'* [eye: dial.], *zrachok* [pupil of the eye], *zrak* [the look of something], *zini* [eyes], *zirki* [stars], *zrit'* [to behold], *zetit'* [to stare at], *zor* [dawn], *zeritsa* [pupil of the eye], *zorlivets* [far-seer], *zenki* [eyes], *zorok* [sharpsighted].

Names for universal reflectors: *zeml'ia* [earth], *zvezdy* [stars]; *ziry*, another word for stars, *zen'*, another word for Earth. The ancient exclamation "zirin" may possibly have meant "to the stars." The Earth and the stars all shine by reflected light. The word *zen'*, which means both Earth and eye, and the word *ziry*, which means both star and eye, demonstrate that both Earth and stars are understood to be universal reflectors. The season of the year when Earth reflects the greatest amount of the sun's light, when it most perfectly fulfills the function of a mirror, bears the name *zima* [winter] (*zimnyi kholod* [winter cold]). The Earth as a universal mirror in which the sun sees itself reflected. More words: *zyrit'* means to look; *zekholnik* is the pupil of the eye; *zekhlo, zekhol'nitsa* is a window, the eye of a building; *zarit'sia* [to look longingly at], *zetit'* [to stare at]. But we emphasize that *zen'* is a general word for both Earth and eye, while *ziry* is a general word for both star and eye. *Ziny* are eyes (a beautiful word).

Reflected rays: *zaria* [dawn], *zori* [daybreak], *zarevo* [glow], *zarnitsa* [heat lightning], *zolok* [dawn: dial.] (*zaria* means generally the reflection of the sun, of a fire, or of lightning), *zarevnitsy* [threshing fires]. The reflection of a storm at sea is *zyb'* [swell], *zybun* [bog] is wetland where every step causes a wave, a reflection that mirrors the step. *Zoi* [echo] is a reflection of sound. *Zolok* is another name for dawn. *Znoi* [scorching heat] is heat radiating from stones or reflected by a wall. The shiniest substance is *zoloto* [gold] (*zerkal'nyi zem* [earth-that-mirrors]). The call of the cuckoo consists of two syllables: the second of them is a muffled reflection of the first, whence other names for the cuckoo: *zegzitsa, zozulia. Zvon* [bell], *zyk* [loud cry], *zuk* [a cry or sound, dial.], *zvuk* [sound]—these are a series of acoustic reflections. Compare *zychny golos* [loud voice], one able to echo back from mountains or walls. *Oznob* [chill], and *ziabnut'* [to shiver] are a mirror of the cold. *Zybka* [cradle] rocks reflectively for a long time; *zud* [itch] refers to reflected sensation. *Zmeia* [snake] moves by reflecting the waves of its own body. *Zoloto* [gold] is *zerkal'naia glina* [earth-or-clay-that-mirrors].

In wintertime the earth reflects rays, and so that season of the year is called *zima* [winter]. In summer it swallows them up. But where do they go, these rays of summer? They too become reflected, in complicated ways, and these types of summer reflections, rays reflected by the universal mirror, also begin with z. Here are the types of reflection we mean: (1) direct reflection—*znoi* [scorching heat]; (2) indirect reflection—*zelen'* [vegetation, green plants], *zerno* [seed], *zel'e* [vegetation, herbs; archaic, gunpowder], *zetka* [rye], *zlak* [cereal grains]. These are annual collectors and reflectors of the sun's rays; they grow green in the summer and die in winter. *Proziabat'* [to vegetate] means to grow.

It is a known fact that the green matter of plants is a complicated mechanism that gathers the scattered rays of the sun into fascicules of little suns (carbohydrates and such). Whence both *zel'e* (in its archaic meaning as gunpowder) and *zelen'* [green plants] must be understood as suns constructed anew from scattered rays of light, and *zelen'* [greens] and *zerna* [seeds] as depositories of solar rays; the sun itself is a great wholesale warehouse, with each green leaf one of its subdivisions. The significance of green-hued substances has been made clear by the work of Timiriazev. The astonishing thing is that language knew about Timiriazev's discoveries before Timiriazev.

Zem [earth] is the eternal reflector upon which people live. If *zen'* means eye, then *zem* is the majestic *zen'* of the nighttime sky: compare *ten'* [shadow] and *tem'* [darkness]. The other reflecting points of the black night sky are *ziry* and *zvezdy* [stars].

The essence of reflection is this: by means of a mirror a fascicule of rays is formed that corresponds exactly to the original. The result is a pair, two nexuses of a given unit, separated by emptiness. Whence the relationship of *ziianiia* [yawning] and *zerkalo* [mirror]: a candle yawns, and so does its reflection in the mirror. The earth yawns when an earthquake splits it in two.

[1915: NP 346]

Analyzing the Word

Together we walked, my teacher and I, back and forth in deserted rooms where the chalky figures of gods glimmered in the white dawn of time, bending over us their frowning awesome faces, their long twisting curls.

And he said: See, I draw on the blackboard *lasty* [flippers] of a wailing seal, *lapa* [webbed foot] of a goose; or I draw a man in a great wide *lad'ia* [longboat] or *lodka* [little boat]—and he sails; a man on *lyzha* [skis] and he moves; *lopata* [shovel], *liamka* [towrope] of a barge hauler, *lepestok* [petal] of a waterlily, *latka* [patch], *list* [leaf] of a birch-tree, *lopukh* [burdock], *lopast'* [vane] of a propeller, the plane of *letchik* [pilot], the wing of *letun'ia* [flyer], *lapot'* [bast shoe], *ladon'* [palm] of the hand, *laty* [armor], *lyky* [bast bark], *led* [ice], *loshad'* [horse]—and everywhere I observe, even in *livna* [downpour] and *luzha* [pond], that *l* is the initial letter of those names where the force of gravity, proceeding along a certain axis, spreads out over a surface that transects that axis.

We are dealing here with broad surfaces that form media of support for sailing and flying, and for moving on land (on skis) and light [*legkie*] bodies. For this reason *l* indicates the conversion of the motion of points from movement along a given straight line to movement over a surface that lies transverse to the straight line. For example, a drop of rain falls, then becomes part of a pond. And the pond is a liquid, plate-like body that lies transverse to the path of the raindrop. *Lug* [meadow] and *log* [gully] are places where ponds form. The plane of *lapy* [paws], *lyzhy* [skis], and *lodka* [boat] is transverse to the direction of a man's weight. The striving of a body (even a stream of water) to become two-dimensional, the expansion of two dimensions of a body at the expense of the third—such is the essence of the letter *l*. In this case the axis of the diminishing third dimension corresponds to the axis of the falling force: *l* means increase of length and breadth at the expense of height, the transformation of a three-dimensional body into a two-dimensional one, into area. Of course while the drops are actually falling, one dimension governs them. Would it not therefore be better to define *l* as the conversion of points from one-dimensional to two-dimensional bodies caused by a cessation of motion, that is as the point of conversion, the point of contact between a one-dimensional and a two-dimensional world? Isn't this where the word *liubit'* [to love] comes from? For this is what happens in love: the consciousness of one human being is falling along a single dimension; the world is one-dimensional. Then a second consciousness appears, and a two-dimensional world with two people in it is created lying transverse to the first one, just as the plane of a pond lies transverse to the falling rain.

Les [forest] is covered with *listva* [foliage].

And here is the deep meaning of the word *liudi* [people]: the path of one human being must be directed at a right angle to the largest possible area of another human being, and once it penetrates, like a spear through a suit of armor, must communicate the force of its blow to the entire progress of the second being.

I have already provided a dictionary of *l* words, but there are many more. During *lov* [fishing expedition] the fish rush headlong into the transverse plane of the net. Or take the word *lebed'* [swan]: its neck resembles water poured from a pitcher, and its wings resemble the waves caused by the falling water. And so it is called *lebed'*. (A swan is something poured out, a vision of the pouring rain.)

Now consider animals with spreading antlers: *los'* [elk], *lan'* [deer], *zhuk-lukan* [staghorn beetle]. *Led* [ice] floats like a boat, wider than the same weight of water. Now let us consider *luk* [bow]: the straight arrow transmits the bow's force to the transverse line of the bowstring, and the bowstring returns it. The pressure of the arrow is entirely similar to the pressure of a raindrop upon the transverse line of the pond. And does not a falling ray of sunshine behave in the same way?

Los' [elk] with his antlers like *lopasti* [blades], and *lan'* [deer]; *ladon'* [palm], the hand's *lopast'* [blade]; broadened water is *led* [ice]; the horse strikes *laty* [armor]; *lob* [forehead] is a broad spreading bone; *latat'* [to patch]; *lepeshka* [wafer] is a flat object; *lepen'* [a cutting], *lad'ia* [shallop], *lodka* [boat], *loskut* [rags and patches], *letaiushchaia latukha* [paper kite in flight], *lubok* [popular woodcut], *lozhka* [spoon], the state of *lezhanie* [lying down], when the whole body stretches out over the broadest possible area, permitting the legs and feet to rest, *lishai* [lichen], *lemekh* [plowshare], *liazhku* [thigh], *lokhta* [bat], a broad stick of wood—all these words are stars in the *l* sky and fall toward a single point.

Here is the force condition: a falling point transmits its motion to a line intersecting the path of the point at a right angle; a point whose trajectory sets in motion the line that intercepts it at right angles. If a capital T turns upside down, it will be called *L*.

Take the military formation called *lava* [cavalry charge]: this is a formation where the movement of a cavalry detachment evolves into an extended line that attempts to broaden itself to the limit in a direction transverse to the path of the attack.

From this we may imagine that in love, as is partly apparent from the words *liuli* [word from a wedding song, also a cradle word], *Lel'* [a pagan love god], *lialia* [term of endearment for a child] and as in the cross, the soul of one individual encounters the soul of another at right angles to produce the greatest possible growth of the second individual, and transmits its movement to him.

Over twenty kinds of manmade structures begin with the letter *kh* [x]: *khram* [temple], *khlev* [barn], *khoromy* [mansion], *khizhina* [shack], *khalabuda* [cabin], *khata* [hut], *khibarka* [hovel], *khalupa* [hutch], *khiba* [shanty], *khutor* [farmstead], *khaz* [house: dial.], *khiza* [shack], *khanulia* [hut: dial.], *khrana* [storeroom: dial.], *khlamina* [tumbledown buildings], *khut* [house: dial.], *khorun* [kennel: dial.], *khabulia* [shed: dial.], *khizyk* [lean-to: dial.], *khoronusha* [hidey-hole], *khalat* [dressing gown], *kholodnik* [cold cellar] (*po-khorony* [burial]).

There you have twenty buildings, most of them having to do with hunting or rural life, which shield man from inclement weather and wild animals. The attacked point of man hides or protects itself in a building from the attacking point of rain or snow. Buildings serve as protection, hence we can define this letter as a barrier plane between one point within its circle of protection and another moving toward it. *Kh* includes the point in flight, the barrier plane in its path, and its goal beyond that barrier. More candles on the Christmas tree of a great nation. Whence *khrabry* [brave men], the military defenders of mankind. The roofs of *khoromy* [mansion], *khata* [hut], and *khiba* [shanty] stop the points of snow and rain and cold and wild animals: man protects himself with roofs.

The movement of a helpless point as it protects itself from a more powerful one by means of a barrier: *khovat'sia* [to hide oneself] (*khovun* [hider], *khomiak* [hamster]), *khoronit'sia* [to hide], *khutit'* [to bury: dial.], *khukhtat'* [to dissemble: dial.], *khunut'sia* [to bury: dial.], *khilit'sia* [to be unwell].

Here are names for a powerful, destructive point: *kholod* [cold], *khor'* [wolverine], *khrat* [insolence: dial.], *nakhrapom* [high-handedly], *khabalda* [impudent person: dial.], *(na)khal* [insolent person], *okhal'nik* [mischiefmaker], *kham* [boor], *khudoi* [bad], *khishchnik* [predator]—these are all things against which we seek the protection of *khata* [house, home, hut].

Here are names for a helpless point that requires protection: *khilyi* [puny], *khrupkii* [delicate], *khima* [simpleton: dial.], *khiryi* [puny: dial.], *khoryi* [ill], *khira* [ailment: dial.], *khinda* [illness], *khandra* [depression], *khil'* [sickness], *khlibkii* [frail], *khir'* [ailment: dial.]; *khluda* [rubbish: dial.], *khilina* [bad weather], *khoroshii* [good], *khudoba* [leanness].

Someone who designs buildings is *khudozhnik* [artist]; to breathe through a barrier causes us *khrapet'* [to snore]. The protective acts of another are called *kholia* [caring]. A plant that grows as a result of man's artificial care and protection is *khleb* [grain]: The aid of men serves to protect it as a building does. *Okhraniteli* [guards] and walls in time of war are *khrabry* [brave]; *khmary* [cloud formations] are structures of sun and sky. *Khizha* [sleet], *khiz* [foggy rain]. *Khmory* or *khmury* [overcast] (cloud formations). *Khari* [mug] and *khukhol'* [mask: dial.] are structurings of the human face. Edifices made of hair: *kholka* [forelock], *khokhol* [topknot], *khvost* [tail]; and *khobot* [proboscis], *khakhun* [wastrel], *khaz* [fop], *khokhrik* [spendthrift], *khukhriak* [prodigal], *khekhonit'* [to pretty up: dial.], *okhorashivat'sia* [to get dolled up]—all these terms relate to an architecture of the human face built of powder and rouge.

Those living walls, a prince's bodyguards, are *khrabry* [brave men]. Souls concealed behind defensive postures: *khitryi* [sly], *khitrets* [sly person], *khukhnat'* [to be hypocritical: dial.], *khukhtat'* [to disparage: dial.]. *Khlad* [cold] is something to protect oneself against (to take care). *Khlam* [trash] is something we don't need to take care of. Someone *khitryi* [sly] is someone with concealed desires.

Khitrets [sly person] may hide his will behind his words; a man in *khizhina* [shack] may hide from *kholod* [cold]; a dead man is *pokhoronen* [buried, hidden away] from the living; people *khovaiutsia* [hide] from an enemy; the sun hides behind *khmara* [dark clouds]; a horse's eyes are hidden behind *kholka* [forelock]; the mind of a sober man is obscured by *khmel'e* [drunkenness], the body by *khvost* [a tail] or *khokhol* [topknot]; a leader takes shelter behind the shoulders of *khraniteli*, *khrabry* [bodyguards, brave men]; a human personality is concealed behind the front of *kharia* [face]; the gods hide themselves away in the sanctuary of *khram* [temple]; a man in *khizha* [shack], *khiba* [hovel], *khata* [hut] hides from sickness and death; *khvastun* [braggart] hides his deeds with his words; we rely on class barriers to hide from *kham* [boor] or *kholop* [serf], and store grain in a building because of *kholia* [our care and labor]—everywhere we play the game of hide and seek, one point hides from another behind a line or a barrier. The task of a barrier is *khovat'* [to hide], *okhraniat'* [to guard], *khoronit'* [to conceal]. And every aspect of this process is expressed by the corpus of names beginning with *kh*.

Roofs and walls stop the points of snow, rain, and the claws of wild animals. *Kh* is a combination of the moving point and the barriers that stand between it and its goal. *Kh* may be defined as the barrier between a moving point and its goal. If the point of force outside this barrier cannot reach the second point, then the bar protecting the second point is also denominated by *kh*.

The following words from the ranks of names beginning in *ch* are names for footgear: *chedygi* [women's boots: arch.], *chekchury* [women's footwear], *choboty* [boots: dial.], *chereviki* [high-heeled boots for women], *chulki* [stockings], *chuviaki* [slippers], *cheverigi* [women's slippers: dial.], *chebotan* [suitcase], *chubary* [women's shoes: dial.], *chupaki* [felt boots: dial.], *chuni* [rope shoes: dial.], *chirki* [shoes: dial.], *chazhi* [fur booties: dial.].

Names for vessels: *chepurukha* [large goblet], *chasha* [cup], *chara* [goblet], *chan* [vat], *chren* [large kettle], *cherpak* [scoop], *cherokh* [large cup], *cherepokh* [shard], *cherep* [skull], *choln* [dugout canoe], *chupka* [small wooden cup], *chupur* [dipper], *chum* [ladle], *chapela* [skillet], *chuman* [birchbark basket], *chinak* [slop basin: dial.], *chilek* [small basket: dial.], *chechen'* [creel], *charuga* [woven grain basket], *charonka* [flat earthenware dish].

Names for garments: *chyga* [long caftan], *chekhol* [underdress], *chukhlashka* [woman's shirt: dial.], *chukha* [peasant caftan: dial.], *chuika* [knee-length jacket formerly worn by men as an outer garment], *chupakha* [bag], *chuprun* [woman's caftan: dial.], *chapan* [peasant caftan:

dial.], *chpag* [pocket], *chokha* [outer dress], *chiruch'* [net bag], *cheche-vitsa* [casing].

Chaiat' [to await hopefully] means to have a heart like an uncovered cup (those who pray using a chalice).

Names for cavities: *chulan* [cellar room], *cherdak* [loft], *chirei* [boil: coll.], *chresla* [loins], *chrevo* [womb], *chelpan* [burial mound: dial.], *chakhotka* [consumption] (an empty chest), *chuma* [plague] (an empty country).

Names of boundaries: *chur* [keep away: coll.], *chuzhbina* [foreign lands], *ochered'* [line], *chislo* [number], *chreda* [succeeding turn], *chet* [even number], *chin* [rank], *chekharda* [leap-frog].

Levers: *cheben'* [?], *chernok* [handle], *chereshok* [handle], *chubuk* [pipestem], *chalik* [trapstick], *chapchur* [boathook: dial.].

Therefore the letter *ch* means one body enclosed by the emptiness of another; these are hollow, empty bodies that contain others in their emptiness. But just as a cup, like a boot, contains a lever (a drop of water won't spill because the lever of the cup's edges maintains its equilibrium), the real force condition contained in the letter *ch* is the following: *Ch,* which appears to be a cup-body for another body, is the condition of equilibrium at the pressure point of a rotating line to which two equally distributed forces are applied. Whence the word *cherezy,* "scales." Footgear, vessels, and garments are all equivalent. They all contain a lever.

"Never forget what I tell you, student mine," said my teacher.

[1915–16: V.198]

A Little Introductory Dictionary
of Single-Syllable Words

	Offshoot words
tra: must, I must; distressing duty	*tral', trul'*
nra: lovely; I like; anything attractive	*norol'*
vra: lying; I don't believe; imaginings, fantasies	*vorol', vral'*
dra: violent, dangerous; I fight	*dorol'*
zra: clear; I see; light	*zorol'*
pra: in harmony with the past; believable; true	*prul'*
mra: death-dealing; I die; nonexistence	*morol'*
kra: mobile; I move; a step	*korol', kral', krul'*
khra: hidden; I can't see	*khrul'*
bra: strong; I grip, I protect, I possess	*borol'*

nra-people, *vra*-people (i.e., writers); *tra*-minded: devoted to duty

bo [for]: cause

to [then]: consequence

vo [in, into]: a demarcated surface and the penetration of its boundaries

do [up to]: the length of a line cut off by a point

so [with]: equality of distance between two moving points

po [upon]: motion over a surface

ko [toward]: diminishing of distance and volume where weight remains constant; direction of motion

mo: the disintegration of one volume into a multiplicity of minute particles

no [but]: a meeting of forces

zo: an area outside a given outline

kho: the presence of one volume within another

[1915–16: NP 345]

313

A Checklist: The Alphabet of the Mind

M [*m*] is the division of a certain volume into an indefinitely large number of parts, equal to it as a whole. *M* is the relation of the whole extent of a line to its members. *Muka* [flour], *molot* [hammer], *mlin* [mill: dial.], *mel* [chalk], *miakii* [soft], *mysh'* [mouse], *mochka* [earlobe].

Λ [*l*] is the conversion of motion from motion along a line to motion over an area transverse to it that intersects the path of the motion. $L = \sqrt{-1}$. *Lob* [forehead], *laty* [armor], *lyzhi* [skis], *lodka* [boat], *let* [flight], *luzha* [pond] (the motion of weight), *lava* [cavalry charge], i.e., a laterally extended formation.

C [*s*] is the movement of several points transmitted from a motionless point, at a narrow angle and in one direction. *Solntse* [sun], *siiat'* [to shine] (rays), *synov'ia* [sons], *soi* [clan] (descendants of a motionless ancestor), *sem'ia* [family], *semia* [seed, semen], *sol* (the ray of a ruler).

К [*k*] is the conversion of forces of motion into forces of cohesion. *Kamen'* [stone], *zakovannii* [chained], *kliuch* [key], *pokoi* [rest], *koika* [bunk], *kniaz'* [prince], *kol* [stake], *kol'tsa* [rings].

Ш [*sh*] is the convergence and reduction in the number of several surfaces while preserving their areas. The union of those surfaces into one. Also the greatest volume within the smallest and smoothest surface. *Shit'* [to sew], *shir'* [expanse], *shut* [jester, buffoon], *shar* [sphere], *shumnyi* [noisy], i.e., hornless. *Shorokh* [powder], *shum* [noise], *shamkat'* [to mumble].

Щ [*shch*] is the largest possible surface for any given volume. A profusion of angles. *Shchert'* [?], *shchel'* [crack, fissure], *shchedrovityi* [pocked], *shcherba* [dent], *shchovba* [?], *shchurit'* [to narrow one's eyes].

З [*z*] is the resonant vibration of distant strings. Separate vibrations with one single origin and with an identical number of vibrations. Reflection. *Zerkalo* [mirror], *zoi* [echo], (echo) *zyb'* [ripple] (the reflection of a storm), *zmei* [serpent], which moves by vibrating. *Zvat'* [to call], *zvezdy* [stars], *zor'ka* [dawnlight], *zaria* [dawn], *zarnitsa* [heat lightning] (lightning's reflection), *zen'* [earth: dial.], *zrak* [the look of something], *ozero* [lake], *zud* [itch], a pain without any origin, reflected pain.

Ч [*ch*] is a casing. A surface enclosing an empty interior, filled up with or containing a volume of something. *Cherep* [skull], *chash* [cup], *chara* [goblet], *chulok* [stocking], *chren* [boiling pan], *choboty* [boots], *chereviki* [high-heeled boots], *cherepakha* [turtle], *chekol* [case], *chakhotka* [consumption].

В [*v*] is a wavelike movement, a turning: *veter* [wind], *vikhr'* [whirlwind], *vit'* [to twist], *val* [groundswell], *volos* [hair], *volny* [waves], *vorota* [gates], *vremia* [time], *voz* [wagon], *vrat* [gate], *volchok* [judaswindow], *vys'* [heights] (something thrown into the heights comes back), *vervie* [cord], *vir* [whirlpool], *vorota vertiatsia* [a gate turns], so does *volchok* [a top]. *Zavyvanie* [howling] involves the revolution of sound. *Vrag* [an enemy] bends a direct line of movement into the ray of a circle. *Ves* [weight, gravity] is the reason the planets revolve around the sun.

П [*p*] is movement born of a difference in pressures: *porokh* [powder], *pushka* [cannon], *pit'* [to drink], *pustoi* [empty]. The conversion of a substance by force of pressure from a state of saturation to one of unsaturation, emptiness, from a compressed state to a scattered one. *Pena* [foam], *puzyr'* [bubble], *prakh* [ashes], *pyl'* [dust]. *P* is the opposite of *k*. *Kuznets skovyvaet* [A blacksmith forges], while *pech'* [stove], *pushka* [cannon], *porokh* [powder], *pyl'* [dust], *pena* [foam], *puzyr* [bubble], *pul'ia* [bullet]—all these dissipate a previously concentrated substance. *P* implies the free movement in one dimension of a substance away from a strong pressure toward a weak one. For example: *Pech'* [stove], *pishchal'* [arquebus], *pushka* [cannon], *pruzhina* [spring], *pravo* [right], *put'* [path], *pad* [school of fish: dial.], *puzo* [belly], *past'* [maw]: an opening for *pit'ia* [drink] and *pishche* [food], *pasti* [to graze], *pravit'* [to rule], meaning to accommodate differences in pressures from individual wills, *palit'* [to blaze]. In a stove [*pech'*] wood is converted into smoke. *Perun* [god of thunder] embodies a maximum of will and pressure.

Ж [*zh*] is the freedom to move independently of one's neighbors. From which we get *zhidkii* [liquid, watery], and *zhivoi* [alive, lively], and everything near the water—*zhabry* [gills], *zhaba* [a toad], *zhazhda* [thirst], *zhalga* [a water-weed]. In *zh* we have the separation of the dry principle, full of movement, from water, the struggle between fire and water. In the opinion of the ancients there was an equals sign drawn between water and time (past). Whence the kinship between *zhazhdat* [thirst] and *zhdat'* [wait]. *Zh* is frequently the separation of water from the fiery element.

X [*kh*] is whatever needs covering (help, protection) in order to grow. *Khily* [puny], *okhraniat'* [to protect], *kholia* [care], *khibarka* [hovel], *khata* [hut], *khram* [temple], *khlev* [cowshed], *pokhishchat'* [to abduct], *khleb* [grain], *khireiushchii* [decaying]. Also *okhraniteli* [guardians], who are *khorobrye* [boastful], *khutor* [farmstead] can also be *khizhina* [shack]; those who destroy fences are *okhal'nichaiushchie* [mischiefmakers], *khaiat'* [to run something down, talk it down]. *Khula* [abrasive criticism], i.e., an intrusion on something already protected; *kholod* [cold]. *Khovat'sia* means to conceal oneself. *Khokhol* [crest of hair] and *kholka* [forelock] both serve to protect the eyes. *Volodat'* [to govern] and *volost'* [an administrative district]—compare *kholodat'* [to turn cold]—refer to common points of warmth and life. *Kh* is whatever cannot exist without shelter, whatever is not able to exist on its own, also *khitryi* [crafty, two-faced, hidden]. Whatever is consigned to different places, i.e., *khleb* [grain] (which is produced through human artifice), *khoronit'* [to bury, inter], *khvost* [tail].

T [*t*] is something that contradicts nature, often a stoppage of motion—*tyn* [palisade], *tol'ko ten'* [only a shadow], *taiat'* [to melt], *tucha* [thundercloud]. *Tochka* [a point]. *Teplota* [heat] results from arrested motion.

Д [*d*] is the transposition of an element from one field of force to another. *Dar* [a gift], *dan'* [tribute], *doch'* [daughter] (one who leaves her own tribe), *delit'* [divide], *drob'* [buckshot], *dolia* [allotment].

T [*t*] is whatever is covered, out of sight and the light of day: *temia* [crown] (of the head), *tyl* [back] (of the head), *tem'* [darkness], *ten'* [shadow], *tucha* [thundercloud], *tiiat'* [to turn dark]. *Tor* [paved road] obliterates nature, a covering material motion, *tyn* [palisade], *tochka* [point]; whatever is *tiazhelyi* [heavy] inhibits motion; *tukhnut'* [to rot] means that the ray of life is extinguished. A raylike approach to life is

316

characteristic of language. Shining has to do with a common fiery point and a multiplicity of rays proceeding from it (the sun). *Soi* [clan] has to do with a common tribal point—one particular ancestor and many descendants.

If *s* is motion out from a fixed point (the path extends outward while the angle remains constant), then *v* is motion around a fixed point (the path is constant in length, the angle changes and increases): *volosy* [hair], *vetki* [branches], *veiat'* [to flutter]. In *voska* [wax] and *vaianie* [sculpture], *vlaga* [moisture] and *voda* [water], the angle of the particles changes, but their common length and their location remain fixed. *Vrashchat'sia* [to turn], *vertel* [spit], *vint* [screw], *vereteno* [spindle], *venok* [wreath], *vikhr'* [whirlwind], *vereia* [gatepost], *val* [billow, swell], all underline the fact that it is precisely these two conditions—constant length and a changing angle—that produce circular motion.

[1916: V.207]

A Second Language

The second language of poetry. Number-nouns. The contradictions between visions of love, the candles of the feast, and the face of the plague
smashing in the window and bringing waves of *Mor-mera* [wholesale
death as retribution] down like a hoof upon the feast—this, after the
punishments inflicted on his friends, is what makes Pushkin's writing
resound with that strength which always obtains when the strings of
Love and Pestilence are stretched next to one another.

And clearly, when Cleopatra values her night at the price of a life
and when the Toastmaster sings, "Itak, khvala tebe, Chuma" [And so I
sing your praises, Plague], what we hear is one and the same sounding
string. The victory of the human voice over the breath of *Mor*—that is
the subject of the Toastmaster's song.

Surely it is no coincidence that the high peaks of this song, the
places where passion and pestilence are united, where the clink of fren-
zied glasses in the presence of the fatal guest finds justification, are built
on one *p* and five *m*'s.

P begins these words: *Perun* [god of thunder], *paren* [boy], *plamia*
[flame], *par* [steam], *porokh* [powder], *pyl* [dust], *pesni* [songs], and the
fiery Pushkin himself. *M*: *mor* [wholesale death], *morok* [darkness], *mo-
roz* [freezing weather], *mertvets* [corpse], *mera* [retribution], *mech*
[sword], *molot* [hammer], *mertvyi* [dead]—a quiver full of the arrows
of Death, that huntress of humans. Life as a mere moment, as the murk
of mortality. Is this clinking of skull goblets and grave songs based on
a fixed numerical law? It is!

Out of the five sections of Mary's song, only the fourth is devoted
to the encounter between *Lad* [harmony] and *Mor*, and it contains five
m's and one *p* also. Her victory over death consists in this: even dying,
Mary loves whatever lives. In the Toastmaster's song, sections four and
five, "*dunovenie chumy . . . naslazhdenie*," each contain 5*m* + 1*p* as their
basic structure.

318

In Lermontov as well, in "Tamara," life is the price of "one night of passion and delight." The first eight sections are devoted to a description of Tamara. But the ninth section "No tol'ko chto utra siian'e" has two *p*'s and five *m*'s. The quatrain of *The Demon* that begins: "*Smertel'nyi iad ego lobzanii*" also has five *m*'s and one *p*. In the whole of *The Feast During the Plague* there are around 150 *p*'s and 250 *m*'s. The sail of victory upon the sea of wholesale death [Khleb.: *Parus pobedy v more mora*] in accordance with the division between the Toastmaster and Mary, is marked by the number-noun 5*m* + 1*p*.

I may have made a mistake, but according to the records in *Feast During the Plague* the *p* occurs 140 times and the *m* 225; 140 + 225 = 365, the number of days in a year.

[1916: V.210]

four

VISIONS OF THE FUTURE

Here, written between 1916 and 1922, are proclamations and visions of the future of Planet Earth, as Khlebnikov imagined it in the vertiginous years of the world war, two revolutions, and the civil war in Russia. In 1916 Khlebnikov with his friend and disciple Grigory Petnikov founded the Society of 317, intended to be an association of creative scientists, writers, and thinkers from various countries who would form a world government and oppose the evils wrought by political states. Soon Khlebnikov's name for himself and his group of friends evolved into the Presidents of Planet Earth, "inventor/explorers" who took a stand against the "investor/exploiters" of this world.

Khlebnikov sees the beginnings of the new government of Planet Earth in the merging of Russia with the unified countries of Asia. He envisages a society in which young people, artists, and scientists will play a special role in breaking down old patterns of thought, established political boundaries, outmoded notions of time and history. A benign technology will facilitate radical changes in agriculture, communication, and travel. The essay "The Radio of the Future" foresees the global communication network of present-day television, while "Ourselves and Our Buildings," "Swanland in the Future," and "A Cliff out of the Future" describe with accuracy and a certain amount of wit the wonders of late twentieth-century urban architecture and city planning.

The summation of Khlebnikov's theoretical ideas is to be found in "Our Fundamentals" and "Excerpt from The Tables of Destiny." Here the possibilities of a universal language created from fundamental linguistic units, and a scale of time based on multiples of 317, are woven together in a single program. In Khlebnikov's projected "sonic art of the future," art is so deeply rooted in nature that it has the power to change the human condition.

The Trumpet of the Martians

People of Earth, hear this!

The human brain until now has been hopping around on three legs (the three axes of location)! We intend to refurrow the human brain and to give this puppy dog a fourth leg—namely, the axis of TIME.

Poor lame puppy! Your obscene barking will no longer grate on our ears!

People from the past were no smarter than us; they thought the sails of government could be constructed only for the axes of space.

But now we appear, wrapped in a cloak of nothing but victories, and begin to build a union of youth with its sail tied to the axis of TIME, and we warn you in advance that we work on a scale bigger than Cheops, and our task is bold, majestic, and uncompromising.

We are uncompromising carpenters, and once again we throw ourselves and our names into the boiling kettles of unprecedented projects.

We believe in ourselves, we reject with indignation the vicious whispers of people from the past who still delude themselves that they can bite at our heels. Are we not gods? And are we not unprecedented in this: *our steadfast betrayal of our own past,* just as it barely reaches the age of victory, and our steadfast rage, raised above the planet like a hammer whose time has come? Planet Earth begins to shake already at the heavy tread of our feet.

Boom, you black sails of time!

> Viktor Khlebnikov, Maria Siniakova,
> Bozhidar, Grigory Petnikov,
> Nikolai Aseev

"LET THE MILKY WAY BE SPLIT INTO THE MILKY WAY OF INVENTOR/ EXPLORERS AND THE MILKY WAY OF INVESTOR/EXPLOITERS"

Here is the slogan for a new holy war.

Our questions are shouted into outer space, where human beings have never yet set foot.

We will brand them in powerful letters on the forehead of the Milky Way, stamp them upon the circular divinity of businessmen—questions like how to free our winged engine from its fat caterpillar, the freight train of previous generations. *Let age groups separate and live apart!* We have broken open the freight cars attached to the locomotive of our daring—and they contain nothing but tombstones for the young.

There are seven of us. We want a sword forged from the purest steel of youth. Those who have drowned in the laws of the family and the laws of trade, those who know only the expression "I consume," they will not understand us, since none of those things concerns us.

The right to form worldwide organizations according to age groups. Complete separation of age groups, the right to a separate way of life and separate activities. The right to have everything separate right up to and including the Milky Way. And out of the way with the uproar of age groups! Long rule the resonant sound of discontinuous time periods, white and black tablets and the brush of destiny. All who are closer to death than to birth must surrender! They must bite the dust when we attack like wild men in this time-war. But *we* have studied the soil of the continent of time, and we found it fruitful. But unrelenting hands from *back there* grabbed us, and they keep us from carrying out our beautiful betrayal of space. Has there ever been anything more intoxicating than this betrayal? You! What better answer is there to the danger of being born a man than to *carry off time?* We summon you toward a land where the trees speak, a land where there are scholarly unions as regular as waves, a land of springtime armies of love, *where time blossoms like the locust tree* and moves like a piston, where a superman in a carpenter's apron saws time into boards and like a turner of wood can shape his own tomorrow. (Oh, equations of kisses—You! Oh death ray, killed by the death ray in the trough of the wave.) We young people were moving toward that land, and all of a sudden some bony figure, someone dead, grabs us and tries to keep us from losing the feathers of the idiot TODAY. Is that fair?

Raise high the winged sails of time, you government of young people, now comes the second time we raid the flame of the investor/exploiters. Be bold! Push yesterday back, take away its bony hands, let the attack of a Balashov gouge out those horrible eyes. This is another sock in the eye for the vulgar inhabitants of space. Which is greater: S/T or N/R? The investor/exploiters in snarling packs have always slunk behind the inventor/explorers, now the inventor/explorers drive the investor/exploiters away.

Every industry of present-day Planet Earth—from the point of view and in the language and style of the investor/exploiters themselves—is "a steal" from the first inventor/explorer: Gauss. He founded the study of lightning. Yet while he was alive he didn't even get 150 rubles a year from his scientific work. Your memorials and laudatory articles try to justify the glee you feel at stealing him totally blind. And to pacify the rumblings of your conscience (which is suspiciously located in your vermiform appendix). Your supposed idols—Pushkin and Lermontov—met their deaths at your hands, in a field at the edge of town like rabid dogs! *You* sent Lobachevsky to be a parochial schoolteacher. Montgolfier wound up in a madhouse. And what about us? The militant vanguard of the inventor/explorers?

Here are your triumphs! Enough of them to fill several big books!

That is why the inventor/explorers, in full consciousness of their particular nature, their different way of life and their special mission, separate themselves from the investor/exploiters in order to form an independent government of *time* (no longer dependent on space), and put up a line of iron bars between ourselves and *them*. The future will decide who winds up in the zoo, inventor/explorers or investor/exploiters, who winds up chomping at the iron bars.

V. Khlebnikov

Orders

I. All the illustrious participants in Futurian publications are hereby promoted from the ranks of human beings to the ranks of Martians.

Signed: Velimir I, King of Time

II. The following are invited to become honorary nonvoting members of the Martian Council: H. G. Wells and Marinetti.

323

Subjects for Discussion

"Alloo, Alloo, Martians!"

1. How can we free ourselves from being dominated by people from the past who still retain a shadow of power in the world of space, without soiling ourselves by coming into contact with their lives (we can use the soap of word-creation), and leave them to drown in the destiny they have earned for themselves, that of malicious termites? We are fated to fight with *rhythm and time* for our right to be free from the filthy habits of people from past centuries, and to win that right.

2. How can we free the speeding locomotive of the younger generation from the insolent freight train of the older generation, hitched on without our permission?

Old ones! You are holding back the fast advance of humanity, you are preventing the boiling locomotive of youth from crossing the mountain that lies in its path. We have broken the locks and see what your freight cars contain: tombstones for the young.

You've hooked your earthling wagon to our star, our locomotive and its defiant whistle, hoping for a free ride!

[1916: V. 151]

A Letter to Two Japanese

Dear distant friends,

I happened to read your letter from Kokumin-Shimbun, and I wondered if perhaps it wouldn't be out of place for me to answer it. I decided it wouldn't, and so I hereby pick up the ball and toss it back to you, and invite you to join the ballgame of the younger generation. You have stretched out your hand to us and so we take your hand in ours, and now the hands of the young people of two countries are joined across the whole of Asia, like the arc of the Northern Lights. And our very best wishes go with the handshake! I don't think you know much about us, but the fact is I feel that you are writing to us and about us. The very same ideas about Asia that have occurred to you so suddenly and so intelligently are quite familiar to us. It often happens that two strings begin to sound in unison, even though quite distant from one another and even though no musician has touched them; some mysterious sound they both share seems to bring them to life. And you even speak directly to the young people of our country in the name of your young people. That is a direct response to our ideas of a worldwide organization of young people and conflict between generations—because each generation has a different way of walking, a different way of talking. I can more easily understand a young Japanese speaking archaic Japanese than I can some of my countrymen who speak contemporary Russian. Perhaps a great deal depends on the fact that the young people of Asia have never once shaken each others' hands, have never sat down together to exchange opinions and decide on a common course. Because if the term *fatherland* has any meaning, then so does the term *sonland,* and we must preserve them all. And the important thing now seems not to involve ourselves in the life of our elders, but to build our own separate life alongside theirs. And another thing we share, which we feel strongly even though we say nothing, is this, that Asia is not just some northern land inhabited by a multinomial of nations, but is in fact a kind of patchwork of written characters, out of which must materialize the word *I*. It may be that no one as yet has really written it down, in which case isn't it our shared destiny, with whatever pen, to write it now, now that its time has come? Let the hand of the universal writer consider the matter! And so let us uproot a pine tree in the forest, let us dip it in the inkwell of ocean, and let us write down our signature sign: I AM FROM ASIA. Asia has a will of her own. And if the pine tree breaks, we will use Mount Everest. So then. Let us take each others' hands, and take the hands of two or three Indians, and Dyaks, and let us rise up out of the year 1916, a circle of young people united not because their countries are neighbors, but because they belong to the same generation. We might be able to arrange a meeting in Tokyo. We, after all, are latterday Egyptians, if we think in terms of transmigration of souls, while you often sound like the Greeks of old. And when a Dyak turtle hunter nails up in his hut a postcard reproduction of Vereshchagin's painting *The Apotheosis of War*, then he becomes a member of our group. But the wonderful thing is, you tossed the ball to us, and it touched our hearts. It's wonderful because that gives us the right to take the next step, which is vital for us both and needed your courteous initiative—because when the ball is returned, the ballgame begins.

Sincerely yours, dear Japanese friends,
V. Khlebnikov

Here is an agenda of topics we might discuss at the first meeting of an Asian congress:

1. Joint support for inventor/explorers in their struggle with investor/exploiters. The inventor/explorers are close to us; we understand them.

2. Establishment of the first Higher Instruct of the Futurians. It will consist of several (13) locations rented (for 100 years) from the inhabitants of the space dimension, scattered along the seacoast or high in the mountains near extinct volcanoes in Siam, Siberia, Japan, Ceylon, the Russian Arctic, in mountainous deserts where life is difficult and there is nothing to invest in or to exploit, but where it is easy to invent and to explore. The radio-telegraph will unite each location with the next, and lessons will be transmitted by wire. We must have our own radio-telegraph system. Communication by air.

3. To arrange within two years for regular attacks upon the minds of the inhabitants of the space dimension (not on their bodies, only their minds and souls), to hunt down their sciences, and defeat them with the deadly arrow of new inventions and explorations.

4. To found the *Daily Journal of Asia,* for poems, inventions, and explorations. This will speed up our flight and make us the swifts of the future. Materials will be printed in any language, telegraphed in from every point. All contents will be translated within the week. It will become a spur for speed, as soon as it appears daily in the hands of the Futurians!

5. To consider the feasibility of a railroad that encircles the Himalayas, with branch lines to Suez and the straits of Malacca.

6. To study Asian classicism, and discard the Greeks. (Vidjai, the Ronins, al-Masih al-Dajjal.)

7. To breed animals of prey, to deal with people who are turning into rabbits. To breed rivers full of crocodiles. To analyze the intellectual capabilities of the older generation.

8. To set up, in these picturesque properties under temporary lease, camps of inventor/explorers, where they can live exactly the way they want and feel. And to require the inhabitants of nearby towns and villages to feed them and respect them.

9. To ensure the transfer to our hands of that part of the general resources which is our due. The older generation have never learned to squeeze out enough respect for the young, and in many countries young people lead a life worse than the dogs of Constantinople.

10. In all the rest we shall let the older generation proceed as they see fit. Their business is business, raising families, and investment and exploitation. Ours is invention and exploration, the arts, knowledge, and struggle with them.

11. To destroy languages by besieging their secrets. The word will be no longer for everyday use, but for the Word alone.

12. Concern for architecture. Portable habitats, with moorings for zeppelins; framework-buildings for the habitats.

13. The language of numbers will be the crowning accomplishment of the youth of Asia. We can use a number to designate every action and every image, and by allowing a number to be projected by a powerful spotlight, we can communicate with each other. In order to establish a dictionary for all Asia (for the traditions and images of all Asia)

we rely on personal contact between members of the Assembly of Children of the Future. The language of numbers is especially suited to radio telegrams. Number-talk. The mind will free itself at last from the meaningless waste of its strength in everyday speech.

[1916: V.154]

Lalia Rides a Tiger

You are the northern goddess of Belorussia, your lashes are snowy, your eyes are blue and your brows are black—your laughing hair blown back on the arms of wind, you whisper to the warriors of Time: Tell me, hunters, had enough? He has only this moment abandoned the deer with its horns flung back wildly, and the air-boys cover your body with woven mats of air—for you bathe eternally in the black and gray eyes of human beings, whether joyful or sullen—you leap upon the tiger's back and he moves, a slink of stripes among the fir trees, and you force him to leap forward like an angry spear toward the future—which is still before the iron gates. But don't the sheep of the future bleat at the awful siege, the clang of the iron of the tiger's breast against the iron of the gates? Yes, we are the Belorussian Lalia, who so often has wreathed the auroch's horn with her delight, and we are also the tiger, the grim gold of the Ganges. Which is why we are as joyful as the children's word *tsatsa,* and monstrous, like the drunkenness of cannon drunk on themselves, dancing a witches' dance. Your golden braids trailing on the back of the beast—they are our first pure Beliefs. "On the terrifying peak of Beliefs" (Petnikov).

Broken claws and scratches on the breast—our dead comrades—

The despairing Troy of our hearts
Has yet to control the fires of time.
Don't turn aside in wild disarray—
Forward, comrades, forward!
(Aseev, to Bozhidar)

They—these comrades who left us early on—were men who held the sacrificial knife to their own throats and carried bundles of faggots for their own pyres. May their memory be praised once again. The voice of Vladimir Cloudakovsky, with its terrific hammer force, would crush anyone who did not perceive in his voice the smile of Lalia riding her tiger. And the gloomy warrior funeral feast, the sword festival in his voice—it is only a small craft rowed by the warriors, but Lalia rides in it. When he says "Hey, Heaven! Take your hat off, here I come!" that is the tiger, clanging once more against the walls of the gate, and when he says "I wear the sun as a monocle in my softly smoldering eye," she asks the question: "What shall I do with suns and monocles?" We know with an absolute conviction that we will not be repeated on Planet Earth. We mean to leave a monument to ourselves—we don't want people to say "they vanished like the Obry,"—so we have established the government of time (a new stone figure on the steppes of time: crudely carved but powerful), and we propose to the governments of space either to accept our existence peacefully and leave us alone, or to engage us in a struggle to the death. People until now have fought with their bodies, with shoulders and arms and legs—we are the first to discover that shoulders and arms and legs are boring second-rate moving parts; the good parts are in the brain box. Which is why we have started plowing up brains. Brainplowers. For us your brains are only deposits of sand, loam, flaky bituminous shale. We already think of you and your behavior as no more than inert elements, so unnatural is everything you do, everything you have perpetrated upon this poor earth. We are so far no more than the beginning. As Kruchonykh once said, "All things may pass away, but we will have no end." We are like fishermen: our catch is your free will and your creeds and your equations. We are like Keepers of the Imperial Larder: we are in a position to nourish a great people for an entire year with just one of our poems. We are seam-stresses: we stitch together national traits into a single middle-class garment so that at least there's something to bundle up the frozen earth. (What, those long yellow legs! Gentlemen, you're getting old!) How's that again? What will happen when we raise ourselves still a few steps higher on the social ladder? And now that we hear friendly, familiar voices from the distant shores of Japan (*Kokumin Shimbun* in Tokyo, the *Chronicle* in Moscow), we claim for ourselves a proud title: Young People of Planet Earth. And there's a chance that one hundred years from now we will still be that. And may the road ahead be a bright one for that new title. The government of time illuminates humanity's high-way with people rays. It has already crushed all former knowledge into a ball of filthy paper. Its cradle exploit. Of course you consider it "private playacting" (Evreinov), but we are at least advancing toward a goal of some sort. We are like foam hurled back into the sea, or like seven of the best Hyksos horses, with black bodies and snow-white manes, urged on toward the victory pillar by the hand of the charioteer. We have become experts in many fields, better than you think. Consider: for five years already we have been engaged in a war between the best people of a great nation (because one of us is better—either you or us—modestly we suggest that it's you). And what's the result? You wind up in *Russian News* recognizing our achievements as blinding, extraordinary . . . . .

Mayakovsky made Gorky cry with his unprecedented piece, *A Cloud in Trousers*. He hurls the reader's soul beneath the feet of elephants he has maddened with his hatred. His voice lashes them into a rage. Kamensky in his beautiful *Stenka Razin* has worked expertly at the task of settling a flowering branch with a hundred nightingales and larks, so that out of it all the real Stenka Razin emerges. Khlebnikov was drowning in a swamp of calculations, and they saved him by force.

> Light the pathway for approaching youth,
> A tribe not even born;
> I am happy to live now,
> To hold the reins for time.

Thus wrote Aseev in his debut, with restrained pride, acknowledging the existence of still greater pride (Aseev and Petnikov, *Letorei*). Petnikov introduced Novalis and worked on an investigation of the roots of the Russian language. A fire lit in a distant camp of words consecrated with the name of Bozhidar, different rays from those of the north. *Letorei* and *Oi Konin* are like ice breaking up on the Don. Bozhidar, who continues to guide two or three individuals toward Planet Earth, has left us rare and beautiful words on the "unique cognitive missile" and "assemblies of extrasensory output." He began to fly and came to grief against the walls of transparent fate. A bird has fallen, and blood drips from its beak. "The image of a missile looms like an obsession within us." "We wing our way like weightless fliers, making all things one, engulfing them in the seamless veil of omniscience." Those are his beautiful words. Bozhidar can be appreciated in the sympathetic vibrations of the hearts of those who knew him . . . . .

"Has such a will remained unfulfilled, has the path been lost to its step?" asks Aseev, as he answers,

> Look out, look up, in sharp-eyed pain,
> We sound the alarm, the spasmodic alarm,
> We come, we come to save you.

Grief is fertile soil for the will. And to the hundred rivers of the Russian anvil the hammers of Nippon now respond. We are advancing toward our shared goal, the solution to the riddle of the will of Asia: AS + TS + U.

[1916: V.212]

An Appeal by the Presidents of Planet Earth

We alone are the Government of Planet Earth. Which comes as no surprise. There's no doubt about it. We are uncontestable and recognized by everyone.

We have rolled up your three years of war into a single conch shell, a terrifying trumpet, and now we sing and shout and we roar out the terrible truth: the Government of Planet Earth already exists. We are it.

We alone, standing on the rock of ourselves and our names, with the ocean of your evil eyes beating all around us, have dared to call ourselves the Government of Planet Earth. We are it.

What insolence, people will say, but we will smile upon them like gods.

We hereby state that we do not recognize any overlords who call themselves governments, states, fatherlands, and other such business establishments and publishing houses, who have built the mercenary mills of their well-being beside the three-year-long waterfall of your beer and our blood, the streams made in 1917 of blood-red waves.

You cover the eyes of War with a homespun blind of words about the death penalty, mouthing the word "homeland" and setting up frontline court-martials.

Ahhl—aboard! Who will be our friend and comrade on this great journey?

We praise the trainloads of loyal subjects of her Holiness Spring and her people, who cling like swarms of bees to trains about to collapse beneath the weight of their new passenger—*Peace*. We know it is Spring who calls her people and sees them and smiles a sad smile.

So say we, ambassadors and commissars of Planet Earth. And you governments of space, calm down, fix the kerchiefs on your heads and stop wailing as if you were attending your own funerals; nobody's going to hurt you. You will be able to enjoy the protection of our laws, you will become simply private associations, on an equal footing with anti-gopher societies, Dante societies, groups in favor of railroad sid-

333

ings, or societies for the dissemination of information on the latest advances in threshing machines.

We promise not to lay a finger on you.

Our difficult assignment is to be switchmen on the tracks that join the Past and the Future.

You simply stay as you are—voluntary agreements between private persons, totally unnecessary, unimportant, boring, and dull as a toothache in the mouth of an old lady in the seventeenth century.

If you are so moral, you governments, then why these sacrifices for the gods, why are we crushed in your jaws, we soldiers and workers?

And if you are evil, then who among us will raise a finger to prevent your destruction?

We are endowed with reason, and we contemplate death with the same equanimity as a farmer who contemplates replacing one plow with a better one. Your space government of sinister plunder, you kings and kaisers and sultans, is as different from our society as the hand of an ape burned by its unknown fire god is different from the hand of a rider calmly holding the reins of bridled fate.

And that's not all. We are founding a society for the protection of governments of space from savage attack by the young rulers of Planet Earth. And this new class will crop your ears.

They are young and impolite—forgive any gaps in their upbringing. We are a special type of weapon. Comrade workers, do not complain because we follow a special path toward our common goal. Each type of weapon has its own design and its own laws. We are architect-workers.

Let these words be a gauntlet whose time has come:

THE GOVERNMENT OF PLANET EARTH

whose black banner of unrule was raised by the hand of man and has been already snatched up by the hand of the universe. Who will tear down these black suns? The burning colors of these black suns? The enemy?

By right of preeminence and by assertion of our right of seizure, WE are the Government of Planet Earth. We and nobody else.

signed: V. Khlebnikov

G. Petnikov

We hope that this list will soon bear the brilliant names of Mayak-ovsky, Burliuk, and Gorky.

Admission to the Government of our star is granted to: [list of names, including Sun Yat-sen, Rabindranath Tagore, Wilson, Kerensky].

[1917: V.162]

Letter to Grigory Petnikov

You know that our goal, a goal we have attained already, solving with the sound of strings what is usually solved by cannon fire, is to grant power over humanity to the world of the stars, by eliminating unnecessary intermediaries between them and us.

Into streets torn by the lion's jaws of revolt we go like a martyr unwavering in her faith and the meekness of her upraised eyes (eyes that direct lightning flashes on the sea of terrestrial stars).

The worldwide thundering of revolt—can it terrify us, if we ourselves are a revolt more terrifying still? You remember that a government of poets has been founded and encompasses Planet Earth. You remember that the sounding string of tribes has united Tokyo, Moscow, and Singapore.

We imitate the waves of the sea, white-capped by the storm, now uniting and rising up, now subsiding into multitudinous distances. You remember that we have succeeded in discovering the harmony of our destinies, which enables us to hold humanity in the palm of our thoughts and raise it to the next stage of existence.

Still it moves, this wanderer of the centuries.

How the harmonies we found have tied the letter U into the thundering of the A string, into the foot soldier's march and beats of the heart, the thunder of the waves, the harmonies of births—these are all similar points of the ray of destiny.

Remember how a foundation was built, solid enough to let us speak of rays of people, or people light, on a line with the black, cold, and burning ray, and the resinous ray of furious lightning. This was done in order to transfer lawmaking power to the scientist's desk and to exchange the arrogant Roman law, based on word definitions, for the approaching law of the Futurians, which consists of equal signs, multiplication and division signs, signs of the square roots of 1 and n, imaginary quantities brought to bear on the substance of humanity.

How we dream of constructing viewing glasses and magnifying lenses for people rays in the elemental agitation of their wars, and of replacing with scientific waves the ordinary barbarous ray of human nature and its blindfolded progressions. All inventions for lesser rays, all the laws of Balmer, Fresnel, Fraunhofer, and Planck, all the art of reflecting, directing, distancing, bringing closer—we swear, we young people, to employ them upon the rays of the human race. Thus will victory be accomplished over space, while victory over time will be attained by means of a movement and transmission of consciousness during a second rebirth. We are determined to die knowing the instant of our second birth, vowing to complete the poem of ourselves.

This is the action of fate's sewing machine—the point of birth is a needle, and in obedience to a law it sews a knot onto the canvas of the human race.

Aryabhatta and Kepler! We see again the year of the ancient gods, great sacred events repeating themselves after 365 years. That is so far the supreme string in the Futurian's scale, and are we not rapt in admiration, seeing that at the end of this growing advance of the laws of origin we find an oscillation of vocalic U and the waves of the A string, the main axis of the sounding world. This is the first section of our pact with heaven for the human race, signed in the blood of the great war.

As far as the second barrier on our path is concerned—multi-language—remember that an overview of the fundamentals of languages has already been accomplished, and a discovery made: that the alphabet is the sound machine of languages, and each of its sounds hides a fully exact and spatial word image. This knowledge is essential in order to transport man to the next stage—a single common language—and that we will do next year.

[March 1917: V.313]

Outline for a Public Lecture and Discussion

(to be given by Khlebnikov and Petnikov)

1. We are sunburnt hunters, at our belt hangs a trap, and in it *Destiny* trembles, a terrified mouse darting its black eyes back and forth. Destiny defined as a mouse.

2. Our answer to war—a mousetrap. The rays of my name.

3. The ray of humanity. Nations as rays. The beautiful waterfalls of number.

4. An armload of the equations of fate. (We are woodcutters in the forest of numbers.) Our arms are aching.

5. The precise carpet of birth. The secret of humanity. The rays of Khlebnikov.

6. The sweep net of generations and its scope. The Laws of Time's workbench. This wanderer of the centuries is exhausted; let us fill his dusty hand with pale blue flowers.

7. Who is the first to have leaped onto the back of untamed Fate? We alone. We need no saddle. We gallop, and our hand resounds against fate. The strokes of our oars. The suicide of states. Who holds out the sword. We are in the saddle.

8. A rope around the thick leg of *War.*

9. Language under siege. *V* as the rotation of a moving point around an immobile one. *Z* as the equality of an angle of incidence to the angle of reflection. Future curls of language and the horror of their simplicity. Harmony and Humany. See my letter to Petnikov.

10. We are a time of measure. Building-beams of time. The beautiful smile of centuries.

11. The blood cell. Its genealogy. Acquaintances. Friends.

12. About helium. The ray of the world. *The World as Poem.*

13. Praise to the *rising sun.* We are repairing the wobbly constellation of the sun; you can hear our hammers at work. Believe in us or

beware. We have come to you from out of the future, from the far reaches of the centuries.

We contemplate your time from the cliff of the *Future*.

We read our poems. Discussion.

[April 1917: V.258]

"We, the Presidents of Planet Earth"

We, the Presidents of Planet Earth, Friends of Fate, Friends of Poetry, etc., etc., have deemed it good on this day the first of June 1918 finally to incarnate an idea that has been of concern to many hearts in the past: to found a Retreat House for those who work with the pen, brush, and chisel. Hidden beneath the wide branches of pine trees, by the shores of deserted lakes, it will gather within its log walls all those barefoot prophets now dispersed by wind and dust across the damp face of Moscovy. The Scythian, the gray aggressor, will retreat to the Retreat House, there in solitude to read the will of the ancient stars.

It will be a monastery—an old one taken over or one we build ourselves—depending on the sympathies of Pierrot, who even now places the penitential skullcap on his tired head and binds the leather thong about his tired loins. Led in our endeavors by the gray Prior of Prayer we will perhaps, out of the hymns of snowstorms and the bells of brooks, reconstruct the old relationship of the Scythian land to the Scythian god.

We call upon all those loyal to our idea to appear and bring aid to celebrate its realization.

Address all letters with suggestions to:

Fyodor Bogorodsky, pilot
22 Tikhonovsky Street
Nizhni Novgorod

Signed and sealed at the point where all roads cross, at 10:33 and 27 seconds according to Predtechensky's watch.

Present: Velimir Khlebnikov, Fyodor Bogorodsky, Predtechensky, Arseny Mitrofanov, Boris Gusman, Ulianov, Sergei Spassky.

[pub. 1918: NP 348]

An Indo-Russian Union

1. The goal of the Society is to protect the shores of Asia from pirates and to establish a single maritime frontier.

2. As we know, the bell that sounds for Russia's freedom will have no effect on European ears.

3. Like social classes, political states are either oppressor states or enslaved states.

4. Until the proletariat seizes power in every state, states can be divided into proletarian states and bourgeois states.

5. The great nations of the Continent of ASSU (China, India, Persia, Russia, Siam, Afghanistan) belong to the list of enslaved states. The islands are the oppressors, the continents are enslaved.

6. Maximize maritime frontiers, minimize land frontiers.

7. A united Asia has arisen from the ashes of the Great War.

8. Clothed in the solid armor of the positive sciences, we hasten to the aid of our common mother.

9. The will of Fate has ordained that this union be conceived in Astrakhan, a place that unites three worlds—the Aryan world, the Indian world, the World of the Caspian: the triangle of Christ, Buddha, Mohammed.

10. The original is inscribed on lotus leaves and preserved in Chatalgai. By a decree of three, the Caspian Sea is declared its protector. We proclaim ourselves the first Asiatics, aware of our insular unity.

11. May the citizens of our island pass from the Yellow Sea to the Baltic, from the White Sea to the Indian Ocean, without ever encountering a frontier. May the tatooed patterns of political boundaries be wiped from Asia's body by the will of the Asiatics. The separate lands of Asia are united into an island.

Citizens of the new world, freed and united because of Asia, we parade in triumph before you. We astonish everyone. Let young girls weave garlands and throw them beneath the feet of the conquerors of the future. Any thorns that attempt to scratch our feet as we proceed toward the future, we will turn them into roses.

Our path leads from the unity of Asia to the unity of the planet, and from freedom for the continent to freedom for all of Planet Earth. We follow that path, not like agents of death but like young Vishnus in blue denim shirts. Our magic weapons are songs and poems.

Asia stands by herself, and see how many suitors surround her—Japanese, English, Americans. Our reply is the drawn bow of Odysseus.

We begin our existence by snatching India from the clutches of Great Britain. India, you are free.

The first three individuals to call themselves Asiatics have set you free.

Remembering the behest of Ceylon, so do we knock at the door of your reason, Island of ASSU.

We have dived into the depths of centuries and gathered up the signatures of Buddha, Confucius, and Tolstoy.

People of Asia, always remember your unity and it will never desert you. We have lighted our lamp. People of Asia, send us the best of your sons to protect the ignited flame.

We call for a congress of the enslaved nations to meet beside the great lake. Great thoughts grow by the shores of great lakes. Here, beside the largest lake in the world, we conceived the idea of the greatest island in the world.

We summon Russia to immediate unification with young China for the education of the world's great interior, Asia, the greater Switzerland.

We sacrifice our hearts to the triangle proclaimed by these races. In so doing we make our names deathless forever and tangle them into the mane of the coursing centuries.

Follow us, all you people!

September 12, 1918, 5:27 A.M., Astrakhan

[TsGALI, f. 527, op. 1, ed. khr.112, l. 1-5]

Asiaunion

The goal of the union is the coming together of the peoples of Asia and organizing a general celebration of the Asiatic peoples.

(a) Reasons for forming the union: the necessity of self-defense for the dismembered parts of a single sacred whole, the Island of ASSU.

(b) In this majestic plan for Asia we see the place of Europe as a satellite revolving around the central sun, Asia.

(c) The unity of the peoples of America. The principles of the French revolution are the cement that holds them together. Asia must develop her own improved principles, which will serve to unite all her peoples.

(d) What should those principles be?

1. Political rayism, as the basis for a world outlook for the peoples of Asia (i.e., principles intended to form the basis for her own life).

2. The combination of the rotary and the retreating movements of humanity creates the motion of a ray.

3. A basic research laboratory for the study of time.

4. This time-lab is to be the Supreme Soviet of the government of Asia.

5. Silence as the fundamental principle of human communication. A person should direct words toward another only when there is something to say.

6. Individuals should dress in simple, light clothes. No one can be internally free if he or she is cramped by an external environment. War against all conventionality, material or immaterial.

7. The Cult of Conscience. One evening a week devoted to a discussion of conscience.

8. Individual Conscience flows into Social Conscience. Conscience as the soul of Asia.

Astrakhan, 1918

[ThGALI, f 527, op. 1, ed. khr.112, l. 6–8.]

Swanland in the Future

Skybooks

In public squares laid out near the gardens where the workers (or creators, as they had begun to call themselves) went for recreation, high white walls resembling white books opened against the dark sky. The squares were always full of crowds, and it was here that the creators' commune brought the latest news to the public by means of shadow printing on shadow books, projecting the appropriate shadow text by means of the projector's dazzling eye. News flashes about Planet Earth, the activities of that great union of workers' communes known as the United Encampments of Asia, poetry and the instantaneous inspirations of members, breakthroughs in science, notifications for relatives and next of kin, directives from the soviets. Those who were inspired by these shadow-book communications were able to go off for a moment, write down their own inspirations, and half an hour later see their messages projected onto those walls in shadow letters by means of the light lens. In cloudy weather the clouds themselves were used as screens, the latest news projected directly onto them. Many people requested that news of their deaths be flashed onto the clouds. For holiday celebrations there were "shot paintings." Smoke grenades of different colors were fired into the sky at various points. Eyes, for instance, were shots of blue smoke, the mouth a streak of scarlet smoke, hair of silver, and against the cloudless blue background of the heavens a familiar face would suddenly appear, marking a celebration in honor of a popular leader.

344

Agriculture: The Plowman in the Clouds

In springtime two skyships were visible, crawling like flies across the sunlit cheeks of the clouds, busily cultivating fields, plowing up the earth below by means of harrows attached to them. Occasionally the skyships vanished from view behind the cloud, and then it seemed as if the laboring clouds themselves were pulling the harrows, hitched to a yoke like oxen. Later the skyfliers flew past like magnificent waterfalls concealed in the clouds, in order to water the plowed fields with artificial rain and from that height to scatter huge streams of seeds. The plowman had found a new place in the clouds, and immediately he was able to till entire fields, the lands of an entire rural commune. The lands of many families could be tilled be a single plowman stationed in the springtime clouds.

Channels of Communication: Spark Writing

Underwater highways with glass walls connected both banks of the Volga at various points. The steppe came more and more to resemble the sea. In summer the boundless steppe was crisscrossed by dry-land vessels that ran on rails powered by wind and sails. Thunderships, skates, and sleds rigged with sails connected one settlement with another. Every hunting or fishing outpost had its own landing field for airships and its own receiver for ray communication with the rest of Planet Earth. As the spark voices spoke their messages from the ends of the earth, they were instantly projected onto the shadow books.

The Eye Cure

Fields planted from the clouds, shadow books that conveyed scientific information from all over the planet, dry-land sailing ships that crisscrossed the steppe like the sea, walls in the public square that became great teachers of young people—all these things changed Swanland radically in only two years. In the shadow libraries the children all read the same book at once, page by page, as it was turned by someone behind them. But places of worship still existed. The most important place of worship was an area sacred to the god of wilderness, where fenced-off preserves were set up. There plants, birds, and turtles all had the right to grow, live, and die. The rule was that all animals were to be kept from extinction. The best doctors had discovered that the eyes of live animals possessed special currents that had a curative effect on mentally disturbed people. Doctors wrote prescriptions for psychological treatment that consisted simply of looking into the eyes of live animals, either the gentle submissiveness of a toad's eye, the gemlike gaze of a snake, or the courageous stare of a lion, and they ascribed to them the same ability that a tuner possesses for adjusting out-of-tune strings. The eye cure became as widespread as mineral baths are today.

The countryside became a scientific commune led by a plowman in the clouds. Each winged creator advanced confidently toward a commune that included not only humans, but all living things on Planet Earth.

And he heard at his door the knock of a tiny monkey's fist.

[1918: T 614]

Ourselves and Our Buildings. Creators of Streetsteads. Proclamor

Swaying beneath the weight of our armor, we poke mankind with the toe of our boot, sit back in the saddle, and point out the way! Then we ram his tired flanks with the little iron wheel attached to our boot, and the tired animal gathers for the jump and takes it idly, waving his tail with satisfaction.

We ride high in the saddle and shout: that's the way we want to go, toward those glass sunflowers in the iron shrubbery, toward cities whose patterns are as harmonious as a fisherman's net stretched out on the beach, cities of glass, shiny as inkwells, who compete among themselves for sunshine and a scrap of sky as if they were part of the vegetable kingdom. "Sunward" is written upon them in the terrifying alphabet of iron consonants and vowels of glass!

And if people are the salt of the earth, shouldn't we pass the salt-cellar (the salt-solar!) sunward? We lay our massive hand upon the contemporary city and its planners and we shout: "Get rid of these rats' nests," and the terrifying rush of our breathing changes the air. We Futurians observe with pleasure that many things shatter beneath our mailed fist. The tables of victors are already hurled down, and the victors are already drinking our *Mares' Milk,* the drink of the steppe; a quiet moan comes from the vanquished.

We will now tell you about your city, and about ours.

I

Characteristics of the supposedly beautiful cities of the bygoners (ancestral architecture).

1. The bird's-eye view: at present, from directly overhead, cities look like currycombs, like hairbrushes. Will it be like that in a city of winged inhabitants? In actual fact, the hand of time will turn the axis

of vision upright, carrying away with it even that piece of architectural pomposity, the right angle. People now look at a city from the side; in the future they will look from directly overhead. The roof will become the main thing, the axis of the standing structure. With swarms of flyers and the face of the street above it, the city will begin to be concerned about its roofs and not its walls. Consider the roof as a thing in itself. It basks in the blue, far from dirty clouds of dust. A roof has no desire to imitate a pavement, to sweep itself clean with a broom composed of lungs, windpipes, and teary eyes; it will not sweep up its dust with eyelashes, or use lungs to sponge the black dirt off its body. Dress up your roofs! Think of them as hairdos, add some pretty pins. People will no longer gather in the vicious streets, whose dirty desire reduces human beings to residue in a washbasin; rather they will throng upon rooftops, beautiful young rooftops, waving their handkerchiefs after a giant levitating air-cloud, sending goodbyes and farewells after their departing friends.

How are they dressed? In suits of armor made from black or white linen, greaves, breastplates, gauntlets, gorgets, all stiffened and ironed, so that they always go around in armor the color of snow or of soot, cold, hard, even though they get soaked through in the first rainfall. Suits of linen armor. Instead of plumes fastened to their helmets, some of them wear smoking pitch. Some of them exchange bold, refined glances of condescension. Which is why the walkway runs higher than the windows and gutters and downspouts. People throng the rooftops, while the ground is left for the transport of goods; the city becomes a network of intersecting bridges, whose inhabited arches connect the residential towers that serve as their supports; the residential buildings serve the bridge as piers and as walls for shaft areas. The city crowds will no longer move about on foot or on their four-legged colleagues; they will have learned to fly above the city, raining their glances upon the place below; above the city will hover a cloud that will test its builder's work, a threat to weak roofs, like a thunderstorm or tornado. People on the rooftops will wrest from any groundling unstinting praise to the roof, and to the street that passes above the buildings. And so, behold its contours! A street high above the city, and the eyes of the crowd high above the street!

2. The city seen from the side: the so-called beautiful cities of the present day, seen from a certain distance, look like scrap bins. They have forgotten the rule of alternation that older structures (Greek, Islam)

knew, alternation of the density of stone with the immateriality of air (Voronikhin's cathedral), the alternation of substance and void; a similar relationship between stressed and unstressed syllables is the essence of a line of verse. City streets today have no perceptible pulse. It is as hard to look at streets all lumped together as it is to read words without spaces between them, or to speak words without stress or accent. What we need is a street with variation, where the heights of the buildings are the accent marks, so to speak, providing a variation in the breathing of the stone. Present-day buildings are built according to the well-known rule for cannon: find a mold and fill it with molten metal. It is the same thing: take a blueprint and fill it up with stone. But in a blueprint there is something that exists and is ponderable, namely the line, which is absent from the building, and contrariwise: the ponderability of a building's walls is absent from the blueprint, which seems empty; so that the reality of the blueprint corresponds to the nonreality of the building, and vice versa. The designers take the blueprint and fill it with stone, i.e., over the course of centuries, without even noticing, they have multiplied the fundamental ratio of stone and void by minus one, which is why the most grotesque buildings may have the most elegant blueprints, and a Scriabin of a blueprint can produce a scrap bin of a building. It is time to put a stop to this! Blueprints are only good for constructing buildings of wire, since the idea of replacing a line with a void and the void with stone is the same as calling the Pope—*il Papa di Roma*—the friend of *Mamma Roma*. The outer surfaces are ruined by a muddle of windows, by the detailing of drainpipes, petty stupidities of design, nonsensicalities, which is why the majority of buildings still in scaffoldings are better than when they are finished. The contemporary tenement apartment building (the art of the bygoners) is an outgrowth of the medieval castle; but castles were freestanding buildings surrounded by air, self-sufficient as hermits, resembling a loud interjection! in the landscape. But here, flattened out by their contiguous walls, depriving one another of decent views, squeezed into the spawn of the streets—what have they come to resemble, with their jumpy patterns of windows, but lines in a book you try to read on a train! Isn't this the way flowers die, clutched too tightly in a clumsy hand, just like these rats'-nest buildings? these descendants of castles?

3. What serves to ornament cities? On the threshold of its beauty stand factory chimneys. The three smoking chimneys on the south em-

bankment of the Moscow River call to mind a candlestick and three candles invisible in daylight. But the forest of chimneys on the lifeless northern swamp forces us to witness nature shifting from one order to another; this is the soft, tender moss of a second-order forest; the city itself becomes a first experiment in a higher-order growth, as yet amateurish. Those swamps are a clearing of silky chimney moss. The chimneys are golden-haired delights.

4. Inside the city. Very few people have realized that to entrust the development of streets to the greed and stupidity of landlords and to give them the right to build buildings is to reduce life to nothing more than unwarranted solitary confinement; the gloomy life that goes on inside a tenement building is hardly distinguishable from solitary confinement; it resembles the life of an oarsmen confined beneath the deck of a galley: he waves an oar in the air once a month, and the monster greed of a dark and alien will proceeds toward its dubious goals.

5. Few have realized as well that traveling is unpleasant and totally devoid of comfort.

II

Remedies from the yet-to-be city of the Futurians:

1. The idea is this: a container of molded glass, a mobile dwelling-module supplied with a door, with attachment couplings, mounted on wheels, with its inhabitant inside it. It is set on a train (special gauge, with racks specially designed to hold such modules) or on a steamship, and inside, without ever leaving it, its inhabitant would travel to his destination. Expandable on occasion, the glass cubicle was suitable for overnight camping. Once it had been decided that the primary building unit would no longer be an incidental, material like brick, but rather these modular units inhabited by individuals, they began the construction of framework-buildings whose open spaces were filled in by the inhabitants themselves with their moveable glass cubicles. And these units were able to be transported from one building to another. Thus was a great achievement attained: it was no longer the single individual who traveled, but his house on wheels or, more precisely, his booth, capable of being attached to a flatrack on a train or to a steamship.

Just as a tree in winter lives in anticipation of leaves or needles, so these framework-buildings, these grillworks full of empty spaces, spread their arms like steel junipers and awaited their glass occupants. They looked like unloaded, unarmed vessels, or like the gallows tree, or like a desolate city in the mountains. And they gave everyone the right to own such a habitation in any city. Every city in the land, wherever a proprietor may decide to move in his glass cubicle, was required to offer a location in one of these framework-buildings for the mobile dwelling-module (the glass hut). And with a whine of chains the traveler in his glass cocoon is hoisted aloft.

For the sake of this innovation, the form and dimensions of all dwelling units were identical throughout the entire country. The number and row of the proprietor's unit was marked on the glass surface. He himself was able to sit quietly reading as they moved him into place. And in this way, we created proprietors: (1) not on the basis of land ownership, but only on the right to a space in a framework-building; (2) not in any one particular city, but generally in any city in the country that takes part in this union for citizen exchange. And all this in order to serve the needs of a mobile population.

Whole cities consisted of such frameworks, products of the joint labor of glassmakers and Ural steelworkers. Every city had such a half-occupied iron framework waiting for glass occupants, like a skeleton without muscles, the cells for the insertable glass cubicles, which are like a currency of volume, appearing empty and dark. And everywhere boats and trains on the move, laden with these glass cubicles, moving them from place to place. Similar framework-hotels were constructed at the beaches, beside lakes, near mountains and rivers. Sometimes one owner would have two or three such cages. Sleeping rooms in the buildings alternated with living rooms, dining rooms, restcrys.

2. Contemporary rats'-nest buildings are built through a combination of stupidity and greed. Whereas their predecessors, the free-standing castles of the Middle Ages, extended their power over the area around them, these sardine castles squeezed sideways next to one another along the street exert their power inward, over the people who live inside them. In the unequal struggle between the many who inhabit a building and the one who owns it, the many, innocent of any bloodletting, nevertheless live in confinement, in the dark prison of these tenements, oppressed by the heavy hand of this combination of stupidity and greed; the only relief available to them has come first from private associations, then from the government. It has been recognized that the city is a focal point for rays of social force, and is thus in certain

measure the property of all the inhabitants of the country, and that in his attempt to live in a city a citizen of the country cannot simply be thrown (by one of those who has just happened to take the city away from him) into the stone huddle of a rats' nest, there to live the life of a prisoner, especially one condemned not by the court system but by the mere facts of existence. But what difference does it make to the prisoner? Even if he doesn't suspect the dreadful uniformity of the living quarters around him, he has been harshly condemned, whether by existence or by the court system; he has been cast into a dark hole like a prisoner of war and cut off from the rest of the world.

It had become clear that the construction of dwellings was legitimately the business of those who would have to live in them. The first beginnings were made when individual streets joined together to form a shareholders' association, in order to construct communal habitats, streetsteads, whose design was based on the principle of alternation of mass and void, thus exchanging the street as a filthy container for a street conceived as a single beautiful habitat; this arrangement was based on the system used in old Novgorod. Here is a view of the great Tver street: a tall townstead built of logs surrounded by an open square. A slender tower connected by a bridge to the neighboring streetstead. Wall-buildings stand next to each other, like three books standing on end.

A residential tower is connected by two suspension bridges to another tall, slender tower just like it, and yet another courtstead. It all resembles a garden. The buildings are connected by bridges, the elevated walkways of the townstead. Thus were the idiosyncratic horrors of private architecture avoided. An organic remedy began to take effect, combatting the arsenic of earlier architecture. Private enterprise still possessed the right to build buildings (1) outside the cities, (2) on the outskirts, in rural areas and wasteland, but even so only for personal use. At a later period governmental authority became involved in streetstead planning, and the concept of the public habitat came into being.

By assuming the authority for urban planning and defining its concern for the problem of houslings and houseability, the government became the senior builder in the land. Standing upon the debris of private architecture, it rested upon the shield of gratitude of those who had suffered torments in the rats' nests of the present day.

They realized that it was ethical to take a profit from the building of glass dwellings. All those who had suffered from the indifferent attitude "sink or swim" were taken under the wing of the architect-government.

The decree against private architecture was never extended to rural dwellings, peasant huts, family dwellings, or farmsteads. The war was being waged only against the urban rats' nests. Land occupied by farm-steaders remained in the hands of its previous owners. The urban hab-itats were: (1) leased out to societies set up by the cities, groups of physicians, travel societies, street associations, parishes; (2) remained with the builder; (3) were sold upon conditions that controlled greed and restricted landlords' rights. This provided an enormous source of revenues. The tall glass towers of the townstead, constructed along the coast and in picturesque locations, became part of the beauty of the locale. And so the government became the chief builder of the nation, and this happened because its resources made it the most powerful of all private societies.

3. What kinds of structures were built? (A word of warning here. We are going to speak now about the marvelous monsters of the Fu-turian imagination, which will have replaced the public squares of the present day, dirty as the soul of Izmailov.)

(a) Bridge-buildings: structures where the arches of a bridge and its support pilings are both composed of dwelling units. Some of these glass and steel honeycombs served as part of an access bridge to neigh-boring structures. This was known as a bridgestead. Support towers and a hemispherical arch. Bridgesteads were often built over a river.

(b) The poplar-tree-building consisted of a narrow tower sheathed from top to bottom by rings of glass cubicles. There was an elevator in the tower, and each sun-space had its own private access to the interior shaft, which resembled an enormous bell tower (700-1400 feet high). The top of the building served as a landing platform. The rings of sun-spaces were closely packed together to a very great height. The glass sheath and its dark frame gave the building its resemblance to a poplar tree.

(c) Underwater palaces: for auritoriums. These were underwater palaces built of thick glass blocks right down among the fishes, with views of the sea, and underwater hatches connecting them to dry land. There, in the silence of the deep, speech and rhetoric were taught.

(d) Steamship-buildings. An artificial reservoir constructed at a high elevation and filled with water, and a real steamship riding the waves, inhabited mainly by sailors.

(e) The filament-building consisted of single rooms connected in a single strand stretched between two towers. Dimensions 20 × 700 × 700 feet. Lots of light! But not much room. A thousand inhabitants. Quite suitable for hotels, hospitals, for construction upon mountain-tops or at the coast. Transparent because of the glass sun-spaces, it had the appearance of a filament or film. Very attractive at night, when it resembled a thread of fire strung between the dark gloomy needle-towers. Built on hilltops. An excellent example of the possibilities of the framework-building.

(f) A similar building with a double strand of rooms.

(g) The checkerboard-building. Where empty room-slots were arranged to form a checkerboard pattern.

(h) The swing-building. A chain fixed between two factory chimneys, with a little dwelling-house hung on it. Suitable for thinkers, sailors, or Futurians.

(i) The strand-of-hair-building consists of a lateral axis with strands of Futurian rooms ascending next to it, to a height of 700–1400 feet. Sometimes as many as three of these strands twine along a steel needle.

(j) The goblet-building; a steel stalk 350–1400 feet high supporting a glass dome containing four or five rooms. Private apartments for those who had retired from the earth; set upon a base of steel beams.

(k) The tube-building consisted of a double sheet of rooms curved to form a tube enclosing a spacious courtyard containing a waterfall.

(l) In the form of an open book; this one consists of stone walls set at an angle, and glass sheets of living modules arranged fanwise between these walls. This is the book-building. The walls are 700–1400 feet high.

(m) The field-building, in which great floors serve to support a tranquil, deserted space, free of interior walls, upon which in artistic disarray are scattered glass huts, lean-tos that don't reach the ceiling, self-contained wigwams and tepees; deer antlers, those rough-hewn products of nature, hung upon the walls and gave each circle the look of a hunter's shack. The corners contained places to bathe privately. Often these floors rose one over the other in the form of a pyramid.

(n) The house on wheels. On a long gas-guzzler with one or more dwelling-modules; living quarters, a secular travelstead for twentieth-century gypsies.

Principles:

1. Fixed framework-buildings, mobile dwelling-modules.
2. Individuals travel by train without ever leaving the living space.
3. The right to private possession of a living space in any city.
4. Construction carried out by the public sector.
5. Regulation for the construction of private houses; an end to streets (as they presently exist); the rhythmic design of habitats, towers as points of interjection in the landscape.

A journey described: I sat in my dwelling-module reading an elegant poem composed of the four words *go-um, mo-um, su-um,* and *tu-um;* I pondered its meaning, which seemed to me more beautiful than many more elaborate passages designed only to destroy euphony. Without leaving I was carried by train across the continent to the seacoast, where I intended to visit my sister. I was aware of scraping noises, of a gentle rocking. That was the steel chain that hoisted me into a poplar-tree-building. Dwelling units in the glass sheath and occasional faces flickered past. A sudden stop. Here in one of the building's empty cells I left my living space. Dressed in the building's style of dress, I stopped at the waterfall and walked out onto one of the small bridges. Elegant, slender, it joined two poplar-tree-buildings at a height of 600 feet. I bowed my head and began to recompute myself, to learn what I had to do in order to fulfill its will. In the distance a filament-building hung between its two steel needles: a thousand glass living units glittered in the air, like a string of trailers suspended between two towers. This was a residence for artists; they enjoyed a double view of the ocean, since the building and its two towers rose near the water. It looked very beautiful in the evening. Beside it a flower-building rose gracefully to an unattainable height; it had a dome of reddish matte glass, lacy railings that formed the edge of the calyx, and staircases of beautifully wrought steel. This was the house where I and E lived. The steel needles of the filament-building and a dense fabric of glass honeycombs glowed in the sunset. From the corner tower, another building stretched away in a lateral direction. Two strand-buildings stretched upwards twining around each other. Before me stood a checkerboard-building. I was full of thought. A grove of glassy poplar-tree-buildings lined the shore. Meanwhile four "Chaika II's" carried an airborne net with bathers sitting on it, and set them down next to the water. It was time for a swim. They rocked side by side on the water. I thought about fairy-tale flying horses, about magic carpets; what *were* fairy tales really, I wondered: merely an old man's memory? Or were they visions of a future only children can foresee? I thought, in other words, about the flood and the destruction of Atlantis: had it already happened, or was it yet in the future? I was rather inclined to think it was yet in the future.

I stood on the bridge; I was full of thought.

[1920–21(?): IV.275]

Proposals

*Grow edible microscopic organisms in lakes. Every lake will become a kettle of ready-made soup that only needs to be heated. Contented people will lie about on the shores, swimming and having dinner. The food of the future.

*Effect the exchange of labor and services by means of an exchange of heartbeats. Estimate every task in terms of heartbeats—the monetary unit of the future, in which all individuals are equally wealthy. Take 365 times 317 as the median number of heartbeats in any twenty-four-hour period.

*Use this same unit of exchange to compute international trade.

*End the world war with the first flight to the moon.

*Establish a single written language for all Indo-Europeans, based on scientific principles.

*Effect an innovation in land ownership, recognizing that the amount of land every single individual requires cannot be less than the total surface of Planet Earth.

*Let air travel and wireless communication be the two legs humanity stands on. And let's see what the consequences will be.

*Devise the art of waking easily from dreams.

*Regard capital cities as accumulations of dust at the nodes of standing waves, according to the theory of resonant plates (Kundt's dust figures).

*Remembering that n^0 is the sign for a point, n^1 the sign for a straight line, n^2 and n^3 the signs for area and volume, find the space of the fractional powers: $n^{1/2}$, $n^{2/3}$, $n^{1/3}$. Where are they? Understand forces as the powers of space, proceeding from the fact that a force is the reason for the movement of a point, the movement of a point creates a straight line, the movement of a line creates area, and the conversion of point to line and line to area is accomplished by the increase of the power from zero to one and from one to two.

*Adopt apes into the family of man and grant them selected rights of citizenship.

*Assign numbers the names of the five vowels: *a, u, o, e, i,* thus $a = 1, u = 2, o = 3, e = 4, i = 5, ia = 0$. A system of notation based on five.

*All the ideas of Planet Earth (there aren't that many), like the houses on a street, should be designated by individual numbers, and this visual code used to communicate and to exchange ideas. Designate the speeches of Cicero, Cato, Othello, Demosthenes by numbers, and in the courts and other institutions, instead of imitation speeches that nobody needs, simply hang up a card marked with the number of an appropriate speech. This will become the first international language. This principle has already been partially introduced in legal codes. Languages will thus be left to the arts and freed from humiliating burdens. Our ears have become exhausted.

*Take 1915 as the first year of a new era: indicate years by means of the numerical expression for a plane $a + b \sqrt{-1}$, in the form $317d + e\sqrt{-1}$, where *e* is less than 317.

*Instead of clothes wear medieval armor, all white, made out of the same material that is now used for those silly starched collars and stiff-front shirts.

*Set aside a special uninhabited island, such as Iceland, for a never-ending war between anybody from any country who wants to fight now. (For people who want to die like heroes.)

*For ordinary wars, use sleep guns (with sleep bullets).

*Introduce into the business of birth the same order and organization that is now reserved for the business of killing; birth battalions, a fixed number of them.

*Redesign chemical and biological warfare so that it merely puts people to sleep. Then governments will earn our admiration and deserve our praise.

*Usher in everywhere, instead of the concept of space, the concept of time. For instance, wars on Planet Earth between generations, wars in the trenches of time.

*Train wrecks would be unavoidable if the movement of trains was organized only in terms of space (the railway network). It's precisely the same with governments; we need a timetable for their movements (as for different trains over the same network of tracks).

*We must divide up humanity into inventor/explorers and all the rest. A class of farseeing visionaries.

*Serious research in the art of combining human races and the breeding of new ones for the needs of Planet Earth.

*Reform of the housing laws and regulations, the right to have a room of your own in any city whatsoever and the right to move whenever you want (the right to a domicile without restrictions in space). Humanity in the age of air travel cannot place limits on the right of its members to a private, personal space.

*Build apartment houses in the form of steel frameworks, into which could be inserted transportable glass dwelling units.

*Demand that armed organizations provide individuals with weapons to dispute the opinion of the Futurians, that the whole of Planet Earth belongs to them.

*Establish recognized classes of geagogues and superstates.

*Let factory chimneys awake and sing morning hymns to the rising sun, above the Seine as well as over Tokyo, over the Nile, and over Delhi.

*Organize a worldwide authority to decorate Planet Earth with monuments, turning them out like a lathe operator. Decorate Mont Blanc with the head of Hiawatha, the gray peaks of Nicaragua with the head of Kruchonykh, the Andes with the head of David Burliuk. The fundamental rule for these monuments to be as follows: the individual's birthplace and his monument must be located at opposite poles of the earth. The white cliffs of Dover can provide a maritime monument (a head rising out of the sea) for Huriet el-Ayn, a Persian woman burned at the stake. Let seagulls perch upon it, beside ships full of Englishmen.

On the great mall of Washington D.C. we must have a monument to the first martyrs of science—the Chinese Hsi and Ho, state astronomers who were put to death for daydreaming.

Erect portable moving monuments on the platforms of trains.

*Create a new occupation—penmen—recognizing that the graphic quiver of handwriting itself has a powerful effect on the reader. The unheard voice of handwriting. Also create a recognized class of artists who work with numbers.

*Utilize the boring eyes of trains as projectors for flashing out schedules of what's happening tomorrow in the arts, like an arrow in swift pursuit.

*Effect an innovation in land ownership, recognizing that the amount of land required for individual ownership cannot be less than the total surface of Planet Earth. Conflicts between governments will thus be resolved.

*Use heartbeats as the units of measurement for the rights and obligations of human labor. The heartbeat is the monetary unit of the future. Doctors are the paymasters of the future. Hunger and health are account books, and bright eyes and happiness are the receipts.

*Base a new system of measurement on these principles: the dimensions of Planet Earth in time, space, and energy to be recognized as the initial unit, with a chain of quantities diminished 365 times by the derivatives a, $a/365$, $a/365^2$. This method eliminates the stupidity of seconds and minutes, while preservng the solar day, divided now into 365 parts; each of these "day days" will equal 237 seconds; the next smaller unit will be 0.65 seconds.

The unit of area will be 59 square centimenters, or $K/365^7$, where K equals the earth's surface.

The unit of length will be $R/365^3$, or 13 centimeters, where R equals the earth's radius. Similarly for weight and energy. What will happen is that many quantities will be expressed by the unit number.

*Employ radio waves to transmit lectures from a Central University to country schools. Every school nestled at the foot of some green hill will receive scientific information, and the loudspeaker will become the teacher for the attentive settlement. A tongue of lightning, as a conductor for scientific truth.

*Deploy the worldwide scientific community in separate authorities, each with a given scientific goal (a struggle with spatially defined authority). For instance, an authority to investigate the question whether there exists any direct contact between people at opposite poles of the earth, if their desires and feelings are connected. Does somebody weep on the banks of the Mississippi whenever somebody rejoices beside the Volga?

Comparisons of tidal waves. Or an authority to investigate the curvature of the earth's surface.

Establishing these projects means creating a special scientific authority for each specific scientific goal.

*Organize a society for all the string players on Planet Earth. The proud Union of Stringplanearth . . .

*Arrange for the gradual transfer of power to the starry sky . . .

*Think of Earth as a resonating plate, and capital cities as dust accumulated at the nodes of standing waves (which England and Japan are already well aware of).

*Considering the advantages of a unified coastal frontier, turn Asia to a unified spiritual island. Anyway there is a second sea above us— the sky. A new commandment: Thou shalt love the new continuity of Asia's seacoast.

*Establish December 25, 1915 New Style as the first day of the new Kalpa.

*Let the laws of everyday existence give way to the equations of fate.

*Let the oriental carpet of names and governments dissolve into the ray of humanity.

*The universe considered as a ray. You are a construct of space. We are a construct of time.

*In order to introduce into the world the great principles of anti-money, to confer upon the board chairmen and directors of great corporations the rank of ensign in the workforce, and to make them accept the pay scale of an ensign in the workforce. The real power of such enterprises thus comes under the control of a peaceable workforce.

[1915 16: V.157]

The Head of the Universe. Time in Space

Two theses:

1. There are ways of looking at a new form of creativity, the art of number pictures, where a number artist can freely draw the inspired head of the universe as he sees it turned toward him. He is not a child; he has no need of the cages and boundaries of the separate scientific disciplines. Proclaiming a free triangle with three points—the world, the artist, and the number—he draws the ear or the mouth of the universe with the broad brush of numbers. He executes his strokes freely in scientific space, and he knows that number serves the human mind in the same way that charcoal serves the artist's hand, or clay and chalk the hand of the sculptor. Working with number as his charcoal, he unites all previous human knowledge in his art. A single one of his lines provides an immediate lightninglike connection between a red corpuscle and Earth, a second precipitates into helium, a third shatters upon the unbending heavens and discovers the satellites of Jupiter. Velocity is infused with a new speed, the speed of thought, while the boundaries that separate different areas of knowledge will disappear before the procession of liberated numbers cast like orders into print throughout the whole of Planet Earth.

Here they are then, these ways of looking at the new form of creativity, which we think is perfectly workable.

The surface of Planet Earth is 510,051,300 square kilometers; the surface of a red corpuscle—that citizen and star of man's Milky Way—0.000,128 square millimeters. These citizens of the sky and the body have concluded a treaty, whose provision is this: the surface of the star Earth divided by the surface of the tiny corpuscular star equals 365 times 10 to the tenth power (365×10^{10}). A beautiful concordance of two worlds, one that establishes man's right to first place on Earth. This is the first article of the treaty between the government of blood cells and the government of heavenly bodies. A living walking Milky Way and his tiny star have concluded a 365-point agreement with the Milky Way in the sky and its great Earth star. The dead Milky Way and the living one have affixed their signatures to it as two equal and legal entities.

2. In several of Malevich's shaded-in sketches, his encrustations of black planes and spheres, I have found that the ratio of the largest shaded area to the smallest black circle is 365. These collections of planes therefore contain a shade year and a shade day. Once more in the realm of painting I had observed time commanding space. In the consciousness of this artist, white and black are sometimes engaged in a real conflict and sometimes vanish completely, yielding place to pure dimension.

[1919: TsGALI, f.665, op.1, ed. khr.32, l. 41]

Artists of the World!
(a written language for Planet Earth: a common system of hieroglyphs for the people of our planet)

We have long been searching for a program that would act something like a lens, capable of focusing the combined rays of the work of the artist and the work of the thinker toward a single point where they might join in a common task and be able to ignite even the cold essence of ice and turn it to a blazing bonfire. Such a program, the lens capable of directing together your fiery courage and the cold intellect of the thinker, has now been discovered.

The goal is to create a common written language shared by all the peoples of this third satellite of the Sun, to invent written symbols that can be understood and accepted by our entire star, populated as it is with human beings and lost here in the universe. You can see that such a task is worthy of the time we live in. Painting has always used a language accessible to everyone. And the Chinese and Japanese peoples speak hundreds of different languages, but they read and write in one single written language. Languages have betrayed their glorious beginnings. There was once a time when words served to dispel enmity and make the future transparent and peaceful, and when languages, proceeding in stages, united the people of (1) a cave, (2) a settlement, (3) a tribe or kinship group, (4) a state, into a single rational world, a union of those who shared one single auditory instrument for the exchange of values and ideas. One savage caveman understood another and laid his blind weapon aside. Nowadays sounds have abandoned their past functions and serve the purposes of hostility; they have become differentiated auditory instruments for the exchange of rational wares; they have divided multilingual mankind into different camps involved in tariff wars, into a series of verbal marketplaces beyond whose confines any given language loses currency. Every system of auditory currency claims supremacy, and so languages as such serve to disunite mankind and wage spectral wars. Let us hope that one single written language may henceforth accompany the longterm destinies of mankind and prove to be the new vortex that unites us, the new integrator of the human race. Mute graphic marks will reconcile the cacophony of languages.

To the artists who work with ideas falls the task of creating an alphabet of concepts, a system of basic units of thought from which words may be constructed.

The task of artists who work with paint is to provide graphic symbols for the basic units of our mental processes.

We have now accomplished that part of that labor which was the thinkers' task; we stand now on the first landing of the staircase of thinkers, and we find there the artists of China and Japan, who were already ahead of us, and our greetings to them! Here is what we see from our place on that staircase: the vista of a shared human alphabet that our place on the staircase of thinkers reveals. For the moment, without advancing any proof, I maintain:

1. B (*v*) in all languages means the turning of one point around another, either in a full circle or only a part of one, along an arc, up or down.

2. X (*kh*) means a closed curve that shields the location of one point from the movement toward it of another point (a protective line).

3. З (*z*) means the reflection of a moving point from the surface of a mirror at an angle equal to the angle of incidence. The impact of a ray upon a solid surface.

4. M (*m*) means the disintegration of a certain quantity into infinitely small parts (within certain limits) equal as a whole to the original quantity.

5. Ш (*sh*) means the merging of several surfaces into a single surface and the merging of the boundaries between them. The striving of the one-dimensional world of any given dimension to describe a larger area of a two-dimensional world.

6. П (*p*) means the increase along a straight line of the empty space between two points, the movement along a straight line of one point away from another and, as in the sum of a point set, the rapid growth in the volume occupied by a certain number of points.

7. Ч (*ch*) means the empty space of one body containing the volume of another body, in such a way that the negative volume of the first

body is exactly equal to the positive volume of the second. This is a hollow two-dimensional world that serves as an envelope for a three-dimensional body—within certain limits.

8. Λ (*l*) means the diffusion of the smallest possible waves on the widest possible surface perpendicular to a moving point, the height vanishing with the increase in width, for a given volume the height becomes infinitely small as the other two axes become infinitely large. The formation of a two-dimensional body out of a three-dimensional one.

9. К (*k*) means the absence of motion, a set of *n* points at rest, the preservation of their relative positions; the termination of movement.

10. С (*s*) means a fixed point that serves as a point of departure for the motion of many other points which begin their trajectory there.

11. Т (*t*) means a direction, wherein a fixed point creates an absence of motion among a set of motions in the same direction, a negative trajectory and its direction beyond a fixed point.

12. Д (*d*) means the transposition of a point from one system of points to another system, which is then transformed by the addition of that point.

13. Γ (*g*) means the largest possible oscillations, whose height is perpendicular to the motion and which are extended along the axis of motion. Movements of maximum height.

14. Н (*n*) means the absence of points, an empty field.

15. Б (*b*) means the meeting of two points moving along a straight line from opposite directions. Their clash, the reversal of one point by the impact of the other.

16. Ц (*ts*) means the passage of one body through an empty space in another.

17. Щ (*shch*) means the laying out of a whole surface into separate sections, the volume remaining fixed.

18. Р (*r*) means the division of a smooth hollow body as a trace of the movement of another body through it.

19. Ж (*zh*) means motion out of a closed volume, the separation of free point systems.

So then, from our landing on the staircase of thinkers, it has become clear that the simple bodies of a language—the sounds of the alphabet—are the names of various aspects of space, an enumeration of the events of its life. The alphabet common to a multitude of peoples is in fact a short dictionary of the spatial world that is of such concern to your art, painters, and to your brushes.

Each individual word resembles a small workers' collective, where the first sound of the word is like the chairman of the collective who directs the whole set of sounds in the word. If we assemble all the words that begin with the same consonantal sound, we observe that, just as meteors often fall from one single point in the sky, all these words fly from the single point of a certain conceptualization of space. And that point becomes the meaning of the sound of the alphabet, and its simplest name.

So for example the twenty names for buildings that begin with X (*kh*), names of entities that protect the point of man from the hostile point of bad weather, cold or enemies, bear the burden of our second claim quite solidly on their shoulders.

The artists' task would be to provide a special sign for each type of space. Each sign must be simple and clearly distinguishable from all the rest. It might be possible to resort to the use of color, and to designate M (*m*) with dark blue, B (*v*) with green, Б (*b*) with red, C (*s*) with gray, Л (*l*) with white, and so on. But it might also be possible for this universal dictionary, the shortest in existence, to retain only graphic signs. Life, of course, will introduce its own corrections, but in life it has always been true that in the beginning the sign for a concept was a simple picture of that concept. And from that seed sprang up the tree of each individual letter's existence.

To me, B (*v*) appears in the form of a circle and a point within it. ⊙

X (*kh*) in the form of a combination of two lines and a point. ⊥
З (*z*) a kind of K fallen over on its back: a mirror and a ray. ⊿
Л (*l*) a circular area and an axis line. ♁
Ч (*ch*) in the form of a goblet. Y
C (*s*) a bundle of straight lines. ≪

But it is your task, you artists, to alter or improve these signs. If you succeed in constructing them, you will have put the finishing touches on the tasks that must be accomplished on this star we all share.

This proposed experiment to convert beyonsense language from an untamed condition to a domesticated one, to make it bear useful burdens, deserves a certain amount of attention.

After all, even in Sanskrit *vritti* means rotation, and in Egyptian as in Russian *khata* means hut.

A program for a single, universal, scientifically constructed language appears more and more clearly as a goal for humanity.

Your task, you artists, would be to construct a suitable instrument of exchange between auditory and visual modes, to construct a system of graphic signs that inspires confidence.

In the alphabet given above I have already provided a universal system of sound "images" for various aspects of space; now we must construct a second system, one of written signs, soundless currency for the marketplace of conversation.

I am confident you will avoid external influences and will follow your own creative paths.

I here offer the first experiments in beyonsense language as the language of the future (with one reservation, that vowels in what follows are incidental and serve the purposes of euphony):

Instead of saying:

> The Hunnic and Gothic hordes, having united and gathered themselves about Attila, full of warlike enthusiasm, progressed further together, but having been met and defeated by Aetius, the protector of Rome, they scattered into numerous bands and settled and remained peacefully on their own lands, having poured out into and filled up the emptiness of the steppes.

Could we not say instead:

> SHa + So (Hunnic and Gothic hordes), Ve Attila, CHa Po, So Do, but Bo + Zo Aetius, KHo of Rome, So Mo Ve + Ka So, Lo SHa of the steppes + CHa.

And that is what the first beyonsense story played upon the strings of the alphabet sounds like. Or:

Ve So of the human race Be Go of languages, Pe of our minds Ve So SHa languages, Bo Mo of words Mo Ka of thought CHa of sounds Po So Do Lu earth Mo So languages, Ve earth.

Which is to say:

Intent upon uniting the human race, but meeting the barrier of the mountain chains of languages, the fire storm of our minds revolves around the idea of a communal beyonsense language and achieves the atomization of words into units of thought contained in an envelope of sounds and then rapidly and simultaneously proceeds toward the recognition throughout the earth of one single beyonsense language.

Of course, these attempts are nothing but a baby's first cry, and the labor all lies ahead of us, but the overall model of a universal language in the future is here provided. It will be "beyonsense."

[1919: V.216]

On Poetry

People say a poem must be understandable. Like a sign on the street, which carries the clear and simple words "For Sale." But a street sign is not exactly a poem. Though it is understandable. On the other hand, what about spells and incantations, what we call magic words, the sacred language of paganism, words like "shagadam, magadam, vigadam, pitz, patz, patzu"—they are rows of mere syllables that the intellect can make no sense of, and they form a kind of beyonsense language in folk speech. Nevertheless an enormous power over mankind is attributed to these incomprehensible words and magic spells, and direct influence upon the fate of man. They contain powerful magic. They claim the power of controlling good and evil and swaying the hearts of lovers. The prayers of many nations are written in a language incomprehensible to those who pray. Does a Hindu understand the Vedas? Russians do not understand Old Church Slavonic. Neither do Poles and Czechs understand Latin. But a prayer written in Latin works just as powerfully as the sign on the street. In the same way, the language of magic spells and incantations does not wish to be judged in terms of everyday common sense.

Its strange wisdom may be broken down into the truths contained in separate sounds: *sh, m, v,* etc. We do not yet understand these sounds. We confess that honestly. But there is no doubt that these sound sequences constitute a series of universal truths passing before the predawn of our soul. If we think of the soul as split between the government of intellect and a stormy population of feelings, then incantations and beyonsense language are appeals over the head of the government straight to the population of feelings, a direct cry to the predawn of the soul or a supreme example of the rule of the masses in the life of language and intellect, a lawful device reserved for rare occasions. Another example: Sophia Kovalevskaia owes her talent for mathematics, as she herself makes clear in her memoirs, to the fact that the walls of her nursery were covered with unusual wallpaper—pages of her uncle's book on advanced algebra. We must acknowledge that the world of mathematics is a restricted area as far as the feminine half of humanity is concerned. Kovalevskaia is one of the few mortals who has entered that world. Could a child of seven really have understood those symbols—equal signs, powers, brackets—all the magic marks of sums and subtractions? Of course not; nevertheless they exercised a decisive influence on her life, and it was under the influence of the childhood wallpaper that she became a famous mathematrix.

Similarly, the magic in a word remains magic even if it is not understood, and loses none of its power. Poems may be understandable or they may not, but they must be good, they must be real.

From the examples of the algebraic signs on the walls of Kovalev-skaia's nursery that had such a decisive influence on the child's fate, and from the example of spells, it is clear that we cannot demand of all language: "be easy to understand, like the sign on the street." The speech of higher reason, even when it is not understandable, falls like seed into the fertile soil of the spirit and only much later, in mysterious ways, does it bring forth its shoots. Does the earth understand the writing of the seeds a farmer scatters on its surface? No. But the grain still ripens in autumn, in response to those seeds. In any case, I certainly do not maintain that every incomprehensible piece of writing is beautiful. I mean only that we must not reject a piece of writing simply because it is incomprehensible to a particular group of readers.

The claim has been made that poems about labor can be created only by people who work in factories. Is this true? Isn't the nature of a poem to be found in its withdrawal from itself, from its point of contact with everyday reality? Is a poem not a flight from the *I*? A poem is related to flight—in the shortest time possible its language must cover the greatest distance in images and thoughts!

Without flight from the self there can be no room for progression. Inspiration always belies the poet's background. Medieval knights wrote about rustic shepherds, Lord Byron about pirates, Buddha was a king's son who wrote in praise of poverty. Or the other way around: Shakespeare was convicted of theft but wrote in the language of kings, as did Goethe, the son of a modest burgher, and their writing is devoted to portrayals of court life. The tundras of the Pechersky region have never known warfare, yet there they preserve epic songs about Vladimir and his hero knights that have long since been forgotten on the Dniepcr. If we consider artistic creativity as the greatest possible deviation of the string of thought from the axis of the creator's life, as a flight from the self, then we have good reason for believing that even poems about an assembly line will be written not by someone who works on an assembly line, but by someone from beyond the factory walls. And by the same token, once he withdraws from the assembly line, stretching the string of his soul to the fullest length, the assembly-line poet will either pass into the world of scientific imagery, of strange scientific visions, into the future of Planet Earth, like Gastev, or into the world of basic human values, like Alexandrovsky, into the subtle life of the heart.

[1919–20: T 633]

On Contemporary Poetry

The word leads a double life. Sometimes it simply grows like a plant whose fruit is a geode of sonorous stones clustering around it; in this case the sound element lives a self-sufficient life, while the particle of sense named by the word stands in shadow. At other times the word is subservient to sense, and then sound ceases to be "all-powerful" and autocratic; sound becomes merely a "name" and humbly carries out the commands of sense; in this case the latter flowers in another round of this eternal game, producing a geode of stones of like variety. Sometimes sense says to sound "I hear and obey"; at other times pure sound says the same thing to pure sense.

This struggle between two worlds, between two powers, goes on eternally in every word and gives a double life to language: two possible orbits for two spinning stars. In one form of creativity, sense turns in a circular path about sound; in the other sound turns about sense. Sometimes sound is the Sun and meaning is the Earth; sometimes meaning is the Sun and sound is the Earth.

Either a land radiant with meaning or a land radiant with sound. And the tree of words clothes itself first in one resonance, then in the other; first it is festive, like a cherry tree decked with verbal blossoms, then it bears fruit, the succulent fruit of sense. It isn't hard to perceive that the time of verbal sound play is the marriage time of language, the courting season of words, while the time of words full of meaning, when the reader's bees hum busily, is the time of autumnal abundance, the time of families and offspring.

In the work of Tolstoy, Pushkin, and Dostoevsky, word development, which was only a bud in Karamzin, has already borne the succulent fruits of meaning. In Pushkin the linguistic North was betrothed to the linguistic West. Under Tsar Alexis Mikhailovich, Polish was the court language of Muscovy. These are historical realities. Pushkin is full of words that end in *-tion;* Balmont of words that end in *-ness.* But suddenly we are witnessing a desire to be free from history—to penetrate to the depths of the word. We have had enough of the historical realities of tribes, of idioms, of latitudes and longitudes. Words have burst into blossom in some invisible tree, leaping into the sky like buds driven by the force of spring, scattering themselves in all directions, and in this we discover the boldness and creativity of the new trends.

Grigory Petnikov in *The Life of New Growth* and *Sunsprouts* precisely and persistently, and with a strong effort of will, weaves his "pattern of wind events"; and the clear, willed coldness of his writing, the sharp, razor-edge intelligence that controls his words, where "in uncompromising life flows the moisture of the Mniester" and where there is "a reflection of utterlessly impossible heights," clearly sets him apart from his fellow flyer, Aseev. "Without fanning the fires of springtime willows," Petnikov's quiet, articulate thinking grows "like the slow flight of a bird winging its way to some familiar evening tree"; it grows like "the patterns of a northern birch branch," clear and transparent. A European mentality hovers over his work, as opposed to the Asian, Persian, Hafiz-like ecstasy of verbal foliage, pure flowering, in the work of Aseev.

Gastev is another story altogether. Here is a fragment of a workingman's fire grasped in its pure essence, no longer you and he, only a solid "I," the fire of a workingman's freedom; here is a factory whistle reaching out of the flames to snatch the wreath from weary Pushkin's brow—a wreath of iron, forged by a fiery hand.

Language, borrowed from dusty book depositories, from daily newspapers full of lies, another's language, not our own, is now at the service of the mind of freedom. "I too have a mind," Freedom cries; "I am more than a body, give me the articulate word, take this gag from my mouth." All ablaze, dressed in gleaming flowers of blood, Freedom has had to borrow dead, delapidated words, but even on these dusty strings she has managed to play the terrifying, often majestic music of worker-power, a music that derives from the triangle of science, our earthly planet, and the muscles of a worker's arm. Gastev looks courageously toward that time when "for atheists the gods of Hellas will awake, giants of thought will murmur children's prayers, thousands of the best poets will throw themselves into the sea," and the We, which includes Gastev's I, cries courageously, "So be it." He walks boldly toward the time when "Earth will begin to sob" and the hands of a worker will contribute to the progress of the universe. He is a cathedral artist of modern labor, who changes the word "God" in the old prayers to the word "I." In Gastev the I of the present prays to itself in the future. His mind is a stormy petrel, which takes its note from the highest wave in the storm.

[pub. 1920: V.222]

Our Fundamentals

Word Creation

Suppose you are in a forest. You see before you oak trees, pine trees, spruces . . . . . the pines mottled with cold dark blues, the wonderful delight of spruce cones, and there in the distance the bluish silver of a clump of birches.

But all this variety of leaves, of tree trunks and branches, was created from a handful of seeds, each one practically indistinguishable from the next; an entire forest of the future can fit in the palm of your hand. Word creation teaches us that all the enormous variety of words derives from the fundamental sounds of the alphabet, which are the seeds of words. From these basic elements the word is formed, and a latterday sower of languages can easily fill his palm with the twenty-eight sounds of the Russian alphabet, the seeds of language. So, for instance, with the basic elements hydrogen and oxygen, you can fill with water the dry bottom of the sea and the empty channels of rivers.

The plenitude of language must be analyzed in terms of fundamental units of "alphabetic verities," and then for these sound elements we may be able to construct something resembling Mendeleev's law or Moseley's law—the latest achievements of the science of chemistry. No public accounting has really been made of the harm caused by improper verbal constructions. This is because there are no account books that record expenditures of popular intelligence. And language has no engineers on permanent duty. How often does the spirit of a language allow for the creation of some direct word, a simple alteration of the consonant sounds in an already existing word? Instead, an entire people uses a complicated and brittle circumlocution and increases the loss of universal intelligence by the amount of time it takes to figure it out. Who wants to travel from Moscow to Kiev by way of New York? And yet what phrase from contemporary literary language is free from such detours? And all because there exists no science of word creation.

If it turned out that there were laws governing the simple bodies of the alphabet, identical for a whole family of languages, then a new universal language could be constructed for the entire family of peoples who spoke them—an express train bearing the mirroring words "New York–Moscow." If two neighboring valleys are separated by a ridge of mountains, a traveler can do two things: blow up the wall of mountains or begin a long and circuitous journey around them. Word creation is the blowing up of linguistic silence, the deaf-and-dumb layers of language. By replacing one sound in an old word with another, we immediately create a path from one linguistic valley to another, and like engineers in the land of language we cut paths of communication through mountains of linguistic silence.

"Bald language" will cover its fields with new shoots. A word contains two parts: pure essence and everyday dross. We may even imagine a word that contains both the starlight intelligence of nighttime and the sunlight intelligence of day. This is because whatever single ordinary meaning a word may possess will hide all its other meanings, as daylight effaces the luminous bodies of the starry night. But for an astronomer the sun is simply another speck of dust, like any other star. And it is a simple, ordinary fact, a mere accident, that we find ourselves located so close to the sun in question. And our Sun is no different from any other star. Set apart from everyday language, the self-sufficient word differs from the ordinary spoken word just as the turning of the Earth around the sun differs from the common everyday perception that the sun turns around the Earth. The self-sufficient word renounces the illusions of the specific everyday environment and replaces self-evident falsehoods with a star-filled predawn. So: the word *ziry* means both *stars* and *eye;* the word *zen'* means both *eye* and *earth.* But do eye and Earth have anything in common? Evidently, for this word signifies not the human eye, and not the Earth we humans inhabit, but some third entity. This third entity has been covered over by the everyday meaning of the word, in merely one of its possibilities but the one most obvious to mankind: perhaps *zen',* used to mean a mirrored device, a reflecting surface.

Or take the two words *lad'ia* [boat] and *ladon'* [palm]. This predawn allows us to perceive the sidereal meaning of the word: a broadening surface onto which the path of some force is directed, like a spear striking armor [*laty*]. Thus the night of everyday reality permits us to see only the dim meanings of words, similar to the dim visions we see at night. We may even describe everyday language as shadows of the great laws of the pure essential Word, falling upon an uneven surface.

There was a time when language united people. Let us return for a moment to the stone age. Nighttime. A fire. Black stone hammers at work. Suddenly, footsteps: each man rushes to pick up his weapons, freezes in a menacing position. But then out of the darkness comes the sound of a name they know, and immediately they understand that one of their own is approaching. "Us! One of us!" rings through the darkness with every word of their shared language. Language unites them like a familiar voice. Weapons are a sign of cowardice. If we think deeply about it, we realize that weapons are only a supplementary dictionary for dealing with those who speak a different language. A pocket dictionary.

Like costumes designed to terrify those who belong to another tribe, languages deserve the same fate as tigers in a provincial zoo, who spend their time picking up expressions of astonishment from people and then exchange the day's impressions: "So what's new with you?" "I'm getting two rubles a day." "That's not bad."

We may even have reason to believe that in some fatal way science is now following the path that language has already taken. Lorenz's universal law says that a body flattens itself in a direction diametrical to the point of stress. But this law is the very content of the "simple name" *l*—whether the *l* name means strap [*liamka*], vane [*lopast'*], leaf of a tree [*list dereva*], ski [*lyzha*], boat [*lodka*], paw [*lapa*], puddle of a cloud burst [*luzha livnia*], meadow [*lug*], stove bench [*leshanka*]. In all cases a force ray of motion spreads out across the wide transverse ray of a surface, until it achieves a point of equilibrium with the counterforce. Spreading over the transverse area, the weight ray becomes lighter and does not fall, whether this force ray assumes the weight of a sailor or skier, the heaviness of the vessel against the chest of a barge hauler, or the path of a raindrop in a cloud burst, crossing the surface of a puddle. Did language know anything about the transverse oscillation of a ray, a vortex-ray? Did it know that

$$R \text{ equals } \sqrt{1 - \frac{v^2}{c^2}}$$

where *v* is the velocity of a body and *c* is the speed of light?

It is evident that language is as wise as nature, and only now with the growth of science are we discovering how to read it. It may occasionally serve to solve abstract problems. Let us try then to use language to measure the length of waves of good and evil. The wisdom of language has long ago revealed the luminous nature of the universe. The "I" of human language coincides with the behavior of light. A fire shines through the patterns of human behavior. Man lives in "this world," in the light of day with its maximum speed of 186,000 miles per second, and dreams of an "other world" where the speed of light is greater. The wisdom of language has advanced beyond the wisdom of science. In the following columns the luminous nature of human behavior is desribed in language and man is interpreted as a luminous phenomenon. The study of man is here presented as part of the science of light.

The Other World	*The Relative Principle*
telo [body], *tusha* [carcass]	*ten'* [shade]
delo [act], *dusha* [soul]	*den'* [day]
tukhnut' [to go off, in the sense of go bad]	*tukhnut'* [to go off, in the sense of extinguish]
voskresat' [rise from the dead, rekindle the spark of life]	*kresalo i ognivo* [flint and steel, used to kindle a spark]
groznyi [threatening]	*groza* [thunder]
molodost' [youth], *molodets* [young man]	*molniia* [lightning]
soludka [sweetroot], *sladost'* [sweetening]	*solntse* [sun], *solniia* [sunning]
soi [clan], *sem'ia* [family], *syn* [son], *semia* (semen)	*siiat'* [to shine], *solntse* [sun]
temia [crown of the head], *tyl* [back, rear], *telo* [body]	*tiiat'* [to darken; by analogy with *siiat'*]
cherti [devils]	*chernyi tsvet* [color black]
merzost' [abomination]	*merznut'* [to freeze]
styd [shame]	*stuzha* [severe frost]
kholostoi [unmarried]	*kholod* [cold]
zhit' [to live]	*zhech'* [to burn]

The Other World	The Relative Principle
peklo [hellfire]	*pech'* [furnace, oven]
pylkii [ardent]	*plamia* [flame]
gore [sorrow, woe]	*goret'* [to burn]
grekh [sin]	*goret', gret'* [to give off heat]
iasnyi um [a clear, lucid mind]	*iaski* [stars: dial.]
iarost' [fierceness, furor]	*iarkoe plamia* [fierce flame]
iskrennii [candid]	*iskra* [spark]
sviatoi [saint], "*svetik*" [darling]	*svet* [light]
zloi [wicked]	*zola* [ashes]

If light is one of the aspects of lightning, then these two columns describe the lightninglike, luminous nature of man and, consequently, of the moral world. Shortly we will be able to construct an equation for abstract moral tasks, based on the fact that the principle of "sin" is located at the black, burning end of the spectrum, and the principle of good at the bright, cold end. Black devils—the demigods of hell, where the souls of sinners burn—are they not all waves of an invisible hot light?

And so in this example linguistics paves the way for the natural sciences and attempts to measure the moral world by treating it as a chapter in the study of rays.

If we take a pair of words like *dvor* [court] and *tvor* [creation], and we already have the word *dvoriane* [courtiers], we can form the word *tvoriane* [creatiers] to mean creators of life. Or, if we already have the word *zemlerob* [plowman, tiller of the soil], we can create the word *vremiapakhar'* or *vremiarob* [tiller of time], and thus have an exact word to describe those who cultivate time the way a plowman cultivates his field. Consider these words: *miropakhar'* [one who plows the universe], or *nravo, nravda* . . . you can see that in this latter case, when the letter *p* of *pravo* [right], *pravda* [truth], and *pravitel'stvo* [government] is replaced by the letter *n*, we pass from the realm of the verb *pravit'* [to rule] to the sphere of influence of the verb *nravit'sia* [to like, to love]. There is also the possibility, when we change *p* to *n*, of *nravitel', nravitel'stvo* [lovernor, lovernment].

From the word *boets* [warrior] we can construct *poets* [singgior], *noets*, and *moets*. From the names of the rivers Dnepr and Dnestr—streams with rapids and swift currents—we can build the words *Mnepr* and *Mnestr* (Petnikov's creations), the latter a quietly flowing spirit of personal consciousness, the former one that flows through the stops and barriers of *p* and *r*, and the beautiful word *Gnestr*, meaning a swift downfall, from *gibel'* [ruin], or *volestr*, from *vol'ia* [will] and speak of the people's *volestr*, or *ognepr* and *ognestr*, from *ogon'* [fire], or *Snepr* and *Snestr*, from *son* [a dream] and *snit'sia* [to dream]. *Mne snilsia Snestr* [I dreamed a swift, rushing dream].

We already have the word *I* and the words *me, my*. From them we can bring to life the word *Mi*, meaning the intelligence from which words proceed. From the word *vervie* [rope, cord] we can conceive of the words *mervie*, and *mervyi*, meaning dying, and *nemervii*, deathless. The word *kniaz'* [prince] permits the word *mniaz'*, one who thinks great thoughts, also *lniaz'* and *dniaz'*. One sound resembles the other.

A *zvach* is someone who calls [*zovet*]. A government [*pravitel'stvo*] that wants to be based on being liked [*nravitsia*] may call itself a *nravitel'stvo*. From *pravda* [truth] we get *nravda*. The word *peter*, from the verb *pet'* [to sing], corresponds to *veter* [wind]: "That is the pleasant patter [*peter*] of the wind."

The word *zemets* [member of the zemstvo] gives us the word *temets*. And the other way: *zemena—zemianin, zemesa*. The word *britva* [razor] gives us the right to construct *mritva*, meaning a deadly weapon. We say someone is *khiter* [sly]. But we can also say someone is *biter* [dy]. Using the word *biven'* [tusk] as a model we can say *khiven'*. "An ear of grain is the *khiven'* of the fields."

Consider the word *lebed'* [swan]. This is sound writing. The swan's long neck reminds us of the arc of falling water; its wide wings recall the water that forms the flat surface of a lake. The word *lit'* [to pour] furnishes *leba*, meaning poured water, while the ending of the word recalls *chernyi* [black] and *cherniad'* [a kind of duck]. Consequently, from *nebo* [sky] we can form *nebed'* [skyan, skygnet] and *nebiazheskyi*. "Over the forest that evening flew a pair of *nebedi* [skyans]."

You recall that occasionally a misprint affords us a certain freedom from the world as it is. A misprint, born involuntarily from the typesetter's will, suddenly gives meaning to a new entity; it is one of the forms of collective creativity and may thus be hailed as a desirable assistance to the artist. The word *tsvety* [flowers] allows us to form *mvety* [*fleurs du mal*], powerful in its unexpectedness. *Molozhava* and *molozhavyi* [young-looking] yield the word *khoroshava*, from *khoroshii* [good]: "the goodling of springtime," and *kholozhava*, from *kholodnyi* [cold]: "again the coldring of autumn"; *borozda* [furrow] and *prazdnik* [festival]; *morozda* [furrozen] and *mrazdnik* [frostival]. If there are stars [*zvezdy*] then there can be *mnezdi*. "And the light of the *mnezdi* shines upon me." *Chudo* [wonder], plural *chudesa*, yields the words *khudesa* [wickeden], *vremesa* [timen], *sudesa* [sagen], *inesa* [otheren]:

> Whorlen of the world-wide will,
> the otheren of graygrow time,
> stillfallen blanketing the field—
> the selven that are names of mine.

"So otheren effaces laboren." *Polon* [captivity] provides *molon*. On the pattern of the word *likhachi* [coachmen], we can have a name for warriors: *mechachi*. *Trudavets, gruzd', trust'*.

Word creation is hostile to the bookish petrifaction of language. It takes as its model the fact that in villages, by rivers and forests, language is being created to this very day; every minute sees the birth of words that either die or gain the right to immortality. Word creation transfers this right to the world of literary creativity. A new word must not only be uttered, it must be directed toward the thing it names. Word creation does not contradict the laws of language. Internal declension is another method of word creation.

If contemporary man can restock the waters of exhausted rivers with fish, then language husbandry gives us the right to restock the impoverished streams of language with new life, with extinct or nonexistent words. We believe that they will begin to sparkle again, as in the first days of Creation.

Beyonsense Language

Word meaning in ordinary natural language is clear. Just as a boy at play is able to imagine the chair he sits on is an actual thoroughbred horse, and as long as he plays, the chair replaces a horse for him, so whenever we speak or write, according to the conventions of human conversation, the little word *sun* replaces the radiant majestic star. The radiant orb is replaced by a verbal toy but shines calmly on and readily assents to the dative and genitive cases its verbal replacement may require. But this equivalence is only a matter of convention; if the real thing were to disappear and only the word *sun* remained, then of course it would be unable to shine down and warm the Earth, and the Earth would freeze and turn to a snowball in the hand of the universe. Similarly, a child playing with dolls may shed heartfelt tears when his bundle of rags and scraps becomes deathly ill and dies; or may arrange a marriage between two rags figures indistinguishable one from the other, except perhaps for their blunt flat heads. While the child is playing, those rag dolls are live people with feelings and emotions. So we may come to an understanding of language as playing with dolls: in language, scraps of sound are used to make dolls and replace all the things in the world. All the people who speak a given language are the players in this game. For people who speak a different language, these sound dolls are simply a collection of scraps of sound. And so a word is a sound doll, and a dictionary is a collection of toys. But language developed naturally from the few basic units that make up the alphabet; consonants and vowels were the strings in this game of musical dolls. And if we take a combination of these sounds in an unrestricted order, such as *bo beh o bee,* or *dyr bul shchyl,* or *manch! manch!* or *chee breo zo!,* then we obtain words that do not belong to any particular language but that do say something; something elusive but real nevertheless.

We humans play with the musical doll *sun;* we pull the ears and whiskers of a great star with out pitiful mortal arms every time we put it in the dative case, something the real sun would never submit to. The word scraps we have just cited offer us nothing like a doll to replace the sun, but they are still scraps of the same material, and as such they do mean something. But since they yield nothing directly to our consciousness (you can't play dolls with them), these free combinations, which represent the voice at play outside of words, are called beyonsense. Beyonsense language means language situated beyond the boundaries of ordinary reason, just as we say "beyond the river" or "beyond the sea." Beyonsense language is used in charms and incantations, where it dominates and displaces the language of sense, and this shows that it has a special power over human consciousness, a special right to exist alongside the language of reason. But there does in fact exist a way to make beyonsense language intelligible to reason.

If we take any given word, say *chashka* [cup], we have no way of knowing what each separate sound means in terms of the whole word. But if we take every word that begins with the sound *ch*—*chasha, cherep, chan, chulok,* etc. [cup, skull, vat, stocking]—then the common meaning that all these words share will also be the meaning of *ch,* and the remaining letters in each word will cancel each other out. If we compare these words beginning with *ch,* we see that they all mean "one body that encases or envelopes another"; *ch* therefore means case or envelope. Thus does beyonsense language enter the realm of sense. It constitutes itself a game based on an alphabet that we have postulated— a new art form—and upon its threshold we now stand.

Beyonsense language is based on two premises:

1. The initial consonant of a simple word governs all the rest—it commands the remaining letters.

2. Words that begin with an identical consonant share some identical meaning; it is as if they were drawn from various directions to a single point in the mind.

Let us take the words *chasha* [cup] and *choboty* [a kind of boot]: the sound *ch* governs both words. If we make a list of words that begin with *ch*—*chulok* [stocking], *choboty* [a kind of boot], *chereviki* [high-heeled boots for women], *chuviak* [slipper], *chuni* [rope shoes: dial.], *chupaki* [felt boots], *chekhol* [underdress] and *chasha* [cup], *chara* [magic spell], *chan* [vat], *chelnok* [barque], *cherep* [skull], *chakhotka* [consumption], *chuchelo* [stuffed animal], then we observe that all these words coalesce at the point of the following image: whether we speak of a stocking [*chulok*] or a cup [*chasha*], in both instances the volume of one body [foot or water] fills up the emptiness of another body which serves as its surface. Whence magic spell [*chara*] as an enchanted casing or envelope that holds motionless the will of the thing enchanted—like water as far as the magic spell is concerned; whence also *chaiat'* [to expect], that is, to be a cup for water that is yet to come. Thus *ch* is not merely a sound, *ch* is a name, an indivisible unit of language. If it turns out that *ch* has an identical meaning in all languages, then the problem of a universal language is solved; all types of footgear will be known as foot-*che,* all types of cups as water-*che.* That is clear and simple.

In any case, the word *khata* [hut] means hut in Russian and also in Egyptian, and *v* signifies "turn" or "return" in the Indo-European languages. If we take the word *khata* as our model, we find *khizhina* [shack], *khalupa* [hutch], *khutor* [farmstead], *khram* [temple], *khranilishche* [depository] we see that the meaning of *kh* is a boundary line between one point and another point in motion toward it. The meaning of *v* is to be found in the turning of one point around another fixed point. Whence *vir* [whirlpool], *vol* [ox], *vorot* [gate], *v'iuga* [snowstorm], *vikhr'* [whirlwind] and many other words. *M* is the division of a single quantity into infinitely small parts. The meaning of *l* is the conversion of a body stretched along the axis of movement into a body stretched in two directions perpendicular to the axis of motion. For example, *ploshchad' luzhi* [the surface of a pond], *kaplia livnia* [a drop of rain], *lodka* [a boat], *liamka* [a tow-rope]. The meaning of *sh* is the merging of surfaces, the elimination of the boundaries between them. The meaning of *k* is a fixed point that holds together a set of moving points.

Beyonsense language is thus the universal language of the future, although it is still in an embryonic state. It alone will be able to unite all people. Rational languages have separated them.

Affirming the Alphabet

Words that begin with *l*: *lodka* [boat], *lyzhi* [skis], *lad'ia* [boat], *ladon'* [palm of the hand], *lapa* [paw], *list* [leaf], *lopukh* [burdock], *lopast'* [blade, vane], *lepestok* [petal], *lasty* [flippers], *liamka* [tow-rope], the art of *let* [flying], *luch* [ray], *log* [gully], *lezhanka* [stove bench], *prolivat'* [to pour out], *lit'* [to pour]. Let us consider a sailor in a boat: his weight is distributed over the broad surface of the bottom of the boat. The point where force is applied is spread out over a wide area, and the wider that area the less the weight. The sailor loses weight. For this reason we may define *l* as the decrease of a force at any given point brought about by an increase of the field of contact. A falling body comes to rest when it comes into contact with a large enough surface. An example of such a shift in the social order is the shift from Tsarist Russia to Soviet Russia, since in the new order the weight of power was transferred onto an incomparably wider area of those bearing power: a sailor—the state—is supported by the boat of broad popular sovereignty.

And so we see that every consonantal sound conceals a particular image, and is in fact a name. As for vowel sounds, we can at least say about *o* and *y* that their arrows of signification fly in opposite directions, and they impart opposite meanings to pairs of words (*voiti* [to enter] and *vyiti* [to leave]; *soi* meaning clan and *syi* meaning individual, an indivisible entity; *bo* to express purpose and *by* to express volition, free will). But vowels have as yet been less thoroughly examined than consonants.

A Mathematical Conception of History. The Futurian Scale

We know the systems of the Hindus, the Chinese, the Greeks. Each of these peoples has its own distinctive conception of what constitutes a beautiful sound and uses a particular musical scale to unite the vibration of strings. But the deity that governs all of these scales is number. The scale of the Futurians uses a particular register to unite both the great vibrations of humanity that call forth war and the beats of each individual human heart. If we conceive of all mankind as a string, then the most diligent and thorough study reveals that there is an interval of 317 years between soundings of the string. The most suitable method for determining that interval is to study similar points in time. Let us peruse the pages of history. We observe that the Napoleonic Code came into existence 317 × 4 years after the Code of Justinian (A.D. 533). That two empires—the German and the Roman—were founded 317 × 6 years apart: Germany in 1871, Rome in 31 B.C. The struggle for dominion at sea, between the islands and the continent, England against Germany in 1915, had a precedent 317 × 2 before—the great war between China and Japan in 1281, during the time of Kublai Khan. The Russo-Japanese war of 1905 occurred 317 years after the war between England and Spain in 1588. The great migration of peoples that took place in 376 had a parallel 317 × 11 earlier, the migration of the Hindu peoples in 3111 B.C. (the era of Kaliyuga). And so we see that this 317-year period is not some chimera of an idle mind, not a fantasy, but is ponderable just as a year is, an earth-day or a sun-day.

The scale consists of the following accords: 317 days, a twenty-four-hour period, 237 seconds, an infantry man's march step or a heartbeat (which are identical in time), a single vibration of the A string, and the vibration of the lowest sound in the alphabet, *u*. A foot soldier in the German infantry, according to military regulations, must take 80 or 81 steps a minute. Consequently in a twenty-four-hour period he takes 365 × 317 steps, or exactly as many steps as there are days in 317 years—the time of one single vibration of the string of mankind. The average female heart beats at exactly the same rate. If we divide this time of one step into 317 parts, we get 424 vibrations per second, or one vibration of the A string. This string serves as the central axis of the art of music. If we take 70 beats per minute as the rate of the male heartbeat, and assuming that beat to be a year, for which we are to find a single day, we discover that day in the vibration of the same A string: in the average beat of the male heart it occurs 365 times. This scale forges into a single register wars, years, days, steps, heartbeats—that is, it ushers us into the great sonic art of the future. In the German and French medieval system the A string did not correspond, but this does not change the facts of the case. According to the studies of Shcherba, the *u* sound makes 432 vibrations per second. If we take the series of 133 × 225 years for the vibrations of continents, conceived as platelike strings, 317 years for vibrations of the string of war, a year, 317 days for the life of memory and feelings, a day, 237 seconds, 1/80 and 1/70 of a minute and 1/439 and 1/426 of a second, then before us stretches a chain of time periods, $a_1, a_2, a_3, a_4 \ldots a_{n-1}, a_n$, joined according to the law that a_n is 365 or 317 less than a_{n-1}. And this series of diminishing time periods is the Futurian Scale.

Imagine a young man with quick, restless eyes, holding a stringed instrument something like a balalaika. He plays. The sounding of one string produces shifts in humanity over a period of 317 years. The sounding of the second produces steps and heartbeats; the third produces the main axis of the sonic world. What you have in front of you is a Futurian and his "balalaika." Riveted to its strings is the flickering phantom of humanity. But the Futurian plays on, and he believes that the harmony of his strings can replace the disharmony of nations.

Once science had learned to measure light rays, studied them in the light of numbers, it became possible to manipulate their movement. Mirrors bring the view of a distant star into the proximity of the writing desk, they give visible measure to infinitely small things that were previously invisible, and they make people, in relation to the world of a single ray of light, into all-powerful divinities. Let us suppose that a wave of light is inhabited by intelligent beings who possess their own government, their own laws, even their own prophets. Would not a scientist who uses a mirrored device in order to control the path of the waves seem to them an all-powerful divinity? And if that particular wave has its own prophets, they would glorify the power of the scientist and flatter him, saying: "You breathe and the oceans move, you speak and the waters retreat." And they would regret that they could not do so themselves.

Now that the great rays of human destiny have been studied, rays whose waves are inhabited by human beings, where a single stroke is of a century's duration, the human mind hopes to apply such mirrored control devices to them as well, to construct a power that consists of double convex and double concave lenses. We may even hope that scientists will be able to manipulate the century-long vibrations of our gigantic ray as easily as they do the infinitely small waves of a ray of light. Then the human beings who populate the ray's wave and the scientists who direct the path of those rays, able to change their direction at will, will be one and the same. Of course this task still lies ahead of us. Our task at present is merely to point out the regularity of human destiny, to provide a theoretical description of it as a ray, and to measure it in time and space. Our purpose is to transfer legislative power to the scientist's desk and to replace the crumbling wood of the thousand-year-old Roman law with the equations and numerical laws that govern the behavior of rays. We must remember that in the final analysis man is a bolt of lightning, that the mighty lightning of the human race does indeed exist—and the lightning bolt of Planet Earth as well. Is it then so surprising that nations totally unaware of each other's existence are bound to one another by exact laws?

Let us take, for example, the law of the births of similar people. It states that a ray, the crests of whose waves mark the birthyears of great individuals with identical destinies, completes a single vibration in 365 years. So therefore if Kepler was born in 1571 and his life, which was devoted to proving that the Earth revolved around the sun, can be taken as a high point of several centuries of European thought, then the year 476, 365 × 3 years before him, saw the birth of Aryabhatta, the "summit of Indian thought," who in the land of the yogis proclaimed the identical revolution of the Earth. In Copernicus' time very little was known about India, and were it not for the fact that people are bolts of lightning, joined to each other by regular connections, we might be surprised at the idea that Kepler, who had the same life task as

Aryabhatta, was born after a predictable interval of time. Similarly the greatest logician of Greece, Aristotle, who tried to establish the laws of exact thinking, the art of reasoning, was born in 384 B.C., 365 × 6 years before John Stuart Mill in 1806. Mill is the greatest logician of Europe—or of England, properly speaking.

Or let us take the names Aeschylus, Mohammed (the Koran is a collection of verses), Firdausi, Hafiz. These are the great poets of the Greeks, the Arabs, and the Persians, the type of individual who appears only once during the entire period of a given people's destiny. A Flying Dutchman with a single destiny, who appears on the oceans of different peoples. Take the years of their births: 525 B.C., A.D. 570, A.D. 935, and A.D. 1300—four points in time, divided by the splash of a wave into 365-year intervals. Or consider philosophers: Fichte in 1762 and Plato in 428 B.C., 365 × 6 years earlier, after six strokes of fate. Or two founders of classicism, Confucius in 551 B.C. and Racine in 1639: Here six of our measures unite France and ancient China: one can imagine the fastidious smile on the face of France and the disdainful expression "Fi donc"—France has no love for China. Such data demonstrate the superficiality of our ordinary understanding of states and nations. These exact laws pass freely through states without marking them, just as x-rays pass through the muscles and show us the imprint of the bones: they strip away from humanity the ragged garments of the state and provide clothes of a different pattern, cut from the starlit sky.

At the same time, they foretell the future, not through the foaming mouths of the ancient prophets but by using cold rational calculations. Now, thanks to the discovery of the birthray wave, we can say in all seriousness that in a certain year a certain individual will be born, someone, let us simply say, whose destiny will be similar to the destiny of someone born 365 years earlier. And then our attitude to death will change as well: we stand at the threshold of a world in which we will know the day and hour of our rebirth; we will be able to look upon death as a temporary plunge into the waves of nonbeing.

And there will be a concurrent shift in our attitude to time. Suppose time to be a series of points $a, b, c, d \ldots n$. Until now we have derived the nature of one point in time from the nature of its nearest neighbor. As a result of this type of thinking, the operation of subtraction was concealed: we used to say: points a and b are similar, and if we subtract b from a it is impossible to get closer to zero. The new way of considering time brings to the fore the operation of division and maintains that distant points may be more identical than two neighboring ones, and that a couple of points t and p are similar if t and p can both be divided by u without a remainder. For the birthlaw $u = 365$ years, in the case of wars $u = 365 - 48 = 317$ years; the founding dates of states are multiples of 413 years, that is 365 + 48 years; thus the founding of Russia in 862 is 413 years after the founding of England in 449; the founding of France in 486 is 413 × 3 years after the founding of Rome in 753 B.C. With this conception of time we come closer to the nature of numbers, that is, to the world of discontinuous disconnected quantities. We began to understand time as an abstract problem of division in the light of the Earth's situation. An exact and thorough understanding of time leads to a dual conception of humanity, since the collection of attributes ascribed earlier to the gods is attainable by means of a thorough study of oneself, and such a study is nothing other than humanity believing in humanity.

It is amazing that even an individual considered separately bears the impress of this same reckoning. Petrarch wrote 317 sonnets dedicated to Laura, the number of vessels in a fleet is often equal to 317, and the human body contains 317 × 2 muscles, 634, or 317 pairs. A human being has 48 × 5 = 240 bones in his body, and the surface of a blood corpuscle is equal to the surface of the earth divided by 365 to the tenth power.

*   *   *

1. Glasses and lenses that redirect the rays of destiny—this is the coming lot of mankind. We must divide ourselves in two, and be both the scientist who manipulates the rays and the tribe inhabiting the waves of the ray controlled by the scientist.

2. As the rays of destiny are gradually revealed, concepts like "nation" and "state" will disappear, and mankind alone will remain, all of whose points are lawfully linked together.

3. Let a man who rests from his daily labors go read the cuneiform of the stars. To understand the will of the stars means to unwind before the eyes of all men the scroll of true freedom. They hang above our heads in a night that is much too dark, these tables of the laws to come. And is not the purpose of division to dismantle the wires of states and governments that intervene between the eternal stars and the ears of mankind? Let the power of the stars be wireless.

The scale of the Futurians is one of the paths. At one end it sets the heavens vibrating, and at the other it hides in the beats of the human heart.

[1919: T 624]

The Radio of the Future

The Radio of the Future—the central tree of our consciousness—will inaugurate new ways to cope with our endless undertakings and will unite all mankind.

The main Radio station, that stronghold of steel, where clouds of wires cluster like strands of hair, will surely be protected by a sign with a skull and crossbones and the familiar word "Danger," since the least disruption of Radio operations would produce a mental blackout over the entire country, a temporary loss of consciousness.

Radio is becoming the spiritual sun of the country, a great wizard and sorcerer.

Let us try to imagine Radio's main station: in the air a spider's web of lines, a storm cloud of lightning bolts, some subsiding, some flaring up anew, crisscrossing the building from one end to the other. A bright blue ball of spherical lightning hanging in midair like a timid bird, guy wires stretched out at a slant.

From this point on Planet Earth, every day, like the flight of birds in springtime, a flock of news departs, news from the life of the spirit.

In this stream of lightning birds the spirit will prevail over force, good counsel over threats.

The activities of artists who work with the pen and brush, the discoveries of artists who work with ideas (Mechnikov, Einstein) will instantly transport mankind to unknown shores.

Advice on day-to-day matters will alternate with lectures by those who dwell upon the snowy heights of the human spirit. The crests of waves in the sea of human knowledge will roll across the entire country into each local Radio station, to be projected that very day as letters onto the dark pages of enormous books, higher than houses, that stand in the center of each town, slowly turning their own pages.

Radioreadingwalls

These books of the streets will be known as Radioreadingwalls! Their giant dimensions frame the settlements and carry out the tasks of all mankind.

Radio has solved a problem that the church itself was unable to solve and has thus become as necessary to each settlement as a school is, or a library.

The problem of celebrating the communion of humanity's one soul, one daily spiritual wave that washes over the entire country every twenty-four hours, saturating it with a flood of scientific and artistic news—that problem has been solved by Radio using lightning as its tool. On the great illuminated books in each town, Radio today has printed a story by a favorite writer, an essay on the fractional exponents of space, a description of airplane flights, and news about neighboring countries. Everyone can read whatever he chooses. This one book, identical across the entire country, stands in the center of every small town, always surrounded by a ring of readers, a carefully composed silent readingwall in every settlement.

But now in black type, news of an enormous scientific discovery appears on the screens; a certain chemist, famous within the narrow circle of his followers, has discovered a method for producing meat and bread out of widely available types of clay. A crowd gathers, wondering what will happen next.

Earthquakes, fires, disasters, the events of each twenty-four-hour period will be printed out on the Radio books. The whole country will be covered with Radio stations.

Radioauditoriums

Surges of lightning are picked up and transmitted to the metal mouth of an auto-speaker, which converts them into amplified sound, into singing and human speech.

The entire settlement has gathered around to listen. The metal trumpet mouth loudly carries the news of the day, the activities of the government, weather information, events from the exciting life of the capital cities.

The effect will be like a giant of some kind reading a gigantic journal out loud. But it is only this metal town cryer, only the metal mouth of the auto-speaker; gravely and distinctly it announces the morning news, beamed to this settlement from the signal tower of the main Radio station.

But now what follows? Where has this great stream of sound come from, this inundation of the whole country in supernatural singing, in the sound of beating wings, this broad silver stream full of whistlings and clangor and marvelous mad bells surging from somewhere we are not, mingling with children's voices singing and the sound of wings?

Over the center of every town in the country these voices pour down, a silver shower of sound. Amazing silver bells mixed with whistlings surge down from above. Are these perhaps the voices of heaven, spirits flying low over the farmhouse roof? No . . . . .

The Mussorgsky of the future is giving a coast-to-coast concert of his work, using the Radio apparatus to create a vast concert hall stretching from Vladivostok to the Baltic, beneath the blue dome of the heavens.

On this one evening he bewitches the people, sharing with them the communion of his soul, and on the following day he is only an ordinary mortal again. The artist has cast a spell over his land; he has given his country the singing of the sea and the whistling of the wind. The poorest house in the smallest town is filled with divine whistlings and all the sweet delights of sound.

Radio and Art Exhibits

In a small town far away, a crowd of people gathers today in front of the great illuminated Radio screens, which rise up like giant books. Why? Because today Radio is using its apparatus to transmit images in color, to allow every little town in the entire country to take part in an exhibit of paintings being held in the capital city. This exhibit is transmitted by means of light impulses repeated in thousands of mirrors at every Radio station. If Radio previously acted as the universal ear, now it has become a pair of eyes that annihilate distance. The main Radio signal tower emits its rays, and from Moscow an exhibit of the best painters bursts into flower on the readingwalls of every small town in this enormous country, on loan to every inhabited spot on the map.

Radioclubs

Let us move up closer. Majestic skyscrapers wrapped in clouds, a game of chess between two people located at opposite ends of Planet Earth, an animated conversation between someone in America and someone in Europe. Now the readingwalls grow dark; suddenly the sound of a distant voice is heard singing, the metallic throat of Radio beams the rays of the song to its many metallic singers: metal sings! And its words, brought forth in silence and solitude, and their welling springs, become a communion shared by the entire country.

More obedient than strings beneath the violinist's hand, the metallic apparatus of Radio will talk and sing, obeying every marked pulse of the song.

Every settlement will have listening devices and metallic voices to serve one sense, metallic eyes to serve the other.

The Great Sorcerer

Finally we will have learned to transmit the sense of taste—and every simple, plain but healthful meal can be transformed by means of taste-dreams carried by Radio rays, creating the illusion of a totally different taste sensation.

People will drink water, and imagine it to be wine. A simple, ample meal will wear the guise of a luxurious feast. And thus will Radio acquire an even greater power over the minds of the nation.

In the future, even odors will obey the will of Radio: in the dead of winter the honey scent of linden trees will mingle with the odor of snow, a true gift of Radio to the nation.

Doctors today can treat patients long-distance, through hypnotic suggestion. Radio in the future will be able to act also as a doctor, healing patients without medicine.

And even more:

It is a known fact that certain notes like "la" and "ti" are able to increase muscular capacity, sometimes as much as sixty-four times, since they thicken the muscle for a certain length of time. During periods of intense hard work like summer harvests or during the construction of great buildings, these sounds can be broadcast by Radio over the entire country, increasing its collective strength enormously.

And, finally, the organization of popular education will pass into the hands of Radio. The Supreme Soviet of Sciences will broadcast lessons and lectures to all the schools of the country—higher institutions as well as lower.

The teacher will become merely a monitor while these lectures are in progress. The daily transmission of lessons and textbooks through the sky into the country schools of the nation, the unification of its consciousness into a single will.

Thus will Radio forge continuous links in the universal soul and mold mankind into a single entity.

[1921: IV.290]

A Cliff out of the Future

People sit or walk, hidden in patches of blind rays by luminous clouds of radiant silence, of radiant stillness.

Some of them are perched in high places, high in the air, in weightless chairs. Sometimes they paint, daubing away with their brushes. Whole companies of others carry round glass panels for floors and tables.

Other people walk on air with the help of walking sticks, or move swiftly through the air-snow over the surface of the cloud crust on skis of time. A great air walk, an elevated highway crowded with skywalkers, curves across the sky above the poles of low towers for lightning compressed into coils. People move upon this weightless path as upon an invisible bridge. Either side is a sheer drop into the void; the path is marked by a thin black ribbon of earth.

Like a sea serpent swimming in the deep with its head raised high above the surface, a building appears, breasting the air as it swims, shaped like a reversed letter L. A flying serpent of a building. It swells like an iceberg in the Arctic Ocean.

A sheer glass cliff, a vertical street of dwellings, rising at an angle in the air, garbed in wind—a swan of these times.

People sit on the balconies of the building. They are gods of serene thought.

"The Second Sea is cloudless today."

"It is. Our great teacher of equality, the Second Sea above our heads; you must raise your hand to point it out. It extinguished the fire of states once pumps and fire hoses were attached to it. That was very hard to do back in those days. That was the great service the Second Sea has rendered us. As a sign of gratitude, man's face has been stamped on one of the clouds forever, a kind of postcard sent to a friend."

"The combat between the islands and the lands deprived of sea-coasts has ended. We are all equally rich in seacoast, now that we have the Second Sea above us. But we were shortsighted then. The sands of stupidity had buried us in great mounds."

I sit here smoking a ravishing thought with an entrancing odor. A resinous sense of well-being enfolds my mind like a blanket.

We must never forget the moral duty every human owes to the citizens of his own body. To this complicated star built of bone.

Human consciousness governs these citizens, and it must never forget that human happiness is the totality of the grains of sand of happiness of all those subject to its government. Let us always remember that every hair on a human head is a skyscraper, and from its windows thousands of Sashas and Mashas look out at the sun.

This is why sometimes just taking off your shirt or going for a swim in a creek in springtime is a source of more happiness than being the greatest man on earth. Taking off all your clothes to loaf on a beach, trying to turn back the receding sun—all that means you are letting daylight into the artificial night of your own internal government; tuning the strings of that government, of that great resonating soundboard, to the key of the sun.

You must not act like Arakcheev toward the citizens of your own bodies. Don't ever be afraid of lying naked in a sea of sunlight. Let's undress our bodies, and our cities as well. Let's give them glass armor to protect them from arrows of freezing weather.

Conversation across the way:
"Have you got any food matches?"
"Sure, let's light up and smoke our supper."
"Want some sweet smoke? Zigzag brand?"
"Yes. These are imported from far away, from Continent A."
The edible smoke is superb, the patches of blue sky are enchanting. A quiet little star is locked in single combat with the bright blue sky.

Bodies are beautiful, once they are freed from the prison of clothes. Within them a pale blue dawn struggles with a milky one.

But the equation of human happiness was found and solved only after people understood that it twisted like a delicate hopvine around the trunk of the universe. To listen to the rustling of water reeds, to recognize the familiar eyes and soul of a friend in a crab at the seashore as it scuttles sideways, claws raised, always on the alert—something like this often gives us more happiness than all the things that bring us fame or the renown of, say, a military commander.

Human happiness is a secondary sound; it twists, turns around the fundamental sound of the universe.

Happiness is the pale moon circling the earths that go around the sun, circling the cow eyes of a little kitten as it scratches its ear, circling the coltsfoot in springtime, circling the splash of the sea waves.

These are the fundamental sounds of happiness, its wise fathers, the vibrating iron rod that antedates the family of voices. More simply, the axis of rotation. And this is the reason that city children cut off from nature are always unhappy, while for country children happiness is familiar and as inseparable as their shadows.

Man has taken the surface of Planet Earth away from the wise community of animals and plants and now he is lonely; he has no one to play tag or hide-and-seek with. In his empty room, surrounded by the darkness of nonbeing, there are no playmates and no games. Who can he play with? He is surrounded by an empty *no*. The souls of animals banished from their bodies have invaded him, and the plains of his being are now subject to their law.

They built animal cities in his heart.

Man seems to be choking to death on his own carbon.

It was his luck to have a printing press that did not have enough of the many twos and threes needed to print a reckoning. For without these numbers the Beautiful Program could not be written. As animals fell into extinction, each took with him to the grave the private numbers of his species.

Entire entries in the ledger book of fortune vanished like pages torn out of a manuscript. Twilight loomed on the horizon.

But a miracle happened: courageous minds have awakened the sleeping soul of the sacred gray clay that covers the earth in layers, awakened it as bread and meat. Earth has become edible, and every clay pit has become a table laid for dinner. The beautiful gift of the right to live has been given back to animals and plants.

And once more we are happy: a lion lies curled in my lap, asleep, and I sit here smoking my supper of air.

[1921–22: IV.296]

From the Notebooks

Tasks for the Presidents of Planet Earth

A timetable for capital cities.
Reorganization of weights and measures.
Reorganization of the alphabet.
An end to languages, which resemble a claw on a wing.
Previewing the future.
Reckoning labor in units of heartbeats.
Man as a point of space-time.
More than half the human body consists of water.

*   *   *

Languages for present-day humans are a claw on a bird's wing: an unnecessary remnant of prehistory, the claw of days gone by.

An Internationale of human beings is conceivable through an Internationale of scientific ideas.

He has no feeling for measure. To agree to print [illegible] is simply bad taste. Combining unusual words becomes extremely boring after five lines, which is why you cannot write novels that way—nobody will read them, they have to [illegible] and anyway you can't pour out an unbroken stream of lyricism ten pages long. It won't work.

It is necessary to universalize one's birth, one's ancestry. Necessary to keep white the gleaming root.

Hand and consciousness are the same thing.

Just as the gleaming white [illegible] root is part of the green grass, so also, for a true conception of humanity, we cannot break man's links with the universe and to the freedom in which humanity was born, like a cup.

400

All we need do in order to construct the universe is gaze into the first three numbers, like a crystal ball. The laws of the universe correspond to the laws of mathematics. All things fly toward nothingness, two butterflies flutter in the flight of words: yes and no, a cloud of divine butterflies, a cloud of dawnings.

The law of the conservation of ink governed the scribe who wrote out the manuscript of the universe. This dark black deer is a black star of storm-clouds.

Human beings have always computed time with the sword, writing in the blood of fighting men. Wars will come to an end when human beings learn to compute time in ink.

War has turned the universe into an inkwell full of blood and attempted to drown the poor, pitiful writer in it. And the writer attempts to drown war in his inkwell, war itself. A controversy of beliefs, the clash of wills.

Who will win?

March 21, 1921

The pen of war has dipped too often into the inkwell of humanity.

Which is better—a universal language or universal slaughter?

The formula of the alphabet is the formula of a body of spatial quantities, fellow travelers of the solar system.

I lie in wait for number like a cat waiting for a mouse.

The nature of rotation lies in this: the sum of the divisors of a number should equal the number itself—the fundamental truth of rotation.

People will understand that there is a timepiece for humanity and a timepiece for the individual.

Igor Soporianin. Boreianin? Soporific Drowsyanin. Stuporianin. Igor Yousleepyawnin.

Freedom is double, it follows 2, the duo sign.
Make way! Let 2 through!
Control is triple and trouble, it follows 3, the trio sign.
Toil, tomb. T'other.
Self-immolation? Where the animal number has grown as well.
Make way! Let 2 through!
Deep dale of decency.
Day, duty, descendants.
3—taint and toil, tomb and treason.
3—third factor in a conversation—them.
3—torrent and tempest.
A treacherous trail.
3 Germans *Tot*.
3—tyrannical trio: pa and ma and mother-in-law, who terrorizes without the excuse of blood ties.
2 damsels, a duet of darlings with the future in their eyes.
2 means deliberation.
Tumor, toad, taboo.
There is no greater freedom than a straight duangle.
There is no greater prison than a triangle. It is a closed expanse.
Diference and triference.
Dear and tear.
2 is a duo, doodling down the dale.
3 is treason, trespass and travail.
A dulcimer duo.
A dusky dell.
A panpipe's drowsy dream.

The equations of my soul: I was born October 28, 1885 $+ 3^8 + 3^8 =$ November 3, 1921; at the Red Star in Baku I predicted the Soviet Government, December 17, 1920 $= 2 \times 3^8 - 317$; I was elected a President of Planet Earth on $3^8 + 3^8 - 3^7 - 48 =$ December 20, 1915 (from birth) or $2 \times 3^8 - 3^7 - 48$. On the day of the battle of Tsushima I conceived the idea of overthrowing the state by means of an idea; on the day of the surrender of Przemysl I entered the domain of chemistry.

The future escapes us because we are lazy.

Power, the laws of states, is a closed body in space. The spatial yes.

The State and the Law are closed principles. We perceive them as enormous blocks, some sort of mass of beasts in space, with a positive whole number.

But for closure, three points are required: they define the closed area.

Freedom is the absence of closure for bodies in motion.

We perceive freedom as an emptiness, as the absence of limits, as the negative volume that accomodates movement. An expanse, an open field for free functioning operations. But this kind of movement without spatial limitations is determined by two points. They fully determine the location of a straight line in space.

The path of freedom, of life, of growth, lies through the power of two. The path of power, of death, of struggle, "the closed expanse", lies through the power of three.

"Expansive" is a word used to describe freedom, but expanse is a two-dimensional space. Descriptions of the state—as a block, an enormous mass—use a three-dimensional space.

Harmony helped the singing savage from losing his way in the chaos of words, offered him a choice, helped him cope with the large numbers of language.

Words have a special power when they have two meanings, when they are living eyes for a secret, when a second meaning shines through the cloudy pane of everyday meaning.

October 25, 1921

The Sea. The Death of the Future. The Break-up of the Universe. Saian. Rusalka and Vila. Sorrow and Laughter. Horse. Three Sisters. The Lightning Sisters. Ladomir. Razin. The Scarlet Saber. Garshin. An Abridged Shakespeare. Night in the Trenches.

Sound writing.
   This branch of art is the culture medium out of which the tree of a universal language may some day grow.

m—dark blue	*z*—gold
l—white, ivory	*k*—sky-blue
g—yellow	*n*—light red
b—red, flame	*p*—black with red highlights

On the nature of friendship.

Do rules of friendship exist? Mayakovsky, Kamensky, Burliuk, and I were perhaps not friends in the closest sense, but destiny has bound our names together like straws in a broom.

And what do we find? Mayakovsky was born 365 × 11 days after Burliuk, counting leap years; between me and Burliuk there are 1206 days, between me and Kamensky, 571 days. 284 × 2 = 568. Between Burliuk and Kamensky, 638 days. Between me and Mayakovsky, 2809 days . . . . .

The art of mathematics has no symbols for rendering the movements of a quantity of time, and until such symbols are constructed or re-shaped—until we *create* such symbols—it isn't possible to record these movements. Very often we are faced with the problem of transferring one and the same operation into spatial terms, for example, combining two sightings of one and the same operation that can be observed from two points of view.

Poems must be written according to Darwin's theories.

December 7, 1921. I can feel the gravestone upon my past. My poetry looks like someone else's.

Verhaeren's poems, Whitman's lyrics and [illegible].
Blok's epic. Wells's prose.

5 curse words become an endearment.
The 100th miracle is a humdrum affair.
Poison cures and kills (a powerful poison is edible). A current of low intensity or one of very high intensity has no effect on an individual.
Sound and color are invisible and inaudible beyond either end of a patch of sound (or color). Too loud a sound is just as inaudible as too weak a one.

A work written with the new word *only* will not effect the consciousness . . . . .

And so his labors are in vain!

The force of a word (if the problem is to measure its magnitude) is similar to the action of a ray on a powder magazine beneath a great capital city (let's say London). The detonation depends not upon force, but on measurement (exactitude). The footsoldier's march step destroys the bridge he crosses. A weak, incomprehensible word may yet destroy the world.

Oh, the duel between destiny and man!

Jiu-jitsu with the state.

1. Spit in death's eye, no matter what form it comes in.

2. If your back is toward the future, turn it toward the past.

3. Break up the powers of an autocracy bashful as a girl by means of laws of time that a child can understand.

4. An end to language conceived as a duty.

5. To smash the shell of language everywhere and forever. Words for singing.

6. Armor made of numbers.

7. Growth of possibilities for arbitrary human behavior. To take away right after right.

   Regiments of songs.
   A trench dug out into the universe.

Kant with his thinker's forehead, beetling like the steep bank of a river over a chin wrinkled as a baby's fist tucked into a collar.

Moving in a direction transverse to time, we can easily see the mountains of the future.

Such a movement is familiar to the mind of a prophet; it is the elevation of height relative to the breadth of time, i.e., the creation of an added dimension.

Speaking metaphorically: the number tree is one and the same in the plane of time and in the plane of weight, with the same twistings, the same ancient twigs that centuries have gazed upon . . . . .

Pushkin

Let us attempt to perceive in Pushkin an exterior surface that reflects the laws of time. On October 10, 1824, he finished "The Gypsies," where he glorifies the freedom of those who live outside the law and the state; therefore according to our law we should expect a reverse wave after $3^6 + 3^6$ days, and in fact on October 8–9, 1828, he finishes "Poltava," where we find the image of Peter the Great, forger of the young nation, hammer of autocracy, binding the Russian barrel with the hoop of Poltava, the Poltavian hoop, that found in Pushkin a resounding nightingale.

Or the other way around: "The Prisoner of the Caucasus" was finished on May 15, 1821—a poem where the savage orient comes alive in the primitive life of mountaineers, a poem full of uncompromising freedom and savage power, and $3^6 + 3^6 - 2^2$ days after that on May 9, 1823, he began *Eugene Onegin,* the portrayal of a landowner poisoned by the west, a reverse event. "Prisoner" depicts the Russian's encounter with the East; *Onegin* his encounter with the "educated West."

Pushkin fully justifies his standing as a sophisticated young frog and the oscillating law of time is easily confirmed by his writings.

November 9, 1828—"The Upas Tree," a murderous parable about the autocracy, 2^5 days after "Poltava."

September 4, 1826, "The Prophet."

January 6, 1835, three Anacreontic Odes.

The Equation of Gogol's Soul

Gogol was born on March 19, 1809. 2^{13} days later ($= 8192$) we are in the year 1831, August 22, 1831, to be exact, the day, that is, when the courageous spring of youth welled up in Gogol's life, when he wrote a long letter to Pushkin full of fraternal enthusiasm, hoping to meet him, and received an answer. It was just at that time that he wrote his delightful *Evenings on a Farm near Dikanka,* where the bright springtime of the Ukraine, her rusalkas and their shining pagan eyes lie concealed behind every line of Moscow type.

Thus did the sunflower of his "I" turn toward life, toward life and love.

And the other way around: after $3^8 + 3^8$ days came a general period in the year 1845, March 1, 1845, to be exact, days, that is, when Gogol (February 24, 1845) made up his mind to live "not for fame" and not for anything enterprising but in His Holy Name, and not by making people laugh but by consoling them.

Like a sunflower, Gogol turned to the Lord with all the leaves of his soul, rejecting his "Tales of Little Russia" with their sounds of kisses and the babble of rusalka-talk. The stern, holy figure of the Lord replaced the sinful rusalka in his soul, when three replaced two in the time equation.

The base of two yielded tales with the rusalkas splashing about in them, while three yielded thoughts of God and the universal twilight beyond the ego. Let us say the day of his birth is the Siberian campaign—the capture of Isker by Yermak's men. (Let us make Yermak's name stand for Gogol's "wah.")

$3^{10} + 3^{10}$ days after the capture of Isker came the reverse event—the battle of Mukden. And Kuropatkin instead of Yermak.

Gogol's turning to God was his Mukden, and his piety was a retreat from his birth, the surrender of his territories to the rod of death, thus similar to Kuropatkin's action. Either the will to God relates to the will to live as -1 to $+1$, and God for Gogol represents existence before birth and the onslaught of piety therefore represents an inverse movement away from life toward that world before birth, or life and piety are mutually opposed life-moves . . . . .

As long as rulers continue trading in the blood of their subjects in order to preserve their own peace and quiet, there will always be a multitude of fools who hope to find in the government of Planet Earth a milch cow with a tasty udder, and who depart disenchanted—and in their midst we alone remain steadfast as a rock. Friends, let us proceed to construct a common language for all of Planet Earth!

More than the sanctified bleating of sheep, more than the beyonsense of the pure human voice intersected by lightning bolts of thought, we must examine what has been done in this sector by the multitude of centuries.

We will pick flowers on Mars, we will give Planet Earth the gift of foreseeing the future. Herald of the glory of art, the end of the glory of the gods.

Human dust on my violin—exhausted wars.

Things I have studied

Animals.

The alphabet.

Numbers.

Family.

Burliuk.

My friends.

People.

The seasons of the year.

Nights in Persia.

Nights in Astrakhan.

Publishers who want to cheat me, hoping I'll be stupid enough not to notice, who don't see my laughing mouth silently whispering. For godssake, cheat me all you want, but if you cheat me again by one yard, you'll be cheated forever by two.

I am winning the game against the dark cliff, I pile up Kerenkis for my right to be cheated, you are only a blade of grass upon it. What a fascinating sight, my ace covering the nine of that threatening cliff.

Publishers come to see me in the hospital pretending they're my brother in order to steal my manuscripts and make a mess of them, publishers who can't wait for me to die so they can wail over the grave of a poet. And all these years you let my poems lie around. Damn you all!

Even the mind of Aristotle was unable to draw any distinctions in the problem of yes and no—the boundaries between the realm of equality and the realm of inequality—and he gave it up. But his reservations do not exist for us. We see precisely that yes and no, being quantitatively equal, possess an identical numerical measure, but there is a 180° difference between them—no has made a turn of 180°, yielding two straight lines, i.e., yes and no are ordinary tin, bronze, an alloy made from a lump of inequality and a lump of inequality: reckoning by numbers they are equal, reckoning by angle they are unequal.

It would no doubt be possible to write a long book on the subject, but that may be precisely the form it can't exist in.

The moment We become our divinity, the streams of all thoughts will begin to flow from the heights of one single thought.

But we are not gods, and for that reason we will flow like rivers into the sea of a shared future. To flow from wherever each individual's experience is located, some like the Volga, some like the Terek, some like the Yaik, into the common sea of a single future.

We will manage to avoid medieval arguments about the number of hairs in God's beard.

Art habitually makes use of desire in the science of wielding power. I have a desire to take something before I actually take it. He said that art had to achieve the same status as science, and industry, Technology with a capital T. But a thousand years before the invention of the airplane, wasn't there the magic carpet? And the Greek Daedalus two thousand before? Captain Nemo in Jules Verne's novel sailed in a submarine a half a century before the Germans' mighty victory at the [illegible] islands. Wells's invention of the time machine.

If an artist must take a back seat to science, life, events, then how is he supposed to foresee, foretell, forewill? And what is so astonishing is this passion for making sure everything is in its assigned place, like the policeman in a parking lot as people leave a society ball . . . . .

Judges are entitled to exercise all rights except the right to be innocent as children in the areas of their particular jurisdiction.

Is it true that the footsteps of an unchaste youth are inaudible?

Mallarmé and Baudelaire have already spoken about the sound

correspondences of words, and about eyes for auditory visions and sounds for which a dictionary exists.

In my essay "Teacher and Student" seven years ago, I too gave some understanding of these correspondences.

B is a bright red color, which is why lips say *bo beh o bee; veh eh o mee* is blue and that's why eyes are blue; and *pee eh eh o* is black. No wonder Toporkov was bewildered and laughed; he couldn't read these [illegible] and looked at the poem the way a wild Caucasus donkey looks at a locomotive because he didn't understand its meaning and significance.

[1914–1922: V.265–276]

The Wheel of Births

Theses

1. It is not the planets' fault that we do not hear them. The wheel of births is in no way at fault because our hearing cannot distinguish the sound it makes, the metallic whoosh of its vanes. We may ask how it is possible to discover a general law for the births of similar individuals who champion one and the same cause if they are born in different states and as members of different nations. But humanity was long ago united by the state of lightning, which plaits the hair of all peoples into one braid. We may imagine an observer from another planet who is able to perceive all mankind quite clearly, but who can distinguish neither nations nor states.

2. According to Bucke (in *Cosmic Consciousness*), Jesus was born six years before the start of the Christian era, in 6 B.C., 365 years after Mencius. 365 × 4 years after Jesus, in 1454, came Savonarola, "friend of the poor, scourge of the rich." 365 × 5 years after Jesus, in 1819, Walt Whitman was born, and Karl Marx in 1818. Another example: Karl Marx came 365 × 8 years after the Brahmin Buddha, according to the *Bhagavata Purana*.

So Whitman is identical with Jesus, spattered by sparks from the factory workbench rather than by seaspray and the dust of the road. Industrial workers in grimy clothes have replaced gray-haired old fishermen. Remember that Mencius, the great Chinese sage, taught that "the people are greater than the gods, and the gods are greater than emperors"; he set emperors in the last place in his hierarchy and ascribed to the people the creation of the gods.

3. Jesus and Savonarola were executed. The star of equivalence rose accurately after a period of 365 years. And let us not ignore the beauty of Karl Marx's appearance 365 × 8 years after Buddha and 365 × 5 years after Jesus.

4. After all, the ancients referred to the period of 365 years as a "god year," while the triangle woven of lightning that unites the sun, the Earth, and a fixed star will become equal to itself again after a god year. They are mistaken who consider time as a continuous quantity: it is discontinuous in the way that numbers and that two neighboring points can be qualitatively different, while remote ones can be identical. Where two births are concerned, time is identical so long as the period that separates the two birth points can be divided evenly into god years—365 years.

[1919: TsGALI, f. 665, op. 1, ed. khr. 32, l. 40]

Order from the Presidents of Planet Earth (Presplanearth)

Order One: The older solar worlds, Jupiter, Saturn, Uranus, the sun's rivals, in order of decreasing mass, shall move according to Law A: so that their seasons change from one to another according to an equation based on three, as the nth root of the number of days. Three is the vehicle of death, of decay; for the older worlds, the base of the equation is three.

Law A:

$$x = \frac{3^{7+n} - 1}{2} + 1053 + \frac{n - 1}{2^{n-2}}\left(\frac{3^5 + 3}{2}(-1)^{n+1} - 3^2 - 3\right);$$

$$\text{or } x = 365\,(365^{n-3} + 3^{n+1} + 3) - 48\,(3n - 2).$$

Answer: $n = 1$, $x = 4332$, the Jupiter year; $n = 2$, $x = 10{,}759$, the Saturn year; $n = 3$, $x = 30{,}688$, the Uranus year. In units of a year this law of seasonal change takes the following form: $x = 3^{n+1} + 3^n$ years or 123,084 years (1 year or $365 = 3^5 + 3^4 + 3^3 + 3^2 + 3 + 3^0 + 1$ days).

    Order Two: The equation for the change of seasons of younger stars (in order of increasing mass) shall be based on the number two:

$$x = (11 \times 2^{(n+2)}) + [3(n-1) \times 2^{(2n-n^2+4)}] + 2^{(4n-12)}$$

Solution: $n = 1$, $x = 88$ (Mercury: Trader); $n = 2$, $x = 224$ (Venus: Sweetheart); $n = 3$, $x = 365$ (Earth). This equation, which stands firmly on the base of two, reveals the agreement between these three stars! It forms the foundation for an association of three stars with differing behavioral traits (Trader, Sweetheart, Wife).

    Order Three: Concerning the coming of the Comrades of the Sun. "The flying government of the solar world." Let us note:

$$\frac{3^{m+1}}{2} = 3^{m-1} + 3^{m-2} + 3^{m-3} + 3^{m-4} \ldots 3^2 + 3^1 + 3^0 + 1;$$

and $1053 = 3^6 + 3^5 + 3^4 = 3^{3+3} + 3^{3+2} + 3^{3+1}$.

These orders are intended not for humans, but for suns! (innovativordering, creativordering, a shift in order-aiming).

And as Presidents of Planet Earth we ask: If we must give orders, who better to give them to, humans or suns? And we are astonished to observe that suns fulfill our orders without objections or fuss.

Frankly, Comrade Sun, we, PRESPLANEARTH, would prefer revolt and rebellion!

Our world is boring.

Jan. 30, 1922
Signed: Velimir the First

[1922: V.165]

"There is a phrase"

There is a phrase people still use to describe certain parts of Planet Earth: No white man has ever set foot there. This was true of the whole dark continent until only recently.

The same sort of thing might be said about time: No thinking being has ever set foot there. Not even the most powerful freight train could transport everything mankind has so far written about space, while everything written about time could be put into a letter and easily transported beneath the wing of a carrier pigeon. The entire contents would consist of little more than a few casually tossed-off remarks, some of them quite accurate. I am not referring to purely verbal studies dealing with this question; they draw no conclusions and provide poor fuel for the steamship of learning.

The fact is that the first appearance on earth of a science of time and the origins of the science of space are separated by approximately seven "god-years"—that is, by seven 365-year periods—which is a convenient measure of large periods of time, of large canvases of time.

The science of time ought to follow the same path as the science of space: it should avoid preconceived ideas, and open its mind and its ears to the voice of whatever experience may lie ahead of it. As long as we are not confused by a ringing in our ears and the feverish voices of delirium, the voice of experience will of course be heard. Our task is to perceive with open eyes the entire extent of experience that lies within the scope of man's reason.

We know that the origins of the science of space are to be found in the experience of carpenters and surveyors in antiquity, who needed to determine fields of equal area in assigning plots to landholders. These people of science had to make rectangular and triangular fields equal in area to circular ones, and resolve the problem of finding equal areas for fields of unequal shape, a problem that nature states in terms of hills and valleys.

It is the opposite for time—the exact laws of time will be able to solve the problem of equality by virtue of an equitable division of areas of land in time, the problem of apportioning the exercise of power, and the demarcation of generations. Thus will truth be advanced in time.

The pure Laws of Time teach us that all things are relative. They make human behavior less bloodthirsty, endow it with a strange nobility. They help us to select collaborators and pupils, allow us to trace the straightest and shortest path toward this or that point in the future, help us to avoid following a false, meandering road in delusory pursuit of actuality.

Each nation in the days of its ascendance will be able to understand its future as a tangent to the point of its present. Each nation will be able cruelly to disabuse itself of the virtue of former primitive methods of foretelling the future. These laws will provide equitable boundaries for every movement: for example, by placing dividing lines between generations, they will simultaneously permit us to see into the future, since the Laws of Time are not dependent on the point where the observer is located. The road open before the science of time is the study of the quantitative laws of a newly discovered world. The construction of equations and their study.

A first glance at these equations of magnitudes of times reveal several distinctive traits inherent only in the world of time, traits that deserve to be enumerated.

[1921–22: IV.312]

Excerpt from *The Tables of Destiny*

The fate of the Volga may serve as a lesson for the study of destiny. The day the Volga riverbed was sounded was the day of its subjugation, its conquest by the powers of sail and oar, the surrender of the Volga to mankind. The sounding of Destiny and a thorough study of its dangerous places should make its navigation a calm and easy matter, just as sailing the Volga became safe and easy once buoys with red and green lights marked the danger spots—the rocks, shoals, and sandbars of the river bottom. In the same way we can study the fissures and shifting shoals of Time.

Analogous soundings may be made in the stream of Time, establishing the laws of time past, and studying the channel of time to come; by sounding Destiny we proceed from the lessons of past centuries in order to arm the mind with new eyes, eyes of the intellect, that can make out events still in the distant future.

It has long been a commonplace that knowledge is a kind of power, and to foresee events is to be able to control them.

Here are two equations: one concerns and outlines the destiny of England; the other provides a basic time outline of India.

It is important to remember that in general opposed events—victory and defeat, beginning and end—are united in terms of powers of three (3^n). The number three is the wheel of death, as it were, for the initial event.

Moscow, January 16, 1922

"CROWNED WITH DAWNS"

A WAKE AT THE NEIGHBORS'
(THE HOUR OF BURIAL)

I discovered the pure Laws of Time in 1920 in Baku, the land of fire, in a tall building that housed the naval dormitory where I was living with Dobrokovsky. The exact date was December 17th.

417

A huge slogan "Dobrokuznia" was scrawled at an angle on the wall, a heap of brushes lay beside buckets of paint, and a constant refrain in my ears insisted that if someone named Nina would only show up, then out of the city of Baku would come the name of Bakunin. His enormous tattered shadow hung over us all. A sculptor began a bust of Columbus in a lump of green wax and unexpectedly produced a head of me. It was a good omen, a sign of good hope for someone sailing toward an unknown land, toward the continent of time. I wanted to find a key to the timepiece of humanity, to become humanity's watchmaker, and to map out a basis for predicting the future. All this took place in the land where man first encountered fire and tamed it into a domestic animal. In the land of fire—Azerbaijan—fire changes its primordial appearance. It does not fall from heaven like a savage divinity, engendering fear; rather it rises from the earth like a gentle flower and almost begs us to pick it and tame it.

On the first day of spring in 1921 I went as a supplicant to the eternal fires. Caught unawares at night by the fast-dropping twilight, I slept in the open steppe, on the bare ground, among clumps of grass and spiders' webs. The terrors of night surrounded me.

I discovered the equation for the inner zone of heavenly bodies of the solar system on September 25, 1920, at the Prolekult conference in Armavir, on the back benches of the meeting hall; during all the inflammatory business speeches, I computed the times of those stars in my notebook.

This equation for the first time fettered the stellar magnitudes together and made them subject to one general law, in tandem with the community of human beings.

I first resolved to search out the Laws of Time on the day after the battle of Tsushima, when news of the battle reached the Yaroslavl district where I was then living, in the village of Burmakino, at Kuznetsov's.

I wanted to discover the reason for all those deaths.

I remember springtime in the north country and the clink of bridle and stirrups; they used to make the horses trundle them across the fields in a special barrel, in order to give the rusty iron the silvery glitter of a new bridle and harness. The poor old horses in the north had to drag around a barrel filled with their own chains.

I had a true and reliable helper in my task—the chance encounter, in that famine of print, with the very book I could not do without.

It was an old gray mare, Comrade Graylegs, who gave me a chronicle of the events of 1917–1920; it was this that allowed me to begin calculating days, which was the next step.

I can still hear the panting breath of that traveling companion of mine.

I am firmly resolved, if these laws do not win a place among humans, to teach them to the enslaved race of horses. I have already expressed this firm resolution in a letter to Ermilov.

The first truths about space sought the force of social law in the surveyor's art, in order to determine the taxes upon circular or triangular plots, or to make an equitable division among the inheritors of a piece of land.

The first truths about time seek points of support for the equitable demarcation of generations, and transfer the desire for equity and law into a new dimension, that of time. But in this case as well, the motivating force is that same old desire for equity, the division of time into equal time-estates.

Humanity, as a phenomenon caught up in the flow of time, was aware of the power of time's pure laws, but feelings of nationality were strengthened by recurring and opposed dogmas, all attempting to depict the essence of time with the paint of words.

Doctrines of good and evil, Ahriman and Ormuzd, eventual retribution—all these express the desire to speak of time before any measure for it was available, using only a bucket of paint.

And so the face of time was painted in words on the old canvases of the Koran, the Vedas, the Gospels, and other doctrines. That great face is adumbrated here also in the pure Laws of Time, but this time with the brush of number, and thus we take a different approach to the task of our predecessors. The canvas contains no words, only precise number, which functions here as the artist's brush stroke depicting the face of time.

Thus in the ancient task of the time-painter a certain shift has occurred.

Time-painting has abandoned the indeterminacy of words and now possesses an exact unit of measurement.

Those who think they can ignore the pure Laws of Time and still make correct judgments will seem like the old tyrant who had the ocean whipped because it destroyed his ships.

They would do better to study the laws of navigation.

First I discovered the characteristic reversibility of events after 3^5 days, 243 days. Then I continued to increase the powers and extents of the time periods I have discovered, and began to apply them to the past of humanity.

That past suddenly became transparently clear; the simple law of time suddenly illuminated it in its entirety.

I understood then that time was structured in powers of two and three, the lowest possible even and odd numbers.

I understood that the true nature of time consists in the recurrent multiplication of itself by twos and threes, and when I recalled the old Slavic belief in the powers of "odd and even" I decided that wisdom was indeed a tree that grows from a seed. The superstition is all in the quotation marks.

Once I had uncovered the significance for time of odd and even, I had the sensation of holding in my hands a mousetrap in which aboriginal Fate quivered like a terrified little animal. The equations of time resemble a tree, simple as a treetrunk in their bases, and slender and complexly alive in the branches of their powers, where the brain and living soul of the equations are concentrated; they seem to be the reverse of equations of space, where the enormous number of the base is crowned by one, two, or three, but never anything further.

These were, I decided, two opposite movements within a single stretch of calculation.

I envisaged them very concretely: for space, I saw mountains, enormous stone masses as a base upon which the power perched like a bird of prey in repose, the bird of consciousness—compared to equations for time, which seemed like slender treetrunks and flowering branches with living birds fluttering in them.

For space, time seemed an inflexible exponent; it could never be greater than three, while the base was alive and limitless; for time, on the contrary, the foundations were fixed as two and three, while the exponent lived a complex existence in the free play of values. Where I had previously been conscious of the empty steppes of time, there had suddenly sprung up orderly multinomials based on three and on two, and I felt like a traveler before whom suddenly appeared the crenelated walls and towers of a city no one even knew existed.

In the famous old legend, the city of Kitezh lay sunk in a deep dark lake in the forest, while here, out of each spot of time, out of every lake of time, arose an orderly multinomial of threes with towers and steeples, just like another Kitezh.

Series such as $1053 = 3^{3+3} + 3^{3+2} + 3^{3+1}$, where the number of members is the same as the base number, the exponent of the leading power is twice three, and the other exponents diminish by one, or the well-known number $365 = 3^5 + 3^4 + 3^3 + 3^2 + 3^1 + 3^0 + 1$, have on the one hand disclosed the ancient relationship of the year to the days and on the other hand have given a new meaning to the old legend of the city of Kitezh.

A city of threes with its towers and steeples rings loudly from out of the depths of time. An orderly city with numerical towers has replaced previous visions of spots of time.

I did not dream up these laws: I simply took the live magnitudes of time, tried to divest myself of existing notions, to see what were the laws by which these magnitudes changed one into the other, and constructed equations based on the experience. And one after the other, the numerical expressions for magnitudes of time revealed a strange kinship with the expressions for space, at the same time that they moved in a reverse direction.

Number is a cup into which we may pour the liquid of any magnitude whatsoever, while the equation is a device that yields a string of magnitudes where the fixed numbers are the motionless nuts of the equation, its framework, and the magnitudes m and n are the mobile elements of the contrivance, the wheels, levers, and flywheels of the equation.

In my mind I would occasionally compare the numbers in an equation whose magnitudes were fixed with the skeleton of a body, and the magnitudes m and n with the muscles and flesh of a body, the whole suddenly brought to life like animals in a fairy tale.

In the equation I distinguished muscular structure from bone.

And behold, equations of time appeared as mirror images of equations of space.

Equations of space came to resemble extinct fossilized animals with huge skeletons and tiny skulls: the brain is the crown of the body.

If the expression for volume is A^3, A here can increase to infinity, but the exponent will always be three.

Three is the fixed magnitude, the bone of the equation; A is its liquid part. For two inverse points in time the expression $3^a + 3^a$ or

$3^n + 3^n$ (or simply 3^n) is very distinctive. Such a time-clamp unites event and counterevent in time.

An event of movement A and its reverse $-A$: here the fixed base is three and the infinitely increasing exponent is n. Isn't this a reverse flow of the computation?

What the ancient doctrines spoke of, what they threatened in the name of vengeance, now becomes the cruel and simple force of this equation; its dry language contains all the force of "Vengeance is mine, and I shall repay" and the terrible, unforgiving Jehovah of the ancients.

Indeed, the law of Moses and the entire Koran is very probably contained in the iron force of this equation.

But think how much ink we save! What a rest for the inkwell! In this we see the growth of progress through the centuries. With the colors of blood, iron, and death we can adorn the phantasmal outlines of the time-clamp of 3^x days.

Behavior and punishment, act and retribution.

Say the victim dies at the initial point.

The killer will die after 3^5.

Suppose the initial point was a step of conquest, marked by a major military success for some wave of humanity. Then the second point, after 3^n days, will mark an end to that movement, the day of its rebuff, a day that shouts: Whoa! Stop! Even though all during these 3^n days the whip of fate kept cracking to shouts of: Hey! Giddyap! Forward!

So the day of the battle of Mukden, February 26, 1905, which stopped the Russian advance to the East, an advance that began with the taking of Isker by Yermak and his band, occurred $3^{10} + 3^{10} = 2 \times 3^{10}$ after the taking of Isker on October 26, 1581.

The battle of Angora on July 20, 1402, which established a limit, a fixed threshold to the western push of the Mongols, occured 3^{10} after the Tatars' enormous success, their conquest of Kiev on December 6, 1240, which marked the beginning of the approach of the East, when the East turned to the West and removed its warlike visor.

The battle of Kulikovo Field, August 26, 1380, stopped the westward drive of the Eastern populations, those waves of Huns, Slavs, Magyars, Polovtsians, Pechenegs, and Tatars. But it occurred $3^{11} + 3^{11} = 2 \times 3^{11}$ after the sack of Rome by Alaric on August 24, 410, when Rome was burned to the ground. The taking of Constantinople in 1453 by the Turks set limits to the ancient Greek drive to the East. But this event, the fall of the Greek capital, happened $3^{11} \times 4$ after the year 487 B.C., when the Greeks had conquered the Persians and surged into the East.

The Roman drive toward the East began around the year 30 B.C., when Rome became master of the Mediterranean and subjugated the Eastern capital, Alexandria (August 4, 30, the taking of Alexandria by Octavian).

That year marked the full flowering of Rome, the essential step toward the East; 3^{11} days later brought the year 455 (July 12, 455), the year of Rome's fall and destruction.

The East shattered its opponent's sword: Bulgaria was conquered by the Turks at the battle of Trnovo on July 17, 1393; 3^{11} days later a reverse event occurred: she was declared independent by the treaty of Berlin on July 13, 1878. Here the law of 3^n unites the point of enslavement, of hands in chains, and the point of independence.

Let us now demonstrate our truth, that an event upon reaching an age of 3^n days changes its sign to the reverse (the yes-integer factor as an indicator of direction gives place to a no-integer factor [$+1$ and -1]), that upon completion of the time sequence represented by the numerical structure 3^n events stand in the same relation to each other as two trains proceeding in opposite directions along the same track, by means of the modest powers of n.

The large exponents are concerned with the dance and drift of states, their baton controls the great hopak of invasions and movements of peoples; while the small ones concern the lives of separate individuals, controlling them by means of retribution or by shifts in the structure of society, translating into numbers the ancient original, the old tables written in the language of words: "Vengeance is mine, and I will repay."

So the military agent Min put down the Moscow uprising on December 26, 1905; he was killed 3^5, 243 days later, on August 26, 1906.

The avenging hand of Konopliannikova, or Fate itself, pulled the trigger of the revolver that shot him.

Autocrat Nikolai Romanov was shot on July 16, 1918, $3^7 + 3^7$ after he dissolved the Duma on July 22, 1906.

The American president Garfield was killed on July 2, 1881, 3^5 days after his election to the post on November 2, 1880.

The attempt upon the life of the governor-general of Poland,

Count Berg, took place 243 days after the beginning of the uprising; in other words, Judgment Day, the day of vengeance, took place 3^5 after the event that called for that vengeance.

The freedom fighter Robert Blum was executed on November 9, 1848, 3^5 days after the beginning of the 1848 uprising (March 13, 1848).

The tsarist government's debts were recognized by Soviet Russia on November 6, 1921, $3^6 + 3^6 = 1458$ days after the beginning of Soviet power on November 10, 1917, when they had been declared null and void.

The Miliukov–Kerensky government of March 10, 1917, was set up 3^5 days before the government of Lenin and Trotsky on November 10, 1917.

The defeat of Wrangel, Kolchak's successor, and the end of the civil war occurred on November 15, 1920, 3^6 days after Kolchak's proclamation of himself as "provisional head of state" on November 17, 1918.

The abandonment of the front line by the troops and the disbanding of military units on December 7, 1917, occurred 3^5 days after Miliukov's declaration on April 9, 1917, about "war to the end" and loyalty to the Allied Powers.

Universal Education Day, August 11, 1918, occurred $3^5 + 2^2$ days after the Tolstoyan mood of the period of troop disbandment on December 7, 1917.

The English struck at the Continent 3^n days after the battle of Hastings, when their island was invaded by an army from the Continent.

The battle of Hastings, which represented the victory of Continent over Island, took place on October 3, 1066; the indigenous population was totally defeated, the island occupied by hordes of Danes; $3^9 + 3^9$ days later occurred the battle of Glenville, when the English defeated the French on June 13, 1174.

3^{10} days later occurred the naval battle of Bornholm, July 22, 1227, when the English avenged themselves on the Danes by defeating their recent conquerors. The island was avenged. Thus in turn were the French and the Danes defeated at sea 3^n days after the reverse event— the defeat of the English.

Thus do yes and no constantly reverse themselves.

We have seen the military duel of East and West; we have seen how the sword falls from the hands of one of the two combatants 3^n days after a successful attack, when one or another capital city is turned to rubble and ashes.

Isker, Kiev, Rome, London form one series. The battles of Mukden, Angora, Kulikovo Field, and Bornholm resounded 3^n days after the first series.

Threshold, obstacle, and stoppage were put to movement; victory is given to the conquered, destruction to the conqueror. The event makes a turn of $2d$, two right angles, and forms a negative turning point of time. The midnight of the event becomes its noonday and reveals the regular working of the timepieces of humanity, ticking in the capital cities of states long blown to dust.

Those who have no ordinary watch, would do well to wear the great timepiece of humanity and pay heed to its regular movements, its tick-tick-tick.

After a lapse of time of 3^n days the second event moves counter to the first, in reverse, like a train speeding in the opposite direction, threatening to derail the purpose of the first event.

The "truth" is, and we put the word in quotation marks for those who still care to doubt it, that events are spatially determined; specifically, the direction of motion of a force becomes a dependent variable of the count of days, that is to say the natural quantities of time. Here we have a quantitative connection, discovered through experiment, between the principles of time and space. The first bridge between them.

It derives from a careful study of the live quantities of time and the law of numbers by which these quantities convert one into another.

If we compare the live natural volumes of blocks of wood with right-angled and equal sides, these volumes will convert one into another according to the law of A^3 or n^3, where n or A is the length of a side according to the law of volumes, then the exponent 3 (a fixed number, fettering the quantities) is the solid bottom and fixed banks of the equation, while the base A is the moving water, the flow of the equation, and any quantity whatsoever may be proposed for it: A is the river of the equation.

For the law of live areas, by which areas merge one into the other, the relation A^2, n^2 applies, and here the fixed number is 2.

Quantities of time, however, merge into each other according to a law of 3^n days and 2^n days: here we have an unrestricted exponent, free as the wind, and a restricted base, the 3 or 2.

The river of the equation flows through the powers, and its banks are the base: 3 is a fixed number, while n is free and may be any possible number.

The delightful notion occurs that in fact there is no time and no space; there are only two different ways of counting, two inclines to the same roof, two paths through a single edifice of numbers.

Time and space together seem to comprise a single tree of mathematics, but in one case the imaginary squirrel of calculation moves from the branches to the base, in the other from the base to the branches.

These operations on quantities demonstrate the art of determining the greatest possible equality by means of the smallest possible inequality.

How many centuries would it take to determine (write out) a number, where a column of three 3s is the exponent of a 3, counting by tens?

Whereas here we are able to define it in an instant, extracting it from the sequence of others, by having recourse to equalities of a higher order.

We might call this the law of the least consumption of ink, the "ink-conservation" principle.

The impulse to find the smallest possible numbers is another law, a kind of Nirvana, the teachings of Buddha in the realm of numbers.

In the calculation that time makes, a gravitation to the numbers that surround the world of nothing (that is, one, two, and three) determines the structure of the base; its fixed bases are threes and twos. In spatial equations three, two, and one are the exponents.

And the base, on the contrary, goes to infinity.

Could we possibly refer to time as space turned upside down?

Raising to a power represents extreme economy in the use of ink; a succession of centuries can be written out (extracted from a sequence of others) with two or three strokes of a pen. This art lies at the foundation of both spatial calculation and the calculation of time.

But where space is concerned, it is the exponent that is created by the propensity toward the smallest possible numbers, the greatest proximity to zero; in the case of time it is the base.

Spatial Quantities

	In the base	In the exponent
The constraint of three or two		x
Infinite increase of the number (numerical freedom)	x	

	For Time	
	In the base	*In the exponent*
Two or three constrained	x	
Infinite increase of the number		x

In other words, space and time are two inverse directions of the same calculation, that is M^n and N^m.

In the lives of individuals I have noticed an especially turbulent time-period with the structure 2^{13} and 13^2. It calls forth triumphs beneath the sign of Mars or Venus, it doesn't matter which.

So Boris Samorodov, who raised the revolt on the White ships in the Caspian, did so $2^{13} + 13^2$ days after his birth.

As I see it, the spirit of courageous deeds was called up in him by two to the thirteenth power, counting from his birth.

If indeed the pure Laws of Time exist, then they must govern without distinction everything that is subject to the flow of time, be it the soul of Gogol, Pushkin's *Eugene Onegin,* the planets of the solar system, shifts in the Earth's crust, the terrible change from the kingdom of reptiles to the kingdom of men, from the Devonian age to an era marked by the interference of man in the life and structure of Planet Earth.

In fact, in the equation $x = 3^n + 3^n$, the interval of time for negative shifts, if we make $n = 11$, then x will equal the time between the destruction of Rome in 410, by peoples from the East, and the battle of Kulikovo Field, which put an end to the advance of those same peoples, a rebuff to the East. If we let $n = 10$, we get x equal to the time between Yermak's expedition and the retreat of Kuropatkin: these points represent the beginning and the end of Russian penetration of the East.

If we let $n = 18$, we get the time between the Tertiary age and our own. And finally if $n = 23$, then $x = 369, 697, 770$ years, or the interval between the Earth's Devonian age, when reptiles were the lords of creation, and the present day, when the Earth is a book with the shrieking title "Man." And does not this secret language based on three serve to explain the superstitious terror that man feels for reptiles, our frequently inoffensive enemies?

Between the Devonian age and our own, according to the determinations of Professor Holmes, there has elapsed a period of $3^{23} + 3^{23}$ days.

That period of time marks the change from the domination of glitter-scaled reptiles to the domination of naked man in his soft envelope of skin. Only the hair on his head, like a wind blowing from centuries gone by, recalls his past. Considered from this perspective, people can be thought of as anti-reptiles. The crawlers on the ground were replaced by human beings, who fall and rebound constantly, like a ball. According to the pure laws of time, whose herald and trumpeter I hereby announce myself, both the life of the earth's crust and shifts in the structure of human society are equally subject to the very same equations.

Here is the law of English seapower: $x = k + 3^9 + 3^9 n + (n - 1)(n - 2)(2^{16}) - 3^{9(n-2)}$, where k = the day in 1066 when the island was conquered by the Danes at the battle of Hastings. If $n = 1$, then x falls on the year 1174, the year of the struggle with France; if $n = 2$, then x comes out as 1227, the year of the struggle with Denmark; if $n = 3$, then x comes out as 1588, the year of the Spanish Armada.

All these wars guaranteed to Albion domination of the seas. And this was indeed to have been expected, because the equation is built on the base of three and its initial point was an English defeat.

Day Unit	In Years	
	Taking a year equal to 365 days	*Taking a year equal to 365¼ days*
$2^0 = 1$		
$2^1 = 2$		
$2^2 = 4$		
$2^3 = 8$		
$2^4 = 16$		
$2^5 = 32$		

Day Unit	In Years	
$2^6 = 64$		
$2^7 = 128$		
$2^8 = 256$	a year minus 109 days	a year minus 109 days
$2^9 = 512$	1 year and 147 days	1 year and 147 days
$2^{10} = 1024$	3 years minus 71 days	3 years minus 72 days
$2^{11} = 2048$	6 years minus 142 days	6 years minus 143 days
$2^{12} = 4096$	11 years and 81 days	11 years and 79 days
$2^{13} = 8192$	22 years and 162 days	22 years and 157 days
$2^{14} = 16,384$	45 years minus 41 days	45 years minus 52 days
$2^{15} = 32,768$	90 years minus 82 days	90 years minus 104 days
$2^{16} = 65,536$	179 years and 201 days	179 years and 156 days
$2^{17} = 131,072$	359 years and 37 days	359 years minus 53 days
$2^{18} = 262,144$	718 years and 74 days	718 years minus 106 days
$2^{19} = 524,209$	1436 years and 148 days	1436 years minus 212 days
$2^{20} = 1,048,576$	2872 years and 296 days	
$3^0 = 1$		
$3^1 = 3$		
$3^2 = 9$		
$3^3 = 27$		
$3^4 = 81$		
$3^5 = 243$		
$3^6 = 729$	2 years minus 1 day	2 years minus 2 days
$3^7 = 2187$	6 years minus 3 days	6 years minus 4 days
$3^8 = 6561$	18 years minus 9 days	18 years minus 13 days

Day Unit	In Years	
$3^9 = 19,683$	54 years minus 27 days	54 years minus 40 days
$3^{10} = 59,049$	161 years and 284 days	161 years and 244 days
$3^{11} = 177,147$	485 years and 122 days	485 years and 1 day
$3^{12} = 531,441$	1456 years and 1 day	1455 years and 2 days
$3^{13} = 1,594,323$	4368 years and 3 days	4365 years
$3^{14} = 4,782,969$	13,104 years and 9 days	

The life of centuries in the light of 3^n.

The eternal duel, illuminated by the torches of 3^n.

The staff of victory changes hands, passed from one warrior to another.

Waves of two worlds, the alternating spears of East and West, clashing through the centuries.

March 5, 3313 B.C. Conquest of India by the Aryans. Wave of Whites from the West.	$3^{13} + 3^7 - 2 \times 3^5$	November 10, 1256. Conquest of Baghdad by Mongols under Hulagu; wave of Mongols pouring from the East.
August 24, 410. Alaric sacks Rome, capital of the West. Wave from the East pours into the West.	$3^{11} + 3^{11}$	August 24, 1380. Battle of Kulikovo; acts as a dam against the people of the East; rebuff to the East.
July 2, 451. Rout of Attila, rebuff to the East.	$3^{12} - 2^7$	February 26, 1905. Battle of Mukden, rebuff to the East.

October 26, 1581. Yermak conquers Isker, capital of Siberia. Wave against the East.	$3^{10} + 3^{10}$	February 26, 1905. Battle of Mukden, halt to Russian advance to the East.
September 3, 36 B.C. Battle of Naulochus, Roman wave in the West.	$3^{19} + 3^{11}$	September 26, 1904. Battle of Shakha, halt to the West.

Let us make the bones of these times speak; let us clothe them with the flesh of human life and grant to the cliffs of time the voice of events in $3^n + 3^n$ days.

August 24, 410. Alaric takes Rome; Wave from the East against the West.	$3^{11} + 3^{11}$	August 26, 1380. Battle of Kulikovo Field; halt to the peoples of the East.
October 26, 1581. Yermak takes Isker; Russian wave against the East.	$3^{10} + 3^{10}$	February 26, 1905. Battle of Mukden, rebuff to Russia.
October 3, 1066. Battle of Hastings, subjugation of England.	$3^9 + 3^9$	June 13, 1174. Battle of Glenville; island England defeats the Continent.
May 18, 1899. Hague peace conference of kings.	3^8	May 9, 1917. Peace proposal of labor at Petrograd Soviet of Workers' Deputies.
July 22, 1906. State Duma dissolved by order of Nikolai Romanov.	$3^7 + 3^7$	July 16, 1918. Nikolai Romanov executed.
November 1, 1917. Beginning of Soviet power in Russia.	$3^6 + 3^6$	November 7, 1921. A shift to the right, negotiations on the assumption of Russia's debts.

December 26, 1905. Uprising in Moscow, put down by Min.

3^5

August 26, 1906. Min assassinated by Konopliannikova.

May 21, 1792. The king deals with foreign powers.

3^4

August 10, 1792. Taking of the royal palace.

The 19th century in the flaring torchlight of 2^n days and 3^n days. The growth of events after 2^{14} days.

June 19, 1815. Waterloo, rebuff for the West. Victory of the Eastern half of the continent over the Western half.

$2^{15} - 3^2$

February 26, 1905. Mukden, second rebuff to the West. The direction of the event is exactly the same; victory for the East.

"The little mailed fist of Germany" in 1870. September 2, 1870 = Sedan. 2^{14} days later Bismarck's winged words about "blood and iron" began to fly like zeppelins, and like the teeth of the magic dragon became a war in the air, on sea and land, underground and underwater; they hissed across the trenches like a poisoned wind, like exhalations of death.

2^{14}

"The big mailed fist of Germany," July 11, 1915, world war. Germany's iron fist, which once threatened only France, now threatens the whole of Planet Earth.

432

November 14, 1860. 2^{14}
Taking of Peking
(the sea peoples be-
siege the continent
of Asia).

September 23, 1905.
The Russo-Japanese
war. Second victory
for the sea. Conti-
nent is conquered.

[pub. 1922: Markov III.471–484]

Everyone, Everywhere, Attention!

Freedom! Futurian freedom! Here it is at last! So dear, so long desired! Fallen from a flock of birds. Our beautiful vision, our revelation, clothed in numbers.

A gift to all the governments of Planet Earth (all are equal—no favorites, no rejects): the right to be destroyed 3^n days after their victory. And equally to rise up and take to the sky, singing, 2^n days after the fall that smashes their wings on the rocks of fate. To fall into the abyss 3^n days after standing on the heights.

Of course others before us have tried to write laws, have tempted their weak forces in the proclamation of laws.

Poor fools! Did they think it was easier than writing poems? But they saw lawmaking as the workhouse of stupidity (Disraeli). Defeated in their first enterprise, they proceeded to the second, as if to the point of least resistance.

Poor fools! The chief ornament of the law, in their opinion, was the barrel of a rifle. They perfumed their code of laws with gunpowder and thought this was the epitome of good taste and elegant behavior, the only seasoning for the art of "proclaiming laws."

They mixed the eloquence of their laws with the eloquence of gunfire—what filth! What depraved habits of the past! What servile adoration of the past!

They accuse us of being merely the hundred-and-first hoof on the lawmakers' path.

What black slander!

As if anyone before us had devised laws that could never be broken! We alone, standing on the rock of the future, give laws that may be disregarded, but cannot be disobeyed. They cannot be broken.

Try and see if you can break them!

Even we admit that we cannot do it!

Who can break our laws?

434

They have been carved not upon the stone of desires and passions, but upon the stone of time.

All of you! Repeat in unison: "No one!"

They are straight and strict in their outlines and have no need to lean upon the sharp stick of war, which wounds whoever relies on it.

[1920–1921: V.164–165]

JOURNALISM

From August 1918 to January 1919 Khlebnikov was living in Astrakhan at his parents' home and devoting some of his time to work as a civilian correspondent for a local military newspaper, Red Soldier. *The four short pieces that follow were all printed in the newspaper from September through December 1918.*

The Union of Inventors

A Union of Inventors has opened in a place of deep spiritual stagnation, the city of Astrakhan. It is slowly trying to earn its "right to exist" and to serve as a resource point for the invention of new forms of food, like fish meal or squash-blossom tea. The opinion has already been expressed that it is possible to make "lake soup," since ponds that have begun to dry up are full of minute living organisms, and such water, after being thoroughly heated, is very nourishing: the taste recalls that of meat broth. In the future, once the edibility of the various varieties of these microscopic water-borne organisms has been established, they will be bred artificially in lakes, and every lake will resemble a large kettle of lake soup, accessible to all.

We are confident that regional centers of scientific thought will not ignore this possible source of a supplementary food reserve.

The sharp goad of universal intelligence, acting in response to population growth, will constantly and urgently stimulate all vital areas marked by sluggishness and stagnation.

[1918: NP 349]

Opening of the People's University

Report

Yesterday marked the inauguration of the Advanced Evening Courses open to the public; present in the People's Auditorium were its future students and many sympathizers with the task of public education.

Comrade Bakradze informed those present about the task of the new center for learning—to afford working people the possibility of devoting their evenings to the pursuit of education.

Professors Usov and Skrynnikov presented the views of contemporary science on the origin of life on Earth and the influence of the planet upon its living creatures.

A number of congratulatory messages were read, including one from students in the Intermediate Courses.

Reflections

In his introductory remarks Comrade Bakradze observed that by establishing a temple of higher education to be open evenings, the workers' government was opening a path to the Sun of Science for those whose days were divided into three equal periods—work, leisure, and sleep—and who, since they work during the daytime, must use their evening leisure to satisfy their thirst for knowledge.

The workers' government that replaced the tsarist order did so on behalf of workers, who had up to now been excluded. Let all who had previously seen the temple of science only through a narrow crack now enter through its wide-open doors! Whatever advances might be necessary on the path to world freedom, nothing can threaten monuments to workers' rights like this just-opened evening temple of science. In this instance the path taken by the workers' government is the correct one.

Professor Usov made a speech on the origins of life on Earth. He pointed out that minute particles of life-bearing dust might be brought to Earth on one of the meteors that fall with such commotion and noise. Like a kind of heavenly mail delivery, each such stone falls like a letter from a nearby star. Is it not the task of the Man of the Future to take up in his own hands this rudimentary offspring of nature, and with the worker's hammer to forge proper relations with neighboring worlds, which are doubtless also inhabited, though perhaps not with people like ourselves?

There is reason to think that perhaps those individuals are right who want the Great War to be concluded by the conquest of the moon. Until then, however, "messages from out there" reach us in the form of stones from the sky.

Professor Skrynnikov devoted his talk to a discussion of the first step of life on Earth. We were made aware of "messages from the future."

Involuntarily, our thoughts turn to the future, when the worker's hand will construct undersea palaces in order to study the ocean depths; when upon Mount Bogdo there will probably arise a castle for studying the skies of Swanland—human intelligence besieging the secrets of the world of the stars; numberless wells drilled into a desert will cover sandy marshes with gardens and plants, recalling the miracles worked by the French in the Sahara, and orderly rows of poplars will hold fast the sandy marshes at the mouth of the Volga, which so much resembles Belgium; it will all become one flourishing garden, one rural commune covered with gardens, a step toward creating a united community on Planet Earth.

There is reason to think that the great waves of Russia, China, and India meet here at the mouth of the Volga, and that this is surely the proper spot to erect a temple for the study of the laws of heredity, in order to establish through the interbreeding of tribes a new species of people, future inhabitants of Asia, and a careful examination of Hindu literature will remind us that Astrakhan is the window to India.

We can even begin to imagine a time when a single newspaper-of-the-air will instruct the whole of Planet Earth by radio, broadcasting via gramaphone recordings the lectures of the best minds of humanity, a supreme council of Warriors of Intelligence.

The evening concluded with a message of congratulation from the future—from the students in the Intermediate Courses.

[1918: NP 350]

Opening of an Art Gallery

Sunday, December 15, marked the opening of a picture gallery established by P. Dogadin. The collection has been put together with great taste and illustrates many currents in Russian painting, although nothing to the left of the World of Art group is represented.

We find here even the venerable Shishkin with his dry, moribund painting. This painter has a servile eye; he perceives nature like the lens of a light-writing device, servilely and exactly. He has reconstructed nature as a mute, a soulless slave, rejecting artistic mediation or the dictates of individual will.

The bold, colorful rebel Maliavin, the "Razin of red canvases," is represented by a restrained sketch entitled *Women*. This artist flaunts the color red in his canvases with an unheard-of freedom—out of this pagan twilight advances a sunblacked woman from the Russian fields—and these canvases first accustomed viewers to the red flag of the revolution; the red banner of his soul whips in the wind as it advances to greet the present.

Repin is here, with all his ineffectualness and his own particular saccharine softness: his subject is *Prometheus*.

Benois, impersonal and mediocre in all respects as always, is represented by a view of Peking at dusk. And let us not forget to mention Sapunov's drooping *Roses* and Roerich's *Rocks*.

There is a large and beautiful piece by Nesterov, *Beyond the Volga*, full of a waning beauty, proud, silent. Another of his paintings, *The Vision of the Child Bartholomew*, shows the boy in peasant shoes with a herdsman's whip and a golden halo surrounding his blond hair, standing enchanted before his vision—a venerable old man from the beyond, an apparition in a monk's cowl leaning against a tree. This painting is the gem of the entire collection.

Surikov's head of an archer is a sketch for his *Stenka Razin*.

There are several pieces by Serov—his powerful, "bloody" brushstroke—and Somov, master of the refined brush of the "urbanite." There is one beautiful painting by Teodorovich-Karpovskaia. The great Vrubel is represented by a sketch for his *Swan Queen*. Vrubel, the Mickiewicz of painting, introduces his own note of pagan legend and pride in color into Maliavin's scarlet rages, Nesterov's quiet renunciation and retreat from life, Surikov's invincible austerity.

The artistic forces of Ashtrakhan, now united in an artists' collective, are represented by the colorist Kustodiev, by Maltsev and Kotov. Kotov's *Verochka,* full of sunlight, awash in color, is an enormously optimistic piece.

The collection also includes letters by Tolstoy, Scriabin, Dostoevsky and others. The collection fixes on Russian painting halfway between the Wanderers and the World of Art. Perhaps at some future time, beside Benois, we will see the indomitable nay-sayer Burliuk or the beautiful martyr Filonov, not yet well known, who sings hymns of urban suffering; and perhaps there will be room on these walls for Larionov's Rayism, for the objectless canvases of Malevich and the Tatlinism of Tatlin. It is true that their work is frequently less a matter of painting than bold attempts to blow up the very foundations of painting; they are guided by this or that exploded precept of art. Just as a chemist can split water into hydrogen and oxygen, so these artists have split the art of painting into its component forces, sometimes emphasizing the principles of paint, sometimes of line. This trend in painterly investigation is totally absent from Dogadin's collection.

[1918: *Literaturnoe obozrenie* 2(1980), III–II2]

The Astrakhan Gioconda

You have all probably seen old paintings that time has darkened to a warm gold, covered with a silken skin, a kind of powder, a patina of gold dust. You immediately recognize the hand of a great artist, even though the canvas is unsigned. In Italy, the land of historic painting, such canvases are the treasures of their native cities, guarded as a man would guard his one remaining eye. Do you recall Leonardo da Vinci's *Gioconda*? It was abducted by some crazed admirer, and after a thousand adventures it was finally returned in triumph to its native city. Cities that have preserved such old paintings over the years provide their best possible frames, a frame of living people, the city's inhabitants—how could any wooden frame be better?

Astrakhan has a Gioconda of its own. A Madonna from the brush of the great Leonardo da Vinci himself: forgotten, unrecognized, it was part of the Sapozhnikov collection, when it was unearthed by the famous painter Benois and sold by him to the Hermitage Museum for 100,000 rubles—as sweetly and easily as you please. But should not this painting be considered one of the supreme attractions of the city of Astrakhan? If so, then the painting deserves to be repatriated to its second homeland. Petrograd has enough artistic treasures. To take this painting from Astrakhan is like taking his last lamb from some poor shepherd.

The Astrakhan Art Gallery, by the way, is located on Kutum, across from the Ibov building.

[1918: *Literaturnoe obozrenie* 2(1980), 112]

Index of Khlebnikov Titles

General Index